THE R

THE ROBINS

An Official History of
Hull Kingston Rovers

Roger Pugh

Scratching Shed Publishing Ltd

Registered in England & Wales No. 6588772.
Registered office:
47 Street Lane, Leeds, West Yorkshire. LS8 1AP
www.scratchingshedpublishing.co.uk
ISBN 978-0993510120

All photos courtesy of the *Hull Daily Mail* unless stated

A catalogue record for this book is available from the
British Library.

Typeset in Oriya MN Bold and Palatino
Printed and bound in the United Kingdom by
Latimer Trend & Company Ltd,
Estover Road, Plymouth, PL6 7PY

This book is dedicated to the group of young pioneers who
founded the Kingston Amateurs rugby club in 1882

A note on statistics

All the statistics used in this book have been compiled with the help of the Rugby League Record Keepers Club, Hull Kingston Rovers' historian Dave Sherwood and Hull FC statistician Bill Dalton. They reflect all appearances in Hull Kingston Rovers 'first class' matches, following the advice of Professor Tony Collins of the International Centre for Culture and Sport at De Montfort University about which games should be classified as such.

These can be summarised as being all Northern Union and Rugby League first team competitions and tour games, but not war league games and friendly matches. References to drop-goals relate to drop-goals kicked since the one point drop-goal was introduced in domestic rugby league in 1974/75.

Contents

When the Red Red Robin
goes Bob Bob Bobbin' Along

When the red, red robin comes bob, bob, bobbin' along, along
There'll be no more sobbin' when he starts throbbin' his old sweet
song
Wake up, wake up you sleepy head
Get up, get out of your bed
Cheer up, cheer up the sun is red
Live, love, laugh and be happy
What if I were blue, now I'm walking through, walking through
the fields of flowers
Rain may glisten but still I listen for hours and hours
I'm just a kid again doing what I did again, singing a song
When the red, red robin comes bob, bob, bobbin' along
When the red, red robin comes bob, bob, bobbin'
When the red, red robin comes bob, bob, bobbin' along
There'll be no more sobbin' when he starts throbbin'
There'll be no more sobbin' when he starts a throbbin' his old
sweet song
Wake up, wake up you sleepy head
Why don't you get up, get up, get out of bed, cheer up
Live, love, laugh and be happy
What if I were blue, now I'm walking through fields of flowers
Rain may glisten but still I listen for hours and hours
I'm just a kid again, doing what I did again, singing a song
When the red, red robin comes bob, bob, bobbin'
When the red, red robin comes bob, bob, bobbin' along
Along, along, along, along, along.

Al Jolson, 1926

Author's note

I FIRST saw Hull Kingston Rovers play in 1968. I was a schoolboy in Leeds then and had been introduced to rugby league by a school friend, Bob Carter, an ardent Leeds fan who was the son of the football secretary at Headingley. I didn't consciously decide to follow the Robins, it just happened. I saw them play the Loiners and that was it. Rovers lost the first three games I watched live but truly supporting a team is not about winning and losing. Something indefinable grips you, you can't help it, it's just there and I became an ardent fan.

Surely, no one in their right mind would choose to board the emotional rollercoaster that is the lot of the diehard. The ecstasy and the despair, the false dawns and dashed hopes, the long trips back after losing away, having your heart in your mouth for seemingly an age as your team hangs on to a narrow lead - only to be pipped at the death, the impotent frustration at a refereeing injustice, the mocking comments of the fans of your deadliest rivals after a humiliating defeat, the inane utterances of those who would not know a full-back from a prop-forward but who believe that they have a unique insight into the inadequacies of your team. However, all these setbacks are forgotten in the exhilarating highs experienced after seeing a trophy held aloft, a derby win, a great away victory against a top side, a winning comeback when all seemed lost.

Most of my early Rovers games were the away ones in the West Riding that I could get to by bus but I managed to engineer a move to Hull in 1971 – ostensibly to go to the teacher-training college – so I was able to become a Craven Park regular too. By 1976, I was working in the civil service in Hull, alongside a fervent Rovers fan with whom I bought my first season ticket for the main stand at the beloved but somewhat eccentric old ground that was then home. Only in the '90s, by which time I had a young football-loving son and my job took me out of town a lot, did my attendance fall away somewhat. I admit too, that it took me a long time to think of the current ground as home. However, over the last ten years, Gavin has also taken an interest in rugby league and we renew two season tickets as a matter of course.

Writing a book has always appealed to me, and when I was able to take early retirement from the civil service in 2012, I resolved to have a go. There could only ever be the one subject for my first effort. It is a story worth telling. Of a journey, often against the odds, from the most humble of beginnings to today's Super League, of triumphs and adversity, characters and loyal servants, great players and journeymen, heroes and the occasional villain.

The club has many younger supporters whose memories will not stretch back to the triumphs of the 1980s, even the struggles of the 1990s – let alone the fascinating '60s and '70s – and there will be few who remember the great side of the 1920s and the struggles that followed. Three years ago, a much-loved club stalwart of over 400 matches died. A contributor to the fans forum wrote, 'I'd never heard of him – but RIP anyway'. This book is for him and all those like him, so they can know more about the bedrock on which this proud club is built.

I have tried to record the club's history in as objective a way as I can, so that those who follow the team today will know more about what went before. Any errors in fact are entirely mine, as are any opinions. The matches I have featured are my choices – there could have been twice as many – the players and officials I have singled out as 'greats' are those who, in my opinion, by their special contribution to the club, the affection they earned, or their sheer dedication and longevity, are worthy of special mention.

I hope that all those who are interested in Hull Kingston Rovers will enjoy this book – but above all, I hope that it does justice to our great club.

Roger Pugh, March 2016

Bibliography

A Social History of Hull Kingston Rovers – P. & R. Schofield

A Tale of Two Roads: An early history of Hull FC and Hull KR –
Mike Ulyatt (Hutton Press)

All the Wrong Moves – Terry Clawson (The Book Factory)

Big Artie: The Autobiography –
Arthur Beetson with Ian Heads (ABC Books)

British Newspaper Archives - *www.britishnewspaperarchive.co.uk*

The British Rugby League Records Book –
Dave Farrar, Peter Lush & Graham Williams (LLP)

Calm in the Cauldron: A Rugby League Journey –
John Dorahy with Tom Mather (LLP)

Daydream Believer – Stanley Gene with Stuart Wilkin (T H Media)

History of Rugby League – series edited by Irvin Saxton (Irvin Saxton)

Hull: A Divided City – Mike Ulyatt (Hutton Press)

Hull Kingston Rovers: A Centenary History 1883-1983 –
Mike Ulyatt (Lockington Publishing)

Hull Kingston Rovers Football Club Ltd –
Directors Reports & Accounts (Hull K.R. RFC)

Neil Fox: Rugby League's greatest point scorer – Robert Gate (LLP)

KHCT 1899-1979 –
Philip A. Vine (Kingston upon Hull City Transport)

Peter Fox: The Players' Coach – Graham Williams & Peter Lush (LLP)

Old Faithful: A History of Hull Football Club –
Mike Ulyatt with Bill Dalton (Hutton Press)

Queen Elizabeth The Queen Mother: The Official Biography –
William Shawcross (Macmillan)

Roger: The Autobiography –
Roger Millward with Mike Sterriker (Riverhead Publishing)

The Story of Hull – Alan Avery (Blackthorne Press)

The Sunday Times Illustrated History of Twentieth Century Sport –
Nawrat, Hutchings & Struthers (Hamlyn)

Trinity: The History of Wakefield Trinity RLFC –
Mike Rylance (League Publications Limited)

We are Hull KR: Back from Oblivion –
Mike Sterriker (Riverhead Publishing)

Acknowledgements

I OWE a huge debt of thanks to many people for their help with this book but none more so than my friend, lifelong Rovers supporter and historian Dave Sherwood. Dave has supported the Robins since the 1950s, and has an amazing recall of detail; matches, players and even of our first meeting at Widnes in 1975! He holds what I am convinced must be a record for a Rovers supporter of not having missed a single game in over a quarter of a century, from September 1979 to April 2005 – a staggering total of 935 consecutive matches broken only by the club starting to play games in France. There should be medals for that kind of loyalty and endurance. Dave, who acts as unpaid club historian and writes articles for the club programme, has shared with me his memories and archive material and has spent many hours helping me to research this book. I hope the book is worthy of his unstinting efforts.

Professor Tony Collins, Director of the International Centre for Culture and Sport at De Montfort University (and

The Robins

Rovers fan) has given me invaluable advice and encouragement, as well as the benefit of his knowledge about the very early years. Local rugby league statistician Bill Dalton, despite being a Black and White, has put aside any sporting differences to lend me his extensive match-by-match statistical records and summaries and to advise on matters connected with Hull FC. Local rugby league personality Alan Parker has loaned me his priceless collection of rugby league literature. Amy Devanney and her colleagues at Huddersfield University have given me generous access to their amazing rugby league archives and the late Richard Bailey of the Rugby League Collectors Federation provided me with the Rugby League Record Keepers' summaries for Hull Kingston Rovers. The Hull History Centre has also been an invaluable research resource for Dave and myself.

I would like to record my particular thanks to my friend and neighbour Jim Mitchell, picture editor at the *Hull Daily Mail*, for his generous help and for allowing me access to the *Mail*'s photograph library, and to the *Hull Daily Mail* for enabling me to use the photographs and quotations attributed in the book. Enormous thanks too to Paul Fletcher, Stuart Quinn, and Matt Dass of Eon Visual Media for sharing with me – and allowing me to use – their priceless collections of photographs and memorabilia.

My grateful thanks are also due to the Robins' chairman Neil Hudgell for his help and support and to current and former officials Chris Draper, Max Gold, Colin Hutton, Peter Johnson, Barry Lilley, Colin McNicol and Ron Turner. Former players Alan Burwell, Len Casey, Michael Dobson, George Fairbairn, Paul Fletcher, David Hall, Phil Lowe, John Millington, Roger Millward MBE, Jason Netherton, Wayne Parker, Mike Smith, Mike Spivey, Brian Tyson and Johnny Whiteley have also generously shared their time and memories. A special thanks too to the ever-helpful Lloyd Lee in the club shop.

I am similarly indebted to Gary Holland, of E.W. Brown and Son, lifelong fan and former Rovers VCR operator Kelvin Hannath, friends and fellow supporters Len Beecroft, Steve Dunn, Mike Knappett and Steve Myers and to Lester Jones, Sam Littlefield, Martin Smith and Mike Smith, who have all helped me in invaluable ways.

Lastly, but certainly not least, to my wife Kirsty and my son Gavin, for their unfailing help, patience, suggestions, support and proofreading throughout.

Foreword – by Colin Hutton

MY association with Hull Kingston Rovers stretches back to November 1957, when I was the licensee of the Avenue pub on Chanterlands Avenue and had a visit from several gentlemen who it transpired were Rovers' directors. My playing days at the Boulevard were nearing their end and they wanted me to take the job of player-coach at Craven Park. As it happened, I joined the club just as coach, but my involvement with the Robins has continued now for almost 57 years.

During that time I have also been general manager, director, chairman and now life president. Although there have been some ups and downs over the years, the club has always been very good to me and overall it has been a wonderful experience that I would not have missed for the world. I have many treasured memories of great players, great games and great times with Rovers. In particular, I was very privileged to be chairman in the club's centenary year in 1983-84 when we won the Championship and Premiership double.

Since then the club has been through some very difficult periods but it has pulled through, and I believe that it is in very good hands today under Neil Hudgell and Rob Crossland. I see no reason why there should not be more successful times to enjoy in the future.

The club's history is a fascinating story, and this book is long overduc. I believe that it does our great club full justice and recommend it to all Rovers' supporters.

Colin Hutton
President
Hull Kingston Rovers RFC

A Word from the Chairman

MY journey with Hull KR started in the mid-1970s, just before the beginning of the golden era for the club. I grew up in East Hull in the shadows of Craven Park, near to vice-chair Rob Crossland, who in those days used to run Saturday morning errands for Colin Hutton from The Zetland Arms public house on Portobello Street.

I held the very privileged position as a twelve-year-old of being a ball boy to a team of all-time greats. I had a birds' eye view of us lifting the Floodlit Trophy at Craven Park in 1977, the catalyst to a decade of success, and which to this day lives longest in all my fondest memories of the club.

In 40 years I have witnessed the great times, being spoilt in those formative years by silverware and individual honours galore. I have been at some remarkable games several of which feature in this book. I have witnessed relegation to the bottom tier of the professional game and was present at Wembley in 1986 when the rot well and truly set in, starting nearly 20 years of decline, leading to administration and near extinction.

Above and beyond that in terms of adversity and heartbreak is the loss of Craven Park in 1989, a move from which to this day I do not think we have fully recovered. Roger's book gives a detailed account of the events of that time, well-researched and putting to bed some of the myths behind the move away from our spiritual home.

The book represents the first proper, all-inclusive history of our great club and acts as a nostalgic reminder as well as an excellent reference source for its many followers. It also gives due credit to some of the many unsung heroes from down the years including, during my time, the Reverend John Leeman, Keith Lyon and Adge Cutler.

For all those reasons I would like to congratulate Roger on the book and commend it as a 'must have' for all Rovers supporters.

Neil Hudgell
Chairman
Hull Kingston Rovers RFC

1. 10-5

May 1980

THERE have been 221 competitive derby games between Hull FC and Hull Kingston Rovers since the Robins joined the Northern Union, and although nine of these have been in Cup Finals, none have gripped the imagination of therugby league world and generated the level of interest in the same way as did the Wembley clash of May 1980.

A local rivalry

Saturday 3 May 1980. The Iranian Embassy in Central London was under siege by terrorists, Great Britain and USA were testing nuclear weapons in the Nevada desert and Dexy's Midnight Runners had just reached number one in the charts with 'Geno'. In other sport, Liverpool had retained the League Championship for a second season, Hull City narrowly avoided relegation to the bottom tier of the Football

League and those at Twickenham were celebrating Bill Beaumont leading England to their first Grand Slam for 23 years.

As the day dawned, however, all other events faded into insignificance for the rugby league followers of the city of Kingston upon Hull. All that was on their minds was the clash with their bitter rivals at Wembley in the final of the State Express Challenge Cup. It was not that Hull FC and Hull Kingston Rovers had not met in a cup final before, they had – four times by then, with the score standing at two-all. But this was the big one – rugby league's annual showpiece occasion at Wembley Stadium, televised live to the nation on BBC1 and played out in front of a capacity 95,000 crowd. To comprehend the importance of the game, it is necessary to understand the rivalry between the two sets of fans.

Their numbers may be less, but the intensity of the division between them is right up there with those in football – Celtic and Rangers, Everton and Liverpool, the two Manchester clubs and Arsenal and Tottenham. It is not always a friendly rivalry, often bitter and hostile. Hull Kingston Rovers and Hull FC; 'the Robins' and 'the Airlie Birds'; the 'Red and Whites' and the 'Black and Whites'. In Hull, even those who have no interest in the game are one or the other, there is no, neutral halfway house. Sometimes, fans of the losing club in a derby match may not be seen for several days afterwards. Kelvin Hannath was the Robins' video operator in the '80s and is one of the diehards. 'I don't have friends who support Hull FC,' he says, 'Only acquaintances. Put it this way, if the wife had been a Hull FC fan, we wouldn't have married.'

The Hull derby is the biggest in rugby league. There may be others between near-neighbours in the sport but none compare with this one. For many supporters, winning the derby games and finishing above their rivals in the league table are more important than any other successes. Traditionally, West Hull is FC territory and East of the city home to Rovers, but this was not always so. The evolution of the place and its transient population in recent years has led to many families moving across these boundaries. Despite that, and the growth in the number of 'mixed families', the intensity today is as strong as ever. Both clubs feed from the competition, interest and passion it generates. 'It has been the lifeblood of both clubs,' says former Rovers' secretary Ron Turner.

The rivalry has generated a fund of stories that have become folklore amongst the supporters. Traditionally, Hull FC has always been the better-supported club but Rovers' Wembley chairman Bill Land had an explanation for that. Responding to a Black and White fan who was crowing about the fact, Land asked: 'Have you read your Bible, son?' As he had not, Land informed him that for every wise man there are two fools.

Even after an early pre-Northern Union derby, the press commented on 'the bitterness between the two sets of supporters.' Despite that, and occasional incidents apart, there is no significant history of violence between opposing fans and May 1980 was to maintain that tradition of deep-felt, but generally well-behaved, respective passion. Many derbies have left a mark, but none was as important to the clubs, their players and fans, as this one.

In his book *Hull: A Divided City*, Michael Ulyatt chronicles 90 years of Hull derbies and gives a final word to a referee, the late Ron Campbell of Widnes. 'When I was in the middle of a Hull derby,' he said, 'I would not have changed places with anyone in the world. To me it was the only place to be .... in front of a packed crowd roaring on

The Robins

their favourites, and shouting abuse at me. My skin used to crawl with the excitement.'

The build-up

From the week after the Robins won their semi-final against Halifax on 22 March, there started an insatiable clamour from supporters for tickets and the club's allocation of 30,000 quickly sold out. Rovers then benefitted from qualifying for the final a week before their opponents. Secretary Turner received a phone call from Wallace Arnold Tours, offering him a further 1,000 that they no longer needed as none of the West Riding clubs would be there. Armed with a cheque, he set off for Leeds to pick up tickets that were to disappear more quickly than it took him to collect them.

It was to be the first of two such trips for him for, as the final approached, he received a further phone call, this time from the Rugby Football League headquarters asking if he could take their remaining stocks. The club was still being besieged with requests and he did not need asking twice.

As cup fever took over the city, Rovers' vice-chairman Percy Johnson was interviewed on BBC *Look North* at his Corn Exchange pub in the Old Town. 'This final is the finest thing that's happened to this city,' he said. 'It has put Hull on the map.' There was certainly no shortage of interest in the game outside the city. The Rugby Football League's fears that it would not capture the imagination of the wider rugby league-watching public were proved groundless. The game attracted interest far and wide and was fully sold out. Jim Geraghty, the boss of Australian side Cronulla, for whom the Robins' captain-coach Roger Millward played in 1976, arranged a 21,000 mile round trip just to be there.

At 9.30am on Wednesday 30 April, 1980 at the Craven

4

Park home of Hull Kingston Rovers, hundreds of Rovers' fans cheering and waving the team off on their historic trip, shattered the peace of a grey and grizzly morning. Their destination was the Runnymede Hotel in Egham, just to the west of what is now the M25. The Robins learned lessons from the 1964 trip when the team stayed in central London on the night before the game, and this leafy suburb was to be their base for the next five days. After that enthusiastic send-off, the team relaxed watching *The Good, the Bad, and the Ugly* on the coach video. There would have been several contenders for each of those roles amongst the passengers.

In Surrey, with the help of a locally based Castlefordian who was a great fan of Millward, Rovers had the clubhouse and facilities of Windsor RUFC put at their disposal for training sessions. This generous but simple act of hospitality would not raise an eyebrow in the 21st century but such co-operation between the two rugby codes was almost unheard of in 1980 and permission had to be obtained from rugby union headquarters, who consented provided that it was kept 'low profile'. There, Millward put the team through its paces and the finishing touches to his preparations with the help of his assistant, Johnny Moore.

In contrast to the occasion of the Robins' first Wembley appearance 16 years before, Millward had a full squad of players at his disposal, although there were serious concerns about a shoulder injury to second-row forward Phil Lowe, sustained against St Helens a couple of weeks earlier. The focus in training was on Rovers' own game, Millward did not overly concern himself with what the Airlie Birds could do, he knew their game well enough from the three previous encounters that season. Honours from those were even, a win to each side and a draw. Aside from training, the players spent their time taking early morning walks, on the

5

pitch-and-putt course, aiming to impress on the pool table – unsuccessfully trying to beat veteran centre Bernard Watson – and mingling with the locals for a quiet drink at the pub.

Some supporters, making a long weekend of the occasion, started to travel south on the day after the team but the main exodus out the city started in earnest on the Friday before the game. Two rail specials left Hull Paragon station that day, followed on the Saturday morning by a further 24, carrying over 20,000 fans of both clubs to the capital, in addition to the many thousands more that travelled by car and coach. Local coach operators struggled to meet the demand from pubs, clubs and works trips and hired in vehicles from all over the north of England. Turner took charge of two coaches that left on the Friday taking the players' wives and girlfriends and club guests to a hotel in Bagshot, just under ten miles from where the players were staying.

It was estimated that not far short of a third of Hull's population was Wembley-bound and a local wag placed a famous sign on Boothferry Road on the Saturday morning asking, 'Will the last person to leave please turn the lights out.' A good omen for the day was how the fans of each club travelled, joked and drank together on their great pilgrimage. Beneath the surface, however, emotions were very different. Local bookmaker Len Beecroft had supported the Robins since the 1950s and recalled wanting them to triumph so much on that day that he did not care if they never won another match.

Millward's team selection contained no surprises. He picked what he clearly saw as his best starting 13, the one that had comfortably beaten Halifax in the semi-final and had played together at Hunslet three weeks earlier. Rovers had struggled to field a settled side that season, and those three occasions were the only ones that this same team had taken the field together. Due to injuries, Millward himself was making only his 10th start of the campaign and hooker David Watkinson only his sixth. As Millward was in his familiar stand-off role, with his trusted lieutenant Allan Agar alongside him at scrum-half, he picked Steve Hartley in the left-centre position that he had occupied on numerous occasions in the previous 18 months.

The doctor cleared Lowe to play and he packed down in the second-row with fellow international and regular partner Paul Rose. Len Casey, who was at loose-forward, remembers that the players were on £1,300 a man to win the cup, over ten times the normal match amount at the time.

It was the fruition of a dream for Millward, who had seen his hopes of a Wembley appearance dashed so many times throughout the previous 15 years. Hannath recalled that: 'The emotional reaction of Millward, and other senior players like Agar and Clive Sullivan, after the semi-final win over Halifax, showed how much reaching Wembley meant to them.' Sullivan, at 37, was the oldest player in the final. Only prop-forward Brian Lockwood had played - and won - at Wembley before and, for the golden oldies, there would not be many more chances.

Sullivan and Casey were the only men on the field who had played for both Hull clubs although Rose was to do so when he moved 'over to the dark side' two years later. Rovers' 15 included nine players born in the Hull area, of whom six had come through their junior set-up, whilst three were from the West Riding, and one each from Barrow, Cardiff and York.

The Robins had started the season as the reigning champions but had finished only in seventh place this time. Hull FC, led by former Rovers' scrum-half and coach Arthur

The Robins

Bunting, had been promoted from the Second Division the previous year and had made an excellent return to the top flght, finishing third. They too were able to field their first choice starters although centre Graham Evans, who would have been one of their substitutes, fell awkwardly whilst playing football in training on the Thursday and was ruled out. The Airlie Birds relied heavily on their West Riding imports, nine in all, with only the long-serving Keith Tindall and Brian Hancock originating from the Hull area. The teams were:

> **Rovers:** David Hall; Steve Hubbard, Mike Smith, Steve Hartley, Clive Sullivan; Roger Millward, Allan Agar; Roy Holdstock, David Watkinson, Brian Lockwood, Phil Lowe, Paul Rose, Len Casey. Subs: Phil Hogan, John Millington.

> **Hull FC:** Paul Woods; Graham Bray, Graeme Walters, Tim Wilby, Paul Prendiville; John Newlove, Clive Pickerill; Keith Tindall, Ronnie Wileman, Charlie Stone, Charlie Birdsall, Sammy Lloyd, Steve Norton. Subs: Brian Hancock, Vince Farrar.

Match day

At the Runnymede Hotel on the morning of the game, hooker David Watkinson summed up the mood of the players at breakfast. Never noted for his sense of humour, he responded to the waiter's '...and what would you like today, sir?' with, '...a winners' medal.' After the players had spent the morning relaxing, Rovers' team coach left the hotel at around lunchtime. Metropolitan Police outrider PC Robert Cooper met them a few miles from Wembley and provided them with their escort to the stadium. It would have done the superstitious members of the team no harm at all to know that, in the five years he had been undertaking this duty, PC Cooper had always accompanied the winning team. Another good omen was that the Robins would use the North dressing room, they had been in the South when they lost to Widnes on their previous appearance.

By 2pm, on Wembley Way, a sea of red and white and black and white was beginning to swell as the fans advanced on the stadium. Hull FC historian and statistician, Bill Dalton, recalls seeing over a hundred coaches discharging their passengers bedecked in their team's colours. He noticed only two or three coaches that obviously carried supporters of only one team, the vast majority were all full of those of both clubs happily travelling together.

Dalton believes that it would be very different over 30 years on, as the nature of the rivalry has changed in the intervening years. Another life-long supporter, Steve Myers, says: 'I remember the surprise shown by the Londoners that these two groups of rival supporters could mix together with no trouble.' Sadly, in some quarters, the good-natured banter has been replaced by the distasteful and disrespectful name-calling and unpleasantness promoted by social media dialogue. The rivalry provides a life-blood to both clubs but it has to be underpinned by mutual respect.

Inside the ground, as the seats filled up, *It Ain't Half Hot Mum* stars Windsor Davies and Melvyn Hayes led the community singing. BBC commentator Eddie Waring informed TV viewers that the gate receipts were near to £500,000 and that, in addition to their share of the gate, the winners would receive £12,555 from sponsors State Express. Millward, who later admitted that walking on the pitch as the ground filled up had 'made the hairs stand up on the back of his neck', said he had little to do in his pre-match talk except remind the players they had to go back to Hull at the end of the day. They all knew how much the game meant anyway. He warned them to be careful because referee Fred Lindop had made an error in failing to send off a player in his previous final and Millward did not think he would make the same mistake again. In that one point he was proved wrong but perhaps it was appropriate that Lindop, who had been in charge of more Rovers' matches than any other official, should referee what was arguably their most important game.

The atmosphere reached boiling point when the teams entered the stadium behind chairmen Bill Land of Rovers and Charles Watson of the Airlie Birds and they were met with a crescendo of noise. Years later, Casey watched Russell Crowe walk into the Coliseum in *Gladiator* and remembered walking out at Wembley. 'It was just like that,' he said. 'It was an amazing feeling.'

Waring's co-commentator, Alex Murphy, felt that the Robins were looking the more relaxed of the two sides. The teams and officials were presented to Her Majesty Queen Elizabeth the Queen Mother, who stopped for a word with every player. At 3pm, Agar got the game under way, kicking off deep in to the Hull FC half, where Woods fielded the ball and made 10 yards before being halted by Lowe and Rose.

After dominating the early exchanges, Rovers scored their only try as early as the eighth minute. A penalty for offside in their own half enabled Millward to find touch 35 yards out. Watkinson took the tap and combined with Roy Holdstock, Agar and Lockwood, who delayed a brilliant pass to send Steve Hubbard steaming through a gap, whilst Lowe embarked on an excellent decoy run. Hubbard, coming inside from his wing, accelerated past three defenders to score 15 yards in from touch on the opposite side of the field.

The irony was that they had practiced this set move many times on the training ground, yet with no success. It is fair to say that no one in the team had any confidence in it but Millward wanted to keep it as an option just in case. The tap was in exactly the right place, so, on a hunch, he called it. It worked to perfection. After Hubbard scored, the touch-judge drew to the attention of referee Lindop an infringement on Hubbard as he scored the try. Although Hubbard missed with the conversion, he kicked the ensuing penalty for the late challenge from in front of the posts to put Rovers 5-0 ahead.

In the 13th minute, Hull FC's Wileman was guilty of a crude, high, off-the-ball tackle on Millward. The incident left Millward with a broken jaw. Rovers were awarded a penalty and Wileman got a severe 'talking to'. In any other game, he would probably have 'walked', but like Keith Hepworth in the 1970 final, he benefitted from the leniency of the Wakefield official. After receiving treatment, Millward carried on. He knew straightaway that his jaw was broken again – it had happened twice before that season, part of the reason why he had missed so many games, but he was absolutely determined to carry on. This was the culmination of all that he had worked for and there was no way that he was going to miss any of it if he could help it. It was bravery of the first order by the little man, however, sadly, he was unable to play to anything like his full potential. 'I couldn't remember much of the next 10 to 15 minutes,' he says. 'It was so blatant, but I shook his hand afterwards – I never bore grudges.'

From the penalty, Watkinson and Lockwood sent Holdstock on the charge. The latter was halted by a three-man tackle in which Stone was penalised for throwing a punch, and Hubbard's kick made it 7-0 after 15 minutes. The Airlie Birds looked out of control at this stage and the next to be penalised was Birdsall, for a foul tackle on Lowe. Gradually, though, they managed to get a grip on their game and started to build some attacks of their own. After stopping one with a textbook tackle on Bray, Millward again needed treatment and, without question, in any other game he would have left the field.

There were some warning signs for the Robins as they started to lose some discipline after their bright start. Murphy commented that they had stopped doing the basics but, generally their defence held firm and, until the 28th minute, all the Airlie Birds had to show was a missed penalty by Lloyd. Then, they won a scrum 10 yards from the Rovers' line and, from Wileman's quick heel, Newlove created a gap for Wilby to score ten yards in from touch, despite the attentions of Hubbard and Casey. Lloyd missed the conversion after several attempts even to keep the ball upright for his kick. His pre-match analysis about the 'nasty swirling wind' in the stadium proved to be correct.

The best chance in the remainder of the half fell to Rovers when Agar, Casey, Millward, Mike Smith and Lowe combined, but Rose was tackled a couple of yards short of the line. Then, just as the half-time hooter was about to sound, the forwards created the position for Millward to drop a goal from 30 yards and the Robins had an 8-3 lead.

The second period was one of near misses. Four tries were disallowed, two to each side, and both felt hard done by. At least Lindop was consistent, if there was any doubt at all in his mind, he denied the score. Final passes also went astray and excellent cover defence meant try-scoring opportunities were at a premium. In the end, the only further scores were a penalty goal to each side. Lloyd managed his only successful kick from four attempts in the 51st minute to narrow the score to 8-5 and, as the game entered the last 15 minutes, Hull FC started to exert some pressure in Rovers' 25. At this point, seeking fresh impetus, the Robins brought on John Millington in place of Rose and he put in some powerful drives and strong tackles. In the 75th minute, Hubbard made no mistake from 30 yards when Lloyd was penalised for an obstruction on Millward. That gave Rovers the five-point cushion that ultimately proved enough in a game where generally defences had been on top.

The Airlie Birds' final chance came in the last seconds when six players handled to put Bray clear but he was brilliantly tackled into touch by Sullivan. Hubbard injuring his leg in turning to chase his opposite number and had to be stretchered off before play could be resumed. Rovers won the scrum and drove the ball out of defence only for Casey to be penalised at a play the ball, and the Black and Whites got one last chance. Nevertheless, Rovers' defence held firm and it was all over. The Robins had finally won the Challenge Cup at their 73rd attempt. Before the game, their attack was considered Rovers' main strength but their defence had overcome.

The contest, although lacking nothing in atmosphere, excitement and incident, was never the rugby spectacle for which the purists had hoped. There was so much at stake and too much tension, which led to many errors. 'It was a game that nobody dare lose,' says Millward. 'There was probably more pressure on the two teams than in any other final.' The fact that Millward was unable to play to his usual standard and the spoiling tactics adopted by Hull FC to nullify the threat of Rovers' creative and speedy backs did not help. Indeed, Rovers' full-back David Hall later described himself as only a spectator. 'It was just a forward battle,' he said.

There were 32 penalties despite Lindop's leniency towards foul play early on. The overall result was that the standard of attacking play never reached great heights and, as *Hull Daily Mail* reporter John Sexton put it: 'It was only in fits and starts that the two sides put together the qualities that had taken them to Wembley…. there were too many mistakes and there have been many better derby games, even with their long-standing tradition for dourness.'

The rugby league press adjudged Rovers' Brian Lockwood to have been the man-of-the-match and he received the coveted Lance Todd Trophy. Perhaps his defence-splitting pass to Hubbard tipped the scales in his favour ahead of his fellow prop Holdstock, who put in a tremendous effort in what was one of his very best games for the club. They were well supported by the tireless efforts of Watkinson and Casey in the forwards. Allan Agar had an excellent game at half-back, prompting well and working tirelessly in defence, as well as shouldering additional leadership responsibility with Millward not firing on all cylinders.

Due to the general lack of attacking fluidity in such a stop-start game, the rest of the backs did not get the chance to shine as they could. Hall had a solid game at full-back, linking up well with play and dealing capably with a variety of kicks that the Airlie Birds tried and Hartley was a constant threat, striving to find the gap that would have enabled him to light up the stadium with one of his 'specials' – the long-distance individual tries that he was noted for. He also had a try chalked off when he supported a four-man move to beat the full-back and cross between the posts early in the second half, only to be recalled for a marginal forward pass.

In front of the Royal Box, Millward was congratulated by the Queen Mother and, watched by TV viewers across the world was presented with the cup. In his book *Roger: The Autobiography*, he described the moment. 'The roar from the

Rovers supporters was deafening. It was a moment that I'd waited my whole career for and one that I'll remember for the rest of my life.' As the players mounted the steps to the Royal Box, bringing up the rear, hobbling painfully on crutches, was Hubbard. The doctor, diagnosing a sprained ankle, quelled fears that his leg might have been broken. There was no way this would prevent him from receiving his medal in person. As the players did the traditional lap-of-honour and paraded the cup to their delirious supporters, Bernard Watson – a Wembley winner with Leeds – and physiotherapist Cliff Wallis helped Hubbard around the stadium.

As the players and fans celebrated, some spared a thought for the Airlie Birds and their fans. They had provided a tough challenge but ultimately their early indiscipline and the tenacious Rovers defence proved too difficult obstacles to overcome. A few of the fans might have known that the score line of 10-5 was exactly as it had been in the first Challenge Cup tie between the two rivals 78 years before – but the Robins had been on the receiving end that day. As is said, revenge is a dish best served cold.

In the immediate aftermath, Holdstock reflected on the speed at which the game passed. 'It seemed to come and go in flash,' he said. It was a feeling shared by many of his teammates but it is doubtful if the Rovers fans, watching on anxiously as their team defended a narrow lead for much of the second half, would have seen it that way. Sitting on the bench, Millington had been worried too. 'As Hull applied more pressure in the last quarter,' he noted, 'I could see some of our lads' heads starting to drop – as soon as I got on I went round shouting at everybody and encouraging them.' Casey told reporter Sexton: 'I knew we were going to win; I never thought we were in any danger once we went in front.' Years later, his view was more like Millward's. 'We just had to win, we daren't lose,' he acknowledged.

Comparing the game to today's derbies, Casey says: 'There were so many local players in our team then. It meant so much more to them than it does to many players today, who are with the club a couple of seasons and then move on.' His point is echoed by 1960s forward Brian Tyson who claimed: 'So many of the players in those days were local lads who had gone to school together and knew each other well – and they didn't want to lose any derby against their old rivals.'

Celebrations

Later, back at the team hotel, there was in Sexton's words: 'A splendid victory banquet, so sumptuous that the chefs earned their applause as they carried in the beef.' Sexton, who had spent the entire trip with the team, from leaving Hull on the coach that Wednesday morning to the triumphant return, was honoured by being asked to propose a toast to, 'Hull Kingston Rovers – the Rugby League Challenge Cup winners.' He is still the only man to have had that privilege. 'There were celebration drinks until the head swam, and the evening all too soon drifted away into sleep,' he wrote.

'The whole day was a wonderful experience,' recalls Turner. 'But it did all seem to flash by. I will never forget the scenes in the dressing room after the game, in particular the arrival of Bobby Ball, who couldn't get over how much Paul Harkin (Rovers' reserve scrum-half) looked like him – and the wonderful banquet for the players, wives, officials and guests on the night of the match.'

The following day started with the trip back-up north, with congratulatory waves and horn blowing from the supporters on the motorway and a rapturous welcome when the team stopped at services on the M1. There was then an open top bus tour of East Hull that culminated at the City Hall for a civic reception. Over 4,000 supporters cheered wildly below as Millward raised the Cup on the balcony. The final stage of the journey was back to Craven Park and the Supporters Club, where players and supporters mingled and celebrated together such a magnificent achievement.

Perhaps some of those present were aware of the periods of adversity in the past when the club had struggled to win any game let alone this huge one, and of how the club had struggled against the odds to even survive. Only they would have fully understood how this great moment was the product of all that had gone before.

*****

2. A Game for Gentlemen

1882-1899

FROM a meeting of a handful of workmates in a back room in a terrace house off Hessle Road in Hull, to becoming full members of the Northern Union in less than 17 years – a remarkable achievement.

Humble beginnings

The origins of the Hull Kingston Rovers Rugby Football Club of today can be traced back to its formation as Kingston Amateurs during the winter of 1882-3.

The world was a very different place then. That summer, in New York, Thomas Eddison started the electrical age by switching on the world's first commercial electricity generating station and, in Britain, Queen Victoria was in the 45th year of her 63-year reign and Gilbert and Sullivan's operettas were the height of popular music. Also, Old

The Robins

Etonians were the last amateur team to win the F.A. Cup, beating Blackburn Rovers in the final at the Oval. The *Sporting Times'* report of Australia's seven-run win over England in a one-off test match, also at the Oval, contained a mock obituary of English cricket, saying that its body would be cremated and the ashes taken back.

Rugby league, of course, did not exist at all. Whilst it is not this book's purpose to chronicle the development of the game of rugby, it may be useful to consider the background and context in which Kingston Amateurs played.

Various different types of football had been undertaken across the country for four centuries, unrecognisable from today's codes of association and rugby football. By the 19th century, early forms of the sport were widely played in the public schools. The popular supposition that the game was founded at Rugby School in 1823, when William Webb Ellis reputedly picked up the ball and ran with it, is almost certainly a myth; players had ball-in-hand long before then. Nevertheless, the public schools were hugely important in its development, not least in producing standardised rules. Devised at Rugby School and published in 1845, they gave birth to the name of 'rugby football'. For many years there were local rule variations but, for the first time, there was a basic framework. After that, young men formed the first rugby football clubs mainly because wanted to continue to play the game they had enjoyed at school.

Until the 1860s, in the main, only the upper and middle classes in the south of England played rugby football but the game then entered a period of rapid expansion, popularised in the best-selling novel *Tom Brown's Schooldays* published in 1859, which brought it to the attention of boys who had not been to rugby-playing schools. There was also an increasing belief that some form of physical exercise was beneficial and team sports were the most popular outlet. In the North, where the industrial revolution had brought increased prosperity, the 1874 Factory Act introduced Saturday half-day holidays and thus gave the working man increased leisure time. As a result, there was a dramatic increase in the number of northern rugby clubs and the balance of power in the game started to shift.

In 1865, the sons of the elite of the city, who had been to public schools like Rugby and Marlborough, formed Hull Football Club which became the leading one in the area. However, the development of the docks and heavy industry saw the city's population more than double in thirty years from 94,000 in 1861 to 199,000 in 1891. That also resulted in an explosion in the number of rugby football clubs.

By the 1890s, Hull was a stronghold, with over forty in the area. Association football was much less popular then and when a league was set up in the Hull area around this time, there were only five teams in it. One of the most significant of the new rugby clubs to emerge in this period, Hull White Star, was formed in 1873 and soon challenged the dominance of Hull FC. The members of both clubs ultimately agreed to merge in 1881, using the FC name and the White Star ground.

The Kingston Amateurs club was just one of those that was formed during this period of expansion. A group of young apprentice boilermakers employed by local firms C.D. Holmes and Amos & Smith, met in a small terraced house in Vauxhall Grove, Hessle Road in late 1882, and resolved to start their own team for the 1883-84 season. By then, Hull was in its heyday as a port with St Andrew's Dock opening in 1883 and Alexandra Dock under construction. Marine engineering was a major industry and C. D. Holmes and Amos & Smith were two of the biggest companies that serviced the trawlers and other ships that constituted heavy traffic in the Humber estuary.

The young men agreed that the club's colours would be red jerseys with a blue band across the chest, white trousers – not shorts at this stage - and red socks. This kit they had to purchase themselves. The Amateurs' first ground was a piece of wasteland in Albert Street, off Hessle Road, the move to East Hull did not take place for over ten years. Albert Street was renamed Gillett Street in 1894 and still exists today, running between Hessle Road and West Dock Street, although evidence of its place in local sporting history is long gone. This ground became known as Flag Edge Touch, due to the flagstones on one side of the ground that denoted the touchline and served as a slightly raised area for spectators. It boasted none of the facilities we associate with a modern sporting arena. The players had to purchase portable goalposts that they erected for home games. The changing facilities were a hedge-bottom, there was a ditch at one end of the ground and a tip at the other. Travellers used the ground as a camp when the Amateurs were not playing and frequently pitched tents on the playing area. However, the ground was local to where most of the players lived and, most importantly, there was no rent to find – a major consideration for those young pioneers.

The club duly started playing fixtures in the Hull and District League in the autumn of 1883 against local sides such as Marlborough, Southcoates, South Myton, Melbourne, Falcons, St Mary's and Three Crowns. The first captain was forward Bob Atkinson and the secretary was a Mr Ashton. Despite their status as newcomers, and their lowly facilities, the club quickly became successful on the field. Although they played only seven matches in that first season, they won six of them and even fielded a reserve team on four occasions.

Even in those early years, the club was progressive and forward-looking, they were not afraid to be proactive and recruit players that would improve them. Young upstarts they may have been, but their early progress was rapid and impressive.

Moving homes

In what was to be a regular occurrence in those early years, the club changed grounds for the 1884-85 season. The number of members they recruited meant that they now had funds and their first rented ground was on Anlaby Road, to the west of the railway line where the flyover now stands.

Around this time, there were moves to put the club on a more 'professional footing'. Officials were elected and rules agreed. Forward W. Cavinder took over as secretary and placed a notice in the local paper, *The Hull Packet*, detailing the 16 fixtures arranged, and inviting clubs of similar ability to help fill the blank dates. In the end, they played 19 games and although records are incomplete, it is safe to say that they won more than they lost. Early regulars in the team, in addition to Atkinson, were Eli Bell, Bob Chapman and J. W. White in the backs; W. Longthorne, J. Hardy, T. Brindle and Cavinder in the forwards.

Even in the club's infancy, there was controversy. There were unsavoury scenes at a game against Hull Forge 'A', when the Amateurs left the field. The committee later placed a notice in the *Packet* to clarify that the team departed, 'in protest against the quarrelsome nature of their opponents.' On the other hand, South Myton did likewise when the Amateurs claimed a free-kick for an offside.

In those days, the result of the game was determined by 'goals' – converted tries today – so that even if a team scored three tries to their opponents one, if none of the three were converted but the opponents enhanced their single try, they were deemed to have won. Each team had an 'umpire,' roughly equivalent to the later linesmen but neutral referees were only appointed to games involving senior clubs.

In 1885, the Hull and Barnsley Railway opened Alexandra Dock and their new line connecting it to the South Yorkshire coalfield. The demand caused by the port's expansion had overtaken the ability of the North Eastern Railway to cope, goods and supplies could not be delivered, ships were unable to receive or discharge cargoes and the port's trade was nearly paralysed. The new line, which passed through Springhead, Little Weighton and South Cave, stopping a few miles short of Barnsley at Cudworth, alleviated the bottleneck.

In their third season, 1885-86, the Amateurs moved home again. Their new ground was at Chalk Lane, which later became Hawthorn Avenue, still a busy thoroughfare between Anlaby Road and Hessle Road to the west of the city. At this time, they decided, appropriately, to change their name to Kingston Rovers. The team continued to gain a formidable playing reputation, winning all their 10 league games, whilst the 'A' team won seven of its 10. Two of the key players, Atkinson and White, the latter an expert drop-goal kicker, were invited to join Hull FC – a great honour at the time. Neither stayed there long, however, both preferring to re-join Rovers. Thomas Milner took over as captain on Atkinson's departure and the on-field success continued. Whilst the fixture list continued to grow, there remained blank dates, on which the club's players often 'assisted' other clubs.

For the first time the club entered the Hull Times Challenge Cup, an important competition for the many clubs in the area. Drawn against one of the leading clubs, Hessle, in the first round, they duly enhanced their growing reputation with a most unexpected win. The club were so short of funds at the time that, although money was collected to hire a horse-drawn vehicle to take the players the five miles or so to Hessle's ground, the club officials were expected to walk. They had a bye in the second round and faced Three Crowns in the third. Despite winning, the Amateurs lost a replay that was ordered following an objection by their opponents, who alleged that encroaching spectators had interfered with play.

A lack of funds did not diminish the club's social conscience and they donated the proceeds from the game against Beverley, in January 1886, to the relief fund for the families of the eight men killed in Albert Dock when a boiler on the steamer *Cartago Nova* blew up.

Meanwhile, in 1886, rugby football's southern-based hierarchy decreed that 'professionalism was a major threat to the ethos of the game', and introduced sanctions to expel any player who was proved to have been paid for playing. They also wanted to face those of their own social standing, not factory workers, dockers and labourers, whom they believed were over vigorous, even violent, in their style of play.

The ruling effectively targeted the northern clubs who regularly paid compensation for loss of pay to train and travel to games – training sessions then often took place on the morning of the game.

That year also saw the introduction of a 'points system' to decide matches, with three points being awarded for a goal (a converted try), and one for an unconverted try.

The rumblings that led to an eventual breakaway did not hamper Rovers' development as a club, however. In 1886-87, their fixture list was enhanced to include games with clubs such as Beverley, and there was further team strengthening. New players included Billy Keith, described some 35 years later as 'one of the most brilliant forwards the club ever had,' and stalwarts Charlie Coyne and William Soulsby. These reinforcements ensured continuing success on the field.

The club entered the new Hull and District Union Cup and lost narrowly to Hull 'A' in the final. As the premier club in the area, it was not surprising that Hull FC fielded only their second team against the young upstarts, albeit that they had been described by the *Hull & Lincolnshire Times* as the best minor club in the area. The occasion was slightly soured by the reported 'excessive bitterness between the rival fans,' whilst Rovers were 'slighted' when Hull FC declined to attend the after-match dinner put on by the organisers at the Salisbury hotel, preferring instead to hold their own celebrations. In direct contrast to today, Hull FC were then an East Hull club, based on Holderness Road, whilst Rovers move to East Hull was still some years away.

In the Times Cup, after beating Central Star and Goole 'A', Rovers lost to York 'A'. A further note of controversy was a Rovers' walk-off following a dispute whilst leading in an 'ordinary' (not league or cup) match at Stepney.

A first trophy

In 1887-88, Rovers moved for the fourth time, to the Locomotive Ground on Hessle Road at Dairycoates. They regularly attracted crowds of 2,000, and faced West Riding opposition for the first time. Founder member Eli Bell emigrated to America and was presented with a silver chain and medal by the club in gratitude for his services. The most significant event though, was that the club won its first trophy, the Times Cup. Rovers beat Selby 'A' in the final on Hull FC's Holderness Road ground, where the price of admission was 6d (2½ pence).

Rovers' team on that historic occasion was:

Milner, Soulsby, Marshall, White, Chapman, Cator, Keith, Stephens, Coyne, Longthorne, Wilson, Hardy, Atkinson, Stephenson, Rose.

Rovers donated their share of the proceeds from the final to local medical charities. The successes during this season precipitated Rovers rise in the ranks of local clubs and, at the end of season dinner, Arthur Yeo of the *Hull Times* described Rovers' success as almost phenomenal, saying that there would be few clubs that could boast such a record.

In 1888, the first victims were found in the London's Whitechapel area of the serial killer known as 'Jack the Ripper'; George Eastman patented the Kodak camera and, on 8 September, the first English Football League matches were played; 'Kenny' Davenport of Bolton Wanderers scoring the first-ever league goal. Rugby union's point-scoring system saw the introduction of kicks for goal following a penalty, which were worth two points if successful.

Kingston Rovers, buoyed by the successes of the previous season, arranged more out-of-town fixtures for the following season including against Castleford Hornets, Doncaster, and Heaton, from Bradford. They went through the season losing just two games, one of which was to York 'A' in the semi-final of the Times Cup. Six-thousand fans watched them draw against Hull 'A' in the final of the Hull & District Union Cup at Holderness Road, and 3,000 people filled the Locomotive Ground to capacity for the replay, which Hull 'A' won.

The Robins

E.E. Ward became the club's president – only when the club became a limited company some years later was the office of chairman introduced – and, by this time, they were regularly referred to as 'the Redbreasts' due to their predominantly red jerseys. During the season, the club pulled off a considerable coup by signing Sam Morfitt from Hull FC, a very talented back despite being only five feet four inches in height.

For the 1889-90 campaign, due to their continuing success and growing support, Rovers again lived up to their name by moving to a fifth, larger ground. This was the former home of one of their main rivals, Athletic, opposite to the well-known Star & Garter pub on Hessle Road. This hostelry, now known as Rayners, was very popular with the seafaring community. The new ground was definitely a step up from their previous homes. It had the luxury of a stand to accommodate 250 supporters and roped enclosures for other spectators. At an early game there, near-disaster was averted when a kick by Soulsby hit the ham sandwich man. Fortunately, it missed his basket and the fare remained intact.

On the field, Rovers won the Times Cup for the second time beating arch-rivals Britannia in the final on Hull FC's ground. Once again, there was controversy in a game against Hull Forge and the clubs were ordered to replay their second round tie on a neutral venue – the Redbreasts winning both games easily. They beat Hull 'A' for the first time but lost in the return game, defeated again in the second round of the Hull & District Cup in front of 6,000 people on Hull FC's ground. Rovers lodged an unsuccessful complaint after that cup defeat because the referee was not the one appointed by the RFU committee.

Rovers played their first Good Friday match against leading Wakefield team, Alverthorpe, who were strong enough to have beaten Hull FC in cup football. Rovers took credit from a narrow 4-2 defeat and a financial bonus from a half share of the £45 gate. This game and the two defeats by Hull 'A' were the only losses in another very successful season. Coyne scored 24 tries and Keith crossed for 20 in only 32 games. In mid-season there was some light relief in the *Hull Daily Mail* letters column caused by a Rovers follower suggesting that Hull FC's first team should play Rovers for 'supremacy of the town.' It provoked robust responses, one suggesting that it would be 'a long time before he witnessed such a match.' In fact, it was just eight seasons before the clubs were in opposition on an equal footing.

By 1890-91, the current name of Hull Kingston Rovers was in regular use, whilst the word Robin first appeared in the nickname and the club were often referred to as the Robin Redbreasts. George Batty became the secretary, a position he combined with that of club umpire. Batty was also the landlord of the Abercrombie Hotel in Campbell Street, Hessle Road, which also served as the club's headquarters.

The first out-of-town signings were made this season, with Williamson and Kilbourne joining from Cleckheaton and West Riding-based R. W. 'Ginger' Jackson, a speedy winger, added. He was also a noted runner and cricketer. Unfortunately, however, star back Morfitt left to join West Hartlepool, although he did guest for the club later that season.

Rovers lost only two out of 26 games all season and Keith, the captain, was the leading try-scorer with 19. By then Bell had returned from America and resumed playing. The club scratched from the second round of the Hull & District cup due to a clash with the return fixture against Buslingthorpe which they chose to honour, duly winning 4-0. The Redbreasts won the Times Cup for the third time in four years, beating Britannia 4-3 in the final, as a result of which they were considered outright winners and allowed to keep the cup. The *Hull Daily Mail* recorded that the home game against Doncaster, or the 'butterscotch town', as they called it, 'commenced with startling punctuality …. only half-an-hour late.'

In 1891, the motor car was first fitted with a starter motor, American Express issued the first travellers cheques and the fictional detective Sherlock Holmes became popular through a series of short stories in *Strand* magazine. John Heath of Wolverhampton Wanderers scored the first penalty in football and rugby amended its point scoring system again. All goals were now worth three points, tries two points and a converted try five points.

That season, Rovers entered the very prestigious Yorkshire Cup, known in those days as 'T'owd Tin Pot', for the first time. Introduced in 1877, despite opposition from the RFU, the first knockout rugby tournament became so popular with spectators that the final attracted much bigger crowds than the early FA Cup Finals. The Redbreasts won their first tie but Dewsbury knocked them out in the second round by the narrowest of margins. Old rivals Britannia were the only local side that Rovers played that season. Overall, they won 21 of 30 matches and Coyne was the leading try scorer, crossing the line 17 times.

In January, the club debuted at the new multi-sport facility at the Boulevard and they were obviously impressed because they decided to hire it for the next three seasons. Then, in February, Rovers played a charity match, in aid of medical causes, against the Alhambra Variety Artistes who all wore costumes, including wigs and hats, much to the amusement of the *Hull Daily Mail* reporter. Later that season the club refused to play in the final of the Times Cup because opponents York would not give up any fixtures to travel to Hull on a Saturday. Rovers, paradoxically, believed that the game must be played on a Saturday to ensure a maximum donation to the charities that would receive the proceeds.

In their first full season at the Boulevard, 1892-93, there was a temporary blip in Rovers' playing successes. Some of the longer-serving players were growing old and the team needed new blood. Twenty-nine games yielded only 16 wins and one draw and they lost 19-0 away to Bradford in the first round of the Yorkshire Cup. However, Rovers beat York in the final of the Times Cup by seven points to nil in April.

In 1893, further tinkering with the points system made all tries worth three points, along with penalty goals, but conversions were now worth only two. In 1893-94, Rovers enjoyed rather mixed fortunes. In the Yorkshire RFU's new 'Intermediate Competition', which comprised mainly West Riding clubs, the Redbreasts won half their league games and finished ninth out of 14. Overall, they won 20 and drew three of their 40 senior matches. George William Lofthouse became the youngest ever player to turn out for the club's senior side at the age of just 14.

By beating Shipley and Hunslet, Rovers progressed to the third round of the Yorkshire Cup, losing 8-4 away to the West Riding club in Leeds. In the first round game against Shipley, controversy again reared its head. Before kick-off, the Shipley captain sent a telegram to the Yorkshire RFU objecting to the condition of the referee, Mr C. Berry, who appeared to be unwell. Rovers, however, were content to play and the game went ahead. Afterwards, Rovers' players were alleged to have been allowed to dodge behind the touch-judges during play without being ruled 'in touch' and, after Berry had allowed a Shipley try, he then changed his mind and disallowed it. The Redbreasts won 7-0 but after Shipley's objection had to replay the game on a neutral ground. This time they won 14-0 and there was no room for debate.

1894 saw the introduction of death duties, the opening of Blackpool Tower and the first man in the UK to be convicted of drink-driving, a London taxi-driver.

Rovers played in what was effectively the third division of the Yorkshire RFU, where they finished third, with 17 wins and two draws from 26 matches. Again, they reached the third round of the Yorkshire Cup, having beaten both Horsforth and Mytholmroyd without conceding a point but lost 13-7 to Hunslet at the Boulevard. Overall, the senior side won 22 and drew two of their 35 games.

The Robins, as they were by then commonly known, showed their community spirit again in January 1895 when they decided to arrange a benefit match for the 'widows and orphans of the poor men lost in the late disastrous gales' – 200 fishermen from Hull and Grimsby had been lost at sea in severe winds at the start of the year. The game was proposed by president Ward and secretary Batty wrote to the *Hull Daily Mail* to seek the support of the public for the game.

Then, during the close season, events drastically altered the whole future of rugby football forever.

The Northern Union – the great 'breakaway'

Back in 1888, in addition to the earlier sanctions on payments to players, the RFU had introduced strict rules to govern the transfer of players between clubs. This had increased dissatisfaction amongst the leading Yorkshire and Lancashire sides. In 1892-93, they had attempted to maintain control over their destinies by organising themselves into leagues and, in April 1895, they proposed to form the Lancashire & Yorkshire

Union of Senior Clubs. The RFU forbade it, saying that they believed that it would be, 'Prejudicial to the best interests of the game.'

As a result, the representatives of 21 senior rugby clubs in Lancashire and Yorkshire held a summit meeting. This historic gathering took place on 29 August, 1895 at the George Hotel in Huddersfield, the home town of one of the leading clubs in the north. Twenty of the clubs present passed a resolution to break away from the RFU to form the Northern Rugby Football Union and establish the principle of payments to players to compensate players for lost wages – broken time payments. There were some individual misgivings but the desire not to be left behind prevailed and the Northern Union was duly inaugurated. The breakaway took place at breath-taking speed and the first NU fixtures were played just nine days after the momentous decision.

Two more clubs joined the original 20 which included Hull FC. A further eight senior clubs joined the new Union the following season, and a whole host of junior sides made the switch in those early years, the Hull & District league being one of the first to join.

For most of the twentieth century, anyone who played or coached in what became rugby league was barred from participating in rugby union.

Remaining loyal to the Rugby Football Union

At the time of the formation of the NU, Rovers were not convinced of its long-term success and took the view that Hull FC's defection opened the door for them to become the leading rugby football club in the area. Once again they moved grounds, but this time it was forced upon them. For their move into the NU, Hull FC needed a larger ground and they had taken a liking to the Boulevard. As the premier club, they were able to offer considerably more rent than Rovers could afford to pay and the Robins had to look for another new home.

They had to make a big choice, either move elsewhere in West Hull and try to compete with Hull FC, or switch across to the hotbed of rugby football in East Hull. On the east side of the city they would be in competition with old adversaries Britannia, but Rovers decided that they would have a better chance of flourishing and took the brave decision to relocate. 'Stay in West Hull and die, or move to East Hull and survive,' was how one press correspondent put it.

So, for the start of the 1895-6 season, the Robins' new ground was the former Southcoates ground at Craven Street, off Holderness Road. By now, rugby was overwhelmingly the most important sport in the city and Rovers were clearly the city's number two club. Despite losing a core of their members and supporters because of the move, they were welcomed into East Hull and gained many new followers, including those of the old Southcoates club. On 8 September 1895, Rovers played their first match at Craven Street, beating Leeds-based side Outwood Church 29-0.

In addition to a new ground, they had a new secretary in Charlie Savage, who was to give loyal service over several years in a key period in the club's development. Now promoted to the Yorkshire RFU's second division, they finished joint second to Shipley. In the Yorkshire Cup, they went one stage further than previously, losing 6-3 at home to Featherstone in the fourth round. Overall, the team won 23 and drew two of 34 games. Sam Morfitt had now returned to the club and became the first Rovers' player to gain representative honours with Yorkshire and England. Perhaps with tongue-in-cheek, president Ward wrote to the Yorkshire RFU during the season to say that as the only local club in membership of the RFU they were the senior club and asking if they were entitled to call themselves Hull Football Club. Needless to say, such a change did not take place.

To put their new ground to full use, the Robins amalgamated with one of the most successful of the handful of local association football clubs, Albany. Taking the name of Hull Town, the Albany club played with some success there on alternate weeks for two seasons. Savage showed that he was a shrewd judge when, in 1897, he noted that: 'Association has been but a minor sport, but .... I have the notion that it will grow, and that it may at some future time be as popular, if not more popular, than is rugby football in the area.' Although Hull Town did not last long, a number of its members were subsequently involved in the establishment of Hull City AFC.

Winning T'owd Tin Pot

In 1896-97, the club adopted its present name of Hull Kingston Rovers, which had been used informally for some years. A team photograph from that season shows that by then white jerseys, with white shorts and red socks, had superseded the red and blue jerseys. Despite the resignation of several sides, the Yorkshire RFU initially denied Rovers a place in the first division but they were promoted when a West Riding team dropped out.

This was to be the most successful season thus far. They had recruited well, in particular, two former Castleford forwards, Jack Rhodes and Anthony Starks, both England internationals. Rovers won the division, losing only three of 26 games and, for good measure, they also beat the 'rest of the league' 26-8 in a challenge match. The season's record of 30 wins from 34 games included a 23-match winning run that was not beaten for over 100 years. However, their outstanding achievement was in overcoming Shipley to win the Yorkshire Cup.

By this stage, the RFU had declared war on professionalism which it believed was the scourge of the game. Rovers' season was soured when they were accused of making 'broken time' payments and offering employment to induce prospective new players to sign for them. This was to be the beginning of the end of the Robins' loyalty to rugby union. The RFU arranged two hearings, pending which the club was suspended from playing.

At the hearing of the Yorkshire RFU, allegations were heard in connection with the club's leading player, Morfitt, Castleford-based players Rhodes and Starks, Keighley-based Blades, Noble, Geenty and McDermott from the North-East, and winger Jackson. The basis of the allegations was that Morfitt used a threat to join Hull FC as a lever to obtain better financial terms; that the West Riding and North-East players were offered inducements or employment to join the club and that Jackson had held negotiations with NU club Holbeck, signing a form agreeing to join them in return for reward.

The hearing found no case to answer except in the blatant case of Jackson, whom they suspended indefinitely. There was much relief and celebration in the Rovers' camp about the verdict but it was to be short-lived. On 19 February, 1897 the club appeared in front of the Professional Sub-Committee of the RFU at York. They found that, by allegedly allowing Morfitt to keep more of the takings from the Plimsoll's Ship public house that he managed in return for staying with the Robins, he and the club had committed breaches of the professionalism rule.

In relation to the recruitment of out-of-town players, the committee felt that the 'disgracefully lax manner' in which the club managed its' finances, and the absence of proper accounts and balance sheet, would render illegal payments to players easy to conceal. This, together with 'evidence relating to the extraordinary migration of players', resulted in Rovers' suspension being extended until 2 March that year. The fact that the club were unable to play any games during this six-week period and thus were forced to fit 14 games into a 46-day period between 6 March and 20 April, makes their league and cup successes that season even more remarkable.

Having remained loyal to the RFU to this point, Rovers greatly resented the action now taken against them. The RFU had also already debarred them from playing against, and seeking the assistance of, the junior NU clubs in the district. This had already hampered their efforts to strengthen and progress. There were also concerns about the standard of opposition that rugby union could offer following the breakaway of the senior clubs.

The Robins decided therefore, to apply for membership of the NU. The decision was not entirely unanimous but the club had continued to make remarkable progress, they remained ambitious and there was a general feeling that there was nothing to be gained from remaining in the Yorkshire union. Accordingly, president Ward wrote to the Yorkshire RFU to tender the club's resignation.

It was clear from recorded discussion at the subsequent RFU meeting on 24 May, 1897 that had not Rovers resigned, they would have been expelled. The Yorkshire Cup had to be returned immediately upon resignation, so its stay in East Hull was short but sweet.

The Robins

Yorkshire Cup Final, West Riding ground, Meanwood Road, Leeds, 17 April, 1897
Hull Kingston Rovers 11-5 Shipley

The records of the two clubs that season pointed to a relatively easy win for Rovers but they had played 15 matches in the six weeks leading up to the final and, although they were able to field pretty much a full-strength side, the players must have been fatigued. Shipley got off to a good start and were the better team in the first half.

Just before half-time, Town scored a try that Emmott improved to put Shipley 5-0 ahead at the break. Despite Rovers' pressure, Shipley still led as the game entered its last quarter and it was looking ominous for the Robins. Then Sam Morfitt scored from an interception, Sparvieri added the goal and the West Riding club, tiring by then, lost some of their heart. Their defence collapsed and George Fletcher put Rovers ahead following a forward rush. Spavieri's conversion attempt hit the crossbar and rebounded back into the field of play.

The Hull Daily Mail *commented that: 'It was a good attempt considering the heavy conditions and slippery ball.' Just before the final whistle, burly Jack Rhodes ended any doubt about the result by scoring Rovers' third try, Sparvieri again failing to convert.*

> ***Rovers:*** *J. Spavieri; D. Morfitt, S. Morfitt, T. Ripton (capt), H. Tullock; C. Coyne, G. Fletcher; A. Starks, J. Rhodes, A. Kemp, J. Geenty, P. McDermott, M. Gledhill, J. Noble, R. Blades*

The Robins returned to Hull by train to a tremendous reception. As the Mail *reporter put it: 'Carr Lane, Anlaby Road, Midland Street and the station yard were a seething mass of humanity, and there was scarcely any moving.' The players had to struggle through the crowd to reach the waiting wagonette, in which they carried the famous old cup aloft in triumph around the city.*

Joining the Northern Union

In 1897, a stampede of an estimated 100,000 gold prospectors descended on the Klondike and Yukon areas of Alaska. In Britain, Queen Victoria celebrated her diamond jubilee and Kingston upon Hull was given city status.

By then, the NU comprised 30 senior clubs, split into two leagues, the Lancashire and Yorkshire senior competitions. On 20 May, the Yorkshire Senior Competition (YSC) committee agreed to recommend Hull Kingston Rovers for full membership in 1897-98. However, an anticipated vacancy in their competition did not materialise, as a planned merger between Liversedge and Heckmondwike collapsed.

The club's failure to gain admittance to the YSC was a serious setback. Several leading players, including Morfitt, Starks, Rhodes, Albert Kemp and Thomas Ripton were unhappy about the club's fixtures for the coming season and asked for transfers. Although the Robins were able to participate in the newly-introduced Challenge Cup, they had to arrange whatever friendly matches they could with other NU clubs to make up their fixture list.

At the Annual Meeting, the club was in crisis. President E.E. Ward, who had held the position for nine years, and to whom, according to the *Hull Daily Mail* correspondent, the club almost entirely owed its early success, retired from the post. H. Mollekin, who had already 'rendered yeoman service to the club' according to the *Mail*, was his replacement. Then secretary T. Ward resigned his position due to pressure of business and Charlie Savage resumed the job. The members proposed Morfitt as captain and, despite his initial reluctance, he was persuaded to take on the role.

The importance of Mollekin, Savage and Morfitt in keeping the club going and raising morale after its setback cannot be underestimated. They even managed to strengthen the team by bringing in the Tudhoe and Durham scrum-half Billy Guy, along with an assortment of players from Featherstone, Goole and other local clubs. Hull FC sought to sign the players who had asked to leave but all except Morfitt withdrew their requests. The NU asked the club for its reasons for refusing Morfitt his transfer, which were accepted, and he too agreed to stay. It is likely that the club's 'A' team ceased to function at this time.

For the 1897-98 season, the NU had abolished line-outs and standardised scoring so that tries were worth three points and all goals two, a system that was to last for 77 years. NU games were still 15-a-side and retained the familiar rugby union loose rucks following the tackle. Rovers' first fixture under NU rules was a 31-0 friendly win at home to Compton, and the first side they faced in a competitive game was Marlborough in the Challenge Cup. The historic match resulted in a 46-0 win for the Robins, with Morfitt scoring four tries. The team progressed to the fourth round, in which they drew 0-0 against Widnes at the Boulevard, where they had somewhat controversially decided to play the tie in an effort to maximise gate receipts. In the replay at Widnes, Rovers conceded their first points and lost 6-5.

By the end of the campaign, Rovers had won 24 and drawn four of their 34. At the end-of-season AGM, Savage commented on the difficulties endured at the start of the season, saying that the club had, 'Been on its last legs' but pulled through.

In 1898-99, there still being no vacancy in the YSC,

Rovers were placed in the inaugural Yorkshire second XV competition. They won all of their 17 matches, scoring 389 points and conceding a mere 18, keeping a clean sheet in 13 of their 17 games. Again, no fewer than 21 friendly fixtures against fully-fledged NU clubs supplemented the league games and two Challenge Cup ties. In a play-off, Rovers beat Heckmondwike – who had finished bottom of the YSC – 21-3 at Headingley, thus qualifying for full membership of the NU. In the cup, after a first round home win over Manningham, interest ended at Broughton Rangers.

Overall, it was the Robins' best season in terms of results but, at the AGM, Savage described the league programme as being 'ridiculously easy'. A testimonial was granted to Morfitt, the leading goal-kicker and try-scorer, at the end of the following season.

The 'Davis affair'

The curious 'Davis affair' took place when Davis, a local man unattached to any club, approached Rovers about the possibility of playing for them. There was not immediately a vacancy in the team but he subsequently played against Widnes. Satisfied with what they had seen, the club paid him 'a small sum of money' and he signed the required forms. Rovers were then very unhappy to learn that Davis had signed for Hull FC and wrote to the NU to complain, saying that he was their player.

They were then even less happy when the NU, who took the opposite view, fined them £50.

The club had now completed their first 16 years of progress at breakneck-speed, a difficult journey often achieved against the odds and the expectations of doubters. They had undergone five ground moves, two name changes

The Robins

and a turnover of personnel at all levels. Now they were to become full members of the NU after two years in waiting. They had managed to retain the nucleus of their side and felt they had grounds for being optimistic about the future. In short, they were eager to go.

*****

3. Laying Foundations

1899-1915

IN their first 16 seasons in the Northern Union, the Robins reached three cup finals and twice finished third in the league behind the great Huddersfield and Wigan teams – only four times failing to win more games in a season than they lost.

First impressions

In 1899, the second Boer War between the United Kingdom and the Boers of the Transvaal and Orange Free State, was brewing in South Africa. At home, Edwin Sewell became the first motorist to be killed in a road accident and Marconi successfully transmitted a radio signal across the English Channel. The population of Hull had risen above 200,000 and, largely due to its importance as a port, the city was entering a period of prosperity that lasted until the after the start of World War I. The first Hull City Tramways services ran along

The Robins

Anlaby Road and Hessle Road. In sport, association football was rapidly expanding world-wide – the English Football League by now comprised two divisions of 18 clubs each and, in the NU, Batley were the reigning Yorkshire Senior Champions, beating Hull FC to the title by a single point.

After the frantic changes of the previous 16 seasons, Rovers were now to enjoy a period of relative stability. Their next ground move was still over 20 years away and they were able to concentrate on establishing themselves as a force in the NU.

Their first season as full members, in 1899-1900, was highly successful. They finished sixth out of 16 clubs in the YSC, winning 15 and drawing four of their 30 league matches despite falling away at the end of the season, when they failed to win any of their last five games.

The Robins' first NU league game was at Bradford on 2 September, 1899 where they lost by three points to nil – no disgrace against the competition's winners that season. After drawing at Castleford the following week, they played Hull FC in their first home fixture on 16 September – the inaugural competitive game between the first teams of the rivals. Rovers won 8-2 and later completed the double over their neighbours with a 3-0 away win, and finished one place above them in the YSC. Rovers beat Millom in the first round of the Challenge Cup but lost their second round tie at Rochdale 13-5.

Rhodes missed only two of the 32 games and other regulars were Debney, Fletcher, Kemp, Starks, Stephenson and Windle in the forwards; Smith at full-back, Tullock on the wing, Guy at stand-off, and Morfitt in the centre. Early stalwart Charlie Coyne played his last game at home to Manningham on 3 March. A reflection of the marked difference in the way the game was played then and now was

44

that in 32 matches only 47 tries were scored – ten of these by Morfitt – and 24 goals were kicked. The game contained much less handling and 'kick and rush' or dribbling was prominent, whilst the heavy balls used at the time made goal-kicking more difficult.

Although not all attendances are recorded, they fluctuated to quite a large degree. 14,000 watched the derby game at Craven Street and there were at least four other five-figure gates, but only 4,000 watched the Castleford game. By this time, Rovers were still wearing white shirts but with dark shorts. 'Breaches of professional rules' were commonplace in the game and the Robins were fined £100 and deducted two points for playing full-back Herbert Sinclair without correctly notifying the NU of his change of employment in the opening weeks of the season. The player himself received a rather draconian three-year ban and secretary Savage was severely censured for his conduct in the matter, his evidence being declared 'not at all satisfactory'. Forward Cole missed the entire season due to a ban imposed when he signed for both Rovers and then amateur club Featherstone at the same time.

Northern Union, Craven Street, Hull,
16 September, 1899
Hull Kingston Rovers 8-2 Hull FC

A crowd of 14,000 paid nearly £500 at increased admission prices for the privilege of watching the first NU derby match between the two clubs. Although unimpressive in their previous two games, Hull FC were strong favourites but it was Rovers who drew first blood with what the Yorkshire Evening Post *described as 'a beautiful try' by Anthony Starks after just five minutes. After this, the Rovers forwards got the upper hand in the scrums and in the loose, and whilst the visitors did get into good positions, they did* not look dangerous. *Albert Kemp, George Fletcher, Jack Rhodes and Starks repeatedly made inroads into the Hull FC defence, and Kemp gave Rovers a 6-0 lead when he scored a try shortly before half-time.*

According to the Yorkshire Evening Post, *the second half started, 'Fast but even' and the Boulevarders got the encouragement of a penalty goal by Billy Jacques, who was later to play a big part in Rovers' 1920s successes. They pressed hard but were unable to crack the Robins' defence. In the end, Herbert Tullock's penalty sealed Rovers' win. The Post complimented the Robins' forwards, adding that they were the better-organised side and that in Tullock they had the most dangerous back on the field.*

After the match, the Rovers committee and players entertained their opposite numbers to a dinner and smoking concert at the Queens Hotel in Charlotte Street. Rovers President, Mr Mollekin, thanked the players and the public for their exemplary conduct, and commented on the sportsmanlike way that Hull FC accepted defeat. The Hull FC President, Mr Brewer, expressed the opinion that the best team won. Mr Hildreth, their secretary, commented on the good relationships he had always had with Rovers' officials and hoped that the prevalent good feeling between the clubs would continue. He added: 'I hope that Rovers will finish high up the NU, so long as Hull FC are above them!'

> *Rovers: H. Sinclair; S. Ruddeforth, H. Tullock, T. Ripton, R. W. Jackson; W. Guy, J. Levett; A. Kemp (capt), A. Starks, J. Rhodes, G. Fletcher, J. Stephenson, J. Noble, J. Debney, A. Windle.*
> *Hull FC: G. Sillis; C. Lempriere, J. Driscoll, J. Tanner, W. Jacques; D. Franks, H. Thompson; F. Cornish, R. Parkinson, G. Voyce, R. Rhodes, F. Gorman, H. Wiles, W. Dale, P. Fildes.*
> *Referee: P. Farrar (Halifax)*
> *Attendance: 14,000 (£500)*

In his annual report, the secretary commented that it had been 'a feat of merit' to finish sixth in their first season in the YSC, particularly given the injuries to key men that resulted in a total of 43 players being called upon. The turf on the ground had been re-laid and spectator accommodation increased. The club designated the last match of the season as a benefit for Coyne for his 'excellent service' and it held a match between A. Stark's XV and A. Kemp's XV to raise funds for the Fishing Fleet Disaster Fund. Two areas that the club did need to address were the growing debt and increasing the depth of the playing strength, where the lack of adequate reserves had cost some games.

Despite a good start that resulted in 18 points coming from the first 13 games, 1900-01 saw a small slip in league position down to eighth out of 16, under new captain Anthony Starks. The highlight was a 7-5 home success over Bradford, who won the competition for a second year running. Although the Robins managed just 6.5 points per game, their defensive record of 5.6 points conceded per game was impressive. In the Challenge Cup, Rovers progressed to the fourth round with wins over Salford, Maryport and Brighouse, before falling 7-2 at Castleford in a replay.

Windle led the way with 32 appearances from the 35 matches and Cole returned to the forwards where he joined the regulars from the previous season. A notable new arrival was Billy Phipps, who made his debut in December and soon became a familiar figure at centre. At the end of the season, there were also debuts for two players that were to be stalwarts of the side in years to come. George Henry 'Tich' West made his first appearance at home to Batley on 6 April and retained his place for the last two games, whilst Alf Carmichael, 'Bunker' as he became known, made his bow at full-back at Brighouse in the last match of the season. Now retired, Coyne assisted Savage with the administrative duties.

At the end of that season, the clubs that had finished in the top six positions in the Lancashire and Yorkshire senior competitions decided that they wanted to form a combined top division, with regional competitions running in parallel as a second tier below. They could only obtain the majority in the NU Committee necessary to do this by expanding the top division to 14 and including a seventh club from each of the two competitions. The new top division was known as the Northern Rugby League. All the Lancashire clubs were content with this but the Yorkshire clubs outside the top tier were not and imposed a boycott of NRL clubs.

A season in exile

1901 marked the end of the country's Victorian era when the Queen died in January after a 63 year reign. The country also endured a wretched summer during which Yorkshire won a second successive cricket County Championship, bowling out Nottinghamshire for just 13 along the way.

Having finished eighth in the YSC the season before, Rovers missed out on joining neighbours Hull FC in the top division, due to points difference that was just six inferior to that of seventh-placed Brighouse. The absence of derby games was unacceptable to both clubs and they arranged 'friendly' derbies instead. This breached the Yorkshire clubs' boycott of the NRL and they expelled the Robins from the YSC. However, there was no shortage of Lancashire clubs who invited Rovers to play in their competition. Rovers agreed to join in order to gain promotion. They were heavily subsidised for the additional travelling incurred and the move eventually worked out to their advantage.

The Robins finished fifth out of 13 clubs in the Lancashire Senior Competition in 1901-02, fourth being missed out on only due to a further two-point deduction for a rules breach. Their very impressive points difference of 195 was bettered only by winners Wigan. There was a new club record 71-0 home win over Radcliffe and a 43-0 home triumph against Altrincham, in which Starks scored five tries to create a new club record. A curiosity in the return fixture at Radcliffe was that Rovers played two men short – which presumably accounted for their more modest 16-0 win. This remains the only occasion when the Robins have failed to field a full complement of players in a first team game. In the Cup, a home win over St Helens was followed by a home defeat to Hull FC in the two clubs' first Challenge Cup meeting – coincidentally by a 10-5 score line.

Welsh stand-off Jim Barry and winger Tich West both established themselves during the season. Meanwhile, infamous winger Jackson returned after missing the previous two seasons but, after scoring eight tries in his 15 appearances, disappeared for good. Others to play their last games that season were forward dependables Debney and Rhodes.

The rules breach occurred when the club played Windle against the League's direction, for which they were fined one guinea in addition to the points deduction, whilst the player was suspended for a hefty six months. In addition, the NU fined Rovers 10 shillings for a late start against Rochdale on 10th April. The club were also required to post warning notices about player behaviour after fighting broke out in both fixtures with Widnes.

At the AGM, Savage was persuaded to continue as secretary despite having decided to resign, but the club headquarters had changed as he was now licensee at the

The Robins

Durham Ox in Blanket Row, just off Queen Street. It was then a very busy part of Hull's old town near to the fruit market, less than a quarter of a mile from where 1970s vice-chairman Percy Johnson held court at the Corn Exchange.

A First Division club

More changes in league structure took place for 1902-03. After meeting with the Lancashire competition clubs, the NRL proposed to bring all the senior NU clubs into a straight two-division structure with 18 in each division. Rather than miss out, the YSC clubs agreed to the proposal and ended their boycott but, because of their action, the NU made them join the new structure in the second division. As Rovers had played in the Lancashire competition the season before, they qualified for a place in the top tier.

Rovers finished 14th out of 18 clubs and, for the first time in their history, the Robins lost more matches than they won – only two wins coming from the first 11 fixtures. Second Division York beat them at home 6-2 in the first round of the Cup. Again, Rovers reserved one of their best performances for a better side, beating inaugural first division winners Halifax 6-0 at Craven Street.

West missed only three of the 35 games and Jimmy Gordon made his debut in the centre. The club's first real star player, Sam Morfitt, made his final appearance in March. Two other long-serving players to retire were centre Thomas Ripton and winger Herbert Tullock. Starks was appointed captain of Yorkshire.

A *Yorkshire Evening Post* report of the home game with Bradford gives a flavour of those early NU games. It commented on a fast and even first half, with high-kicking and 'kick and rush' tactics prominent, and that despite the energy Rovers put into attack, Bradford's second half wind advantage was decisive.

The accounts, presented at the AGM, showed a net profit of £82 with gate receipts and subscriptions totalling £2,441 and players' wages and bonuses accounting for £1,110. The club had cleared most of a £300-plus debt carried over from 1901-02. A proposal for a salaried secretary but an overall reduction in officials, was agreed.

The Greats – No 1
Sam Morfitt - *see Hull KR legends gallery*

Signed from Hull FC in the 1888-89 season, Sam Morfitt was Rovers' first real superstar. Born in Hull in 1869, he played his early rugby with Holderness Wanderers, Three Crowns and Southcoates before joining FC. In 1888 he crossed to Rovers but left for a spell with West Hartlepool during the 1889-90 season, although returning to guest for the Robins later that season. His guest appearance against Hull Forge in the 1890 Times cup-tie resulted in the game being replayed, when the cup committee upheld Forge's objection about his eligibility. Whilst at West Hartlepool, he won Durham county honours, played for the North of England and won four of his six full England caps. He returned to Rovers by the 1895-6 season, and subsequently played for Yorkshire.

Only 5ft 4in tall and weighing 10st 6lb, he started his career as a skilful and tricky half-back. Later, he worked on his speed and Rovers rewarded him with centre spot, in which he played most of his later club and representative football. His all-round pace and skill were more important in that position than defensive strength and the ability to break a tackle. Sam played in Rovers' first six seasons in the NU, making 83 competitive appearances over that period, kicking nine goals and scoring 29 tries. He played his last game at Warrington on 21 March, 1903. His younger brother Dan also played regularly for the club. Sam Morfitt died, aged 85, in January 1954.

The 1903-04 season saw Rovers return to the black in terms of their playing record, defeated in only one of their first 11 games this time. Despite a loss of form in mid-December, the Robins won four of their last five matches to claim eighth place out of the 18 First Division clubs. The early season run included a 9-3 success against eventual champions Bradford and Rovers' first-ever win at Wigan, 5-0. The *Yorkshire Post* recorded that the latter match took place in splendid weather with unusual interest generated by the fact that Rovers were the first Yorkshire team to visit Wigan that season.

Both derby games resulted in away wins, Hull FC successful 3-2 at Craven Street in December when both sides had a man sent off and Rovers taking revenge with a 7-2 win at the Boulevard in April. For the second time, Rovers finished above their neighbours in the league – this time by five places – but lost at home to Leeds in the first round of the cup.

Harry Shann became the team's first official 'trainer', the equivalent of a coach today. Carmichael began to challenge Sinclair for the full-back position although he did not make it his own for another three seasons. Along with Fletcher, Sinclair only missed two games, moving to centre when Carmichael had an 11-match run at full-back. Jimmy Gordon deputised as captain when Starks was absent though injury or representative commitments. The code's first international match took place when England played Other Nationalities at Wigan in April and Starks had the honour of being named the first England captain.

Rovers had completed six seasons in the NU and had

comfortably established themselves in the top flight. The secretary's report recorded it as: 'The most successful season in the history of the club .... considering the depression of trade in the city, the financial success was even more remarkable.' It referred to a terrible injury list with Sleep out for five months, West and Starks each suffering three separate injuries and several other players were missing for significant spells. In this context, the league position was as remarkable as the £622 profit made. At the AGM it was acknowledged that, for the first time in its 20-year history, the club was free of debt, it had more property than ever before as well as £50 cash-in-hand. One issue, however, was that difficulties in finding suitable employment was hampering player recruitment efforts.

A first Challenge Cup final

In June 1904, Hull City AFC was founded. They played their first season at the Boulevard, which they shared with Hull FC. On 21 October, the 'Dogger Bank incident' took place. Russian warships attacked a fleet of Hull trawlers, completely unexpectedly and without provocation. One trawler, the *Crane*, was sunk, two trawlermen lost their lives and 30 others were injured. The Russians had mistaken the fishing fleet for the Japanese Navy, with whom they had experienced recent skirmishes. Their action caused a major diplomatic incident and a threat of war between England and Russia.

It was in the 1904-05 season that the Robins made their first appearance in a major final, when they reached the decider of the NU Challenge Cup. In the league, they ended 12th out of 18 clubs. The season did not start auspiciously as Rovers lost five out of their first six matches, including a 4-6 loss away to eventual wooden-spoonists Runcorn. But they then won 11 out of the next 16 league games up until the end of January, including an 8-0 success in the Boxing Day derby at the Boulevard. After that, the Challenge Cup dominated the remainder of the season but at the expense of the league, in which they won only a further three fixtures. The return derby at Craven Street resulted in an 11-6 defeat.

In the first round of the cup, the Robins were drawn away to Cumbrian junior club Brookland Rovers, whom they paid £80 plus a half share the gate to make the long trip to Hull. Rovers' reward was a then club record 73-5 win, in which winger Tich West scored 11 tries and kicked 10 goals for a personal tally of 53 points, which is still a rugby league world record. In the following rounds, they beat Leeds and Hunslet at home and, against all expectations, Broughton Rangers 10-6 in the semi-final at Belle Vue, Wakefield. All three of these clubs finished higher in the league than the Robins. In the final, although a strong Warrington side beat them, it was a very fine achievement.

Rugby League Challenge Cup Final, Headingley, Leeds, 29 April 1905
Hull Kingston Rovers 0-6 Warrington

Despite their league record against Warrington that season, when both sides won their home league games against the other – Rovers convincingly 13-0 and Warrington narrowly 4-2 – the Robins were still rank outsiders on the day. They did remarkably well to reach the final, as relative newcomers to the NU. A big crowd of well-wishers gave them a send-off to Headingley, with hundreds lining Park Street bridge to wave as the train passed. It was reported that the train was pulled by same engine, with the same crew, that took the team to the semi-final, and that the driver and fireman had been kitted out in white Rovers jerseys – although how long they

54

remained white on the footplate of a steam locomotive is very questionable. The playing kit had continued to evolve, and was then white jerseys and blue shorts.

Warrington were without influential forward Jack Preston, who was injured, whilst Rovers forward Richard Townsley had been unemployed for several weeks and was prevented from playing by the then 'working clause'. The game itself was unremarkable. After early Warrington pressure, the Robins produced the first move worthy of note when half-backs Jim Barry and Jimmy Gordon combined to provide an opening for Billy Phipps, who sent Tich West on a run for the line, only to be tackled by Warrington's star wingman Jack Fish. The Warrington forwards then started to get the upper hand, and created a couple of openings that Rovers managed to snuff out. Fish failed with an ambitious penalty attempt in the 25th minute, and a couple of minutes later Isherwood intercepted Barry's pass to West, heading the ball away in football style. The alert Fish raced up to grab the loose ball and he beat the Rovers cover before slipping near the touchline in his attempt to round full-back Herbert Sinclair, and was tackled. Towards the end of the half, the Robins produced some pressure and Barry made a spectacular run, but Hallam and Fish managed to scramble clear his kick to the line.

In the second half, Warrington took control after Fish's early break. The Wires won a scrum near the Rovers' line, Davies and Isherwood sent Fish charging for the line, and the winger scored a controversial try when it appeared that he was held in the combined tackle of Sinclair and West before wriggling his way over. Fish's conversion attempt scarcely left the ground but, ten minutes later, Brooks burst through an opening in a tiring Rovers' defence, drew Sinclair and passed on to Fish, who sprinted over unopposed near the posts for his second try. This time Hallam's attempted conversion hit the upright. The Robins tried valiantly to get back into the game, with Fish twice denying West, whilst Warrington also twice came close.

The Robins

The Manchester Guardian *commented that Warrington, 'by far and away the better team,' 'won well and deservedly.' A couple of hundred fans turned out at Hull Paragon station that evening to welcome home the players, and it would be twenty years before there was another Challenge Cup final trip.*

Rovers: H. Sinclair; W. Madley, A.W. Robinson, W. Phipps, G.H. West; J. Barry, J. Gordon; A. Starks (capt), A. Kemp, W.T. Osborne, A. Spackman, A. Windle, G. Ellis, F. Gorman, D. Reed.

Warrington: J. Hallam (capt); J. Fish, D. Isherwood, G. Dickenson, T. Kenyon; D. Davies, E. Brooks; A.S. Boardman, G. Thomas, F.H. Shugars, G. Jolley, W. Belton, A. Naylor, W. Swift, J. Harmer.

Referee: J. Bruckshaw (Stockport)

Attendance: 19,638 (£1,270)

West established a new club record with 28 tries, almost half the total scored by the team, and forward John Ellis played in all but one of the 39 games. The nucleus of a fairly settled side was full-back Herbert Sinclair, wingers West and Madley, centre Billy Phipps, half-backs Gordon and Barry, whilst in the forwards, in addition to the old campaigners Kemp and Starks, the regulars were Ellis, Gorman, Osborne, Spackman and Townsley.

Three of the longest-serving players made their last appearances for the club during the season. Between them, half-back Billy Guy and forwards George Fletcher and Albert Kemp had made over 400 appearances for the Robins. All had also played in the pre-NU days and had been very influential in establishing the club in the Union. Former skipper Kemp retired after the Challenge Cup final and the club awarded him a benefit match. Amongst several new faces, forward Arthur Spackman, who made his debut at Runcorn in the first game, proved the most valuable acquisition.

At the end of the season, Fred Langley became the club's first official chairman, and C.H. Duggleby replaced the stalwart servant Charlie Savage as secretary when the latter stood down for the final time.

For the first time, Rovers played games on Good Friday as well as Easter Saturday, with a Bank Holiday Monday game thrown in for good measure. During the season, two clubs refused to fulfil their fixtures at Dewsbury due to the smallpox outbreak in the town. The NU expressed strong disapproval of their actions, and threatened 'substantial damages' against any clubs who followed suit. The disease was far from uncommon in those times.

Hull Kingston Rovers RFC Ltd

The following season, 1905-06, saw Hull City make their football league debut only a year after their formation, with a 4-1 home win over Barnsley. They eventually finished a commendable fifth in Division Two.

Under club president John Moore, the AGM took the decision that Rovers should become a limited company, which occurred on 11 September, 1905. Langley remained chairman, but the new secretary was George Johnson, who was to retain the role until just after World War I, and who was responsible for the publication of the club's first formal Annual Report at the end of the season.

At that stage, the NU was tinkering with its' rules and competitions in an effort to make the game more attractive and introduced the Lancashire and Yorkshire Cups. Two clubs, though – Birkenhead and Lancaster – resigned, leading to a discontinued Second Division, which had endured three rather traumatic seasons. Accordingly, a single league format was introduced that continued until the 1960s.

The Robins

The problem was that 31 clubs was far too many for each to play the other twice, but they did not want to lose the home and away fixtures with their traditional rivals – not least for financial reasons. So, in the new set-up, each was required to play a minimum of 20 fixtures that must include reverse games with all clubs within their own county, and they were allowed to play as many other matches as they wanted. The number actually played varied between 20 and 40, with league positions decided by the percentage of points gained against games played. Leigh won the league with 80 per cent (48 points from 30 games), but they attracted criticism for not facing the stronger Yorkshire clubs. They did play Rovers and beat them twice, albeit quite narrowly.

The Robins themselves won 22 out of their 36 games and finished seventh, a creditable achievement, particularly as the seven Lancashire clubs they played home and away included Leigh, Oldham and Wigan, who were the top three from West of the Pennines in the final table. Rovers gained increased satisfaction as their Boulevard neighbours finished only in 17th place.

The Robins won 5-4 there on Boxing Day and returned in February to play a friendly in aid of the local unemployment fund. The city may have been prosperous, but there was no welfare state then, only the workhouse. Rovers won the friendly 5-0, but the Airlie Birds extracted revenge with a 17-4 Good Friday win at Craven Street. The two clubs reached an agreement to pool and share the receipts of the derby games – the first of several similar arrangements.

It was in this season that the first concentrated Christmas and New Year programme took place, with the Robins playing six games in ten days between 23 December and 1 January, with a 50 per cent success record.

In the new Yorkshire Cup competition, they reached

the semi-final, where they lost to Hunslet after a replay. Fog caused the abandonment of the first match at Craven Street after 63 minutes with the visitors leading 12-3. Despite Rovers' appeal, the county committee gave Hunslet ground advantage for the replay and Rovers lost 14-3. In the Challenge Cup, there was no repeat of the previous season's heroics. After beating Dewsbury and Brighouse, the latter in a replay after a 0-0 away draw, a rare score line even then, they lost 15-0 at Batley in the third round.

During the season, the Robins signed winger W.F. 'Fred' Jowett and centre Dan Rees from Swansea rugby union club. Jowett was a current Welsh international and had toured Australia and New Zealand with the 1904 British Lions. Rovers reportedly agreed to pay Rees two pounds and ten shillings per game, win or lose, and to find him a job. Another new signing was forward Jim Gath from Heckmondwike, who played in 42 of the 45 first team games, one more than the ever-dependable Windle.

Thanks to being able to field a reasonably settled side, the 31 players used was the lowest since the club joined the NU. The first Rovers' annual gala took place at Craven Street in July 1906, becoming a regular event until after the First World War.

Two ground-breaking rule changes were introduced by the NU in 1906-07; the reduction to 13 players per side with the dropping of the two 'wing forwards' and the introduction of the play-the-ball after a tackle – thus removing the 'loose ruck.'

To answer the criticisms of Leigh's title win the season before, the NU introduced end-of-season play-offs. The top four clubs met for the honour of calling themselves champions. In that first season, Halifax won the play-offs and also topped the league.

The Robins

Rovers' record slipped somewhat that season, finishing half way in 13th spot following six more resignations from the league. Abnormally bad luck with injuries meant that only five of the 1905 cup final side played in over half the games. The Robins had a poor start with only one win in the first seven matches before the Yorkshire Cup sparked a revival, and a six-match winning run which included progress to the final and a narrow defeat to Bradford.

Whilst Rovers were undoubtedly somewhat unlucky to have lost that game, the rest of the season was unremarkable as they failed to achieve any consistency. Both games against Liverpool City took place at Craven Street as City, who struggled through the season winless, sacrificed ground advantage in the hopes of benefiting from a larger gate. The two comfortable wins gained against them put Rovers' points difference into the black.

There was no Challenge Cup run; after taking revenge on Bradford by knocking them out in the first round, Rovers were beaten 17-0 in the second round at Huddersfield. The Fartowners were then languishing in the bottom half of the table but, within five years, had put together one of the sport's most formidable teams.

Carmichael was now the established full-back and kicked 44 goals – a then club record that he subsequently bettered several times. Former Pontefract winger W.H. Dilcock arrived for the last 13 games and scored 13 tries to finish joint top of the try-scoring chart with Tich West.

Attendances had declined slowly since the first season in the NU, with the home derby game failing to attract a 10,000 attendance for the first time and a low of just 1,000 for the second Liverpool home game. Despite that, chairman Edwin Ombler reported a £269 profit at the AGM and reported that due to increased cup revenue, the directors were, 'well satisfied with the financial outlook'. He added that they recommended the formation of a strong reserve team in order to improve the club's playing strength and mitigate the effect of injuries.

Yorkshire Cup Final, Belle Vue, Wakefield, 1 December 1906
Bradford 8-5 Hull Kingston Rovers

Rovers suffered a blow in the run-up to the final when their inspirational captain, Anthony Starks, was ruled out due to pneumonia. Their opponents Bradford, despite having won the NU Challenge Cup the previous season, were struggling both on the field and off it – their style of play and big heavy pack were not well suited to the new law changes and, like the Robins, they had suffered a poor start to campaign. They were also rapidly losing support, partly to neighbours Bradford City who were riding high in the second division of the Football League. The week before the final, the two sides met at Craven Street, Rovers winning 17-8, after which game Bradford's tactics for the final were undoubtedly hatched.

In excellent conditions, and with over 4,000 supporters behind them, Rovers immediately went on the attack and in the early exchanges, Bradford scarcely got out of their own half. Bradford's tactics were physical and direct and clearly designed to knock the Robins out of their stride. A penalty for offside saw Bradford take the lead after almost half an hour and that signalled a flurry of chances. Rovers were quickly back on the attack and Barry and Phipps put West over for an unconverted try. Then, after both sides had missed with kicks, Bradford scored a good try through Brear and a second when Dechan crossed in the corner from Connell's kick immediately on the restart. Neither was converted and Bradford led 8-3 at half-time.

The Robins

*Rovers dominated again after the break and should have
levelled but, after a flowing move, West dropped a good pass
when clear. The same player then missed a penalty from in
front of the posts and Rovers went a man down when
Hambrecht had to leave the field. Despite several other
chances, all the Robins could manage was a penalty goal
from Madley.*

*It was widely reported in the press that the better side had
lost – but that would have been of little consolation to the
Robins, who had to wait fourteen more years before winning
their first NU trophy.*

> **Rovers:** *A. Carmichael; G.H. West (capt), W.
> Phipps, D. Rees, W. Madley; J. Barry. A.
> Lofthouse; J. Gath, H. Sherwood, A. Windle, C.J.
> Hambrecht, H. Smith, A. Spackman.*
> **Bradford:** *Gunn; Dechan, Mosby, Hesletine,
> Connell; Surman, Brear; Feather, Greenwood,
> Mann, Laidlaw, Walton, Francis.*
> *Referee: W. McCutcheon (Oldham)*
> *Attendance: 10,500*

The first tourist games

1907 was the year in which the birthplace of British
motorsport and aviation, Brooklands, the world's first
purpose-built motor-racing circuit, was opened in Surrey. Not
too far away, the RFU paid £5,572 for a 12-acre site at
Twickenham, which became their headquarters.

In 1907-08, Hunslet and their 'terrible six' pack became
the first team to win all four cups available in a season – the
Championship, Challenge Cup, Yorkshire Cup and Yorkshire
League trophy. The Yorkshire and Lancashire league trophies
were awarded to the clubs that gained the most league points
in matches against the other clubs their own county.

The Robins saw a strong revival in fortunes. They finished in sixth place out of 27 clubs and, most encouragingly, won ten of their last 13 games. The improved league form was achieved despite the fact that, once again, they were unable to field a settled side. New half-back Arthur Booth was ever-present and Carmichael kicked 81 goals to beat his previous season's record. Whilst a derby double was conceded to Hull FC, the Robins again finished ten places higher than their neighbours in the league. However, there was no cup success, with defeat in the first round of both cup competitions.

Rovers played an overseas touring team for the first time when 7,000 spectators saw them lose 6-3 to Albert Baskerville's pioneering New Zealand 'All Golds'. The tourists were bolstered by guest Australian Dally Messenger - the scorer of one of their two tries – the leading rugby player in the southern hemisphere. After 35 games in England and Wales, the tourists returned home via Australia, where they played a further ten times, and are widely credited with establishing the sport in the Antipodes.

The tour match must also have inspired Rovers because in their next game they comfortably beat eventual champions Hunslet 23-11 to start their successful end-of-season run. Another of the old stalwarts, former skipper Anthony Starks, ended his very distinguished Rovers career in the Yorkshire Cup defeat at Leeds in November, while the colourful former Harrogate RUFC forward or winger Charlie 'Slasher' Brain made his debut at home to Bramley in October. Future club chairman E.W. Brown made a try-scoring debut on the wing at Dewsbury in the second game of the season, but only made two more appearances. A team photo of the time shows that the white shirts had now given way to red ones, still with dark shorts.

The Robins

Following up on the recommendation at the previous AGM, Rovers reintroduced a second team. It was captained and coached by Jimmy Gordon, now at the end of his playing career. They played 27 games, including two against Hull 'A', and although it made a £130 loss, the directors considered this money well spent.

The club held a benefit for former player William Soulsby and one of the outstanding players of the club's early years, Charlie Coyne, died during the season – less than eight years after playing in his last game.

The Greats – No 2
Anthony Starks - *see Hull KR legends gallery*

Anthony Starks was born in the Castleford area in 1873. He joined the Robins in 1896 from Castleford, then a junior side.

He was 5ft 11½, tall by the standards of the day, and weighed just over 13st in his prime. A skilful and hard-working forward, he was a powerful runner with a good pair of hands, who was also a useful kicker both in the loose and from the mark. A fine player and a gracious sportsman, both in victory and defeat, Starks led Rovers both as captain and by example in their early NU days.

That he had only one international appearance to his name, when he captained England against the Other Nationalities at Wigan in the very first NU international match in 1904, is more of a comment on the lack of representative opportunities in his heyday than on his ability. One of the NU's first great players, he also earned 23 Yorkshire caps – in addition to his two England and 13 Yorkshire rugby union caps.

Starks captained the Robins for several seasons, and was only the second player after Windle to pass 200 appearances for the club – finishing with 208 in the Northern Union. He kicked 72 goals and scored 31 tries, captaining the club in its first Challenge Cup final appearance in 1905. The 16-2 first round Yorkshire Cup defeat at Leeds on 9 November, 1907 marked the end of his illustrious playing career.

Remaining in Hull, he subsequently served for a spell on Rovers' board. In 1946, nearly 40 years after his last game, Starks was presented with a 'benefit' cheque for £272, which had been raised by the club and its supporters. By this time he was 72 and disabled by a leg injury sustained during World War II. It was an eloquent testimony to the esteem in which this great servant of the club was held. He died in 1952.

Following in the footsteps of Ebbw Vale and Merthyr Tydfil the season before, four more Welsh clubs joined the NU for 1908-09 but not one of these newcomers survived two seasons.

Now wearing white shorts with their red shirts, the Robins endured a rather indifferent season. After winning only one of their first seven games, they also suffered a five-match losing run over the Christmas and New Year period, and again went out in the first round of both cups. A highlight was the 8-3 win over reigning champions Hunslet at Craven Street on 16 January but they finished 16th out of 31 clubs in the league. On Boxing Day at the Boulevard, the Black and Whites inflicted on Rovers their then heaviest derby defeat, 33-7, but the Robins turned the tables at Craven Street, winning 35-4. That 31-point margin stood as a record for Rovers over the Airlie Birds for over 98 years.

The most notable match of the season was the first visit of an Australian touring team on 21 November, when 7,000 spectators paid £230 to see the Robins win 21-16. Rovers' points came from Carmichael, who kicked five goals, with tries from Booth, Brain and Pratt and a dropped goal from Gordon. This time Dally Messenger featured on the wing for his own country. Other members of the visitors' three-quarter line were centre Jim Devereux, who stayed on to play for Hull FC after the tour, and Albert Rosenfeld, who became a member of the great Huddersfield side of that era.

It was a difficult first tour for the Australians. In a very hard northern winter, they played 45 matches and lost the Test series 2-0 - the first match was drawn – all this prompting tour manager James Giltinan to write back home: 'We are having nothing but rain, snow, sleet and cold ... why, you cannot feel your hands and feet; and the referees are cruel ..... (they) don't give us anything at all.'

New signing G. Unsworth, a back-row forward, made most appearances, one more than new team captain Carmichael. An otherwise unmemorable 27-11 defeat at York on 3 April saw back-row forward Arthur Moore make the first of his 337 appearances for the club. The most significant of a number of other debuts was that of strong-running forward Bill Sandham against Hunslet in November.

The broken leg sustained by record-breaking winger Tich West in the Yorkshire Cup defeat at home to Batley on 10 October, the second of his career, enforced his retirement. Beverley born and bred, standing only 5'6" tall and weighing only 10 stones, West was a fast and elusive player. He played 218 games for the Robins, scoring 98 tries and kicking 45 goals. It was a cruel quirk of fate that injury prevented him becoming the first player to score 100 tries for the club – it would be 17 more years before this target was reached. His eleven tries in a match against Brookland Rovers remains a rugby league record, however.

Another veteran, Andrew Windle, made his final appearance in the following match, at home to Oldham. Windle made a then club record 238 appearances, having made his debut in the first NU game at Bradford. Along with

Kemp, Starks and Fletcher, all by now retired, he had formed the cornerstone of Rovers' pack.

The annual report commented that, 'the season was the most disastrous from the point of view of injuries within the directors' recollections.' Two players broke legs and, in all, 42 players played in the 35 matches. Retiring chairman Ombler said at the AGM that further team strengthening was needed, and that the club had potential targets in mind. John Moore was elected chairman, and former great Anthony Starks joined the board.

In football, 1909-10 saw Manchester United move into their 'luxurious new stadium' at Old Trafford, destined to become home to the domestic showpiece of the 13-a-side game while Hull City had an excellent season, finishing only one point away from promotion to Division 1 of the football league.

The Robins started brightly, winning six out of their first seven games including a 15-11 win over Oldham, who finished top of the table and won the Championship play-off. After that their form was patchy, and the team eventually finished 11th out of 28. Once more, both derby games produced home wins, but lack of cup success continued, with first round exits in both competitions.

International forward Alfred Mann, who had led the rough tactics against Rovers in the 1906 Yorkshire Cup decider signed from Bradford, along with his half-back colleague Tommy Surman. Mann and the dependable Carmichael were ever-presents throughout the season. With 78 goals, Carmichael was the league's top goal-kicker, an achievement that he repeated over the next three seasons. He was the first-ever Rovers' player to finish top of the NU goal, try, or point-scoring charts.

Welshman Jim Barry, who had made his debut in the

The Robins

first match of the 1901-02 season, played his last game at home to Wakefield Trinity on 20 November. For eight seasons he had been the club's number one half-back, scoring 41 tries in 208 games.

The annual report again bemoaned an 'unparalleled run of injuries' and commented that the small profit of £9 14s 5d was 'solely attributable to an extraordinary run of ill luck.'

Director John Wilson was nominated for the NU management committee.

Lofty heights

During the summer of 1910, a Great Britain team set sail to tour Australasia for the first time, winning all three tests – two in Australia and one in New Zealand. Nevertheless, despite there being some top-class players in their ranks, particularly in the 1920s, it was to be over 50 years before a Rovers player won a place on a Great Britain tour.

In 1910-11, Ernest Gill replaced Harry Shann as the trainer and the Robins had their best season in the NU so far. They were just one win short of qualifying for the Championship play-offs for the first time, with a 68.18 per cent record, compared to fourth-placed Widnes' 68.33 per cent. After losing their opening three games, they were downed only once of the next 12, and ended the season with a then club record nine-match winning run, which would have been extended had Merthyr Tydfil not conceded their home game on 4 March. Uniquely to this day, both derby games were drawn – 8-8 at the Boulevard and 5-5 at Craven Street. Following these two draws, a friendly game to decide the 'local championship' was arranged, which the Robins won 37-8.

There were cup wins for the first time in four seasons as Hunslet and Halifax were beaten in the Yorkshire Cup but

Rovers lost 12-2 in the semi-final to a strong Huddersfield side at Fartown. It was the same old story in the Challenge Cup though – a hard-fought 7-9 first round defeat at home to second-placed Oldham.

A settled side is often a successful one, and Rovers used only 29 players in their 37 games. Skipper Carmichael was at full-back; Dilcock, Hughes, Thomas and Hyam in the three-quarters; and Moore, Mann, Huskins, Blackmore, Sandham and Spackman were the nucleus of the pack. It was only at half-back, where Surman missed most of the season through a serious injury, that the Robins struggled to find a satisfactory combination.

Carmichael was again ever-present and re-set the club's goal-kicking record for the third time in five years – this time breaking the three figure barrier with 116. In addition to being the NU's leading goal-kicker with 129 in all, he was also the leading points-scorer with 261 and was presented with a gold watch to mark his achievement.

A club record 127 tries were scored, with winger Dilcock leading the way for the second season running, this time with 19. Whilst the quality of the team was undoubtedly improving, there was a general increase in points-scoring in the league, as clubs responded to the rule changes the NU had introduced to speed up the game. League leaders Wigan scored 650 points in 34 matches; five years earlier, leaders Leigh had posted only 245 in 30.

Notwithstanding the relatively successful season, in his AGM address chairman Moore accused 'certain players' of having thrown away the club's chances of glory by 'kicking over the traces' on the night before games. They were a disgrace he said, and should not pull on a Rovers jersey again. Despite this, the practice of players meeting in the Queens Hotel on the Friday night before the game and discussing tactics for the following day, was one that persisted for many years prior to World War II.

In 1911, the NU standardised playing times at 40 minutes each way, with an interval of not more than five minutes – timings that remained unchanged until a ten-minute half-time break was introduced in the 1970s.

The Robins surpassed their previous season's performance in 1911-12, finishing third in the league behind only the great Huddersfield side and a powerful Wigan outfit. They also won all their home league games for the first time ever. The highlight of the season was the home game against champions-to-be Huddersfield on 16 December, in which Rovers inflicted a six-try victory over their illustrious opponents by 32-10 in front of 7,000 spectators. Ten days later, they gained an 18-5 home win over Hull FC to claim a first derby double since 1902-03, and the Robins ended the season seven places above their old rivals.

Rovers reached the final of the Yorkshire Cup, in which they were comfortably beaten 22-10 by Huddersfield in front of a 22,000 crowd at Belle Vue, Wakefield. The game was as good as over in the first half, when Huddersfield scored four tries to lead 16-2. Rovers badly missed key forwards Mann and Sandham, who were both suspended.

The Robins won a Challenge Cup tie for the first time since 1907 when amateurs Beverley visited Craven Street and were dispatched 34-5. The second round brought a 3-3 home draw against Warrington and Rovers lost the replay 3-0 four days later. Lacking several first team regulars, the club's first Championship play-off game resulted in a 41-3 drubbing at Wigan. A second tour match was played against Australia, with the tourists claiming a narrow 5-2 win in January that was the club's only home defeat of the season.

The side remained relatively settled, with only 27

players being used over the 43 games and Surman providing some stability again at half-back. Carmichael, Sandham and William Huskins each missed only three games. Carmichael again broke his club record by kicking 127 goals; he also topped the league's goal-kicking chart for the third year running and was again the league's leading points-scorer. The 597 points scored in league matches was a club record that, although equalled in the halcyon days of the 1920s, was not beaten for over 50 years.

Arthur Spackman left at the end of January to join Keighley. Since making his debut on the first day of the 1904 season, he had given stalwart service over 222 games. Both Carmichael and Moore were selected to play for England.

Another season's profit, of over £200, was put to good use at the season's end when the club pressed forward with ground improvements. The pitch was dug up and reseeded, and the old best stand – often referred to by regulars as the 'orange box' or the 'worst stand' after improvements to other parts of the ground – was demolished and a new impressive structure built in its place.

1912 was the year in which the RMS Titanic struck an iceberg in the North Atlantic and sank, with the loss of 1,517 lives. In cricket, it was the only time ever that England played a triangular Test series at home – Australia and South Africa providing the opposition. England won the tournament with four wins and two draws from their six matches. At the time, Test matches in this country were played over only three days, but in order to produce a result, the final, decisive game in the tournament was the first 'timeless' test, and lasted four.

The Robins maintained their third-placed league position in 1912-13 – once again behind Huddersfield and Wigan. An 18-0 derby success at Craven Street was followed by a narrow 7-5 defeat at the Boulevard on Boxing Day and league doubles were recorded over Batley and Leeds for the first time. Although the Robins were again beaten by Wigan in the Championship play-off semi-final, they made a much better fist of it this time before going down 16-3.

For a second season running, Challenge Cup hopes came to an end at Wilderspool in the second round, where the Robins lost 13-6 to Warrington. Hopes were raised of a Yorkshire Cup run when the cup-holders and reigning Champions Huddersfield were dispatched 11-3 at Craven Street, but in the second round Rovers surrendered a 7-3 half-time lead and were pipped 11-10 by Leeds at Headingley. Thomas Cook's organised a supporters rail special for the Leeds cup-tie at a cost of 2s 3d per head (roughly 11 pence) – even though the game was played in the afternoon, the return trip did not leave Leeds until 22.45!

Once again, the club reaped the benefit of a settled side – only 24 players were used in 37 games and a nucleus of eleven played in two-thirds of them. Newly signed former Newport RUFC centre R.G. Hicks and skipper Carmichael missed only one match each. Another newcomer, Leonard Trump, stepped into the pack vacancy left by Spackman's departure and played in 33 games. Back-row forward Sandham scored 25 tries, a then club record for a forward, whilst his six in a match against Coventry is still the best match tally for a Rovers' forward. Carmichael's reduced goal tally of 86 was still enough for him to be the NU's leading goal kicker again.

The strange 'Coulson affair' took place; Rovers and Wigan both believing that they had signed the Durham rugby union captain W.H. Coulson. In the press, Coulson said that there was 'absolutely no truth in the rumour that he had signed for Rovers' and that it was 'a case of impersonation.' Coulson never played for either club, and the Robins were even fined half a guinea for entering a wrongful registration.

In 1913, the NU introduced a ban on overseas imports from Australia and New Zealand, but that was too late to halt the progress of Huddersfield's Australian winger Rosenfeld who finished the season with an incredible 80 tries – a record surely unlikely to ever be broken.

Edwin Ombler took over from Moore for his second spell of office as chairman, while John Wilson, now elected to the NU management committee, took over temporarily from Johnson as secretary, due to the latter's ill-health. The 'A' team were second in the Yorkshire Senior Competition and the Robins had now completed the first thirty years of their existence with their two finest seasons to date.

After consecutive top-four finishes, Rovers' league form slipped a little in 1913-14 when they reached only sixth place, neighbours Hull FC overtaking them to finish fourth. The Robins were again unbeaten at home in the league, with two games drawn. Once again, the derby games finished even, with each side winning its home fixtures. There were second round defeats in both cup competitions – Rovers drawing the short straw in the Challenge Cup in the shape of Huddersfield, who won 17-2 at Craven Park.

The Christmas trip to Oldham that had been endured with a conspicuous lack of success over the last five seasons was now replaced by a trip to league leaders Wigan. The change of fixture brought no change of luck, but the return fixture a week later on New Year's Day was something of an epic, Rovers running out 8-6 winners. The game inspired an anonymous writer to prose and the *Hull Daily Mail* published his match report in poem under the title of 'The Battle of Bunker's Hill'. That was a reference to the nickname of the slope at one end of the ground – most probably in tribute to Bunker Carmichael.

Although it had been possible to field a fairly stable

The Robins

pack, the back division was not so, particularly in the middle of the season, and results were inconsistent. A notable new arrival was half-back Tommy McGiever from Leigh.

At the end of the season, Great Britain sailed off on their second Australasian tour, where they avenged the 3-0 home whitewash the Aussies had inflicted upon them in 1911 by the same score line. They also won a one-off Test in New Zealand before returning home. At Rovers' end-of-season AGM, a profit of £204 was reported. Chairman Edwin Ombler retired, expressing disappointment that some of his fellow directors had not put in as much time and effort as he had. Former player Anthony Starks left the board at the same time. Some dissatisfaction was expressed about some of the team's displays, particularly away from home.

Wartime

World War I broke out on 4 August, 1914 on which day the Privy Council declared war on Germany. William Shawcross, in his biography of the Queen Mother, records that the audience at the London Coliseum that night was 'filled with people exhilarated by the prospect of war' and that the Queen Mother later recalled there were people dancing and shouting in the streets, genuinely believing that it would be all over in about a month. Perhaps that attitude explains why the war did not, at first, affect matters at home too much and in common with other sports, the NU committee met and decided to continue as normal. The all-conquering Huddersfield side topped the table for the fourth consecutive season and they went on to emulate Hunslet's 1907-08 feat by winning all four trophies available to them.

The Robins' dip in form of the previous season continued and they finished 11th out of 25 in the league.

Rovers gained an unwanted record on 9 December, when they conceded 50 points for the first time, going down to their then heaviest defeat, 52-11 at Huddersfield. A defeat by the same margin was also suffered at Wigan in January – the score this time 46-5. Rovers also conceded a league double to Hull FC for the first time since 1907-08, who, to rub salt in the wounds, also beat them in the second round of the Yorkshire Cup.

Goal-kicking forward W.T. Wootton arrived and largely displaced Carmichael from the kicking duties. The latter fell ill and was unable to play after Christmas, so Mann took over as captain at the beginning of January. Winger Harold Lord finished as top try scorer for the second successive season, this time with 15. He, along with a number of other regulars, including three-quarters Len Fussey and David Vaughan and forwards James Lowe and Leonard Trump, never played for the club after that season. Wootton played in every game, whilst Mann and Huskins missed only one game each.

By the end of the season no end to the war was in sight, home conditions were worsening, and, in common with other sports, all official rugby league competitions were suspended. The situation affected the season's gates and despite the 10,000 attendances for the Huddersfield and Hull FC games, the average home attendance was below 5,000. The suspension of all cheap rail fares affected Rovers, who still used the train to transport players to games. Rovers' increased players' match fees at the start of the season but they subsequently agreed to a game-wide 25 per cent cut. Increased travel costs and reduced receipts from all sources contributed to the Robins making a loss of £525 over the season. Even the proceeds of the club's gala, a continual source of profits well in excess of £100 in previous seasons, were down to £85.

At the Robins' AGM in July 1915 the new chairman,

The Robins

J. T. Collier, reported that 27 players were already serving their country; one, Phil Thomas, was killed in action, and Charlie Brain was taken prisoner at Mons. A plan to improve the changing facilities had already been shelved due to the war. Club secretary George Johnson offered to take a pay cut and as compensation, he was found 'other business.' In the same month, half-back Idris Dean, who had played his last game for Rovers in January, took the club to court to recover £24 for 16 weeks non-employment pay that he believed was due to him.

After much discussion at NU headquarters, war emergency leagues were organised over the next three years, based loosely on the Lancashire and Yorkshire competitions, and run on amateur lines. Rovers competed in all three under the captaincy of Mann whenever he was available. It was a very difficult period for all clubs and the Robins were no different. The difficulties of operating in wartime conditions were exemplified by Rovers' game at Leeds in 1915-16. Due to rail delays, the side arrived late, causing a 45-minute delay to the kick-off. They had only ten men at the start and although the other three arrived later, only 15 minutes were played in the second half to ensure the players could get back to Hull. It was impossible to do other than run at a loss, and by 1917-18, despite relaxed registration rules, it was a struggle even to put out a side. Rovers and Barrow cancelled the fixtures between the two clubs due to the substantial increase in rail fares. That season Rovers won only one out of 25 games – but by then, top teams like Oldham, and even the mighty Huddersfield, had ceased to function at all.

*****

4. Triumphant Twenties

1919-1930

FOR all of the club's successes and achievements before the first war, its existence was still regarded as somewhat precarious; it was only the successful period in the 1920s, and the bold move to its new home, that really enabled it to put down the roots that would ensure its long-term existence.

An inauspicious restart

The early post-war period was a very unsettled time, with uprisings across Europe and strikes and discontent in Britain. Overall, of the 70,000 Hull men and women who served, a tenth were killed and a further 14,000 disabled. However, compared to the Second World War, the city escaped relatively lightly, although 54 people were killed in Zeppelin raids and Holy Trinity Church in the old town sustained serious bomb damage.

The Robins

Against this background, the 1918-19 season opened in September with only eight clubs able to return to action. The Robins told the NU that they 'had no team and no money,' and prepared to return to action the following January by setting up a 'finance club' to raise operating capital. By December 1918, it had accrued £180 and although more was needed, the club believed they could resume playing activities. They began with two friendlies against the Airlie Birds over the Christmas period, followed by a return to competitive action in a shortened county-based league competition. Rovers played seven of the other ten Yorkshire clubs that were operational, both home and away. The kit that was to become familiar for so many years – white jerseys with a wide red band, white shorts and red socks – was introduced.

Half of the 1914-15 season regulars either never played again or did so only on a handful of occasions. 'Slasher' Brain had been in captivity for over four years, only returning to Hull around the time Rovers were returning to action, and played only once more for the club. The first game, at home to Wakefield Trinity, saw the competitive debuts of three stalwarts – three-quarters Gilbert Austin and Jimmy Cook, and forward Frank Bielby. Although the Robins had a five-match unbeaten run from mid-February, their form slipped, and they lost all their last five games, including both league derbies. The Challenge Cup did not reappear until 1920, but a Yorkshire Cup competition was played and Rovers lost in the third round at home to Huddersfield.

Former Bradford forward, Alfred Mann, played his last game for the club in that tie. A fine servant, he had been one of the key players of the immediate pre-World War I period. Mann's robust style had made him an unpopular figure with the fans when he played against the Robins in the 1908 Yorkshire Cup final, but the same quality made him a

78

favourite in his 224-match career at Craven Park. He led the side by example and his career return of 50 tries was most impressive.

In the same game, another stalwart front-rower, William Huskins, also made his last appearance. Originally from Normanton, he made his debut at the start of the 1909-10 season, and played 222 games, mainly at prop. Alf Carmichael played in the first match on the resumption, but his illness had taken its toll and he was forced to retire.

After Rovers' end-of-season AGM in July, E.W. Brown, a Hull City Councillor, local funeral director and, briefly, former player, took over as chairman from J. T. Collier. At the same time, Shrewsbury-born former police sergeant, Tom Williams, became club secretary, succeeding the long-serving George Johnson. The finance fund had been a success, in addition to which the club made a £416 profit over the year. Brown commented that it was: 'A vital point in the history of the club, which was better off financially than for some time.'

However, a cautionary note was sounded about the 'sad state' of the ground. Over the previous two years, the club had completed essential maintenance by purchasing materials and employing the directors' own workmen to complete the work. That saved around £600 in builders' costs but further repairs were anticipated, and the club would not be able spend all its funds on new players. The thrust of recruitment policy would be to look for local talent in the mould of Austin and Bielby.

The NU President J. B. Cooke, attending an end-of-season Hull FC presentation event, commented on the cordial relationships that now existed between the two clubs in the city, contrasting this with his last visit, when he had to smooth over difficulties between the two.

The Robins

The Greats – No 3
'Bunker' Carmichael - *see Hull KR legends gallery*

Alf 'Bunker' Carmichael was the first in a line of excellent full-backs that have served the club with great distinction. Born in April 1883, he worked in the fruit trades in Hull, which is almost certainly where the nickname of Bunker came from. Fruit trade workers often had their wages supplemented by a bunker bag – which was a parcel of fruit.

Carmichael made his debut for Rovers at Batley on 18 April 1903, and became the Robins' regular custodian in the 1906-07 season. He was a solid defender and fine goal-kicker, but typically of most full-backs of the time, his attacking incursions were limited. In fact, of the 12 tries he scored in his 338 appearances, four were from the wing position that he occupied on five occasions during his second season with the club.

However, his goal-kicking was outstanding. In all he landed 723 goals for Rovers, setting a record that stood for over 50 years until another first class exponent, Cyril Kellett, passed it in the 1960s. His record of 14 goals in a match, in a 70-13 thrashing of Merthyr Tydfil in October 1910, is still unbeaten, although three other players have now equalled it. He was the first man to kick 100 goals in a season for the Robins, passing that landmark on two occasions. Perhaps his greatest achievement though, was finishing the top goal-kicker in the NU for four consecutive seasons, between 1909-10 and 1912-13.

Unfortunately, however, ill-health curtained Carmichael's career. He did not play after the end of December in the 1913-14 season, and appeared in only one more competitive match, at home to Wakefield Trinity in January 1919. At the time of his retirement Carmichael had kicked 813 goals – more than any other player at the time. During his career with Rovers, Carmichael left the fruit trade and for a short while became the licensee of the Queens Hotel in Charlotte

80

Street. Sadly however, his health deteriorated and he died in September 1921.

He did leave a legacy, for his son George, or 'Young Bunker' as he was sometimes known, was also a fine player, making his Rovers debut in the 1929-30 season and claiming the full-back position as his own after the retirement of Laurie Osborne at the end of the 1931-32 campaign. Young Bunker left the club in December 1934 to join Bradford Northern, whom he then served with distinction.

The following season, 1919-20, saw the league format return to that of the pre-war years, with clubs playing all the others in their own county and a minimum of three from across the border. As everyone played varying numbers of fixtures at the time, league places were still decided on a percentage basis and the top four clubs played off for the Championship. St Helens Recreation took the place of Runcorn, who did not resume after the war.

Arthur Moore took over from Mann as the Robins' captain and former Hull FC centre Billy Jacques succeeded Gill as the new trainer, but it was a very disappointing season. Rovers lost only once in the first eight games, including an 8-8 draw in the Boulevard derby, but won only twice in the next 20. The Christmas Day derby defeat saw the start of a then club record 10 successive defeats.

Rovers' final league position, 19th out of 25 clubs, was made worse by Hull FC's lofty second-placed finish and play-off success over Huddersfield. The Robins also lost in the first round of both cup competitions.

Nonetheless, there were signs towards the end of the season that there might be better times ahead as the management started to build the nucleus of a strong pack of forwards. Bielby, Moore and Sandy Gibson (who actually made his debut before the war) were joined by new arrivals

The Robins

Bob and Jack Wilkinson - both prop-forwards but not related and brothers Frank and Bob Boagey from the North-East. Bielby was the top try-scorer with eight and winger Billy Bradshaw was the leading goal-kicker landing 21. William 'Mucker' Clark, who had made his debut at scrum half on the first day of the 1913-14 season, became a regular performer, showing his great utility value by playing in the three-quarters, at half-back and in the forwards. Austin was ever-present in his first full season, playing almost exclusively at full-back.

At the AGM, chairman Brown said that whilst the club was in a very healthy position, he now had very serious concerns about the state of the old Craven Street ground, which was in constant need of repair. The club had spent £937 on repairs over the course of the previous season which, added to £1,640 spent on players' wages and transfers, was the reason for the loss. Some of the new players had not been as successful as anticipated, particularly in the backs, and the club were actively trying to recruit. Once again scouting included Wales and unsuccessful offers had been made to two rugby union stars.

By the end of the season, however, the country was facing crisis. Industrial unrest was rife, unemployment had doubled to over 1.3 million and the government had made elaborate plans for distributing food in the event of transport strikes. Although the strikes were called off on 15 April, it was clear that very difficult times lay ahead.

The first NU trophy

Despite some on-field encouragement at the end of the previous season, the Robins' transformation in 1920-21 must have surprised even the most optimistic supporters. They jumped 18 places to top the league table for the first time. A more settled side developed, built on the pack that had started to come together the previous season. It was augmented by C.W. 'Bill' Westerdale, who made his debut at Leeds on 8 January and was to be a stalwart figure throughout the decade. Local full-back Laurie Osborne made his debut in the first game and soon became a regular fixture and the back division also included Cook and Austin, who were both ever-present at centre, together with a new regular half-back partnership of McGiever and Clark.

The season started with a five-match winning run that ended when Hull FC won 15-6 at Craven Street at the beginning of October. This reverse was followed by a 20-14 win at Wigan, the first leg of what was an impressive double as the Riversiders were still good enough to finish fourth in the league. Thereafter Rovers' league form was excellent, with a double over a powerful Batley side, an 8-4 revenge win at the Boulevard on Christmas Day, and only five further defeats all season. A victorious Yorkshire Cup campaign culminated in a 2-0 win against Hull FC in the final at Headingley, Rovers first trophy in the NU. The run to the decider included wins over Bradford, with Gilbert Austin sprinting from behind his own line to score, Leeds and Dewsbury.

The Challenge Cup was again a disappointment, however. Dewsbury gained revenge for their Yorkshire Cup defeat when they beat Rovers 12-0 at Crown Flatt in the first round. As league leaders, the Robins had a home semi-final in the Championship play-off, in which they beat Wigan for the third time that season, emphatically 26-4. In the final, they met the second-placed Airlie Birds for the fourth time in a momentous season. This time the Black and Whites took their revenge with a narrow 16-14 win. Although transport problems meant that only 10,000 spectators attended the title culmination, an amazing total of 91,000 people watched that season's quartet derby encounters. If the attendance at the final was underwhelming, it was plentiful compared to the 13 spectators that attended the game between Leicester City and Stockport County the same day – the lowest-ever recorded Football League gate.

Notwithstanding the disappointing climax, the season under Jacques and Moore had undoubtedly been the most successful in Rovers' history. Centre Cook was the leading try-scorer with 20, whilst Bradshaw and Osborne shared the goal-kicking duties.

During the campaign, director John Wilson resigned from the board when he was appointed secretary of the NU, a post he held until the end of the Second World War. Former secretary Charlie Savage, so influential in the club's early years, died in mid-season and the club flag was flown at half-mast at the home game on 18 December. The Dewsbury home fixture, on 22 January, raised £580 for Carmichael's benefit.

**Yorkshire Cup Final, Headingley, Leeds,
27 November 1920**

Hull FC 0-2 Hull Kingston Rovers
In 1920, the Yorkshire Cup was a major trophy and there were fears that its great sporting traditions might be at risk when these two deadly rivals faced each other in the final. Only a couple of months earlier, two Rovers players had been dismissed at Craven Street in a rough derby and passions ran high. The Hull Daily Mail *appealed to the players for a clean but hard game and to spectators not to incite foul play.*

After taking an early lunch in Hull, the Robins travelled to Leeds by train, using the same one as Hull FC but sitting at the front end rather than the back. Many of the clubs' supporters travelled the same way and there were four special trains laid on. The day itself was dull and wet but at least the thick freezing fog that had dominated the week of the match had abated somewhat. The Airlie Birds, as reigning champions, and with four internationals including the great Billy Batten, were strong favourites. Rovers for their part fielded ten local men, supplemented by the Lancastrian stand-off Tommy McGiever, North-Easterner Bob Boagey at hooker and Northamptonshire-born winger, Billy Bradshaw. The Robins were a strong and physical team but they could play a bit themselves and they were not going to be intimidated by their illustrious neighbours.

As it turned out, the game was no great spectacle as both sides strove unsuccessfully to break down the others' strong defence. Neither were the worst pre-match fears realised and the contest was mainly played in a good but very competitive spirit. It remained scoreless until almost the end of normal time, when Bradshaw fielded a clearance some 45 yards out and 10 in from touch. Although everything was against him – the distance, angle, mud, sodden heavy ball and the onrushing defence – he launched a towering drop-kick that referee Hestford adjudged had cleared the crossbar between the uprights. After signalling a goal, Hestford promptly drew the game to a close.

Back at the City Hall in Hull that evening, where the teams attended a Civic Reception hosted by Lord Mayor J. B. Atkinson, the somewhat retiring Bradshaw was called upon to relive his crowning moment to a huge crowd of supporters. It was too much and rendered him speechless, but his captain, Arthur Moore, had no such difficulty stepping in. It was his proudest moment, he told the fans, to lead a team of local lads to the club's first cup win in the NU and he hoped to play Hull FC again, this time in the final of the Challenge Cup.

Hull FC: E. Rogers; A. Francis, W. Stone, W. Batten, J. Holdsworth; E. Caswell, T. Milner; J. Beasty, H. Hewson, H. Taylor, R. Taylor, J. Wyburn, J. Kennedy (capt).

The Robins

Rovers: L. Osborne; L. Harris, G. Austin, J. Cook, W. Bradshaw; T. McGiever, W. Clark; J.H. Wilkinson, R. Boagey, J.R. Wilkinson, F. Bielby, A. Moore (capt), A. Gibson.
Referee: A. Hestford (Broughton)
Attendance: 20,000

Championship Final, Headingley, Leeds, 5 May 1921
Hull FC 16-14 Hull Kingston Rovers

Arthur Moore got his wish to play the Airlie Birds in a cup final again rather more quickly than expected – but it was in the title decider, not the Challenge Cup. Less than six months after the Yorkshire Cup meeting, the two sides again cossed swords for silverware. By this time though, the situation in the country had deteriorated considerably. Traffic in the port of Hull had dwindled alarmingly due to the depression and there was a severe shortage of coal that caused havoc on the railways. There were late efforts to relocate the game to alleviate the difficulties of travelling to Leeds, and Rovers chairman E.W. Brown was called to NU headquarters where he was asked for his agreement to the tie being transferred to Hull City's Anlaby Road ground. Brown said that he would need to check whether his board concurred but was told that an answer was needed immediately. He felt that he could not take the responsibility of agreeing the change on his own and so the game went ahead at Headingley as planned.

Only one train left Hull and the attendance was half what it had been for the Yorkshire Cup, with only an estimated 600 making the journey over. Despite that, there was an outbreak of fighting at the St Michael's Lane end before the start but order was restored before the teams ran out. Rovers kicked off with a slight breeze behind them and in the Airlie Birds' opening attack, Frank Bielby produced a typically thunderous tackle to halt the formidable Billy Batten on halfway. Rovers then attacked and, from a scrum penalty, 'Sandy' Gibson gave them a 2-0 lead. The Airlie Birds looked more dangerous with the ball, particularly in the backs, and they scored three tries before half-time. Batten put Stone in at the corner, Caswell's good pass sent Devereux across and a rare error from Rovers' full-back Laurie Osborne gifted the big second-row forward Taylor a try. Fortunately for the Robins, all three were scored near the touchline and none converted so, thanks to a second Gibson goal, Rovers went in at the break only 9-4 down.

In the second half, a minor altercation ensued between Bielby and Taylor after the latter had been penalised for an off-the-ball incident. Then what proved to be the decisive score came when Rovers' forwards attempted to dribble the ball through the Black and Whites' defence – a common tactic at that time – but Hull FC forward Wyburn, his head bandaged following a first half knock, scooped the ball up and charged powerfully up field. As Osborne closed in to make the tackle, Wyburn slipped the ball to the supporting Taylor, who scored between the posts. At 14-4 down with 25 minutes to go, and with heavy rain now falling, Rovers threw everything into attack. After 63 minutes, Tommy McGiever's clever kick was gathered by Harold Mulvey at the corner, despite the efforts of Milner. The winger was able to run round to the posts and Gibson converted. Shortly after, the gap was narrowed to three points when Gibson kicked a penalty following a scrum infringement and the Airlie Birds appeared to be tiring. Kennedy gave them some respite with a penalty that made it 16-11 but, from the restart, Rovers roared back again. Louis Harris fielded the ball and made good ground before passing to Jimmy Cook, who burst through for an excellent try. With less than five minutes to go, the conversion attempt went wide from a fairly easy position and with it Rovers' chances of repeating their Yorkshire Cup success.

Jim Kennedy, accepting the trophy, paid tribute to both teams and Arthur Moore, congratulating Hull FC on retaining the trophy for a second year, spoke of his pride in *captaining a side 'of mostly local lads' to their second major final of the season.*

> **Hull FC:** *E. Rogers; J. Devereux, J. Kennedy (capt), W. Batten, W. Stone; E. Caswell, T. Milner; J. Beasty, J. Ellis, P. Newsom, R. Taylor, J. Wyburn, H. Garrett.*
> **Rovers:** *L. Osborne; L. Harris, G. Austin, J. Cook, H. Mulvey; T. McGiever, W. Clark; J.R. Wilkinson, A. Gibson. J.H. Wilkinson, R. Boagey, F. Bielby. A. Moore (capt).*
> *Referee: A. Brown (Wakefield)*
> *Attendance: 10,000*

Meanwhile, even more significant in the long term than any of the on-field successes, the decision was reached to buy a new ground. Chairman E.W. Brown was undoubtedly the driving force behind the project and succeeded in gaining the support of his fellow board members.

In January, with rumour abounding, Brown put his plan to a shareholders meeting. There was no sense, he argued, in continuing to pay 'hand over fist' to keep the tiny old Craven Street ground going. The ground was a disgrace to the NU, he said, with its inadequate stands, primitive sanitary arrangements and putrid dressing rooms. A larger ground would enable Rovers to accommodate more spectators who could not or would not attend matches at Craven Street and it would ultimately pay for itself. At several matches during the season, the gates had had to be closed as the ground was full.

In the face of critics who accepted the principle but felt that embarking upon such an expensive scheme in the poor economic climate was a very risky business, Brown argued that the board were convinced that it was the only way to safeguard the long-term future of the club. Brown won the day and the 'new ground scheme' was launched. The club bought a plot of land further east of the city, on the south side of Holderness Road, adjacent to the Corporation Tramways depot. At an Extraordinary Meeting on 1 April, the 'Craven Park Ground Scheme' was launched to raise funds for the project. The scheme included creating a further 6,000 10-shilling shares in the club, whereby those taking 20 shares were entitled to a pass for the new best stand.

At least the club were in an excellent financial position to take this massive step. At the AGM in the Metropole Hotel in Hull, the chairman reported a record £2,376 profit on the season's operations. There was also a 'most satisfactory' response to the ground scheme. On and off the field, it was a very exciting time for the club.

The coal strike in Britain ended in July 1921 whilst, across the world, the Communist Party was founded in China and Adolf Hitler became Fuhrer of the National Socialist party in Germany, then under martial law following the Munich riots.

Featherstone Rovers were the latest club to join the NU and were to prove awkward opponents for the Robins over the years.

For the Robins, 1921-22 was something of an anti-climax in playing terms. Their form was inconsistent to the extent that only once did they record four consecutive wins, and they slipped to 11th out of 26 clubs in the league. They won 13-3 at the Boulevard in October but the Black and Whites took their revenge by winning 18-0 at Craven Street on Boxing Day on their way to their third consecutive top-four place. In the cups, old foes Dewsbury knocked Rovers out of the Yorkshire Cup at the semi-final stage and, in the Challenge Cup, a narrow first round win over York was followed by a 10-0 defeat at home to the Airlie Birds.

The referee had to halt the game twice against Leeds

at Craven Street in March when spectators tried to man-handle the touch-judges and Rovers' scrum-half Joe McGlone was the first victim of a new crack-down aimed at cleaning up the scrums when he was suspended for two games for putting the ball in unfairly.

The reason for Rovers' inconsistency was not difficult to pinpoint. Minor injuries and other absences disrupted the side, particularly at half-back, and only three times in 44 matches could the club field an unchanged side. Again Austin was ever-present, finishing as top try-scorer with 19. Osborne shouldered the bulk of the goal-kicking duties as Bradshaw's appearances became infrequent. On 27 April, Keighley provided the opposition for Rovers' last match at Craven Street and Frank Boagey scored a hat-trick of tries in a 26-3 win. It had been the club's home for 27 years, but perhaps the rather paltry attendance of 3,000 reflects the lesser affection in which it was held than its successor.

Even at a time of significant unemployment the club still made a profit albeit a more modest one of £779, despite a players' wage increase and a £400 loss on running the 'A' team. At a relatively quiet AGM, Brown said that the profit had been the result of 'strict economy and judicious management.' He paid tribute to Bunker Carmichael who died in September 1921, less than three years after his final appearance.

Brown reported that work on the new ground was progressing well and that it would be ready for the start of the following season. He did, however, have some strong words for a small minority who opposed the scheme and 'had done their best to blacken it in the eyes of the public.' He said that there had been many obstacles that had needed to be overcome, in particular when the NU refused to help. Brown felt that the investment of £500 by the City Council had turned the tide and ensured success of the venture. Over £5,000 worth of debentures had now been sold. The only debate was around the name of the new ground. Eventually, 'Craven Park' narrowly won the vote over 'Kingston Park' after 'Robins Nest' and 'Wilberforce Park' had been eliminated.

A very significant event, in October 1921, had been the formation of the Rovers Supporters Club. This was endorsed by the chairman as being 'a very useful initiative in many ways' and the new organisation quickly proved its worth by raising money towards the cost of the east stand at Craven Park. A founder and early chairman of the Supporters Club was East Hull painter and decorator Sam Littlefield, whose legacy to the club is the now-familiar crest, which he designed and the club duly adopted.

A new home

1922-23 was the season when the Northern Union became the Rugby Football League, when Hunslet's flying winger Harold Buck moved to Leeds for £1,000 in the game's first four-figure transfer and when Hull Kingston Rovers moved to their new Craven Park stadium on Holderness Road.

The first game there was the visit of Wakefield Trinity on 2 September 1922, which resulted in an inauspicious 3-0 defeat, the visitors' Albert Rosenfeld – in the latter stages of a magnificent career – having the honour of scoring the inaugural try at the ground. Winger Louis Harris scored Rovers' first against Featherstone five days later. Much ceremony surrounded the official opening of the new ground on 21 September when, at a ceremony on the car park, chairman E.W. Brown opened the gates to the stadium with a golden key that had been presented to him by the architects.

The Robins

In his speech, Lord Mayor Councillor Wokes said that he 'had never seen a better ground'.

The first derby game at Craven Park, in October, resulted in a 10-7 win for the visitors. The *Hull Daily Mail* reported that they won through their superiority in the backs but that Rovers' forwards, with Jack Wilkinson, Bielby and Clark outstanding, more than matched their opposition. There was an element of controversy when Bielby was awarded a second half try that brought Rovers right back into the game – the Airlie Birds claiming that their player had already grounded the ball. Veteran referee Renton, whose handling of the game the *Mail* described as admirable, explained that the Hull FC player had bounced it. The crowd of 22,282 remained a ground record and Brown declared himself delighted with gate receipts of £1,300, more than £200 greater than the old Craven Street best.

Tragically, however, Rovers director Jonathan Abbott collapsed at the game and died shortly after reaching hospital.

Only nine league defeats were suffered throughout the season and in the second half of it, Rovers showed their best form. The Airlie Birds completed a league double at the Boulevard on Christmas Day but after a 10-5 defeat at Leeds on 27 December, only two other matches were lost all season – one in the first round of the Challenge Cup at Keighley and the other, two games later, in the league at Hunslet. Rovers then embarked on a ten-match winning run that took them through to the end of the season. An 18-5 win at Barrow in the last match catapulted them above Wigan to finish fourth and in the Championship semi-final they made the short trip to the Boulevard to take on their neighbours.

Although they'd conceded a league double to their neighbours, Rovers had won 14-2 in the first round of the

Yorkshire Cup the previous October, their first derby win at Craven Park. In the Championship play-offs, the Robins levelled the account for the season with a convincing 16-2 triumph, to set up a final with second-placed Huddersfield at Headingley. If the Fartowners were not quite the force they had been before the war, they were still formidable opposition, so for Rovers to pull off a convincing win and take their first Championship title was a true cause for celebration. The '20s had started majestically, with a Yorkshire Cup win, a first-placed league finish, an inital Championship and a magnificent new home – all in just three seasons.

Once again there was evidence of the benefits of a settled side. After the end of October, only 37 changes were made in 30 games, compared to 101 in 33 matches over the same period in the previous season. Osborne started all but two at full-back and finished only two short of a century of goals, his best ever tally. Rhys Rees, who made his debut the previous season, and Cook both started every game at centre as did Austin on the left wing, whilst burly right-winger Harris missed only three fixtures. Jack Hoult made his debut in the third game and was established after that, playing at stand-off with either McGiever or McIntyre his playmaking partner.

Seven men were the regular members of what was often referred to as the 'panzer pack', a formidable unit that was the cornerstone of the successes. Prop-forwards Bob and Jack Wilkinson, hooker Frank Boagey and back-rowers Frank Bielby, Bill Westerdale and Arthur Moore were joined by the big South African George van Rooyen, who arrived at the start of the season.

It was a wonderful side that would almost certainly rival any team that Rovers have fielded since.

The Robins

Championship Final, Headingley, Leeds, 5 May 1923
Huddersfield 5-15 Hull Kingston Rovers

If the neutrals felt that this was an unspectacular final, their opinion was not shared by more than 3,000 Robins' fans that made the trip to Headingley. Rovers were at full strength but Huddersfield were missing their veteran captain, the great Harold Wagstaff, who had a stomach ulcer. Whilst Rovers' pack was perceived as their ace, the Fartowners' forwards nonetheless had a weight advantage of one stone per man.

The early tackling was fierce, particularly by Rovers, and scoring opportunities were restricted to penalty attempts. The usually prolific Ben Gronow missed two for the Fartowners and for Rovers, Laurie Osborne miscued from in front of the posts. Arthur Moore stopped Howarth on the line after 25 minutes and seven later Osborne atoned for his earlier miss when he dropped a magnificent long-range goal after fielding Huddersfield's clearance kick from a Rovers forward rush. It was Osborne's 100th goal of the season in all matches. Rovers spurned a try-scoring opportunity just before the interval when Louis Harris broke away but ignored his four teammates in support and was tackled by Huddersfield full-back Thomas. Osborne's goal was all that separated the sides at the interval.

At the start of the second half, Harris was again to the fore with a 50-yard break. Again, it failed to lead to a try but with Rovers visibly increasing in confidence, it was no surprise when centre Rhys Rees sliced through the defence after a fine handling move. Osborne made it 7-0 after 45 minutes. Both sides missed opportunities through over-eagerness. Osborne, who had played well up to that point, made a bad error when he misjudged a kick from Davidge, allowing Clark to hack the ball forward and Williams followed up to score. Gronow landed his first kick from four attempts and the margin was only two points. It was another error that led to the next and decisive try. Huddersfield stand-off Rogers had been injured early on and his immobility forced a positional shuffle in which loose-forward Stamper had to move to full-back. Unfortunately, when attempting to gather a kick ahead, he lost the ball on his own line and Jimmy Cook raced up to score. Osborne missed with a fairly easy kick, but it was 10-5 with 15 minutes to go. Rovers then tried a succession of drop-goal attempts, all of which failed before, in the last minute, the unfortunate Stamper was slow to claim a loose ball and Jack Hoult scooped it up and scored near the posts. Osborne kicked the goal and it was all over.

It was Rovers' first Championship – a victory built on their resolute defence and a fine kicking game. The Hull Daily Mail *said that the man of the match was undoubtedly Rees, who beat five defenders for his try. Skipper Moore lifted a trophy for the second occasion, this time on behalf of a team containing 11 local players.*

> **Huddersfield:** *G. Thomas; G. Davidge, P. Reid, T. Howarth, W. Watts; J.H. Rogers, S. Williams; A. Swinden, B. Gronow, T. Fenwick, D. Clark, A. Sherwood, J.F. Stamper (capt).*
> **Rovers:** *L. Osborne; L. Harris, J. Cook, R. Rees, G. Austin; J. McIntyre, J. Hoult; J.R. Wilkinson, F. Boagey, J.H. Wilkinson, C.W. Westerdale, F. Bielby, A. Moore (capt).*
> *Referee: F. Fairhurst (Wigan)*
> *Attendance: 14,000*

At the AGM, E.W. Brown said that Rovers now had the finest ground in the country with a superb playing area, parking for 300 cars and 14 tennis courts that were in regular use. He paid tribute to the architects, Blanchard, Wheatley & Houldsworth of Savile Street in Hull – adjacent to where the club shop now stands – and said that apart from the roofing, which had been constructed by a Manchester firm, all the labour had been undertaken by local men. Hull BOCM had provided ashes and waste that formed the foundations for the terracing.

Brown admitted that in the early days, his co-directors caused him sleepless nights. Unused to dealing with such large sums of money '...they had issued contracts as if they were dealing in paper bags, although I myself had not the slightest idea where the money was coming from,' he said. The new ground got quick recognition from the RFL as the Yorkshire versus Lancashire game was played there on 7 December 1922 in front of over 8,000 spectators, not bad for a Thursday afternoon. Laurie Osborne was Rovers' representative in an 11-all draw.

Reviewing the season, the *Hull Daily Mail* hailed E.W. Brown as the pioneer behind Rovers brave move, reflecting on the club's precarious existence before and immediately after World War I. 'Only supreme optimists could have believed that the club could not only continue to exist, but would make good, against a background of industrial depression as never before had been experienced,' it said. Their reporter added: 'When things looked blackest, there arose in East Hull a band of greathearts capable of dealing with a menacing situation.' He believed that the bold decision to move the club to a more spacious area where it 'could expand its lungs' was probably the decisive factor in preserving its future. The *Mail* commended the Rovers management on achieving stability in this first season in its new home and the 'splendid consistency of the team that outstripped clubs with more resources.' It concluded: 'With so many young players, it is bound to do as well, if not better, next season.'

On the financial side, the purchase of the ground put

the club £11,392 in debt from debenture stock (£6,150), a bank overdraft (£2,068) and other creditors (£3,174). The season's largest income was a record £9,065 in gate receipts and the biggest expenditures were £2,944 on wages for the players and trainer and £1,909 entertainment tax. That left a profit of £1,884 which, if maintained, would allow the club to pay off the debt at a manageable rate.

After the Lord Mayor's show

After the successes of the previous season, 1923-24 was a disappointment, not only for the Robins, who had to settle for 11th place, but also for Hull FC, who dropped from top to 17th. Even after a victory against Huddersfield, the *Hull Daily Mail* reporter was very critical of Rovers' performance, particularly the backs, and suggested the better side had lost. One consolation for Rovers was a double in the derby games, the first since 1911-12. The 18-9 win at Craven Park on Christmas Day was against the odds as both Westerdale and Boagey were sent off for violent conduct in the first half of a rather robust game. They did take one prisoner with them, but the Airlie Birds still had at least a man advantage for the majority of the game. Indeed, injuries reduced Rovers to nine men for a short while. Skipper Moore and newcomer Harold Binks were outstanding in the host's pack, as were Clark and Jack McIntyre at half-back.

Rovers paid the price the following day, though, when they visited lowly Keighley with just two personnel changes and were comprehensively beaten 18-2, the first of four consecutive defeats. They went out of both cups in the second round, to lowly Barrow in the Challenge Cup and in the Yorkshire Cup at the hands of Batley, who had a wonderful season, finishing second in the league.

The Robins

South African back-rower van Rooyen joined Wigan in November but shortly afterwards a letter he had previously written appeared in the *Johannesburg Star*. It alleged that he had made a mistake in coming to England, was unable to get a job and appealed to the sporting public for money to get back home. The Robins decided to put the facts of the case before the RFL and ask for an enquiry, saying that they had abided by all the conditions of his contract and had offered to assist with the costs of his wife and children returning to Johannesburg, as they did not like England. Van Rooyen said that Rovers had failed to fulfil promises about housing and employment but he was hoping that his move to Wigan would resolve the issue. The RFL exonerated the Robins saying they had done everything they could to assist the player and, to remove any doubt, the club released details of the payments they had made to him.

On 8 December, Austin voluntarily ended his 190-match run of consecutive appearances in order to play for Yorkshire, which he considered a great honour. His run was not only a record for Rovers but also a rugby league landmark that stood for over 50 years. The season marked the debuts of forward stalwarts Harold Binks and Ben Britton.

At the AGM, E.W. Brown reported a season's profit of £419 despite gate receipts almost £3,000 down on the previous season. Brown felt that the financial situation was 'very satisfactory considering the great depression of trade in the city, and the general falling-off of attendances at football throughout the country.' He reported that the total cost of the Craven Park ground was £18,700, of which £8,300 had been paid. Of that, £600 had been raised by the sale of the remaining club assets from Craven Street. A decision was reached that only sports events would be held on the new ground but it was only a short time before an exception was made.

The board was criticised for its non-aggressive policy in relation to signing players and its failure to address poor half-back play. Those shortcomings were blamed for some pitiful gates, as low as 2,000. The chairman defended himself and his board, whilst Moore said that the players bore their share of responsibility.

The club were concerned about the lack of corner flags on some grounds and called for them to be compulsory. 'At Swinton,' Brown said. 'Not only were there no corner flags, but one of the Swinton players ran around a policeman on the touchline to score a try.' Warrington had come up with a new fixture proposal that would mean each club playing every other team in their county once in the first half of the season; the county leagues would then be split in two and the teams in the two top halves and the two bottom halves would then play each other once. This idea might not seem so far-fetched nowadays but it failed to find favour in 1924.

The game against Halifax on 31 March was a benefit match for long-serving skipper Moore who had led the club to two trophies and he received a cheque for £500. Huddersfield, Hull FC and Rovers organised a joint benefit game for former Robins' winger Harold Mulvey who had sustained a broken leg that ended his career whilst at Fartown. Future international loose-forward Jack Feetham made his 'A' team debut at the age of just 14 years and three months.

Scaling new heights

In 1924, the FBI appointed J. Edgar Hoover as its first Director, George Mallory and Andrew Irvine were lost on Mount Everest and the ten millionth Ford Model T was manufactured. In sport, Harold Abrahams ran the 100m in 10.6 seconds to win the gold medal at the Paris Olympics and, in the first test at Edgbaston, South Africa were bowled out for 30 in their first innings in reply to England's 438.

After the relative disappointments of the previous season, the Robins came back strongly in 1924-25, finishing second only to Swinton in the league and winning the Yorkshire League trophy for the second time. They had not only the best defensive record in the Championship but in the club's history, with only 171 points conceded in 34 encounters. Rovers won nine of the first ten league games, including a record 39-2 victory over Hull FC at Craven Park which remained the highest score recorded against the old foe until 2007. They drew the return derby at the Boulevard and followed that with a nine-match winning run that was ended by a narrow defeat at Leeds.

Rovers opened their Yorkshire Cup campaign with a 45-0 thrashing of Halifax followed by a win over York, before a 10-8 home semi-final defeat to Batley. In the Challenge Cup, straightforward home wins over minnows Bramley and Wigan Highfield and a hard-earned 5-0 third round win at mid-table Keighley took the Robins into a semi-final against Leeds at Belle Vue, Wakefield. Bielby scored the only try of the game but the Loiners gave Rovers a scare by whittling away their 7-0 half-time lead, leaving them hanging on to win 7-6. In a disappointing performance in the final at Headingley, Oldham comfortably took the spoils.

By virtue of gaining second place in the league, Rovers entertained Wigan in the Championship semi-final the week before the Challenge Cup decider and scored three tries to none in an impressive 13-4 win. It was in this game that Austin became the first to score 100 tries for the club. Wigan, captained by the legendary Jim Sullivan at full-back, had five internationals in their side but they were no match for spirited Rovers. Swinton won their semi-final at home to St Helens

Recs to set up a final at the Athletic Grounds, Rochdale. Rovers made a few changes to freshen up the team beaten in the Challenge Cup the week before and they certainly worked because they brought the Championship trophy back to Craven Park for the second time in three seasons.

In a wonderful campaign, Austin set a new club record with 37 tries on the wing. Another best was the lowest number of players used, just 23 in the 44 matches. Hoult had moved to centre to replace the departed Rees and Charlie Webb, who had made his debut two seasons earlier, formed the regular half-back pairing with McIntyre. The Christmas Day derby marked the last appearance of the great Arthur Moore, after which Osborne took over as club captain. Andrew Carmichael was the main beneficiary of Moore's departure, claiming the regular loose-forward spot.

In November, the RFL Management Committee appointed a Commission to look into the vexed question of fixture clashes between Hull City and the two Hull clubs, a situation exacerbated by the fact that all three played predominantly on a Saturday at that time. A fairer system was drawn up and a further agreement was reached with the Airlie Birds about pooling the receipts from derby games.

That 1924-25 season represented the peak of Rovers' successes in their early history. What followed was a gradual period of decline. Despite over £2,000 profit made during the season, very little impression had been made on the ground debt which was to be a millstone in future seasons.

The Greats – No 4
Arthur Moore - *see Hull KR legends gallery*

Arthur Moore was born Arthur Mawer in Hull in 1886. He signed for Rovers from junior club Hull St Patricks for 2s

The Robins

(10p) in 1906-07, making his first team debut in the front-row at York on 3 April 1909. Many of his early appearances were at prop, although there was one at scrum-half, but he gradually gravitated to the back row. His career was characterised by being remarkably free of serious injury and aside from the interruption due to his war service between 1914 and 1919, his absences from the team list were rare.

Always an influential figure on the field, Moore made 341 appearances for Rovers, scoring 90 tries. He captained the Robins for over five years from August 1919, leading them to their first two trophy successes. An outstanding forward, he was a strong tackler and determined runner who always led from the front and commanded great respect from teammates and opponents alike. He won one England cap and six for Yorkshire.

A well-earned benefit accrued him over £500, a quite remarkable sum in those hard times. At 39 years of age, Moore made his last appearance for the Robins in the drawn Christmas Day derby of 1924. Later that season he transferred to Dewsbury for a £250 fee and won the Yorkshire Cup with them in 1925. He subsequently retired from playing the following year. Arthur Moore died in 1956.

Internal discord

Before the start of 1925-26 season, there were calls for the club to make special provision for ladies that had supported them loyally since the move to Craven Park. The chairman responded by introducing a new scheme whereby for 17s 6d (87.5 pence) women could purchase a season ticket that would guarantee them a seat in the best stand for all home league matches. He hoped this, and the fact that the club had got rid of the environment at Craven Street where spectators in the stand could clearly hear the obscenities exchanged on the touchline, would encourage more ladies to attend matches. Unfortunately, the move did not have the desired impact.

During the season, director John Work appealed through the *Hull Daily Mail* for better support. He cited the fine set of players the club possessed, the good football they played, that they had a chance of winning three competitions and that they had the finest ground in the league. 'Some of the gate receipts have been ridiculous,' he said. 'They had not even amounted to £200 and it costs over £100 to send the team to play games in Lancashire.'

In the league, the Robins finished in sixth place but were overtaken by their neighbours, who jumped 14 places into fourth spot. Nonetheless, their performances against fellow Yorkshire teams were sufficient for them to retain the Yorkshire League trophy. It was the first half of the season that scuppered any hopes of another top four finish. When Rovers lost 9-4 at the Boulevard on Christmas Day, it was their seventh league defeat of the campaign, one more than they had suffered over the whole of the previous season.

There was an improvement in the second half of the season, with only four defeats in 17 games. They progressed to the third round of the Challenge Cup but hopes ended with a 24-3 defeat to the now powerful Swinton side. Two future Rovers greats, centre Jack Spamer and half-back Harry 'Scrubber' Dale, made their debuts in the closing weeks of the season.

The Easter programme resulted in an incident that could not happen today. After the comfortable Good Friday win over Huddersfield, the directors selected a team to visit Wigan the following day and to play Leeds on Easter Monday. As it transpired, Harris, who was picked at right-wing, was unable to play at Wigan and was replaced by Raynor. The Wigan game resulted in a 13-all draw and, on the return journey, the directors present decided that based on his performance, Raynor should retain his place for the Monday game. When Harris declared fit, expecting to reclaim his spot, a debate ensued that escalated to the directors.

At that point, the decision made on the way back from Wigan was overturned. It so annoyed director Andrew Woods, who was party to the original choice, that he resigned in protest. Woods, however, allowed his name to go forward for re-election at the summer AGM and was re-elected. At their first meeting, however, Woods gave vent to his feelings about some of his colleagues with comments so severe that they caused the rest of the newly-elected board to resign en masse.

The club then entered limbo. Secretary Tom Williams was left in the awkward position of having to keep the club running but only able to act in routine matters. An extraordinary shareholders meeting had to be called in order to elect a new board. Woods said he only had the interests of the club at heart and in order that the impasse could be resolved, he withdrew his nomination. That enabled a new board to be elected and, once again, E.W. Brown was its chairman.

Despite a reduction in gate receipts, the club still managed to make a profit of over £1,000 that Brown felt to be very satisfactory given the bad weather experienced during the season and the general economic climate. He felt that more injuries than in recent seasons, combined with some loss of form, worked against greater success. Brown recorded his disappointment that Craven Park had not been awarded a Test match against the New Zealand touring team the following autumn – the fact that the Boulevard had must have rankled. Brown also thanked the Supporters Club for a £350 donation in addition to the £67 they contributed to the benefit fund for long-serving utility player W. 'Mucker'

Clark. The popular Clark made his debut in 1913 and hung up his boots at the end of the season after playing 163 games.

The ten-day General Strike of May 1926, called by the TUC in support of the mineworkers, affected the transport, docks and power industries. Against a background of violence, volunteers helped to maintain services. In Hull, clashes between police and strikers led to 25 arrests, whilst university students from Keble College, Oxford, came to help keep essential services running.

Challenge Cup Final, Headingley, Leeds, 25 April 1925
Hull Kingston Rovers 3-16 Oldham

In front of 28,000 spectators at a sun-drenched Headingley, Rovers failed to do themselves justice. Most observers thought that the forwards played well, in particular Frank Boagey, Frank Bielby and Andrew Carmichael, but the half-backs had an off-day and the side failed to reproduce the great defensive efforts that had characterised their season. Only Osborne at full-back saved them from a much heavier defeat.

Rovers kicked off against a strong wind and the early stages were even and well-contested, with chances to both sides. Rovers almost scored early on with the forwards dribbling the ball over the Oldham line but the Roughyeds managed to touch it down safely. The Oldham full-back, Knapman, only just failed to put his side ahead when his ambitious wind-assisted drop-goal attempt fell just under the crossbar from ten yards inside his own half. Oldham started to press strongly and, in the 33rd minute, a break was finished off by Farrar who shrugged aside Osborne's uncharacteristically poor effort to push him into touch. In the closing stages of the half, Rovers twice went close and Harris missed with a penalty attempt. At only 5-0 down at half-time, and with Rovers having the wind behind them in the second half, most of the crowd expected them to overwhelm their opponents in the second half.

However, Oldham came out strongly and twice in the first 15 minutes exposed Rovers' defensive frailty, with tries for Farrar and Corsi. At 13-0 down, Rovers fought back briefly. First, Carmichael and Bielby combined to put Jack Wilkinson in for a try and, minutes later, Carmichael almost did likewise for Gilbert Austin but his kick ahead agonisingly beat the winger's dive. Rovers were starting to tire and Oldham took charge with some strong forward play, Farrar and Brough putting Davies in for a try to put the game out of reach with only five minutes to go.

Oldham's Hesketh produced a brilliant display to destroy the Robins' half-backs almost single-handedly. Too many of Rovers' players had an off day and the 16 points they conceded was the highest score recorded against them all season.

> **Rovers:** L. Osborne (capt); L. Harris, J. Cook, J. Hoult, G. Austin; J. Raynor, J. McIntyre; J.H. Wilkinson, F. Boagey, J.R. Wilkinson, C.W. Westerdale, F. Bielby, A. Carmichael.
> **Oldham:** E.H. Knapman; R.B. Farrar, S. Rix, E. Davies, J. Corsi; G. Hesketh, B. Beynon; A. Tomkins, R. Marlor, J. Collins, R. Sloman, A. Brough, J.H. Hilton (capt).
> Referee: R. Jones (Widnes)
> Attendance: 28,335 (£2,870)

Championship Final, Athletic Grounds, Rochdale, 2 May 1925
Hull Kingston Rovers 9-5 Swinton

After the previous week's disappointment, Rovers faced another formidable test. Although they had never won the title, Swinton possessed a very strong side that was soon to lay down a marker in emphatic style, winning three Championship trophies in the following six seasons. To *freshen up the team, Rovers brought in Ralph Rhoades at centre and moved Jack Hoult out onto the wing in place of Louis Harris and in the forwards, Harold Binks and Ben Britton came in for Bob Wilkinson and Bill Westerdale.*

It was a hard fought and exciting tussle. With a slight wind behind them, Swinton took command through their forwards from the start and Jimmy Cook had to be at his best to keep out dangerous winger Brockbank in the opening minutes. Evans was pushed back and prevented from touching down twice and Brockbank had a try disallowed for a forward pass. It looked like a question of how many Swinton would score. Gradually Rovers clawed their way back into the game and after they had missed two penalty attempts, Hoult made a magnificent break only to be denied by Brockbank's excellent cover tackle. Then, after a Frank Bielby obstruction, Brockbank kicked a penalty to put Swinton 2-0 ahead after 31 minutes, and he increased their lead when he finished a well-executed move near the corner-flag two minutes from half-time. Swinton's backs had looked more dangerous and kept the ball in hand more, whilst Rovers had placed too much emphasis on their kicking game.

When the game got under way again, the wind had given way to slight rain. Five minutes into the half, Rhoades made something out of nothing. Failing to gather McIntyre's pass, he coolly dribbled the ball before picking it up ahead of Williams to race over between the posts. Osborne converted to level the scores and that was the inspiration Rovers needed. Their pack stepped up a gear and began to dominate. Under terrific pressure, Swinton were forced on the defensive for much of the rest of the half and although they kept their line intact, Osborne's penalty goal put Rovers ahead after a foul by Beswick on 68 minutes and he then sealed the win with a second goal, following the intervention of a touch judge, eight minutes from time.

It was a sweet success for the Robins, particularly after the Challenge Cup disappointment and a just reward for

107

their tremendous efforts throughout the season. It was
received very enthusiastically by their small contingent of
supporters that had made the difficult journey to the
Athletic Grounds and sportingly by those of Swinton and
the neutrals. The Swinton local paper, The Journal,
commented that whilst their side's efforts were too
individual, Rovers '...had the right team spirit and worked
collectively.'

> *Rovers: L. Osborne (capt); J. Hoult, R. Rhoades,*
> *J. Cook, G. Austin; J. McIntyre, J. Raynor; B.*
> *Britton, F. Boagey, J.H. Wilkinson, H. Binks, F.*
> *Bielby, A. Carmichael.*
> *Swinton: R. Williams; F. Evans, W. Sulway, J.*
> *Evans (capt), C. Brockbank; W. Rees, B. Evans; H.*
> *Entwistle, H. Blewer, M. Strong, J. Entwistle, T.*
> *Halliwell, F. Beswick.*
> *Referee: A. Brown (Wakefield)*
> *Attendance: 21,580*

Castleford were admitted to the league for 1926-27, along with Pontypridd. At Craven Park, pre-season activity included a repaint of the ground in readiness for its forthcoming visit by the Prince of Wales, the future King Edward VIII. After opening the Ferens Art Gallery in the city centre on 13 October, the Prince was entertained by the singing of over 10,000 Hull schoolchildren on the pitch, with thousands of parents and others looking on from the stands. The venue was regularly used for school sports days at the time.

Efforts to recruit players from Wales continued and, in particular, the club was looking for big forwards. In response to shareholder criticisms about early-season fitness, the players' initial training was more rigorous than ever. The *Hull Daily Mail* commented that centre Jim Cook had 'reduced his dimensions very considerably and if this counts for anything, this very erratic player should show his best form very quickly.' Key half-back McIntyre was back in training after his injury-curtailed time the previous year. There was an open to the public practice match between the 'Stripes' (probables) and 'Blues' (possibles), who included three trialists.

In the league, Rovers finished in sixth place again and won all their home league games for the second time. The only blip in the home record was a draw against Halifax in the first round of the Yorkshire Cup, the Robins losing the replay 13-0. There was a magnificent comeback on New Years' Day when, in a fine team performance they recovered from a 15-7 half-time deficit to record their first win over a New Zealand touring team, 20-15. The team was more settled, with Austin and Bob Wilkinson each missing only one of the 42 matches and only 26 players being used in all. With 29 touchdowns, Austin was once again the leading try-scorer and Osborne kicked 77 goals.

The defence improved on the previous season but the margin between failure and success was small, five league matches were drawn and five were lost by six points or less. If just six more points had been gained from those ten games, Rovers would have finished above Wigan, St Helens and Hull FC. Honours in the derby games were shared, with both winning their home fixtures. The pattern of Derby games, played on Boxing Day and Good Friday for three seasons from 1904-05, then in October and Christmas or Boxing Day, changed from 1926-27 until World War II to Christmas Day and Good Friday.

Jack Feetham, still only 17, took another step towards stardom when he made a try-scoring debut in an 18-6 defeat at Wigan on 30 October. Meanwhile, the drawn game at Castleford in December marked the end of the Rovers career of local utility-back Jack Hoult, who had made his debut in the second game at Craven Park in 1922. He played in 172 matches, mainly at stand-off or centre, scoring 74 tries, then moving to York.

St Helens Recs pipped Swinton to finish top of the league for the one and only time in their professional history, which ended just before World War II. Newcomers Castleford came bottom, with fellow new club Pontypridd two places above them – Cas lived to fight another day but the Welshmen did not. The Challenge Cup final was broadcast live on the radio for the first time and veteran referee Frank Renton retired after 30 years in the middle. Renton had refereed Rovers in their first Challenge Cup campaign back in 1898. E.W. Brown proposed that Renton's experience be put to good use as a mentor for young referees, of whom there was a shortage. Meanwhile, serious concerns were being expressed in rugby league circles about the financial situation at Huddersfield, where one of the early giants had now slipped to 23rd place.

After the abolition of the old county leagues in 1902, the Yorkshire Senior Competition name was revived for 'A' team competition. In 1926-27, Rovers 'A' team topped the YSC and won the YSC Shield. The club saw that as vindication of the policy to withstand the reserve team's regular financial losses. Debts had now stabilized around the £7,500 mark and were seen as satisfactory. Sadly, former winger Tich West died just under 20 years after his retirement from playing.

1927 saw the opening of Hull University, aviator Charles Lindbergh completed the first non-stop solo Atlantic flight and the first official Ryder Cup was won by the USA. Swinton became the first Lancashire club to win all four cups open to them.

The Robins finished 13th in the league in 1927-28, their lowest position for eight seasons, and there was a dismal sequence in which the team failed to score in seven out of ten consecutive games. Again, Dewsbury ended Yorkshire Cup hopes, this time winning at Craven Park in the semi-final on 3 November. It was Rovers first home defeat since 6 March 1926, a club record run of 33 games, comprising 30 wins and three draws. Then, in the second round of the Challenge Cup, Warrington achieved a rare 5-0 success at Craven Park, a graveyard for them on so many occasions over its 66 years.

The simple fact was that the team was starting to grow old. Two of the greats, Austin and Bielby, had a well-deserved joint benefit that earned them £81 each and both played their last games for the club. Frank Boagey also made the last of his 218 appearances, in a Yorkshire Cup defeat by Dewsbury. In his heyday, he had been described by trainer Jacques as the finest hooker in the league. New skipper Andrew Carmichael was joined in the pack by Binks, Britton, Feetham and Westerdale. McIntyre formed the regular half-back partnership with Hall, who made 32 appearances in his only season with the Robins. Osborne, although relinquishing the captaincy, remained a pillar of reliability at full-back and he and Westerdale both missed only two of the 44 games.

The Greats – No 5
Gilbert Austin - *see Hull KR legends gallery*

Whilst Gilbert Austin is best remembered for his amazing run of 190 consecutive appearances, he was also one of the club's outstanding three-quarters.

Born in 1895, Austin signed for Rovers during World War I, making a try-scoring debut at home to Wakefield Trinity when official fixtures resumed on 25 January 1919. In his first two seasons, he played mainly at full-back, moving to centre in the 1920-21 season and from 1922-23, he performed mainly on the wing.

The Robins

It was on 8 December 1923, over four years after he had made his debut, that he finally missed a Rovers game so that he could play on the wing for Yorkshire against Lancashire at Oldham. His centre that day was rugby league great, Harold Wagstaff. In all, Austin played four times for Yorkshire, sadly each occasion on the losing side and he was selected for the Great Britain trial match before the 1924 tour to Australasia.

Unfortunately, however, he was somewhat exposed that day in a side that was heavily beaten.

Over his 347-match career with the Robins, Austin scored a total of 163 tries including a then record 37 in the glorious 1924-25 season, in which he touched down six times in a Yorkshire cup-tie against Halifax. Not blessed with either raw pace or tremendous strength, he was an extremely dedicated and reliable all-rounder who knew his way to the try-line and who never gave less than his best.

Austin retired from the game in 1928, making his final appearance for Rovers in a dour 0-0 draw at home to Dewsbury on 7 January 1928. He scored his final try six days earlier in a 9-8 win at St Helens Recs. His consecutive games haul stood as a rugby league record for over 50 years until it was finally beaten by Widnes hooker Keith Elwell in the 1980s.

Gilbert Austin died in 1947 from injuries sustained in a motor accident at the age of just 53.

The Greats – No 6
Frank Bielby - *see Hull KR legends gallery*

It is remarkable that two of the club's legends should make their full debuts on the same day but, because of WWI, the previous 'first class' game had been over three and a half years earlier.

Frank Bielby was born in Beverley in 1897. He played in the second-row of the team that beat Wakefield 22-10 on 25

January 1919 and, like his fellow debutant Austin, he marked his bow with a try.

A local man, Bielby was a fearsome tackler. Supporters at the time used to say that he was the only one in the league who could consistently tackle Hull FC's legendary centre Billy Batten and dump him on his backside. Bielby, though, was much more than that. Though not tall, he was very powerful and no slouch with the ball in hand either.

His career tally of 78 tries in 276 games was a very good return for a forward at the time. He also had the knack of scoring tries when they were most needed, like the match-winners in the third round and semi-final of the 1925 Challenge Cup campaign.

Another asset was his versatility and he appeared occasionally in the three-quarter line in his early days, as well as taking on other pack duties. Bielby played his last game for Rovers in a 19-0 defeat against Bradford Northern at Odsal on 19 February 1928. He then transferred to York, for whom he played for a couple of seasons before he returned to Craven Park, where he was a familiar figure on match days as a gateman for many years. Bielby was also a friend to many generations of Rovers players, always having a word of advice or encouragement for them in their early days. For his many fans, he was one of the finest and most popular players the club has produced.

The last survivor of the great early 1920s teams, Frank Bielby died in 1980.

Midway through the season, the RFL decided to introduce new rules to tidy up the play-the-ball.

The *Hull Daily Mail* reported after Rovers' game against St Helens Recs on 2 January that 'despite the fact that referee Brown lectured the players before the start on the new rule, the players made no attempt to carry it into operation.'

The club made a £787 loss, the first deficit since 1920-

21, largely because of a £1,370 reduction in gate receipts due to the team's slip in form and some very poor weather. The total indebtedness was £7,295, including a £1,000 loan from the RFL. Chairman Brown said that the players had risen to certain heights and then let the club down. He was proud of the 'A' team, who gave hope for the future by retaining the YSC league leaders' shield. He indicated that if a top-class half-back became available, he would be prepared to pay £1,000 to secure his services.

The board had refused an offer from a greyhound company to buy the ground but had agreed a lease that would bring greyhound racing to Craven Park for the first time. The club would receive £300 for the first season and £500 annually thereafter.

Brown castigated those who he felt would rather criticise than contribute, saying there was too much back-biting and criticism of certain players. He appealed to supporters to take the rough with the smooth and said that they could not expect top class players on such small gates. Brown ended by complimenting the *Hull Daily Mail* on their coverage, contrasting it with the situation in Warrington where club representatives had told him they wished their local press would give them similar support.

The most unpopular club in rugby league

Season 1928-29 started brightly, with the team riding high at the top of the table after suffering only one defeat in the first 11 games.

After that, their form became more inconsistent and they lost 10 league matches in all, albeit that five of them were by six points or less. Both derby clashes resulted in away wins and Rovers won the last four league games to ensure a second-placed finish behind a revived Huddersfield. It was to be the club's highest for another 38 years.

In the Championship play-offs, third-placed Leeds were the semi-final opponents at Craven Park. It was the fourth time the two sides had met that season; Leeds winning at Headingley in the league and Yorkshire Cup, whilst the Robins triumphed 5-0 at Craven Park in the league. The play-off produced another tight game in which Leeds scored the only try to win 7-4. The cups proved a disappointment, with first round defeats in both. Once again, the league performances demonstrated the benefits of a settled side. Osborne and centre A.J. Jordan, signed the previous season from York junior rugby league, were ever-presents and, in all, eight players played in 35 or more of the 43 games. Scrubber Dale, who had played only six times in the previous two seasons, now made the stand-off position his own. The problem position in the backs was left-wing, where seven players featured – most of them not natural wingers. Second-row was the other problem area, veteran Bill Westerdale appeared on 36 occasions but 10 other players were used at various stages.

Andrew Carmichael left to join the Airlie Birds early in the season but in Jack Feetham Rovers had a ready-made replacement and Westerdale took over as captain. Rovers wanted a £100 fee for Carmichael but Hull FC were only prepared to pay £75. Carmichael stumped up the balance himself to secure the transfer, being told by his new employers that they would repay him it whenever he needed it!

Old servants Louis Harris, Bob and Jack Wilkinson made their final appearances during the season. J.H. 'Jack' Wilkinson was an old-fashioned prop-forward who never took a backward step and his front-row partner, J.R. 'Bob' Wilkinson a more mobile, ball-handler. Both had made their debuts in 1920 and had gone on to be key members of the 'panzer pack.' Having each played over 250 games for the Robins, they pulled on the shirt for the final time in a 13-4 defeat against Huddersfield at Fartown on 3 November 1928. Solidly-built wingman Harris made the last of his 254 appearances at St Helens Recs on 2 January at loose-forward. He joined the Robins' board in 1937 and served as a director until the 1970s.

The successful league campaign came at a cost to the club's reputation. There were allegations of Rovers' dirty play causing injuries. Throughout their successful period, the Robins forwards had adopted a robust style but in that they were no worse than most. The RFL chairman had attended a game against Dewsbury, after which complaints were made that due to the Robins' over-physical style, several Dewsbury players were unable to play the following week. The chairman expressed surprise about the comments and exonerated Rovers. He said that poor management was the reason why some clubs were struggling and they appeared to be looking for scapegoats.

However, mud tends to stick and at the end-of-season AGM, E.W. Brown said that Rovers appeared to be the most unpopular team in the league and 'the directors were insulted everywhere they went.' He was quite disillusioned by the treatment afforded the club. In hindsight, he regretted his actions following a home game against Batley when, according to the *Hull Daily Mail*, an opposing player 'reeled out of the pack with his hand to his face and fell to the ground.' As referee Robinson was unable to identify the offender, Brown ordered an internal enquiry immediately after the game as a result of which back-row forward George Saddington was given a two-match suspension by the club.

Nevertheless, by January, unhappy about perceived

victimisation and in particular about an incident where Saddington was sent off having apparently done nothing wrong, Rovers wrote to the RFL to complain. Brown's increasing despair caused him, for the first time, to mention the possibility of his stepping down as chairman. He did not court favour with other Yorkshire clubs when he criticised some of them for either fielding weak 'A' teams or not fulfilling reserve fixtures at all. 'It was impossible to improve form and combinations under these circumstances,' he said. His words would soon come back to haunt him.

The club returned to the black with a £672 profit and there was hope that the additional future income from the new greyhound track would make an impression on the longstanding ground debt. Brown commented that there had been a slump in interest in the game, not only in Hull but elsewhere and whilst he was aware of the need to regenerate that interest, it could not be done by recruiting costly players.

One director felt that refereeing standards did not help, saying that at Castleford he had counted the number of times that referee Laughlin had blown to signal infringements but had given up when it reached 70. In the same game, the official called time five minutes early and had to get the players back when the linesman drew attention to his error.

At the end of the season the board decided, as a token of appreciation for the players' efforts, to take the team that played in the last game plus the two reserves, trainer and groundsman, to see Dewsbury play Wigan in the first Challenge Cup final to be played at Wembley.

The 'forgotten final'

1929-30 saw a slight slip to sixth place in the league but there was another Yorkshire Cup triumph to savour. The league form was inconsistent, with an unbeaten eight-match run and seven consecutive wins sandwiched between poor spells. Despite that, the Robins dropped only five points more than the clubs above them. Challenge Cup hopes ended with a narrow first round defeat at Batley and there was no derby victory to savour for the first time in ten seasons, following a 2-2 draw at the Boulevard and an 11-3 defeat at Craven Park.

On Boxing Day, Rovers played against an Australian touring side for the fifth time. Considering that they had a hard game at the Boulevard the day before and had made only one change in personnel, a 10-5 defeat was a pretty decent result. That game featured an outstanding performance by Dale in what was widely held to be his best game for the club. He never achieved international honours and perhaps had a point to prove. As the gate receipts were to be shared with the tourists, Rovers had not been happy about playing the tour match on Boxing Day, wanting a more lucrative holiday game. In the event, they were satisfied with a 12,000 crowd, the joint best for the season alongside the Good Friday derby, which earned them £1,119.

The Yorkshire Cup campaign saw once more high-flying Huddersfield beaten 8-3 at Craven Park in the first round, before Binks' try gave the Robins a very hard-earned 3-0 second round win in an ill-tempered game at Thrum Hall, Halifax in which three players were sent off. In the semi-final at Craven Park, Bramley were comfortably beaten 15-5 to set up a final against Hunslet at Headingley on 30 November. The Myrtle and Flame were favourites, but Rovers showed their best form and prevailed 13-7 in what is termed 'the forgotten final', coming as it did at the end of a very successful decade for the club.

Yorkshire Cup Final, Headingley, Leeds, 30 November 1929
Hull Kingston Rovers 13-7 Hunslet

Very few people gave Rovers much chance when they faced Hunslet in the 1929 Yorkshire Cup final. The south Leeds side were a strong team, playing on their own doorstep and had the greater support on the day. However, the Robins produced a fine display that had Hunslet reeling from the start.

Jack Spamer followed up his own kick-off and tackled Hunslet full-back Walkington in possession. Rovers forced an error and, from the scrum, Scrubber Dale dodged round the blind side and beat the defence to score before their opponents were alive to the danger. Laurie Osborne's conversion made it a sensational start for the Robins as they led 5-0 with only two minutes gone. To prove this was no flash in the pan, in the eighth minute, from another scrum, Dale and Spamer combined well to create the space for Jordan to send his winger 'Tacker' Rainton over for a try. The score was too far out for Osborne to convert, but Rovers led 8-0. Hunslet then hit back with a long-range penalty goal and the tackling became fierce as the two sides fought it out in the middle of the field. Rainton had to leave the action for attention for several minutes after a heavy tackle but the Rovers pack were more than a match for anything that Hunslet could throw at them. Then, with just five minutes to go to half time, Rovers scored a decisive third try when Dale created a chance for Spamer, who touched down by the posts to give Osborne an easy conversion. Rovers went in at the break with a 13-2 lead that was as deserved as it was unexpected.

Hunslet came out strongly in the second half, determined to force their way back into the game, and Rovers had to defend strongly, twice preventing seemingly certain tries. Eventually, however, Hunslet did find a way through and Jenkins scored in the corner. Traill kicked the conversion to make it 13-7 and Hunslet were back in the game. Try as they

*might though, they were unable to break the Robins'
determined defence again.*

*Inspired by Spamer and Dale, the Robins had claimed an
impressive win. However, it would be over thirty years
before another trophy came to Craven Park.*

> **Rovers:** *L. Osborne; G. Bateman, J. Cook, A.
> Jordan, C. Rainton; H. Dale, J. Spamer; B. Britton,
> L. Sharpe, F. Roberts, H. Binks, C.W. Westerdale
> (capt), H. Williams.*
> **Hunslet:** *J.C. Walkington; G. Broughton, J.
> Coulson, H. Beverley, Rhodes; G. Todd, W.S.
> Thornton; D.M. Jenkins, H. Moss, J. Traill, F.
> Dawson, H. Crowther, W.G. Chapman.*
> *Referee: F. Fairhurst (Wigan)*
> *Attendance: 11,000 (£685)*

Prop Britton missed only one game all season and fellow
forwards Binks, Westerdale and Leslie Sharpe played in all
but a handful between them. Westerdale, who continued to
skipper the side, was by now playing mainly at prop. Jack
Feetham became the first serving Rovers player to play for
Great Britain when he scored a try in a 31-8 defeat in the First
Test against Australia at Craven Park on 5 October 1929 in
front of a 20,000 crowd.

Feetham played only one more game for the Robins
before transferring to Salford and was replaced by Harry
Williams at loose-forward. The Australia game was to be
Craven Park's only test match but Feetham later won seven
more Great Britain caps whilst with the Red Devils. He played
the first 103 games of his career with Rovers, scoring 30 tries.

In the backs, Bunker's son, George, made his debut
as cover for Osborne at full-back on 26 September, after which
he was utilised in various back positions. Osborne passed the
50 goals for the season mark for the ninth consecutive year

as he chased Bunker Carmichael's club record total of 723. Right-winger George Bateman finished at the top of the club's try-scorers for the third successive season, his last with Rovers. At the end of the season he left to join Hull FC, with whom he enjoyed considerable success.

Another of the last links with the great side of earlier in the decade was severed when Jim Cook played his last game in a heavy defeat at Leeds in January. He retired after sustaining an internal injury that caused him problems for the rest of his life. The talented but enigmatic centre had been a stalwart of the side since the First World War. Relying on skill and power rather than pace, on his day he was one of the best centres the club has had. Cook played 362 times for the Robins, scoring 116 tries.

'Forward rushes' and 'dribbles' were still commonplace in the game and even by the end of the decade there remained a quaint haziness about kick-off times, particularly for evening matches. Around this time, a Hull baseball team played on Craven Park, which included rugby league players such as Rovers' Frank Blossom and Freddie Miller from Hull FC, augmented by some professional players. The team was quite successful, continuing into World War II and playing friendlies against American servicemen.

On the other side of the city, Hull City, who had comfortably maintained their Division Two status in their first 24 years as a football league club, were relegated for the first time.

Meanwhile, at the AGM, Rovers announced that they made a profit of £382 on the season as a result of strict economies. Chairman Brown said that gate receipts had been £4,612 – half what they had been in the first season at Craven Park. He found it difficult to understand, given that the team had been near the top of the table and had played some splendid football. The club's debt stood at £6,700 and it needed to find £4,500 before the end of the next season. He did not want to issue fresh debentures, and commented on the nuisance of the ten shilling shareholders who he referred to as 'screaming as if they owned the club.'

Brown paid tribute to former chairman John Moore, who had been instrumental in the club becoming a limited company and who had died during the season. Moore had been a stalwart in the Craven Street days and had not approved of the move to Craven Park. He recognised the benefits of the new ground but felt that the timing was not opportune. He had a point. Whilst the club had enjoyed unparalleled success during the past decade, the balance of the debt from the ground move was starting to become a serious concern.

*****

5. An Uncertain World

1930-1945

THE 1930s was the blackest decade of the century, beginning with deep economic depression and ending in a declaration of war in which over 50 million people subsequently perished. Hardly comparably, Rovers' fortunes mirrored the climate in the country and, at their worst point, they too faced a desperate struggle for survival.

The Great Depression

The Great Depression lasted for a large part of the 1930s. Originating in the U.S.A. after the stock-market crash of 29 October 1929, it was the longest and deepest worldwide economic downturn of the 20th century. Its effects on Britain's northern industrial areas were swift and devastating as demand for traditional industrial products collapsed. By the end of 1930, unemployment had risen to about 20 per cent of the workforce and exports had fallen in value by half. In Hull, that downturn was significantly felt. On a brighter note, Hull aviator Amy Johnson achieved worldwide acclaim when she became the first woman to fly solo from England to Australia.

At first sport seemed to escape unscathed. In football, Arsenal won the 1930 FA Cup to start their domination of the first part of the decade, helped by the fact that the effects of the depression were felt much less in London than the rest of the country. The 'little maestro' Don Bradman dominated the summer with his 974 runs in five Tests as Australia won the Ashes 2-1. Their rugby league counterparts, the Kangaroos, were not so successful and suffered defeat in the autumn series in Britain by the same margin.

The biggest change in rugby league was that after 25 years, the percentage system for deciding league positions was finally dispensed with. From 1930-31, all teams played 38 games, consisting of the other 13 teams from their own county home and away plus six teams from the neighbouring one, determined on league positions from the previous season.

That season, Rovers' Lancashire fixtures were against Broughton Rangers, Leigh, Oldham, St Helens, St Helens Recs and Warrington from Lancashire. To allow an even split of clubs, Halifax played as a Lancashire club.

Under this new formula, Rovers ended up 13th, which was to remain their highest finish for 29 years. They also lost in both cup competitions at the first round stage without scoring a single point. A high point in a disappointing season came with a win in the home derby game on Good Friday, in a season's best run of five consecutive victories.

Early in the season, Wakefield Trinity introduced a new pay structure that meant their captain, half-back Jonty Parkin, lost the preferential terms he had enjoyed for the previous six years. His ensuing dispute with the club led to them placing him on the transfer list for around £100, 'in recognition of his valuable service over a long period.' Parkin immediately bought his own transfer and elected to join the Robins, whose players had apparently agreed that he could receive more than the usual match fees. The 34-year-old had captained Great Britain since 1921 and was then the only man to have gone on three Australasian tours. He was undoubtedly a more than useful capture for Rovers and in the second half of the season he formed a successful half-back partnership with Dale, who returned from injury at the end of December.

The Robins were unable to field a stable team, particularly in the three-quarter line where there was much chopping and changing. In the forwards, Britton, Binks and Westerdale made up the usual front row with Sharpe, Saddington and the highly-regarded young loose-forward, Fred Brindle, behind them. At full-back, Osborne did not play quite as often as before but there was a good deputy for him in Bunker's son, George Carmichael, who also continued to provide cover in the three-quarters. The Robins missed the try-scoring of Bateman and in all no fewer than 19 players occupied the two wing positions at one time or another. Amongst them were Billy Batten Jr, the son of the former Hull FC legend and father of future Leeds loose-forward Ray, and Ralph Rhoades, who had returned at the end of the previous season, having not played since October 1925. Spamer played mostly at centre that season but he too made occasional wing appearances. A.J. Jordan, who had been ever-present at centre only two seasons before, played his last game in the Yorkshire Cup defeat to Wakefield in mid-October.

The club had lost £60 per week between November and March which, had it not been for the Christmas derby revenue, could have proved disastrous. E.W. Brown said it would take a lot of effort to put it in a safe financial position.

The Robins

It was a familiar story as he blamed bad weather, poor rugby and the economic situation for lower gates. Brown said that: 'A serious effort must be made at once to rekindle interest by getting together a team capable of providing good, fast football.' However, the players were ageing and some simply were not good enough. The club were not in a position to buy ready-made replacements and would have to develop their own. Brown also felt that some of the pitches had not been conducive to good rugby, for which reason he supported Salford chairman Lance Todd's summer rugby proposal.

The 1931-32 season saw the Robins drop a place in the league table. Just one cup-tie was won, at home to Wakefield in the Yorkshire Cup, but there was a derby double over Hull FC, who slipped to 21st in the standings. The team remained unsettled and Rovers used 32 players in 41 games. The pack was dependent on the same six as last season, with Binks ever-present, but Westerdale had played in less than half the games.

The regular half back pairing was Dale and new skipper Parkin but a young Wilf McWatt played his first five games for the club when he deputised for the veteran international. Carmichael and Osborne shared the full-back duties until Osborne hung up his boots at the end of the season after a glorious career. He finished just five short of Bunker Carmichael's club goal-kicking record. Another of the last links with the glory days, Jack McIntyre, lost his regular half-back place and made the last of his 298 appearances for the club at centre in the 4-2 Challenge Cup defeat at Warrington. In his 10 seasons with the club, McIntyre had often carried the playmaking role. Parkin also ended his short association after the last game of the season at home to Hunslet.

After making 365 appearances, long-serving forward Bill Westerdale made his final one at home to Batley on 9 April. He had been tremendous, a loyal servant.

The season's gate receipts increased slightly on the previous one but at £3,653 were less than half those received in the club's first season at Craven Park nine years earlier. A further loss meant that no impression was made on the overall debt and the shareholders pledged to raise £500 to help strengthen the team. Meanwhile, the *Hull Daily Mail* lamented that having been one of the prime movers in 'one seat per club' on the Rugby League Council, Rovers now rarely took their seat. Future chairman E.E. Mowforth joined the board at the AGM.

The summer rugby debate resulted in a resolution by a handful of Lancashire clubs to submit proposals for a trial league, but the idea quietly died a death. Meanwhile, a debate started about whether referees should give signals to indicate the reason for awarding penalties. The RFL chairman was in favour but secretary Wilson was not, saying that it was 'not the duty of the referee to act as a semaphore steward.'

End of an era

In 1932-33, Hull City won Division Three North and returned to the second tier of English football. In cricket, Douglas Jardine's England team caused a diplomatic incident with their 'bodyline' bowling, designed to negate the strength of the Australian batting – specifically Bradman.

For Rovers, the season brought a further slip down the table to 21st, with Hull FC overtaking them despite conceding a second successive derby double to the Robins. There was no cup success, although Rovers did take Keighley to a replay before losing in the first round of the Challenge Cup. A 54-9 home thrashing of Bradford Northern in April was the highest score recorded at Craven Park at the time. Quite where it came from is something of a mystery, as Rovers had at the time gone

11 games without a win, including a 16-3 loss to the same opponents at Odsal just seven days earlier.

With George Carmichael now the settled full-back, Roland Hill and Jack Smith joining Spamer as regular three-quarters and Dale at stand-off, the backs were a more stable unit although following the departure of Parkin, scrum-half was clearly a problem. New skipper Binks, established in the hooking role, was once again an ever-present in the pack. Saddington and Williams, together with prop W.H. Eddoms and back-rower Ted Tattersfield, gave most support. Promising young loose-forward Fred Brindle was transferred to Huddersfield for £400 in January.

By the end of the season, however, events off the field overshadowed what had happened on it. In March, the club's overdraft had stood at £3,683 and the bank refused further borrowing. The directors were bailing the club out and Brown admitted that Rovers would be lucky to finish the season. The players agreed to forgo wining and draw bonuses and accept a flat £2 per match, whilst the club disbanded the 'A' team in November and cut the secretary and groundsman's wages. In April, the postponed Christmas derby took place at Craven Park, but in torrential rain the gate receipts were just £65, compared to £605 for the Boulevard derby two weeks earlier.

By May, the *Hull Daily Mail* reported that Rovers' plight was causing much concern at RFL Headquarters, and that, 'only personal sacrifices by the directors are keeping the club going.' Even then, Rovers lost £388 on the season. In June, they appealed to the RFL to take up the remaining £750 debenture stock. Fortunately, for once, the plea fell on sympathetic ears and the amount received eased the immediate crisis. The Robins were not the only club in crisis, however, and Leigh made the decision to continue operations only at a meeting in the town at the end of the season.

The Greats – No 7
Laurie Osborne - *see Hull KR legends gallery*

Lawrence William Osborne was born in 1896, a product of the old Courtney Street school and East Hull through and through. He was only ever going to be a one-club man.

He joined the Robins from the Browns' Shipyards amateur club having served in the Royal Navy at the battle of Jutland during World War I. He made his Rovers' debut aged 24 at Hunslet on the first day of the 1920-21 season. By the end it he had made the full-back position his own, occupying it in all but two of his 431 appearances. He proved an extremely reliable performer, ever-present in 1928-29, and rarely missing more than two or three games in a season until his last couple. Osborne had a lot to live up to when he took over at full-back from the great Bunker Carmichael but did so with flying colours.

Slight with a rather laboured run, he was an unimposing figure on the field and did not have a great turn of pace. However, Osborne had three characteristics that made him a first-class custodian; a very powerful kick in the loose, an uncanny positional sense, and was very safe under the high ball. In addition, he was a very fine goal-kicker with a final career tally of 718. Whilst this was five short of Bunker Carmichael's record, his 20 tries gave him a new club record of 1,496 points.

Capped eleven times by Yorkshire, he was a great favourite of the Rovers' fans of the time, and alongside Carmichael, Kellett and Fairbairn, ranks as one of Rovers greatest ever full-backs. At the start of only his second season, he gave Wigan's latest expensive Welsh rugby union recruit, the to become legendary Jim Sullivan such a torrid time with his clever kicks, that Sullivan admitted he considered tearing up his signing-on fee and returning to Wales there and then.

> *Ironically, Osborne's last game was also against Hunslet,*
> *on 23 April 1932 but in a narrow home defeat this time.*
> *Post playing, he took over as manager of the Hull Brewery*
> *Sports Club in Sylvester Street, where he remained until his*
> *retirement.*
> *Laurie Osborne died in March 1953.*

At an eventful AGM, Brown told the shareholders that the bank and debenture interest, together with rates, would mean that the club needed to find over £600 for the next season before they incurred any playing expenses. He pleaded for increased season ticket sales, saying that Huddersfield earned £2,317 from season passes in 1932-33 but Rovers' similar income was just £103, whilst they had given £559 worth of passes to debenture holders. There was criticism from shareholders about the standard of rugby played, the lack of investment in the team and the board's policy of selling better players to keep afloat.

Brown also announced that, after 14 years in the hot seat, he would not seek re-election as chairman although he would remain on the board. In response to the tributes paid to him, Brown said that he had many happy times as chairman, as well as the bad ones, and that he had always done his best. However, he had become '...heartily sick of working under the current conditions,' concluding that it was '...utterly impossible to run first class football at Craven Park.' He said that he could have papered the room with the anonymous letters he had received, he had thrown them all away, but he did recall one that simply said, 'Lloyd George was a hero once, and so were you – now get out of it!'

For the following season, 1933-34, Wigan Highfield moved to White City in London, where they became London Highfield and were the first rugby league team to play under floodlights. Bradford Northern moved into their new home at Odsal Stadium, playing their first game there against Huddersfield on 1 September. With three members of staff, including secretary John Wilson who lived on the premises, the RFL moved into their new headquarters at 180, Chapeltown Road, Leeds.

At Craven Park, the new season opened under a new chairman, W.A. Crockford, and former half-back Jimmy Gordon took over from Billy Jacques as trainer. Jacques had joined the Robins after a 122 match career as a goal-kicking centre for Hull FC and looked after the team over then the most successful period in the club's history. Although his last few seasons had been difficult, for reasons largely outside his control, Jacques does not always get the credit he deserves for his role in the remarkable 1920s successes.

Rovers moved up two places to 19th in the league but lost both derby games for the first time since 1922-23. After an early season defeat in a tour game against Australia, there was a run to the final of the Yorkshire Cup, and a first win in the Challenge Cup since 1928 – albeit against the amateurs of Wigan Rangers. There were more refereeing controversies and Mr Armstrong of Huddersfield so upset the officials of both clubs in his handling of the league match at Dewsbury in November that they jointly wrote to the league to complain. The RFL summoned Armstrong to appear in front of its management committee, but there is no record of this taking place.

The Yorkshire Cup featured some of the best performances of the season with away wins at Featherstone, Leeds and Huddersfield, the latter two finishing well above Rovers in the final league table that season. They played near-neighbours York in the final at Headingley. After a couple of top-half finishes, York had their best ever season in the league in 1932-33, when they finished third and were fifth the following campaign. They were clearly a better side and duly won the trophy for a second time, triumphing 10-4 in front of a 22,222 crowd. Rovers were not disgraced, however, and their share of the £1,480 gate was very welcome.

Front–rower W.H. Eddoms put in a remarkable shift that season playing in all of the 45 games, including the five in ten days over Christmas and New Year and three in four days over Easter. His regular front-row colleagues were skipper Harold Binks and Frank Blossom. Carmichael missed only two games at full-back, whilst Spamer and Hill were the backbone of the three-quarter line. Locally-born John 'Mick' Eastwood made his debut on the right wing on 16 December and was ever-present thereafter. Young Louis Beaumont, the eldest of three brothers who played for the club, made 16 appearances in the centre in his first season in the team. Great Britain chose Dale to play against Australia in the autumn but he was injured in November, missed most of the remainder of the season and did not get another chance.

The season saw the final appearances of stalwarts Harold Binks and Ben Britton. Both made their debuts in 1922-23, played over 330 games for the club and were given free transfers on 22 August 1934. Local man Binks was a versatile, skilful and hard-working forward who made 111 consecutive appearances between 1931 and 1934 and led the team in his last two seasons. The West Riding-born Britton was a big heavy front-row man who was not particularly mobile but whose presence beefed up the pack and invariably resulted in a better supply of ball. Binks moved on to Bradford to play out the end of his career whilst Britton went to Keighley. In addition, Rovers transferred Saddington, who had won two England caps that season, to York to help balance the books in March.

The end-of-season AGM was less eventful than the year before. Encouraging performances in the closing weeks of the season, including a five-match winning run, suggested Rovers were developing the nucleus of a sound team. It had also been possible to run the 'A' team throughout the season. Despite a small loss on the season, gate receipts and season pass sales had increased and the bank overdraft reduced, leading to a mood of cautious optimism. The number of directors was increased from nine to 15 on the basis that, 'the more people there are to push the load up the hill, the easier it will be,' according to the minutes. Secretary Tom Williams retired after 14 years of devoted service and the players presented him with a medal for his helpfulness and consideration. Williams, who had not long been widowed and was not in the best of health, was succeeded by E.E. 'Ted' Haysom.

False hopes and disappointments

At first glance, the optimism expressed at the end of the 1933-34 season did not translate into greater success on the field. In 1934-35, the team slipped four places in the league to 23rd, whilst their Boulevard neighbours continued their climb and finished sixth. After another replay against Keighley, successful this time, interest in the Yorkshire Cup ended in the second round against Wakefield, whilst Hunslet stubbed out Challenge Cup hopes in the first round at Parkside. In a sense, the team had done what the shareholders asked for, they tried to play good football and largely eradicated the rough stuff. Perhaps they were a little unlucky too as six of the league defeats were by five points or less, three in succession from 27 October, and all against decent sides.

The side was unsettled and injuries, indifferent form and suspensions led to 39 players, plus four trialists, appearing in the 42 matches. Ted Tattersfield took over as captain after the departure of Binks. George Carmichael had asked for a transfer and got his wish when Bradford signed him in January, whilst Blossom moved to Oldham before the start of the season. After the departure of Carmichael, Rovers tried five players at full-back, the last of which, Wilf McWatt, gradually made the position his own.

The 'old dependables,' Spamer and Dale, missed only three games between them. Spamer took one of the centre positions whilst Dale had six different partners at half-back, one of whom was Eastwood, who played in five different positions. The mainstay of the forwards were Tattersfield, Williams, Fred Shillito, who had played only a handful of games over the previous two seasons, and young hooker Joe Ramsden, who made the first of his 346 appearances at Batley on 1 September. Eddoms again featured regularly in the front-row before requesting a transfer and did not play after 2 February. Louis Beaumont split his 28 games between centre and second-row.

Thanks to transfer income received, Rovers made a profit of £845 on the season and reduced their bank overdraft to £2,271 – the lowest for ten years. Chairman W.A. Crockford said: 'The club has passed through a difficult period with flying colours,' and he was hopeful of success next season. The chief concern was to find new three-quarters, he noted, and the board were prepared to provide money for 'at least one man of first-rate ability.' They had scouts hunting potential new players all over the West Riding.

Crockford confirmed that one source of income would cease as the greyhound racing promoters at the ground were closing down the operation. Former chairman E.W. Brown resigned from the board after 21 years, thus severing another link with the club's most successful era. In paying tribute to his work for the club, his successor said that whilst ever the club remained in existence, the name of E.W. Brown would be associated with it.

The Greats – No 8
E.W. Brown - *see Hull KR legends gallery*

Ernest William Brown was born in Hull on 11 August 1882 the son of Thomas Dyson Brown, a devotee of local sport, particularly cricket and Hull FC. 'E.W.', as he was known, played 35 games for the Airlie Birds between 1902 and 1907 before trying his luck with Rovers, much to his father's disappointment. E.W. scored a try on his Rovers debut on the wing at Dewsbury on 14 September 1907, but played only twice more for the Robins.

A joiner by trade, he spotted a potential niche for his skills and in 1903 set up his own business in Waterloo Street in Hull as an undertaker, making his own coffins. The following year he married Sarah Ann, with whom he had four children.

Despite having only a fleeting playing career, E.W. became deeply involved in the club and its affairs, sufficiently so to allow his name to be put forward for the board. He was elected a director in 1913 and became the club's chairman in 1919. It was also a very eventful period of his life. In 1920, E.W. purchased the three houses on Beverley Road in the north of the city that the family business still occupies. The following year, he was elected as an independent city councillor for the West Central Ward, a position he held for six years.

As Rovers chairman, E.W. Brown was the driving force behind the move from Craven Street with the purchase of Craven Park in 1922, and presided over a decade of success that was second only to Roger Millward's sides between 1977 and 1986. Over many years, Brown invested heavily in the club of his own time and money. In the end, after 14

> years as chairman, when the success had dried up and the
> club was struggling financially, the pressure and criticism
> finally took its toll and he decided not to seek re-election as
> chairman. He then served on the board, trying to help pull
> the club round, for a further two years before calling it a day.
>   In later years, despite suffering with heart problems, E.W.
> continued to work in his business until the day of his death
> in October 1946 – a true and loyal servant of the city of
> Kingston upon Hull. He was nominated to be the city's next
> Lord Mayor but sadly did not live to take office.
>   The family business on Beverley Road, with its distinctive
> clock, is now run by Gary Holland, E.W.'s great-grandson
> and his wife, both Rovers fans.

A new low

By 1935, the growth of Nazism in Germany gave rise to increasing concerns, often only privately expressed, about the possibility of another war. Much of the north of England was still struggling to shake off the effects of the Depression and Hull's shipping industry suffered severely. Many dockers were unemployed as were those in shipbuilding and the industries that serviced the dwindling fleets.

In sport, one of Yorkshire and England's finest cricketers, Herbert Sutcliffe, played his last innings for his country. The doyen of cricket writers, Sir Neville Cardus, praising his character, application and willpower, observed with his characteristic command of language that, '(Sutcliffe) often had to live above his technical income.'

The 1935-36 season was a baptism of fire for the new trainer Bill Westerdale, who took over from Gordon. Other than Spamer, Dale, Ramsden and Tattersfield too many players were too old or not good enough. The side was constantly chopped and changed – young McWatt, for example, being used at full-back, centre and half-back, Eddoms returned to action and played for all but four of the 40 games with former Hull FC forward Frank Thompson joining him in the front row. However, filling the centre and second-row slots caused a particular headache.

Results suffered accordingly. The club finished in their worst position to date, 28th out of 30, winning only nine league games. The Robins lost in both cups at the first round stage and endured a nine-match losing run between the end of January and the start of April. Meanwhile, the Airlie Birds were riding high; league leaders, Champions, and a derby double.

Encouraged by a local upturn in interest in the game the previous season and by the fact that now the greyhounds had gone Craven Park would be used exclusively for rugby league once more, the RFL allocated it a second international. This was a triangular tournament game between England and Wales, which Wales won 17-14 in front of 17,000 spectators on 1 February. Notwithstanding the extra income, Rovers lost £948 on the season's workings due largely to the loss of the greyhound rent, negligible transfer profits and the poor weather that affected attendances. It had been necessary for the 'A' team to cease functioning again at the end of February.

The board had deliberately avoided selling players in order to try to build a better team and to that end a 'new player fund' had been set up. They reported to the AGM that it was making 'splendid progress.' A new scale of players' payments, aimed at encouraging point-scoring, was agreed. Once again, Rovers complained to the league about referee Armstrong, this time for allowing the home game against Bradford to go ahead when the club felt that neither the ground nor the weather were fit for play. Again, the RFL took no action. Baseball had been played on the ground, earning a small profit, although it proved to be for the one season only.

The Robins

The summer Olympics of 1936 in Berlin became a platform for Adolf Hitler's attempts to legitimise the Nazi regime to the world, whilst that November the BBC started the first television service in the UK. In rugby league, Newcastle replaced Acton & Willesden, one of the two London clubs that had joined the league the previous season. Newcastle themselves lasted just two years.

For Rovers, the 1936-37 season brought a significant improvement in playing fortunes. In the league, they won almost twice as many games as they had the year before, and jumped nine places to 19th. A run of five consecutive wins started on 21 November and they also won four of their last five games.

They were a little unlucky that they played, and lost, twice to Streatham & Mitcham in the early part of the season, the remaining London club subsequently disbanding two-thirds of the way through and all their remaining fixtures were awarded to their opponents.

A second Challenge cup-tie win in three years was recorded when Rovers beat St Helens Recs 13-5 in the opening round but they lost 7-2 at home to Liverpool Stanley in the second. Stanley were enjoying the best two seasons of their largely nomadic and impoverished existence, finishing second the previous season and fourth this.

The team had a touch more stability. A fairly regular pack emerged, with newcomer Ray Maskill joining Ramsden and Thompson in the front-row. Louis Beaumont made up the usual back row with Tattersfield, until he left to join Leeds at the end of January, and Jack Cayzer who signed from Acton & Willesden at the start of the season. Eddoms lost his place early in the season and transferred to Wakefield. Beaumont missed only two of the 41 games played.

The picture in the backs was less rosy with the three-quarter line a particular nightmare but Vic Young joined from Hunslet and was the regular stand-off, forming a partnership with Dale when the latter returned from injury in mid-January. McWatt again had to abandon his favoured full-back role to cover at centre and in the halves, but took over as captain after Tattersfield left.

E.E. Mowforth replaced W.A. Crockford, who resigned as chairman in the early part of the season, whilst former player Louis Harris joined the board. Rovers made a small profit thanks to some increase in gates and the transfers of Eddoms and Tattersfield. The 'A' team had resumed operations again and was third in the YSC, whilst the 'new players' fund' enabled the club to purchase a couple of recruits. The chairman recorded the club's thanks to Hull FC for their £50 donation to the fund. A note of discontent was sounded about the RFL, who were charging Rovers four per cent interest on their loans which was believed to higher than any other such agreements.

Winger John Standage, who joined the club from Halifax during the previous season, sadly contracted meningitis and died at the tragically early age of 23.

Selling the family silver

In the summer of 1937 another Yorkshire cricketing great, Len Hutton, made an inauspicious debut for England against New Zealand, scoring one run in two innings, but quickly redressed the balance by making a century in his second test. In Hull, the Corporation opened its trolleybus system, although it was a further three years before they extended the Holderness Road route past Craven Park.

There was pre-season optimism that 1937-38 would be one of the best since the World War I, with all the players still available from the previous year and an intensive search proceeding for new ones. However, Rovers' league position slipped again, this time to 24th. Thirteen of the 27 league points earned were won away from home which did not help to improve gates. After the Robins beat Keighley on 13 November, they won only two more matches before 19 March, when a 12-11 win over Bradford Northern at Odsal sparked a run of five consecutive wins, including the first derby triumph since April 1933. Rovers lost in the first round of both cups, including a dismal 2-0 home defeat by Keighley in the Challenge Cup. The 'A' team, however, had a splendid season, finishing runners-up in the YSC.

Because Halifax played as a Yorkshire club for fixture purposes, they were allowed some leeway about which Yorkshire clubs they played. They decided they wanted to exchange their 1937-38 fixtures against Rovers for two against Leeds. That meant that Barrow had to play the Robins instead of the Loiners, about which they complained to the RFL. Sadly, that slur did not inspire Rovers, who lost at home to Barrow 29-3 in the middle of their poor run and conceded the double in March.

The trend towards a more settled side continued, however, the Robins even managing to field an unchanged three-quarter line on 19 occasions. Two new signings were Steve Morgan from Swansea RUFC, who made his debut at the end of November and played regularly thereafter, and Hull FC's star centre and captain Joe Oliver who arrived in March. Both McWatt and Eastwood missed only one game and Eastwood finished top try-scorer for the second season running. Up front, Maskill, Ramsden, Louis Beaumont, Shillito and Cayzer formed the nucleus of a workmanlike pack. The club awarded a joint benefit to Spamer and Dale, with the home game against Bramley on 9 April designated as their match.

Unfortunately, crowd troubles marred the season at Craven Park. At the end of the home match against Castleford on 9 October, referee Devine reported that he had been molested by two youths. The RFL warned the club about spectator behaviour and told them to place warning notices. Unfortunately, this seemed to have little effect, because three weeks later, a linesman alleged that he had been struck on the head by a piece of brick. At the subsequent RFL enquiry, Rovers argued that he had fainted due to the cold but that explanation was not accepted by the league, who ordered that the ground be closed for two weeks, stipulating that the Robins could not play games within a ten-mile radius during that period. The home game against Bradford Northern on 6 December was therefore played at Bramley and the 'A' team played one home fixture on their opponents' ground.

Overshadowing playing matters, the board took the decision to sell Craven Park to a greyhound company, who would let Rovers continue to occupy it on a 21-year lease at a rent of £250 per annum. The fact was that since buying the ground, Rovers had quickly paid over half the cost but on the remaining debt they had struggled to make any headway at all. After a further season's loss, it stood at £7,989, including the £2,989 bank overdraft. The directors reasoned that they could completely clear the debt from the £10,750 received from the greyhound company, and they would still have a tidy sum left to bank.

The debentures had fallen due for repayment in December, the club had appealed for holders to renew for a further five years and fortunately 80 per cent agreed. The chairman said that some of the ground money would be available for team-strengthening and that they had offered large fees for two centres but both had good jobs and would not come to Hull unless the club could find them similar employment. The club had paid a substantial transfer fee for Oliver. The annual report described the season as, 'one of the most critical in the history of the club.'

By the middle of 1938, the world was anxiously waiting to see if the Nazis invaded Czechoslovakia and what the repercussions would be. The British government was pursuing its policy of appeasement towards Hitler and it was only the then politically ostracised Winston Churchill and his followers who were urging the government to be prepared for war. Across the country, people went about their business as normally as possible, and the 1938-39 season opened with its usual dose of early optimism. At the end of September, though, the league discussed the possibility of the outbreak of war and decided to carry on as usual unless there were, 'untoward developments'.

As it transpired, it was Rovers best season since 1931-32. They gathered 39 points from 40 league matches, and finished 17th out of 28 clubs. It was not until the seventh game that they were victorious in the league but thereafter, wins started to come regularly and the season finished with a five-match successful run.

Travel sickness was the problem. Rovers won 16 out of 20 home games but only their last two away, at Rochdale and then an impressive 12-8 triumph at fifth-placed Leeds. There were two derby wins, both at home, in the league and the first round of the Challenge Cup.

The better form was based on the work of a solid pack. Second-row forward Len 'Nobby' Clark, who had come into the side towards the end of the previous season, was an ever-present over the 44 games, and he had good support from Maskill, Ramsden, Cayzer and Blanchard, the latter also having made his debut year before. Eastwood was the top try-scorer again, having a good run at scrum-half, but both he and full-back McWatt were frequently called upon to cover in the three-quarter line. By now, Spamer was playing mostly out on the right wing and J. C. Milner, who signed from Wakefield in December, made the left wing slot his own. Oliver was injured in March, whilst Dale featured only in the first three matches and neither played again.

At the AGM, the board reported that they had received all the money for the sale of the ground, had settled the debts and their only liabilities were the 10 shilling shares. They had made a small profit over the season and there was nearly £2,000 in the bank. Former players Fred Barron and Jimmy Gordon were elected to the board, now slimmed down again to nine members as the debt problem had been resolved. Typifying the mistrust felt by some clubs towards the RFL, Rovers alleged that letters they sent to the management committee were not put before them by the secretary.

Elsewhere in rugby league, Wigan chairman Harry Sunderland criticised Halifax and Leeds for trying to buy success, saying that Wigan had 'thousands in the bank, but would not join in with the silly season.' Halifax might have 'bought' the Challenge Cup, but Salford finished at the top of the league for the fourth time in the decade and also won the Championship. At the other end of the spectrum, Liverpool and Rochdale needed help from the RFL to enable them to complete the season, whilst St Helens Recs ceased operations in April.

The outbreak of war

Despite the worsening political situation in Europe by the late summer, Rovers called up their players for training at the end of July and met them to discuss playing terms the following week. The 1939-40 season kicked off as usual and Rovers extended their winning run with a 9-2 victory at Rochdale, followed on September 2 with a 24-2 home success over Halifax. However, by then German troops had invaded Poland and the inevitable happened when Great Britain and France declared war on Germany the following day.

In common with all other sporting activity, the league competition was immediately suspended and that was effectively the end of competitive rugby until 1945. The relaxation of the sport ban allowed the start of Emergency War Leagues on a county basis on October 7. Player registration rules were relaxed to allow them to appear as guests for other clubs to reduce travelling. Several of Rovers' West Riding-based players turned out for clubs nearer their homes, to the extent that utility back Wilf Whitworth played for Wakefield one week and appeared for Rovers against Wakefield the week after.

At the end of the season the Robins' board took the decision, mainly on financial grounds, to suspend activities for the duration of the war. Chairman Mowforth later said that he regretted the original decision to play in the war league. The matches had not been well supported, a situation exacerbated by all home games clashing with those of Hull City, and Rovers lost £611 on the season. As the country's third largest and its major fishing port, Hull was also considered a danger zone and one game at the Boulevard had to be abandoned due to an air raid. Sensible though the decision was, it was portrayed by the prophets of doom as the death of the club.

On 7 August, the Rugby League Council met to consider the forthcoming season. Taking into account the government's wishes that as much football as possible was played to, 'provide recreation and relaxation for the workers,' they decided to run similar war leagues to the previous year. Rovers were one of four clubs that decided not to compete, with three more closing down operations mid-season.

The Greats – No 9
Harry 'Scrubber' Dale - *see Hull KR legends gallery*

*'Scrubber' Dale was one of the best half-backs ever to play
for the club. A talented schoolboy player, he acquired the
nickname 'scrubber' when a sports paper featured him in an
article. Due to his short stature, his nickname at school was
'squibber' but the paper got it wrong and 'scrubber' stuck.
Born in February 1908, he was a product of Buckingham
Street School, joining Rovers from local junior rugby, and
making his debut at stand-off on 27 March 1926 at Hunslet.*

*Dale soon became a firm favourite of the supporters.
Although small in stature, he played above his weight and
was tough and fearless. Very quick off the mark, fast over a
short distance and with skill, cheek and devilry, he was
typical of the breed.*

*Playing in either half-back position, he invariably took the
game to the opposition. He was a born leader, who would
direct and encourage his forwards. It was unfortunate that
Dale came on to the scene as a young player just as the club's
great twenties side had peaked and by the time he was at his
best, Rovers were very much in decline. Perhaps his finest
hour was the 1929 Yorkshire Cup final win, when he inspired
an unfancied Rovers side to victory against Hunslet by
scoring an opportunist try of his own and combining with
Jack Spamer to create Rovers' other two tries.*

*Although that was to be the only domestic honour he won,
the Yorkshire selectors recognised Dale, who earned seven
county caps and his reputation earned him opportunities to
join more fancied clubs. On his one and only selection by
Great Britain, to face the 1933 Australian tourists, he was
forced to withdraw due to a knee injury. Apart from a short
spell with Newcastle towards the end, he remained loyal to
Rovers throughout his career.*

Dale made 306 appearances for Rovers in which he scored

88 tries and kicked 11 goals, marking his final appearance with a try at Leigh on 3 September 1938. He was awarded a joint benefit with his old mate, Spamer, a home game against Bramley in April 1938, from which both men received a then very respectable £84. A docker for most of his working life, Dale sustained a serious head injury whilst working with a bomb disposal unit for the Royal Engineers in World War II and did not enjoy the best of health in later life. After several spells in hospital, Scrubber Dale died in 1970.

Northern RL, Craven Park, Hull, 2 September 1939
Hull Kingston Rovers 24-2 Halifax

What might have appeared just an ordinary league game was remarkable for many reasons. The country was on the brink of war and there was a sense of trepidation about what the future would bring. There was a sense of despair amongst those who had lived through it all 20 years earlier. Already there were preparations for war going on all around them and the match kicked off with the sight of barrage balloons in the sky above.

Whilst Halifax were able to field a full-strength side, Rovers were without new skipper Naylor and the dangerous winger Milner. Milner's absence resulted in the only ever instance of three brothers appearing together in the first team for Rovers. Harry and Bill Beaumont were on the wings and eldest brother Louis was in the second-row.

Rovers started strongly and spurned a couple of opportunities before Bill Beaumont followed up his own kick to score an opportunist try. Wilf McWatt failed with the conversion attempt and then missed a couple of penalties. When Halifax attacked, Mick Eastwood's excellent tackle kept Rovers' line intact. Shortly after that, the visitors' prop-forward Baynham was sent off, followed by Rovers stand-off Steve Morgan. Bill Beaumont then landed a penalty goal, which he quickly followed up with an excellent try when he outpaced the cover to take Eastwood's brilliant kick and score in the corner. McWatt landed a magnificent touchline conversion to give Rovers a 12-0 half-time lead.

The second half opened with Beverley and Cox combining well for the visitors and Jack Spamer had to be at his best to make a try-saving tackle. Within minutes, however, future RFL chairman Hubert Lockwood got Halifax on the board when Rovers were penalised for obstruction. There were then chances for both sides with Bill Beaumont holding Lockwood up over the line before Chadwick followed his teammate Baynham to the dressing room after an over-vigorous exchange. In a move that covered half the length of the field, Spamer beat several defenders and sent Louis Beaumont on a run but the cover got back to stop him.

Harry Beaumont almost got Jack Cayzer in at the corner and another fine tackle prevented Halifax scoring through Bevan. Midway through the half, the forwards carried on McWatt's break from the back and Eastwood finished between the posts. McWatt converted and added a penalty to make it 19-2. McWatt then sidestepped several defenders on a run from his own line before passing on to Louis Beaumont who, with the defence expecting the pass to the supporting Joe Ramsden, cut inside and ran half the length of the field for the try of the match, which McWatt converted. In the closing stages, what was to be Spamer's final appearance was marked by his dismissal, along with the Halifax Maori centre, Smith, after a violent clash. It was an inappropriate end to his long and distinguished career.

As the annual report commented, it was a, 'splendid performance' against the reigning Challenge Cup holders. Having won the last five matches of 1938-39 and now the first two of the new season, Rovers were on a seven-match winning run for the first time since 1930, but it would be almost six years before they beat Rochdale to make it eight on the trot.

Remarkably, all of the Rovers side that day survived the war. McWatt, Ramsden and Len Clark played on until the

1950s, and only Spamer and Jack Cayzer, who moved on to Leigh, never played in the team again.

> **Rovers:** *W. McWatt (capt); H. Beaumont, J. Spamer, W. Whitworth, W. Beaumont; S. Morgan, J. Eastwood; L. Blanchard, J. Ramsden, R. Maskill, L. Clark, L. Beaumont, J. Cayzer.*
> **Halifax:** *H. Lockwood; J. Bevan, C. Smith, J. Treen, A. Bassett; G. Todd, J. Goodall; G. Baynham, H. Field, H. Irving, J. Cox, J. Chadwick, H. Beverley.*
> *Referee: T. Morley (Wakefield)*

The Greats – No 10
Jack Spamer - *see Hull KR legends gallery*

John Thomas 'Jack' Spamer was born in East Hull in 1903 who served the Robins with distinction for over 13 years. Having signed from local amateur club Barnsley United, Spamer made his debut for Rovers at home to Wakefield Trinity on 18 March 1926, scoring a hat-trick of tries in a 29-3 win over Huddersfield in his fourth game. His usual and preferred position was centre but he featured there in only three-quarters of the games he played for the club, also making over 50 half-back appearances and over 70 on the wing.

Whilst there were good players around him at the start of his career, most of his achievements were in a declining or struggling team. He was a great servant in difficult times – an excellent team man, and reliable to the last.

Spamer may not have been the most talented player Rovers ever had but he was as dedicated and loyal as any. Representative honours were few and far between and perhaps his unselfish versatility counted against him. He won two Yorkshire county caps and was selected once for a Great Britain tour trial match. Towards the end of his time, he assisted Westerdale with the coaching duties, including a spell as 'A' team coach.

The war ended Spamer's career at Craven Park and he played his last first class game against Halifax the day before war was declared, later making a further 20 war league appearances. He played 445 games, a club record for almost 50 years, the bulk at an incredible average of 33 per season and scored 145 tries, around one every three matches. It speaks volumes for his commitment, fitness and versatility that he maintained such consistency of performance.

Spamer shared a benefit with Dale in 1937-38 but he fell on hard times in the latter stages of his life and was awarded a further testimonial in 1988. Jack Spamer died in 1991.

Although there was no playing activity, Mowforth and his board were determined to keep the club alive. The club held an AGM each summer as usual, at which they presented a report of activities and finances. In 1941, Mowforth reported that there had been a £133 loss over the preceding 12 months, which was understandable as there was virtually no income, whilst there were still some administrative expenses. He said that over 60 of the players were in the armed forces and felt that the decision to suspend activities had been a very wise one. Earlier in the year, popular former secretary, Tom Williams, passed away after a long illness at his home near the ground. His only son, Cyril, who had helped him with clerical duties before his retirement, was later to continue the family link with the club.

Hull suffered heavy and sustained bombing in the Blitz, from May 1941 to July 1943. During the worst nights on 7-8 May 1941, 454 people were killed in the most severely damaged British city in the war, partly because of its strategic importance as a port. It was an easy target and, if the enemy planes that had flown further west had any bombs left after their raids, they would often drop them on the city on their way home. In total, 1,243 Hull people were killed and nearly half its then 320,000 population made homeless, as over 90 per cent of the city's housing stock was damaged or destroyed. A significant part of the city centre was destroyed during the course of the war.

Two key figures of the 1920s died in late 1941, former trainer Harry Shann, aged 75, and popular centre Jimmy Cook, who had suffered a strained heart in his later playing days that affected him considerably over his last dozen or so years. Notwithstanding, he remained a happy and cheerful figure around North Hull Estate until his death, aged 40.

At a sombre AGM in summer1942, the death in action of former player J. Moore was reported, as was the fact that Pounder and Shillito were missing. Happily, Pounder did survive and even attempted to play rugby again after the war. By the 1943 meeting, when the worst of the bombing was coming to an end, a more upbeat note was sounded. Mowforth said that the club were ready to resume when hostilities ended. W.A. Crockford had actively represented the club at RFL Council meetings and some of Rovers' players were helping to keep other clubs going. The meeting ended with a minute's silence for players missing or killed in action.

In 1944, Mowforth reiterated that the club would be ready when the league resumed. He said that the club had not been asleep and had lined up one or two promising lads.

By May 1945, secretary Haysom confirmed that the directors had decided the club would recommence playing in 1945-46. As they were making efforts to build a side in readiness, he asked aspiring young players to contact him if they would like a trial. At the start of August, pre-season began under the supervision of new coach Stan Adams, a former first grade ref who was a master at Boulevard school, and trainer Ted Jacobs. After six long hard years for club, city and country, there was something to look forward to again.

*****

6. Long Hard Times

1945-1957

THE early post-war period was a very difficult time for Hull Kingston Rovers; they were marooned in the bottom half of the table and had very little money, but the generosity of their football neighbours helped keep them afloat.

Aftermath

Many people expected that once the war ended, life would quickly get back to normal but that was not the case. Winston Churchill, now in opposition after Labour's shock win in the 1945 general election, had correctly predicted that the war would leave the country bankrupt. There was no money to rebuild. Rationing continued and living standards were worse than in wartime. There was an air of depression in the country which eventually turned to anger. It would be many years before Hull's extensive war damage was repaired.

The Robins

Although there was a need for sport and entertainment to brighten up peoples' lives, it was similarly difficult for sporting institutions. The RFL, like the Football League, quickly put in place a full programme once the war ended but it took a lot longer to shake off the air of austerity. Other than St Helens Recs, who had resigned after the 1938-39 season, only Leigh did not resume playing in 1945 and Workington Town were welcomed into the league for the first time.

It was a patchy season for the Robins. They won most of their home league matches but only three away games and finished in 18th place in the league. The highlights were the Craven Park derby that saw the Robins gain a convincing 23-9 win in front of 16,000 spectators, and the 26-7 win over St Helens that featured the four-try home debut of Welsh stand-off Emlyn Richards. Sadly that game attracted only a 3,000 attendance, the average being around 4,500.

The decision had been made to introduce two-leg games in the first round of the two cup competitions. In the Yorkshire Cup, the club's old nemesis Dewsbury prevailed, Rovers' initial one-point advantage proving too slender. After disposing of Manchester amateur side Langworthy Juniors in the first round of the Challenge Cup, Rovers had a home draw against a Salford side that in 1939 had become the first to make successive Wembley trips. After a nil-nil draw, they were well beaten, 38-6, at the Willows.

A record 50 players, plus three trialists, appeared in the 42 matches as the club sought to re-establish a regular side. Skipper McWatt led the way with his 38 appearances at full-back, but the rest of the back division was very unsettled, the only other to appear in more than half the games being former Wakefield player Whitworth. There was more continuity in the forwards, with Clark, Ramsden, Ted Bedford, and new recruits Sid Atkinson and Arthur Wilmot all regulars. Alec Dockar made his debut in the opening game at centre but by the end of the season was established at loose-forward. Welshman Bryn Goldswain, another more than useful capture from Swansea RUFC, played at both centre and back row.

Utility back Mick Eastwood, played his last game at Wakefield on 12 January. He had been seriously wounded whilst serving in the Army during the war and resuming his rugby career had been a remarkable achievement. Playing mostly at wing and scrum-half in an indifferent side, Eastwood scored 68 tries in 205 games. At the end of the season, Louis Beaumont, who made the most appearances of the three brothers, retired after playing 202 games for the club. Mainly a prop or second-rower, he also filled in at the problem centre positions in his early days.

Northern RL, Craven Park, Hull, 13 January 1946
Hull Kingston Rovers 26-7 St Helens

Missing six first team regulars through injury, suspension and service commitments, Rovers surpassed all expectations by serving up their best performance of the season in comprehensively beating St Helens. Had those players been available, new Welsh stand-off Emlyn Richards might not have been called upon to make his home debut. He took full advantage of the opportunity, however, scoring four tries with a combination of speed, sidestep and anticipation that immediately established him as a fans' favourite. There was never a more sensational first appearance at the famous stadium.

Another Welsh newcomer, full-back John Henry Lewis, impressed with his solid defence and intelligent kicking in open play. Winger Bill Beaumont travelled overnight from his army station in Scotland to play and produced one of his best performances, showing a fine turn of speed, and scoring a good try. Former Wakefield utility back Wilf Whitworth kicked two conversions and loose-forward Frank Collinson Rovers' other try. The Robins held a 10-2 interval lead and continued to pile on the pressure in the second half.

Rovers' forwards were beaten for possession in the scrums, the only area of play where they were inferior to St Helens, but they more than made up for it in the loose. Although Saints were far from the power they became in later post-war years, it was still an impressive performance by the Robins.

Rovers: J. Lewis; H. Gee, H. Bratley, W. Beaumont, J. Eastwood; W. Whitworth, E. Richards; J. Dyson, R. Martindale, L. Clark, S. Atkinson, B. Goldswain, F. Collinson.
St Helens: J. Bradbury; A. Gregory, T. Waring, S. Powell, E. Prescott; J. Myers, W. Lee; G. Davies, F. Phillips, J. Hornby, T. Leyland, T. Heaton, N. Birch.
Referee: R. Rawlinson
Attendance: 3,000

The annual report commented that Rovers had, 'lost matches not through lack of enthusiasm, but hard work badly applied.' Chairman Mowforth noted he had refused a £1,000 offer for Alec Dockar and felt that two other first class players had been signed in the former Welsh Rugby Union men Richards and Goldswain. The £41 profit on the season would have been far greater but for the increasingly heavy burden of entertainment tax, that had cost the club £2,812 over the course of the season – nearly as much as the players' wages. It was also recorded that Hull FC chairman Ernest Hardaker thanked Rovers for lending his club players during the war years.

At the end of the season, former Northampton RFC

player Bill Fallowfield succeeded ex-Rovers' director John Wilson as secretary of the RFL. The debate about allowing substitutes started but it would be many years before the idea came to fruition.

On 31 August 1946, Hull City opened the Boothferry Park ground that was to be their home for over 50 years and was to play a significant role in Rovers' history. Since 1906, City's home had been the Anlaby Road ground adjacent to 'the Circle', the home of Hull Cricket Club. In contrast, Rovers had ground problems when the East Stand had to be rebuilt following serious fire damage during the summer.

The 1946-47 season gave Rovers little encouragement as they climbed only two places in the table. With Joe Oliver appointed as coach in place of Adams, the team made an encouraging start and were unbeaten after six games. They then came crashing down with a 50-2 hammering by a powerful Wigan side that went on to claim the league leadership and Championship. That was followed by a 15-11 defeat at the Boulevard in the semi-final of the Yorkshire Cup. A disastrous run of eight defeats in nine games from the end of November, including a 9-5 derby defeat, was ended with a comfortable win over lowly Bramley.

After that the notorious winter of 1947 began to bite and no games were played in February. Following a narrow two-leg defeat to Hunslet in the first round of the Challenge Cup and a drawn game against Huddersfield, a run of five consecutive wins included the Good Friday derby at Craven Park. The bad weather meant that the season was extended to the end of May and Rovers had to play the final six games in 19 days, winning only twice. There were a couple of valiant performances amongst those, notably at York, despite losing Ike Mills in the first minute. Two more injuries then reduced them to ten men for most of the second half but only in the later stages were they beaten. Rovers finished in 16th spot and the Yorkshire Cup wins over Halifax and Huddersfield were to be the last cup successes until 1952.

In the backs, McWatt continued to be a reliable figure at the back, Fred McBain made his debut in early December and the right-wing spot his own, whilst former armed forces back 'Gus' Steele debuted at centre in April. William Beaumont made the most appearances, 39, on the left wing and the previous season's recruits Maurice Daddy, Ron Mills and Richards contested the half-back positions. Yet again, centre was the problem position and twelve players were used in the two spots. Up front, Goldswain, Atkinson and Dockar comprised a very accomplished first-choice back row, Ramsden missed only four games at hooker and Len Hartley, Viv Hill and Arthur Senior were the regular props. Clark missed most of the season through injury and Bedford played his last game for the club in the thrashing at Wigan. A promising young local second-rower, Dennis Scholes, made his debut at home to Liverpool in May.

Northern RL, Craven Park, Hull, 15 March 1947
Hull Kingston Rovers 0-0 Huddersfield

'When Kingston Rovers and Huddersfield walked off at the interval, one half of the pitch was as clean and untrodden as the moment the game started. The other half was a morass; it was the half in which a very surprised Huddersfield team of Australian, English and Welsh internationals had to defend against a wave of ceaseless attacks.' These were the opening sentences of the Hull Daily Mail *report on a remarkable performance by the Robins.*

The game was notable for the first appearances in English rugby league of Australian greats Lionel Cooper and Johnny Hunter for the visitors but it was Rovers' home-grown talent that rose to great heights against this team of stars. They bottled up the visitors' dangerous backs whilst their dominant pack both ruled the scrums and gave the illustrious Fartowners a run-around in the loose.

21-year old full-back Hunter saved Huddersfield on numerous occasions throughout the match with his courageous defence. Late in the game, Rovers were denied the victory they richly deserved when Alec Dockar, playing one of his finest games for the club, intercepted and kicked ahead – only to be brought to ground by Hunter and the referee waved away the claims for a penalty try.

Goldswain had earlier been denied a try as the ball just went dead as he dived for it in the in-goal area, and Cooper went near for Huddersfield in one of their rare attacks.

The Robins have been involved in only three scoreless draws since World War II. All three took place at Craven Park but this was the only one in a league match and the only one that was celebrated as enthusiastically as a win.

> *Rovers: W. McWatt (capt); F. McBain, H. Mills, D. Hutchins, W. Beaumont; M. Daddy, R. Mills; A. Senior, J. Ramsden, V. Hill, B. Goldswain, S. Atkinson, A. Dockar.*
> *Huddersfield: J. Hunter; J. Anderson, B. Madden, A. Fiddes (capt), L. Cooper: G.R. Pepperell, W.G. Morgan; H. Whitehead, R. Nicholson, R. Robson, L. Baxter, D. Thomas, A. Givvons.*
> *Referee: A .S. Dobson (Featherstone)*

A players' terms dispute that threatened the home game with Dewsbury in late November was resolved and the game went ahead but Rovers were angered by the publicity the visitors gave to the issue and complained to the RFL. The league 'deeply regretted' Dewsbury's actions but were unable to take any sanction. A general increase in attendances had led players to demand better terms and Dewsbury themselves, along with several other clubs, had been affected by pay disputes that season. In March, following the February freeze, rugby league clubs were affected by a national ban on mid-week sporting events. The RFL successfully fought this on the grounds that mid-week games would not be, 'detrimental to national efforts,' but games could not be played until there was sufficient light for a 5pm kick-off, 'to avoid workers taking an afternoon off.' It was agreed that the season would continue until 14 June in any case.

Despite their difficulties, Rovers made a profit of £1,519 on the season's operations. None of their key players were sold but there were no significant signings either. Club director W.A. Crockford was elected Chairman of the Rugby League Council.

In 1947-48, Wigan continued to dominate the league, dropping only nine points in 36 games. By this time, the 'kick and rush' tactics had largely faded and whilst there were still long kicking duels between full-backs, the game was played more with ball in hand.

The campaign was something of a disaster for Rovers. They won only ten of their 36 league games and finished in 25th place, fourth from bottom. They won only three of the first 16 league games and lost five games in succession on three occasions. Between the disappointments, there were some surprisingly good performances – a 13-7 win over the New Zealand tourists, watched by a crowd of 12,000; a derby double, and home wins over Leeds and St Helens.

Perhaps the Good Friday derby at Craven Park was the highlight. First half tries by Bowers and Tindall, one converted by Miller, put the visitors 8-0 up but Bill Beaumont scored in the corner just before half time to cut the deficit. A second try by Tindall, converted by Miller, restored the Airlie Birds' ten-point cushion early in the second half and with the visitors' defence on top, there appeared no way back for the Robins. Then, with 10 minutes to go, Daddy raced through a gap and linked with Ike Mills, who put McBain over in the corner. A magnificent touchline conversion from Ron Mills, followed by a superb angled penalty goal, brought Rovers to within three points. Astonishingly, McBain found a gap on the blind side of the scrum to level the scores at 13-13, Ron Mills giving Rovers victory with two excellent penalty goals, the second from just three yards inside his own half.

Centre Bill Jackson joined in the autumn for a then record £1,000 from Workington and made a good impression in his 21 games. Hooker Ramsden made the most appearances, missing only two matches and Dockar took over from McWatt as skipper at the start of the season. McWatt, Ramsden and Clark were recognised with a joint benefit and presented with cheques from the proceeds of the match against Salford in November, as well as each receiving a 'wallet of notes' from the Supporters Club.

An unusual incident took place when a 30-foot tree was blown over by strong winds just in front of the team bus between Rawcliffe and Goole on its return from the game at Castleford in November. Fortunately no one was hurt and the players cleared the road by attacking it with axes and saws – where they obtained these implements from is not recorded.

The club paid tribute to long-serving chairman E.E. Mowforth, who decided to stand down at the AGM, and the new chairman was T.C. Williams. Following the much-regretted resignation of secretary Ted Haysom due to ill health during the season, the board now decided that the post, which had been part-time since 1934, should revert to being full-time. Sidney Dolman, who was employed by travel agent Thomas Cook, was selected from 60 applicants and offered the post in July. Dolman, however, changed his mind and declined. Stan Pleasants, the Hull Harriers athletics club secretary, was appointed in his place.

A false dawn

In 1948, Britain's Labour Government was pursuing its nationalisation policies. Coal and electricity had already been taken under government control and, at the beginning of the year, it was the turn of the railways. The financial situation of the four big railway companies, who had suffered so much damage and neglect during the war, was dire, and nationalisation was inevitable. The National Health Service was being implemented across the country and the National Assistance Act introduced the welfare state. The hugely unpopular bread rationing, introduced due to the severe damage to crops caused by the winter of 1947 was ended but clothing, chocolate and petrol rationing all continued.

The 1948 National Service Act meant that from 1 January 1949, men aged between 17 and 21 in all but a handful of essential occupations were conscripted to serve in the Armed Forces for 18 months. They then remained on the reserve list for four years, during which time they could be recalled to their units. Until 1960, in common with other sporting clubs, Rovers temporarily lost the services of many of their players due to national service.

Whitehaven followed neighbours Workington into the rugby league and the minimum admission price for Rovers' home matches was 1s 3d (just over six pence). Ted Jacobs was appointed coach for the 1948-49 season, succeeding Joe Oliver, and ex-Workington centre Jackson was selected as first team captain. Seeking fresh talent, the club raided the England amateur team, signing full-back Jim Lufford, winger Ernest Burke and back-row forward Harold Welsby.

The season proved rather more successful than the previous one as, despite a poor start, the Robins finished nearly half-way up the league table. After beating Barrow at home in the first game, Rovers lost the next seven league games before beating Bradford Northern on 2 October. From that point, they won 16 of 28 league games and there was even a five-match winning run from mid-November. Both derby games resulted in home wins, there was no progress in either cup competition but there was a fine triumph over the Australian tourists.

The new skipper managed only two games before losing his place through injury. He was unable to get back in the side and moved to Warrington in November. Regular performers in the three-quarters were Richards, who was the top try-scorer for a second successive season, his fellow Welshman, Cyril Smith and Jim Schofield. Apart from them, 14 other players were used in the four positions.

New signings Welsby, who made the most appearances with 35, and Jim Barraclough from York, the younger brother of Alf who had made his bow the previous March, joined Wilmot, Ramsden and Dockar as pack regulars. Ramsden took over the captaincy from the unfortunate Jackson. Welsh international Goldswain, who was a school teacher in Liverpool, played 25 games in the back row before requesting a transfer due to the amount of travelling he had to do. At the end of the season he moved to Oldham for £2,000, a then club record for an incoming fee. Goldswain had played in 121 games for the Robins.

Having made small annual profits since the war, an increased one of £1,174 was reported at the AGM. Reflecting on the playing strength, the chairman said that 11 players had been injured at the start of the season and bemoaned the usual difficulties of travelling, housing and the lack of suitable jobs that hampered efforts to attract out-of-town players to Craven Park. Shareholder A.J. Snelling was unimpressed. 'You have no ground, no team and no policy,' he said. 'You won't get anywhere next year with that team.' There was agreement too that the game needed to be cleaned up and that referees needed to be stricter.

A complaint that was subsequently to be heard all too regularly, about the use of shareholders' proxy votes, surfaced at this meeting. Only 170 shareholders were present but 1,600 votes were cast. Fred Robinson was elected chairman in place of T.C. Williams and H.W. Bentley took over from Stan Pleasants as secretary. In the close season, work was completed on the ground drainage and the playing area was re-seeded, whilst the supporters club opened their new clubhouse at the ground.

Tour match, Craven Park, Hull, 18 October 1948
Hull Kingston Rovers 17-12 Australia

'Rovers were the best club side we have met on the tour.' That was the opinion of the Australian team manager Bill Buckley at the celebration dinner after a thrilling game at Craven Park.

After Froome had missed an easy penalty for the visitors in the opening minutes, Graves quickly atoned with two others, the first from three yards inside his own half, to put the tourists 4-0 ahead. After that, the visitors' pace and skill were nullified by Rovers' unfaltering defence until Graves started a passage of play that resulted in Cowie being awarded a controversial try after a move that appeared to contain both a forward pass and a knock-on. Young Ernie Burke was being given a torrid time on the wing by the powerful Graves but despite being battered and bruised, he never wavered. Wilf McWatt then got Rovers back into the match with a couple of straightforward penalties, before

Graves added a third penalty to put the Australians 9-4 up at the break.

If the first half was exciting, the second was a thriller. The game became fiercer and referee Howgate dismissed big Aussie second-rower Jack Rayner after fighting broke out, followed quickly by Rovers' Jim Barraclough. Inspired by stand-off Gus Steele and centres Cyril Smith and Ike Mills, however, the Robins turned the game on its head. After being twice denied only by the bounce of the ball, Steele sent Burke racing in at the corner to give them the try their mounting pressure deserved. The Kangaroos came back, however, and Horrigan forced his way over to restore their five-point advantage with 17 minutes left.

The Robins were undeterred and Joe Ramsden started a move that saw Smith draw the defence in one direction, then sidestep and set off on a diagonal run before sending Steele in by the posts. McWatt converted to level the scores. Just three minutes later, Smith and Steele combined again and this time another change of direction sent Mills running round behind the posts to give McWatt another easy conversion.

The tourists responded again and tried everything to get back into the game but Rovers' magnificent defence held firm for a famous win – their first over an Australian side since the very first encounter 40 years earlier.

> **Rovers:** *W. McWatt; E. Burke, C. Smith, H. Mills, F. McBain; C. Steele, M. Daddy; A. Wilmot, J. Ramsden, H. Welsby, J. Barraclough, B. Goldswain, A. Dockar (capt).*
> **Australia:** *V. Bulgin; J. Graves, N. J. Hawke, J. Horrigan, P. McMahon; G.K. Froome, C.B. Hopkins; E. Brosnan, K. Schubert, N. Hand, D. Hall, R. J. Rayner, L. Cowie.*
> *Referee: A. Howgate (Dewsbury).*
> *Attendance: 7,757 (£949)*

The Robins

Snelling's prognosis proved depressingly accurate in 1949-50. By Christmas, only seven out of 22 matches had been won and although a 9-0 home derby success then led to a run of four victories in five games, there were only three more after the end of January. One of these, a 12-0 success over fourth-placed Halifax, was the best performance of the season. The Robins lost the return derby at the Boulevard 15-6, and they slipped to 22nd place in the league.

The home form was decent but there was only one away win all season, in the league at Bramley. The first round of the cup competitions were still being played over two legs and, as in the season before, Rovers lost both legs to Warrington in the first round of the Challenge Cup. In the Yorkshire Cup, a narrow home first leg victory over Bramley was overturned at Barley Mow, and the Robins lost 16-10 on aggregate.

Local winger Geoff Tullock and York-born Arthur Payne made their debuts in the first match of the season. Tullock made the right-wing position his own and Payne was a regular in the three-quarters. Tullock was the nephew of Herbert Tullock who played in the early NU days. Former Hull FC back Henry 'Ike' Mills also featured regularly at centre and stand-off and Welshman J.H. Lewis, who had made his debut in December 1945 but played only one game since, then returned to challenge McWatt for the full-back position. The long-serving and reliable 'Nobby' Clark played the last of his 141 games in the Good Friday defeat at the Boulevard.

Prop-forward Alf Palframan, whose father played a handful of games either side of the First World War, made his debut in March and, along with Barraclough, the most appearances. Skipper Ramsden lost his place to promising young hooker Sam Smith in early April and played his final match in the shirt in the derby defeat at the Boulevard.

Another to take his bow was popular Welsh back Richards, whose last appearance was in a dismal 15-2 defeat at Batley in March. He played rugby union for Mountain Ash before the war but had been persuaded to try league during the conflict by the legendary journalist and broadcaster Eddie Waring. Slight of stature but pacy and elusive, he played a handful of games for Leeds in the war league before Waring introduced him to Rovers post-armistice. Playing both at wing and half-back, Richards scored 46 tries in his 112 games for the Robins.

At the AGM, former chairman Crockford lost his seat on the board and future vice-chairman Ron Chester was elected. A season's surplus of over £2,000 was inflated by a profit of £1,455 on transfers. In consequence, the club had a healthy £3,920 in the bank at the end of the season. Chester asked whether it was worth making a profit by selling what good players the club had and remaining bottom of the league. It was not an entirely fair observation as in Tullock, Scholes, Palframan, Barraclough, Dockar and Smith the club undoubtedly possessed some very decent players – even though they badly needed better support.

Retiring chairman Robinson, who was replaced by Wilf Spaven, felt that given the difficulties of getting good players to come to Hull, the Robins would have to depend more on local talent. He said that the club could not continue to buy houses and rent them out uneconomically (three had been purchased by that time), and that procuring suitable employment for imported players was almost impossible. 'I have seen the club in far worse positions than we find ourselves today,' he said. 'I am sure that in the not too distant future the club will be back at the forefront of the game.'

The Robins

Bleak times

1950 saw the start of the Korean War and the Group Areas Act in South Africa established apartheid. It was not a good summer for English sport. The national football team suffered a humiliating 1-0 defeat to the USA at the fourth FIFA World Cup in Brazil, the England cricket team were soundly beaten 3-1 by the West Indies – their first series win in England, and Australia beat the 1950 Great Britain rugby league tourists 2-1 – their first Ashes win for 30 years.

In 1950-51, a Rovers ground season pass cost £1 and a best stand seat cost £2 5s. The Robins did not justify Robinson's optimism and slipped another place to 23rd. The season opened disastrously, with a then record 55-3 defeat at Warrington in the first match. Although Rovers won four of the next seven league games, there was a miserable run before the visit to the Boulevard on Christmas Day. That game resulted in a 3-3 draw and heralded a slightly improved second half of the season, which produced seven wins and a draw from 21 games. Whilst the Robins comfortably won the Craven Park derby 21-4, the Black and Whites still managed to finish five places higher in the table.

Again, the club was stronger in the forwards than the backs, with Jim Barraclough, Smith and Dockar providing the backbone of the pack. Smith and Dockar each missed only three games and Dockar also took over the goal-kicking duties. Frank Moore was signed from Batley in October and became a regular member of the front row.

In the backs, J.H. Lewis, something of a supporters' favourite in his short spell with the club mainly due to his somewhat over-enthusiastic playing style, started the season in possession of the full-back jersey but played only eight more games. The veteran McWatt appeared only twice, playing his last game for the Robins in a 42-3 thumping at Dewsbury in March. He then took over the first team coaching duties and, as a result, after being relegated primarily to 'A' team work, trainer Ted Jacobs resigned in October.

McWatt, who joined Rovers from the old Humberside amateur club at the beginning of the 1930s, had played 328 games for the club almost exclusively in his favoured custodian position. Not blessed with great pace, he was nonetheless a solid and reliable performer in an era when the club had all too few players in that category. A competent goal-kicker, he landed 431 goals to add to his 29 tries.

Despite missing eight games, and having little consistent support in the back division, Tullock scored a post-war record 26 tries that stood for 12 seasons. Amongst ten new arrivals in the revolving door that was the back division were full-back Peter Ingram who followed Moore from Bramley, centre Hugh O'Connor from Halifax, winger Bill Cornforth and ex-Goole RUFC stand-off Brian Spence.

A dramatic slump in finances saw the club lose over £2,000 on the season, with gate receipts down by £1,600 and a significant loss on transfer activity. The annual report noted much enterprise in recruiting at least 15 new players and over 50 trialists had played in the 'A' team, with a commensurate effect on its success, and a 'B' team had also been inaugurated to help develop young players.

In 1951, *A Streetcar Named Desire* and *The Day the Earth Stood Still* were released in the cinemas and the influential comedy *The Goon Show* was first broadcast on the BBC Home Service. The colourful English golfer Max Faulkner won the Open at Royal Portrush, and Juan Manuel Fangio the first of his five Formula One titles.

On 6 October 1951, rugby league's first televised match, between Great Britain and New Zealand, took place at Odsal and on 19 April 1952 the Challenge Cup final was broadcast live on TV for the first time. The initial floodlit match of any code to take place outside London was staged when Bradford Northern hosted the Kiwi tourists and Cardiff and Doncaster joined the rugby league. There was disharmony at RFL headquarters, where some dissatisfaction about the work of secretary Bill Fallowfield led to a clandestine report by the chairman of the RFL council, Sir Edwin Airey, into the running of the league. 'I'm not concerned about what people think of me, it is rugby league that matters and there is a lot needs to be done,' Airey said.

Another small slip in 1951-52 saw Rovers finish 25th out of 31 clubs. After winning their first two matches, the Robins triumphed in only five of the next 30 games, until four victories in the last eight games lifted them out of the bottom three. They conceded a derby double for the first time since 1936-37, losing a home derby for the first time since the war.

In those days the players were expected to make their own way to the local grounds and for the Hull FC players that meant a trolleybus ride up Holderness Road with the supporters. John Whiteley remembers that Christmas Day derby because the service was only operated long enough to take the supporters home and when the Airlie Birds' team emerged from the ground, the buses and trolleybuses were no longer running. None of the players had cars and they could not afford taxis, so they ended up walking back to West Hull. Had the diehard Rovers' fans known that, they might at least have gained a grain of satisfaction.

Amongst another myriad of signings costing in total £4,928, two were particularly significant. Derek 'Rocky' Turner arrived from Ossett RUFC and, after making his debut at loose-forward at Bramley in September, played in every game. His next 11 were at centre but after that he established himself as a formidable back-row regular. After negotiations with Huddersfield's Russ Pepperell had broken down, the club signed Bryn Knowleden from Warrington in January for a new club record £2,000. Knowleden was appointed player-coach with Bill Westerdale assisting him as trainer, and he played a few games at stand-off before settling in the centre position. In November, Scholes left to join Leeds for a somewhat inflated £4,000 fee – double that received for Goldswain. Clearly the Headingley club had been influenced by the three tries he'd scored against them a couple of weeks earlier.

Apart from Tullock, Ike Mills and Ron Armitage, who had arrived from Ossett with Turner, the rest of the back division was again something of a lottery. In the forwards, injuries decimated the seasons of key performers Palframan, Smith and Jim Barraclough. Turner and Tullock made the most appearances, missing only six games each.

At the AGM, Spaven was voted off the board and J.R. Rawson took over as chairman. The Ground Fund was inaugurated, with Alderman Fred Holmes as its chairman and a membership of four directors and two supporters' club representatives. Tribute was paid to club president Ernest Seaton who died during the season and 1920s star Laurie Osborne who passed away on 31 March. Even allowing for the Scholes transfer fee, the season still produced a loss of £401. Despite the lowly league position, the annual report recorded that a 'new wave of keenness and enthusiasm was showing' by the end of the season. The 'A' team had used no fewer than 69 players and, keen to encourage more young players, two summer coaching schemes were initiated, whilst it was hoped to run at least one junior side again the following season.

The Robins

A helping hand

The 1952-53 season resulted in a further slip down the table to 28th and the 1935-36 low of only nine league wins was equalled. Not until Wakefield visited Craven Park on 4 October did the Robins register a league victory. Ironically, their only successes before that were against the same side in the two first round legs of the Yorkshire Cup – their first cup wins since 1946. Rovers played their first ever floodlit game, a league match at Odsal on 19 November. It was far from being a happy experience as they were soundly thrashed 43-0. The best spell of the season, eight wins in 11 games, was kick-started by a 16-9 derby win at the Boulevard on Christmas Day. There were Challenge Cup wins over Doncaster and Swinton but the Robins lost in the third round at Wigan and won only one of their last 12 games. That dismal run included a 13-2 defeat in the first derby game to be played at Boothferry Park.

The annual report recorded that the amounts expended on player recruitment, wages and the crippling entertainment tax, which accounted for £2,241, left the club with practically no funds for running costs during the season. In addition to imposing strict economies, the board contacted Hull City to ask if they might use their ground for the Good Friday game. There was great interest in derby matches, the capacity at Boothferry Park was far in excess of that of Craven Park and the extra income would be crucial. In a magnificent gesture, the Hull City board agreed to loan Rovers their ground at no charge for the game, which was watched by 27,670 who paid £3,280 – a magnificent windfall that enabled the Rovers board to pay all their debts and cover costs to the end of the season without selling any players.

There was at least a little more continuity in team

selection. Palframan and Smith were ever-present in the front row, where they were joined in all but nine games by Moore. Skipper Dockar and Turner were back row regulars but Jim Barraclough again endured an injury-hit season. Eight players were tried at full-back until Dennis Chalkley arrived from Halifax in January. Tullock, Ike Mills, Jock McAvoy from Warrington and former Hull Boys Club back Tommy Sutton were regular performers in the three-quarters; Bryn Knowleden was at stand-off and Daddy and Harry Kirby shared the scrum-half duties. Tullock led the try-scorers for the third year running.

Daddy made his last appearance in the heavy defeat at Huddersfield in the last game of the season. The clash also marked the end of the brief Rovers' careers of McAvoy and Chalkley. Ike Mills played his final game in a narrow home defeat by Keighley in March and Alec Dockar retired at the end of the season.

Despite the Boothferry Park windfall, a profit of merely £15 was made on the season demonstrating how serious the situation might have been otherwise. At the AGM, Wilf Spaven was returned to the board and future chairman Bill Land was also elected. A.J. Snelling took over as chairman from J.R. Rawson. A joint testimonial was held for Daddy, Ike Mills and Ron Mills and, in contrast to the senior team, the 'A' team enjoyed a quite successful season.

The Greats – No 11
Alec Dockar - *see Hull KR legends gallery*

Over the years, Rovers have had a succession of top class loose-forwards and Alec Dockar was undoubtedly one of them. Unfortunately for him though, his time at the club coincided with some of its' bleakest years – never once in that

*time did they win more games in a season than they lost –
and he was denied the chance to play in a really strong side.*

*Born on 28 December 1920, Dockar was a product of
Courtney Street school in Hull. He then joined Craven Park
Juniors and, although he had six trials for Hull FC as a
centre, signed for the Robins as a winger in January 1937.
He appeared for the first team in the emergency war league
in 1939, making a very favourable impression before the
club decided to suspend playing activities at the end of that
season. When his services commitments allowed, he turned
out in war league games for Halifax and, on one occasion
and very much against his will, for the Black and Whites.*

*Returning to Rovers after the war, he made his first-class
debut at right-centre at home to Rochdale Hornets on 25
August 1945. Always wearing his trade-mark scrum-cap,
he played mainly in his favoured loose-forward position but
also turned out at stand-off, centre and once even at full-
back when needed. Dockar was club captain in the 1947-48
season and was recognised with Yorkshire, England and,
once, Great Britain honours.*

*Johnny Whiteley remembers a wag shouting: 'You'll never
be as good as Dockar, Whiteley!' in one of his early derby
games. The two developed a mutual respect and friendship.
Whiteley recalls Dockar as one of the first contemporary
loose-forwards and a strong and intelligent player.*

*Relatively late in his distinguished career Dockar's goal-
kicking talents were recognised and he landed 114 of his 133
goals in his last three seasons. After being awarded a well-
deserved benefit, he retired from the game at the end of the
1952-53 season making his last appearance at home to
Bradford Northern on 20 April 1953. Over eight seasons,
Dockar wore the colours 255 times and scored 53 tries.*

*A printer by trade, Dockar continued to live in East Hull
for many years after his retirement, maintaining an interest
in the game through the Hull Former Rugby League Players
Association, until his death in 1994.*

The lowest ebb

Over a year after she had acceded to the throne, the coronation of Queen Elizabeth II took place in June 1953. The Prime Minister, Winston Churchill, had felt that the event should not be held in 1952 as the economic crisis was then so grave that not a single working day should be lost. It was the world's first major international event to be broadcast live on television and the widespread celebrations gave the country a much-needed boost in spirits.

Any uplifting of spirits at Craven Park was very short-lived. In 1953-54 the Robins finished 29th out of 30 clubs in the league, their lowest ever position on the ladder of professional clubs. The 14-match losing run experienced between 3 October and 26 December remains the worst in the club's history and the five league wins and 12 points recorded are the poorest returns. Whilst Rovers finished below Doncaster on points average, they avoided the ultimate indignity of bottom position, which was the lot of Liverpool City.

On the opening day of the season, the Robins beat Warrington 17-5 at home, their first win over the Wire since 1932. It was undoubtedly the high point, as the visitors then lost only five games all season in finishing runners-up to Halifax. The game had been delayed by ten minutes as a bag containing the visiting players' boots had been mistaken for a mail sack and removed from their train at Manchester. Fortunately the error was realised and the bag dispatched on the next train.

A curiosity is that the three players who scored tries in that game, Tullock, Turner and Jim Barraclough, were all sent off in the 12-0 defeat at Hunslet two days later. There have been several incidences where two Rovers' players were sent off in the same game but this is the only recorded incidence of a trio.

Hunslet also had two men dismissed and when referee Jackson abandoned the game with five minutes left, Rovers had nine men to Hunslet's ten, as a player from each side had also been forced to retire due to injury. After considering the referee's report, the RFL decided that the result should stand and that 'a suitable letter' should be written to both clubs. The game attracted considerable publicity.

There were a few decent players in Rovers' side but strength in depth was woefully lacking and that was badly exposed when injuries occurred. Five players returned from national service but another four were lost. Turner was without doubt the best player and made comfortably the most appearances with 35 from 40 games.

The team was more unsettled than ever. Jim Barraclough, Tullock, Moore and Knowleden, who had now taken over the skipper's role, all missed around half the games. A dozen players made their debuts during the season of which two locals, full-back Terry Buckle and winger Arthur Garry, were to prove the best acquisitions, each going on to make well over a hundred appearances.

The club's directors were concerned that whilst the team could win plenty of possession, they lacked a scrum-half who could use it to good effect. Without funds, a player exchange was the only way forward and Smith and Turner were the only players that other clubs wanted. Believing that in Tong they had a capable replacement hooker, they agreed to let Sam Smith go. He moved to Hunslet just before the Challenge Cup transfer deadline in January, with scrum-half George Ellenor coming to Rovers in part-exchange. Whilst he was not a particularly creative player in the loose, Smith was an exceptional ball-winner in an era where scrums were fiercely contested and he was a very sound tackler. Smith holds the unusual record of playing the most games for the club, 117, without recording any type of score; but his tenacity in a struggling team was priceless against some formidable packs. Whilst with Rovers, Smith gained Yorkshire county honours but the highlight of his career was his subsequent selection as Great Britain's hooker for the inaugural 1954 World Cup.

The home game with Hull FC was again played at Boothferry Park, this time as an evening kick-off under floodlights, the first of its kind, but in front of a lower attendance of 16,720. Although Rovers' board insisted on making a contribution to the match-day expenses, the gate receipts of £1,976 were still particularly welcome and enabled the club to make a small overall profit of £338 on the season's workings.

After the 18-17 defeat at home to Leeds in April the visitors, who had overwhelmed a poor Robins' side 56-5 at Headingley the previous November, presented their hosts with a £26 donation in recognition of their fine sporting efforts in the return game. One positive note was that the youth side, Craven Park Juniors, again won three trophies, in only their second season in existence. During the season, the supporters club also made most welcome donations to the tune of £160. Former founder player and director Eli Bell died at the age of 88 and the club also mourned the death of another ex-player and long-serving director, Fred Barron.

Rovers were reprimanded by the RFL for publishing an article in a match programme that both strongly criticised a referee and encouraged supporters to make demonstrations' against officials. They were told that if any such demonstrations took place at Craven Park, the club would be held primarily responsible.

Thankfully, 1953-54 is best known in rugby league not for the travails of Hull Kingston Rovers but the extraordinary scenes at Odsal stadium in May. A dull draw between Halifax and Warrington in the Challenge Cup final necessitated a replay at Odsal eleven days later, a match watched by an official attendance of 102,569, still a British rugby league record, and many hundreds more climbed over fences to get into the ground. A debate was sparked about two-legged first round cup matches when the Challenge Cup first round was decimated by snow and ice and, from the following season, all cups reverted to single leg ties for all rounds.

A slow climb

In 1954 food rationing in the UK finally ended with the lifting of restrictions on the sale of meat, Boeing's first jet airliner took to the skies and Bill Haley and the Comets released 'Rock around the Clock', credited as the start of rock and roll. In sport, UEFA was formed and Roger Bannister ran the first sub-four minute mile in Oxford.

The first rugby league World Cup took place in France in the autumn of 1954, with England beating the hosts in the final in Paris. At the start of the domestic season, Blackpool Borough joined the competition. There was some improvement in results at Craven Park in 1954-55. In that season, half the Robins' fixtures were against Lancashire clubs because as they had finished bottom of the Yorkshire league the season before and due to the imbalance of Yorkshire and Lancashire clubs, they were regarded as being 'neutral.' Nonetheless, they doubled their win tally from the previous season to ten. Despite again conceding a derby double, they finished in 25th place, just six places behind their neighbours. There were still some very lean periods though and Rovers won only two games between 6 September and 27 December. The 46-10 success over Bramley on 2 October was the first time the Robins had scored 40 points since 1938 but two weeks later a then record defeat, 58-3, was sustained at Leigh. When Rovers visited Blackpool on 27 November they lost 19-3 to give the seaside club their first win in the professional ranks.

Former player Jack Feetham replaced Knowleden as coach in mid-season. The change did not reap immediate rewards and only two wins were gained from the last 13 league games, both over Salford. York were defeated 7-6 in the first round of the Challenge Cup but that was followed by a heavy defeat at Hunslet in the next round. There were, however, some more encouraging displays towards the end of the season. Winger Garry made most appearances with 33 in a team that was no more settled than in the previous year. Nine players were on national service and another dozen players made their debuts.

Jim Barraclough moved to Featherstone after over six years of good service, mainly in the back row and occasionally at centre. A strong runner, Barraclough played 161 games for Rovers, during which time he gained Yorkshire and England representative honours.

Knowleden, who joined the club as player-coach from Warrington in early 1952, played his last game at home to Dewsbury on 13 November and Tong took over as skipper. Only starting his rugby league career at the age of 23, Knowleden quickly gained recognition as a talented centre or stand-off with his home town club Barrow. Moving to Warrington, whom he captained in the 1950-51 season, he won domestic and international honours. Seeking a new challenge, Knowleden joined Rovers as captain-coach at the beginning of 1952. He played 66 games for the Robins where he was one of the few class players in the side and accordingly received some unwelcome attention.

Despite receipts of £2,124 from the home derby game, played at Boothferry Park for a third consecutive year, and the sale of one of the club's three houses for £482, the Robins still lost over £1,000 on the season. The club unsuccessfully wrote to the RFL asking for assistance with the cost of travel to the additional games in Lancashire and they were one of four clubs who complained about the effect on attendances of the televising of the World Cup final.

1955-56 saw further on-field improvement, albeit marginal, and Rovers finished in 24th place – this time out of 30 as Belle Vue Rangers pulled out of the league on the eve of the season. It was by then too late to alter the fixtures and that campaign only saw a return to the percentage system for deciding league places. An experimental floodlit competition, played at football stadia in the London area, was screened by ITV. Eight clubs participated and Warrington beat Leigh in the final.

Rovers atoned for their previous defeat at Blackpool with a double over the seasiders and won 11 league games in all, the highlight being a 21-20 win in the 'Boothferry Park derby' in October. That was also a fourth successive victory for the club, the first time since 1948 the feat had been achieved. The Robins lost the return derby at the Boulevard on Good Friday and four days later they were thumped 68-0 at Halifax, the club's worst-ever defeat at the time. There was no joy in the cups, with a first round Challenge Cup defeat away to lowly Liverpool City and a second round Yorkshire Cup loss to Castleford.

Yet again, it had proved impossible to field a settled team. Garry made most appearances, playing in 33 of the 39 matches and scoring 14 tries – twice as many as anyone else. The other regulars in the backs were full-back Buckle; former Stoneygate RUFC winger Bernard Golder; ex-Hunslet centre Maurice Thornton; Gilbert Austin's nephew, Pat, who played mainly at stand-off and local scrum-half Johnny Parker. Half-back Peter Key returned, having missed the previous season due to his national service in the Far East, where he had played rugby union for Perak. Regulars in the pack were Beverley-born prop Ken Grice, former rugby union back-rower Jim Shires, Tong and Sutton, by now operating in the second row.

Northern RL, Boothferry Park, Hull, 8 October 1955
Hull Kingston Rovers 21-20 Hull FC

Rovers' first victory at Boothferry Park was a real thriller. The Robins had not beaten their arch-rivals since the Christmas Day contest of 1952 and had been given little chance of winning this time.

Playing with a fierce intensity from the start, Rovers tackled and harried their more illustrious neighbours out of the game in the first half. Sam Evans gave Rovers an early lead with a penalty goal and Johnny Parker's drop-goal made the score 4-0. The Robins were unfazed when Hutton's two penalty goals brought the Black and Whites level. Evans had another penalty attempt, his effort missed but Hutton's drop-out went straight to prop-forward Ken Grice who simply drove forward through the Airlie Birds' defence in a thirty-yard run that took him past Hutton to score. It was the try of his career. Evans' conversion made it 9-4 to Rovers at the break.

Evans soon made it 11-4 with another penalty but that seemed to galvanise the Airlie Birds who took complete control. They ran in four tries without reply, through Riches, Scott, Moat and Watts. Fortunately for Rovers, two of those were too wide out for Hutton to convert but the Black and Whites still had a 20-11 lead with just eight minutes to go. Rovers then went on all-out attack to get back into the game but the Boulevarders seemed capable of dealing with everything thrown at them. John Hall started a move that was carried on by Maurice Thornton and Parker and was finished by Alan Bartliffe, who raced in for the try. Evans converted and the deficit was just four points. With time almost up, Parker found touch near the corner-flag, Jim Shires emerged from the scrum with the ball and strode over the line to touch down.

Despite the Airlie Birds' protests, referee Jackson awarded the try and Evans made light of the pressure to stroke the ball over from wide out. However, the drama was still not over as, with the final whistle still not blown, Rovers' skipper Jim Tong was penalised under his own posts. Hutton came forward to take the kick from a position from which he could hardly miss – but he did and the final whistle blew amidst scenes of jubilation from the 'home' supporters.

> **Rovers:** T. Buckle; B. Golder, K. Goulding, A. Bartliffe, A. Garry; M. Thornton, J. Parker; K. Grice, J. Tong (capt), S. Evans, J. Hall, J. Shires, T. Sutton.
> **Hull FC:** C. Hutton; K. Bowman, B. Cooper, W. Riches, I. Watts; R. Moat, T. Finn; M. Scott, T. Harris, J. Drake, H. Markham, W. Drake, J. Whiteley.
> *Referee: J. W. Jackson (Barrow)*
> *Attendance: 16,670 (£1,911)*

The biggest blow, however, was the inevitable departure of loose-forward Derek 'Rocky' Turner to Oldham for £2,750. It had been obvious for some time that the youngster had been destined for better things and in the end Rovers could hold on to him no longer. Nevertheless, comparing the fee to the £4,000 received from Leeds for Scholes four seasons before, the Roughyeds certainly got a bargain.

Turner had become a supporters' favourite in his 140 games and whilst he did not reach his full potential in red and white, he went on to achieve the game's highest honours both as a player and coach.

The last match of the season marked the final appearance of winger Geoff Tullock. The former Withernsea RUFC winger played 167 times, scoring 66 tries. Fast and powerful, he was a handful for opposing defences and made 16 of his appearances in the second row.

Despite a profit of around £1,750 on transfers, the £1,911 receipts from the Boothferry Park game and the sale of another house, the club still made a small loss on the season. Other than the derby game, only two home matches paid their way. Nevertheless, the Ground Fund finances were steadily increasing and the Rovers Development Fund, which was to introduce the highly-successful club lottery, was inaugurated under the control of directors Alford, Chester, Land and Parkinson.

The league's fixture formula was the big issue debated by the clubs at the time. At an Extraordinary General Meeting in March, six possible formulas were outlined, and the clubs subsequently had a postal vote to decide. Rovers opted for a scheme proposed by Wigan, in which a three-division structure would be played in the first half of the season and in the second the clubs would be brought together in single league, with fixtures determined by positions gained to that point. All the dialogue came to very little though, as the clubs eventually voted for a single-tier system with only minor changes to what was already in place. Players' wages were also discussed and a maximum £8 for a win and £4 for a defeat was mooted whilst the age limit for referees was reduced from 55 to 50, where it has remained since.

The summer of 1956 saw the world's first nuclear power station opened at Calder Hall in Cumberland, close to where Sellafield currently stands. The House of Lords defeated a bill to abolish the death penalty and, in cricket, Jim Laker became the first man to take 19 wickets in a Test match, playing for England against Australia at Old Trafford.

The 1956-57 season produced little on-field progress for the Robins. Manager-coach Feetham resigned for business reasons in July and was replaced by another former Robin, Joe Ramsden. Rovers finished 26th in the league, conceded a double to Hull FC, who were runners-up to Oldham, and went out of both cups in the first round. They won five of their first seven league games to raise hopes that were quickly dashed when they descended into a ten-match losing run.

At the turn of the year, as an experiment, the directors introduced a mid-week get-together with the players, at which no punches were to be pulled. This had some immediate success, as a number of issues were ironed out and a four-match unbeaten run ensued. It included a 13-10 win at Huddersfield that was described by the *Hull Daily Mail* reporter as the club's best result for many years. Moving the ball around confidently, Huddersfield quickly opened an 8-0 lead before Brian Coulson took advantage of their over-confidence, intercepted smartly and sprinted away to score. Within minutes, winger Sid Stark levelled the scores when he finished off a good move, and ten minutes from half-time Garry pulled off a second interception and put the Robins 13-8 ahead at the break. In the second half, Rovers simply tackled their illustrious opponents out of the game, and held on for a famous win. Unfortunately though, the improvement could not be sustained and there were only two more wins before the end of the season.

One area of improvement was a more settled back division. Buckle was the regular full-back until he was replaced by former Hull Boys Club player Harold Ellerby at the beginning of January. Regular three-quarters were ever-present winger Garry and, in the centre, former Hornsea RUFC man Norman Hancock and Brian Coulson from Heworth. Brian Beck usually took one of the half-back positions alongside Coulson's brother, Gordon, who joined from York in December and made the scrum-half spot his own. Two young players, who were to serve the Robins for many years, made their debuts – Hull-born David Elliott at scrum-half at Bradford on 6 October and, three matches later, at Salford, Featherstone-based stand-off Cyril Kellett.

It was in the forwards where the problems now lay and injuries played a big part. Grice missed most of the early season before making a try-scoring return at Rochdale on 3 November and eight other players were used at prop. Tong and former Craven Park Junior Laurie Brookfield shared the hooking duties, but a staggering 17 players were used in the three back row positions, with four of those making their debuts and seven their last appearances.

Despite receipts of over £2,000 from the now-regular Boothferry Park derby and the sale of the last club house, the accounts continued to show a loss – this time of £843 on the season. At the AGM, future vice-chairman Percy Johnson was elected to the board. The annual report recorded that the directors once again were disappointed with the performances of the first team and found it very difficult to understand the in and out form in many matches. The 'A' team, on the other hand, showed some excellent form, particularly in winning the YSC cup. In total, eight new signings were made during the season.

The Boothferry Park derby caused ill-feeling at the Boulevard. The game was originally scheduled for Good Friday but switched to an early season, mid-week date so that it could be played there. Hull City already had a Good Friday home game and when the Hull FC v York game had to be postponed in March, City wrote to the RFL asking that it was not re-played on the Easter date so as not to clash. The league, in recognition of the co-operation shown by Hull City in the past, agreed to the request. The Hull FC board complained to the governing body that they were working more for football than rugby. On-field co-operation between the two Hull clubs did not work out any better, as a joint Hull & Rovers XIII lost 37-14 to the Australian tourists.

Since the end of World War II, the club had endured twelve very difficult seasons on and off the field. Without the total income of over £10,000 from the five derbies at Boothferry Park, its very existence would have been threatened. At last, however, better times were around the corner.

*****

7. Resurgence

1957-1968

THE pairing of chairman Wilf Spaven and coach Colin Hutton was responsible for transforming the fortunes of the club from perpetual strugglers of the early post-war period, to one of the leading forces by the mid-1960s.

New leadership

1957 was the year in which Egypt reopened the Suez Canal to shipping, averting a crisis. *The Sky at Night*, now the longest-running documentary and the pioneering soap opera *Emergency Ward 10* were first broadcast on TV. British drivers Stirling Moss and Tony Brooks, driving a British car, the Vanwall, won the British Grand Prix – the last ever won by two drivers sharing the same car.

For the Robins, the 1957-58 season did not begin particularly auspiciously. They were not happy with their fixture list believing that there was an imbalance between the first half of the season, with too many home games and not enough in the second. Nor did they take full advantage either. By the time York arrived at Craven Park on Christmas Day, they had won four and lost five of their home games and, with only three away wins, were firmly rooted in the bottom half of the table.

By then, however, there had been a change of coach. Joe Ramsden shocked the club when he resigned for personal reasons in November. The board decided that they wanted a dynamic young coach who would introduce up-to-date methods and would be in touch with the modern game. Across the city, the Hull FC full-back Colin Hutton was coming towards the end of his playing career and had obtained his Grade 1 coaching certificate. Knowing that he was interested in moving into that realm, Rovers believed that he was their man. Originally, they wanted Hutton as a player-coach but the Airlie Birds wanted a fee, which the club were unwilling to pay.

The issue was resolved when Hutton agreed to join the Robins in a non-playing capacity. Chairman Snelling told him that the club would do their best to bring in the right players. A heavy defeat at Blackpool in his first match in charge underlined the challenge that faced him, but there were encouraging signs when Rovers won seven of the last nine games of the season. There were no cup successes and both derby games were lost, however, discernible change was in the air.

Following Hutton's arrival there were several signings; centres Bill Riley and Joe Mageen arrived from Halifax, Cumbrian back-row forward Doug Holland joined from Workington, former international prop-forward Bob Coverdale switched from Wakefield and ex-Rovers' winger or back-rower

Dennis Scholes, who had by then moved from Leeds to Featherstone, returned to the club. Kellett, whose goal-kicking was becoming an important feature, played most of his football at centre until January, when he got first run at full-back.

As the new signings bedded in, some of the old faces disappeared. Jim Tong, who had made his debut at the start of the 1950-51 season and had played a secondary role to Ramsden and Smith before finally becoming first choice hooker, made his final appearance at home to Rochdale at the start of February. A hard grafter who was a decent ball-winner, solid tackler and a natural on-field leader, Tong played 151 games for the Robins. Others who had played their last games for the club by the end of the season included full-back Terry Buckle, utility back Harold Ellerby, half-back Gordon Coulson, prop Sam Evans, and forward Tommy Sutton.

Sadly, chairman A.J. Snelling died during the course of the season. Wilf Spaven took his position, initially on an acting basis, but which was confirmed at the end of the season AGM. Spaven's partnership with Hutton, supported by an enthusiastic and ambitious board, played a huge part in the rise of the club's fortunes.

The Greats – No 12
Joe Ramsden - *see Hull KR legends gallery*

After Frank Boagey in the 1920s, Joe Ramsden was the next in a long line of first class hookers produced by the club. Born in Hull in July 1915, he joined Rovers from local side Prince of Wales in August 1934 and made his first team debut at Batley on 1 September that year. A very good tackler and excellent ball-winner in the scrum, Ramsden soon became a first team regular.

He volunteered for the RAF in 1939 and, by the time the war ended, he was aged 29. He then resumed his role as

Rovers' first choice number nine and had a spell as skipper, taking over from Bill Jackson in 1948. That year he also shared a benefit with Len Clark and Wilf McWatt. Ramsden was responsible for the early development of younger hookers Sam Smith and Jim Tong, encouraging them and passing on his knowledge. At the end of the 1949-50 season, at the age of 35, he felt that he should give way to the younger men and requested a transfer. Ramsden played his last game for Rovers in the Good Friday derby at the Boulevard on 7 April 1950.

Despite the war taking the best years out of his career, he played a remarkable 346 games for the club and his dynamism and skills earned him 17 Yorkshire county caps over 12 years. He never played for Great Britain, not quite managing to displace the regular hooker, Wigan captain Joe Egan, although he frequently out-hooked him when they came up against each other. On his last appearance for Yorkshire in 1949, he beat Egan 38-23 in the scrums but all Ramsden had to show were over 20 'shadow' selections.

After moving to Keighley for £500 in 1950, he played on for a further four years before coaching them for around 18 months. He then returned to Craven Park as coach at the start of the 1956 season, holding that role until 19 November 1957, when he resigned on a personal 'matter of principle'.

Ramsden never fell out with the club and was a familiar sight at the ground, particularly at the greyhounds. In his later years, he moved to the Bridlington area and he died in September 1996.

A very important development was the launching of the Rovers Lottery which was the brainchild of the Rovers Development Fund. It was to be crucial in financing future team-strengthening but the directors themselves found much of the money for the 1957-58 signings. Overall, the club recorded a loss of £1,735 on the season, despite the £2,476 gate from the derby game at Boothferry Park. A good piece of financial news was the abolition of Entertainment Tax, of which the Robins had paid £17,000 since the end of the war.

The 1958-59 season may have been a disappointment to Spaven and Hutton but transforming an ailing team was not an overnight job. The league position of 18th represented a slight slip from the previous season and the team's form was still inconsistent. There was, however, some cup success, including an emphatic first round Yorkshire Cup win at Castleford and the first Challenge Cup triumphs for four seasons.

There were several important arrivals. John Taylor, who had signed from local side BOCM, made his debut in the back row in the second game and missed only five thereafter and back-row forward Ray Jacques arrived from Wakefield Trinity. The 'Cornish Express,' Graham Paul, came from Penzance-Newlyn RUFC as a stand-off but his pace saw him also used on the wing. Perhaps the most important signing, though, was that of the former Halifax skipper and international hooker Alvin Ackerley for £1,000. 'He started our revival,' acknowledged lifelong supporter Len Beecroft. 'He was our first real professional in the way he approached the game.'

In the Challenge Cup, over 6,000 spectators watched a thrilling battle in the mud as the Robins overturned the odds to beat renowned cup-fighters Widnes 3-2 in the first round. Several hours of steady rain before the game resulted in a hard gruelling battle between the packs in which Rovers just came out on top, with the hard-running Taylor and the strong-tackling Holland leading the way. After a comfortable win over Castleford in the next round, the Robins fell 23-9 to the Airlie Birds in round three.

Kellett had made the full-back position his own and broke Bunker Carmichael's 47-year old points-scoring record for a season with 268, including 128 goals. The other back division regulars were Brian Coulson on the right wing, new skipper Riley at centre, Key, at either centre or half-back and scrum-half Elliott. For the third season running, Coulson was the leading try-scorer and Riley missed only two games.

In the pack, the regulars were Grice, Jacques, Holland and Taylor. Scholes played the last of his 129 games for the Robins in a home Boxing Day defeat to York and left to join Doncaster. He had made his debut back in 1947 and established a reputation as a pacey and strong running winger or second-row forward. Laurie Brookfield, a solid and reliable front-rower, also made his last appearance in that match after playing 69 games for the club.

Finances were improving and for the first time in several years a profit was recorded on the season – a healthy £2,538 thanks largely to £2,744 receipts from the last derby to be played at Boothferry Park before the Football League imposed a ban on their grounds being used for rugby league. The 21-year lease on the ground expired in 1959 and the owners wanted to increase the rent. The board started to consider its options, believing that the way forward was for the club to purchase its own ground. They had identified a potential site for a new one, off Winchester Avenue, about a mile further out of town off Holderness High Road.

In the scorching summer of 1959, *Explorer 6* sent the first picture of Earth from space. Hawaii became the 50th US state and Sir Alec Issigonis launched the original Mini. Cliff Richard and the Drifters (later Shadows) spent six weeks at number one with 'Living Doll' and unseeded Australian Rod Laver reached his first Wimbledon singles final.

The Robins did not make a great start to the 1959-60 season, indeed after a fourth straight loss in August, at home to Featherstone, half the pack never played again. However, performances improved, and for the first time since 1930-31, Rovers won more games than they lost. For finishing in the top half of the table, the players received a bonus pot of £500 to share. The fixture list included clusters of home and away games, at the end of the season, for example, there were four away fixtures, followed by four at home, and finally five away.

Until the last third of the season, Rovers struggled badly away from home. Before mid-February, they won only one away game but an improvement resulted in five more after that.

Amongst several new signings, the most notable was that of Bramley scrum-half Arthur Bunting, who was to have a long association with the club. Two young local players, Len Clark and Terry Major, made their debuts at centre although both were to play a lot of their rugby in the forwards. Despite having a stronger squad of players, Rovers struggled to find the right blend. Paul continued to alternate between the two wing spots and stand-off as several half-back combinations were tried, also involving the former Airlie Birds' Roly Moat, Elliott and Bunting. Peter Key played the first four matches in the centre before moving to scrum-half for two games.

Unfortunately, in the second of those Rovers sustained a heavy defeat at Leigh after which Key lost his place and never regained it. He was a good footballer and tackler who, whilst lacking the pace of a top-class half-back, had been a reliable servant over his 114 games. Holland made his last appearance in a defeat at Warrington in April, where he was sent off, and he later joined Bradford Northern.

Kellett was now established as the first choice full-back and Riley and Coulson remained regulars in the three-quarters. In the forwards, former Wakefield prop Bob Coverdale became the regular No 10 and new skipper

The Robins

Ackerley made the most appearances with 38, missing only two games. Jacques was the regular loose-forward until Cliff Last arrived from Leeds to take his place in January and in the second row, ex-rugby union men Gordon Hackling and Jim Jenkin were the most regular performers.

The board decided to sign a new three-year lease on the ground, but at an increased rent. The plan was to use the time to build a new ground on the Winchester Avenue site, which a benefactor purchased for the club for £1,500. Nevertheless, without the Boothferry Park income for the first time in eight years, Rovers lost £1,893 on the season's workings.

A natural leader

1960-61 saw a further marginal improvement. A decent start with six wins in the first nine games was followed by a couple of poor spells before the team struck a vein of good form to end the season with eight wins in the last nine games. That run included a first derby win in 13 attempts and a first for Hutton over his old club, when they beat the Black and Whites 14-10 at Craven Park. The Robins finished 12th in the table, just one place behind their neighbours, but FC did end Rovers' Challenge Cup hopes in a 16-3 second round defeat at the Boulevard. Once again away form let the club down. Before that end-of-season run, they won only two out of 16 games on their travels.

There were three significant debuts during the season. Young local hooker Peter Flanagan played his first game at home to Oldham on 15 October and the away game at the same opponents in February saw the introductions of loose-forward Harry Poole, signed from Hunslet for a new club record £6,000, and prop-forward Brian Tyson. Flanagan competed with Ackerley for the number nine jersey for remainder of the season, whilst Poole and Tyson immediately became automatic selections. Poole's arrival signalled the end of Last's Rovers career and he left to join Keighley.

Northern RL, Craven Park, Hull, 17 April 1961
Hull Kingston Rovers 14-10 Hull FC

Two brilliant tries by the 'Cornish Express', Graham Paul, inspired Rovers to their first derby win since October 1955, ending a run of twelve consecutive defeats. A 13,000 crowd at Craven Park witnessed a game that the Hull Daily Mail *reporter described as being of 'breath-taking pace'.*

The Robins probed for an early opening but it did not come and Bill Drake missed with a goal attempt for the visitors. Rovers then lost the ball as they tried to break out of their 25 and Hollindrake went in at the corner to open the scoring for the Black and Whites. Two penalties by Cyril Kellett and one from Drake made the score 5-4 to the Airlie Birds before Rovers suddenly burst into life. Harry Poole found touch in the Hull FC half and Rovers won the ball. After John Taylor, Brian Tyson and Kellett had combined well, Paul took Kellett's clever pass, cut inside and beat three men, before stepping out of the tackle of full-back Kershaw and sprinting for the line. Three minutes later, Bob Coverdale and Kellett combined to send Paul away again and this time he beat Kershaw on the outside. Unfortunately, Kellett could convert neither try and the score was 10-4 to the Robins. They could have scored again when a kick ahead ricocheted off Kershaw had not the bounce beaten the two supporting Rovers' players. The Black and Whites came back again but they fluffed a couple of chances to pull a try back before half time.

The second half continued at the same pace combined with some ferocious tackling, referee Wilson then sending both hookers off for technical offences. With Whiteley to the fore,

*the visitors put Rovers under sustained bombardment but
Kellett eased the pressure with another penalty. With eight
minutes to go, Bill Drake dummied his way over for a fine
individual try and the conversion narrowed Rovers' lead to
just two points. Kershaw nearly regained the lead for the
visitors with a weaving run but it was Kellett with his
fourth penalty, this time from half-way, who settled the
issue. The Robins had matched the powerful Airlie Birds'
forwards in the loose and in Paul and Kellett, they had the
match-winners.*

> **Rovers:** A. Mullins; G. Paul, B. Matthews, C.
> Kellett, B. Shaw; D. Elliott, A. Bunting; R.
> Coverdale, P. Flanagan, B. Tyson, A. Thompson,
> J. Taylor, H. Poole (capt).
> **Hull FC:** J. Kershaw; D. Doyle-Davidson, G.
> Matthews, S. Cowan, T. Hollindrake; F.
> Broadhurst, T. Finn; M. Scott, J. Drake, B.
> Hambling, C. Sykes, W. Drake, J. Whiteley (capt).
> Referee: G. Wilson (Dewsbury)
> Attendance: 13,000 (£1,430)

With Coverdale missing only one game at prop, Grice's
opportunities diminished. Taylor reclaimed a regular second
row spot but injury prevented new skipper Jim Jenkin from
making his first appearance until November. Then, when
Jenkin broke his arm in Poole's debut game, Poole, a natural
leader, took over the responsibility. Rovers soon confirmed
him as the official captain and he retained the role throughout
his time with the club.

In the backs, Kellett and the versatile Paul were ever-
presents. In an unsettled back division, Bunting and Elliott
vied for the scrum-half role and a dozen others filled the three-
quarter and stand-off positions during the course of the season.

After playing in 107 games for the Robins, in which

he scored 23 tries, former skipper Bill Riley left to join Dewsbury at the end of the season. He was a very good, reliable and experienced centre who read the game well and was a good play-maker.

A good omen was that without any transfer, Boothferry Park or house sale income, the Robins still managed to make a small working profit. Plans had been drawn up for a £100,000 modern 30,000-capacity stadium at Winchester Avenue and a pitch was laid, complete with lights and a pavilion, that was used for training purposes whilst money was raised to build the ground.

During the season, the RFL appointed a special committee to look into the causes of declining attendances and in April appointed a sub-committee with the wide remit of looking at the game as a whole.

On the world stage, as relations between East and West deteriorated, the building of the Berlin Wall commenced and Russia closed the border between East and West Germany. Hull City appointed experienced former Preston North End manager Cliff Britton as successor to Bob Brocklebank. Britton was to manage City in 406 games – the longest-serving manager in their history.

The 1961-62 rugby league season saw the start of an unlikely association between Rochdale and Fiji. Hornets' chairman Arthur Walker brought two, Joe Levula and Orsi Dawai, to the Athletic Grounds. Their success saw them followed over the next few years by several more including Mike Ratu senior, whose grandson played briefly for the Robins in 2010. Sadly, in common with Craven Park, a Morrison's supermarket now stands on the site of the Athletic Grounds, which staged Rovers' 1925 Championship Final success.

The campaign opened with Rovers and their supporters full of confidence. It was Poole's first full season and they now appeared to have the nucleus of a very good team. There had been a resurgence of team spirit and Hutton had prepared them well, working hard on their fitness. They did not disappoint, reaching eighth place in the league and finishing above their neighbours for the first time in 30 years, as well as claiming a first derby double since 1947-48.

Although they won only one of their first six away games, the Robins then so successfully banished the 'away day blues' that they achieved a club record run of 17 consecutive victories between 18 November and 24 March. As a result, they reached the top four and the semi-final of the Challenge Cup. Club historian Dave Sherwood believes that the 2-0 second round cup win at Swinton was the best defensive performance he has ever seen from a Rovers side. After Kellett kicked a first half penalty, they scarcely got out of their own half but, with Ackerley leading the way, they tackled magnificently and gave away no penalties – fully deserving their £25 per man winning pay.

A 15-3 third round win at Workington was the club's first-ever success at Derwent Park. After an early try by Southward had put the home side ahead, the Robins played some brilliant football to register first half tries by Kellett, Harris and Paul. The forwards took over in the second half and did not allow Town back into the game. After that, the season disintegrated somewhat and Rovers won only three of the last twelve games including an eight-day spell in which they lost to eventual league leaders Wigan, twice, and St Helens. The Robins got back on the winning trail with a 10-9 success at Featherstone. That game saw the debuts of exciting young local back Alan Burwell and experienced former Dewsbury hooker Alan Lockwood, who dropped the winning goal two minutes from the end. In the cup semi-final at Odsal, a weakened Rovers side put up a spirited performance, particularly in defence but Huddersfield edged them out 6-0. The other semi-finalists were Featherstone and Wakefield, the first time Yorkshire had provided all four.

Earlier in the season, a polio outbreak in Hull meant that Rovers were unable to play any matches between 14 October and 11 November and the disappointing end to the season was mainly due to fixture congestion and injuries that resulted. However, the Robins had achieved their aim, a top-half finish and a place in the following season's new First Division and had played entertaining football.

The key to the club's greater success was that they were able to field a largely settled side. Full-back Kellett made the most appearances, missing only one of the 41 games and kicking 112 goals. Major and Brian Burwell, the elder brother of Alan, were the regular centres, whilst local winger Bob Harris won a consistent place. Paul, unfortunately, missed over half the season due to injury, but Elliott and Bunting formed a settled half-back partnership.

Brian Coulson made his last appearance in April. With a scoring record of 73 tries in 142 games, he had been a very useful performer in the three-quarters, but supporters invariably remember more the freak incident when the top of a goalpost, weakened by being struck by the ball, fell off and hit him on the head during a practice match. Fortunately, he was not seriously injured. His departure was compensated by the arrival of the powerful former Barnstaple rugby union three-quarter Mike Blackmore.

In the forwards, Coverdale remained the regular open-side prop but Ackerley, whilst a key figure in the winning run, was injured towards the end of the season and played his last game at Wakefield in April. The experienced former Hull FC prop Jim Drake, was signed in November for £4,000 and he competed with Tyson for the number 10 jersey, as well as allowing Tyson to provide cover in the second row. The regular back three were Taylor, Poole and former Exeter RUFC man Ted Bonner, who made his debut in the first match of the season.

A combined Hull FC and Rovers side beat the visiting New Zealand tourists 17-6 at the Boulevard and, at the end of the season, the Robins and Airlie Birds went on a rugby league promotional tour of the West Country. Colin Hutton was chosen as coach of the 1962 Great Britain team to tour Australasia and John Taylor was selected as a member of the touring party, the first Rovers player to achieve this honour. The 'A' team provided more good news by winning the Yorkshire Senior Competition Cup. A season's loss of over £4,000 was attributable to transfer activity.

The Greats – No 13
Alvin Ackerley - *see Hull KR legends gallery*

Born in November 1927 in Cockermouth, Alvin Ackerley joined Workington Town after the war and moved to Halifax in 1948. As a leading member of the redoubtable 'Fax pack of the 1950s, he gained Cumberland, England and Great Britain honours, touring Australasia in 1958. It was something of a surprise when Halifax allowed the hooker to leave following a pay dispute during the 1958-59 season. His signing for a bargain £750 fee on New Year's Day 1959 was a big coup for the Robins and Halifax' loss was definitely Rovers' gain, especially as he had Championship medals and Wembley final appearances to his name.

A seasoned professional, he was a complete all-round performer in his position. A very good ball-winner, hard tackler and a constant threat from the acting half position, his presence in Rovers' front row commanded respect from all opponents. Historian Dave Sherwood believes that Ackerley was the best hooker Rovers have had – a huge compliment. 'Ackerley just shades it in terms of his all-round performance,' he says.

In November 1961, Ackerley announced his retirement from the game but it was probably the shortest ever because 48 hours later he responded to Hutton's plea and returned to the fold. It was his next game that was dubbed 'Ackerley's finest hour' when, on 2 December 1961, he was carried off in the first half against star-studded cup-holders St Helens, only to return a few minutes later. Ackerley had an outstanding game, repeatedly slicing through the St Helens' defence from dummy-half and leading his side to a famous 12-5 win.

At the end of that season, Ackerley once more announced his retirement – this time for good. He made his final appearance for Rovers at Wakefield on 23 April 1962 after playing in exactly 100 matches for the Robins. He also played a big part in the development of his replacement Peter Flanagan, who was to emulate his achievements at international level.

Ackerley died in late 1973 and was later inducted into the Halifax Hall of Fame.

1962-63 saw a change in the league fixture formula. In addition to the reintroduction of two divisions, two zonal competitions were played, the Eastern and Western Divisional Championships. Playing some excellent football, Rovers won their first 14 fixtures of the season – a club record at the time. In the process, they reached both the Yorkshire Cup final and the Eastern Division final. Their first defeat was a shock home loss to Bramley in a First Division game on 20 October, the first of three consecutive setbacks that included the Yorkshire Cup final and a home league defeat by eventual First Division champions Swinton.

The Yorkshire Cup decider was the Robins' first cup

final appearance since their defeat by York in the same competition in 1933. Unfortunately their hopes were shattered by losing three players to injury during the game, including skipper Poole, and they lost 12-2 to Hunslet at Headingley. However, Rovers returned to Leeds just two weeks later and beat Huddersfield in the Eastern Division final with a much weakened team. After that, their inconsistent form resulted in a 10th place out of 16 First Division clubs. A remarkable feat was that for the only time ever, Rovers defeated their Boulevard neighbours on four occasions during the season, achieving doubles in both the league and the Eastern Division.

There were two main reasons for Rovers' inconsistency after such a good start. The first was the string of injuries to key players. The most significant was the broken arm sustained by the influential Poole. Having only just returned to the side after missing 11 of the first 15 matches with an ankle injury, he was now ruled out the rest of the season, a devastating blow. The second factor was the severe winter of 1963. The Robins were unable to play any games between 22 December and 16 February which, together with a Challenge Cup run that took them through to the semi-final, meant they had to play no fewer than 17 games in 51 days between 12 April and 1 June.

The Challenge Cup run started with a low-key single-point home win over Keighley in the first home game for over two months, made possible by the club using 200 braziers to thaw the frozen pitch. That was followed by a comfortable home win over Featherstone and an excellent, hard-fought 10-7 triumph away to high-flying Widnes. For the second year running though, hopes ended in the semi-final at Headingley, this time with an 18-4 defeat by Wigan. After that, handicapped by the long injury list, attention turned to the fight for First Division survival, which the Robins achieved in no small part due to their reserve strength.

Kellett played all but six matches in his usual full-back position and broke Carmichael's club goal-kicking record with 142. Paul was ever-present on the right wing and scored 34 tries during the season, a post-war club record, whilst Harris was the regular left-winger and scored only one fewer try than Paul. Rovers signed Batley prop Peter Fox from Batley as cover and he came into the side when Jim Drake was injured in April.

Beverley-born prop Ken Grice retired due to injuries at season'e end. He made the last of his 194 appearances at home to Castleford on 6 May, marking the occasion with his 18th try. An old-fashioned prop-forward, he was a solid, reliable grafter. Nothing in his Rovers career gave him greater pleasure than his 30-yard try against Hull FC in 1955.

Club chairman Wilf Spaven was elected chairman of the Rugby Football League for 1963-64 and a further positive note was sounded with a season's profit of over £2,000.

Eastern Division Championship Final, Headingley, Leeds, 10 November 1962
Huddersfield 10-13 Hull Kingston Rovers

The Robins' first trophy win since 1929 came after their injury-hit side rose to the occasion. Free-flowing football established a 13-2 lead before the grit and determination they showed in defending their lead in the second half, against constant waves of Huddersfield pressure, paid off.

Rovers were missing regulars Mike Blackmore, Dave Elliott, Brian Hatch, Ken Grice, John Taylor and their leader, Harry Poole. All of them played in the Yorkshire Cup final two weeks earlier, in which the Robins, with only 10 fit men by the end, put up heroic resistance against a strong Hunslet side.

The Robins

Despite lacking so many key men, Rovers began strongly. In the first 25 minutes, their hard-working defence stopped Huddersfield taking a grip on the game, then Alan Burwell broke through and linked with Terry Major, who sent Graham Paul racing to the line. Cyril Kellett converted from the touchline. Minutes later, Bob Harris exploited Dyson's misjudgement and raced away, with Kellett converting again. Dyson's penalty made it 10-2 at half-time.

Huddersfield dashed any thoughts of an easy win by coming out strongly in the second period but despite being penned in their own half for a long period, the Robins' defence stood firm. Midway through the half, Peter Flanagan started a move just outside his own 25-yard line. Bob Coverdale and Arthur Bunting took over before Burwell sent Paul racing 45 yards to the line, holding off Smales and Dyson to score in the corner. From 13-2 down, Huddersfield came back with two tries in quick succession, one converted by Dyson, to put them within striking distance with six minutes to go. Only some desperate defence prevented them completing their comeback; winger Senior was tackled just short and Rovers held on for a well-deserved win.

Bunting was outstanding in the backs, well supported by Burwell, with Brian Tyson, Ted Bonner and Coverdale leading the way up front, but this was essentially a triumph for teamwork and determination.

Huddersfield: *F. Dyson; K. Senior, L. Booth, R. Haywood, G. Stocks; H. Deighton, T. Smales (capt); B. Rowe, D. Close, K. Noble, A. Kilroy, K. Bowman, A. Redfearn.*
Rovers: *C. Kellett (capt); G. Paul, T. Major, B. Burwell, R. Harris; A. Burwell, A. Bunting; R. Coverdale, P. Flanagan, J. Drake, B. Tyson, P. Murphy, E. Bonner.*
Referee: T.W. Watkinson (Manchester)
Attendance: 6,822 (£1,342)

A Challenge Cup marathon

The 1963-64 season was memorable only for its Challenge Cup campaign. Before that, no impact was made in the Eastern Division, there was a second round Yorkshire Cup defeat and a disappointing league campaign resulted in a ninth-place finish out of 16 clubs. If the Robins had been knocked out of the Challenge Cup in round one, the only consolation would have been the derby double and Hull's relegation – but the cup run put a different complexion on the season.

Overall, the team had not changed greatly from the previous year. Young centre Johnny Moore had forced his way into the team, allowing Blackmore to move to the wing at the expense of Harris. Elliott and Alan Burwell vied for the stand-off position with Bunting the regular scrum-half. Graham Paul scored two tries in the final game at home to Widnes before retiring to the West Country but a speedy local flyer, Chris Young, made a promising debut at the end of the season.

In the forwards, Tyson invariably took one of the prop positions, making the most appearances with 43 from 48 games. Frank Fox arrived from Halifax and John Bath from local rugby union to compete for the other prop position, whilst Flanagan had his first full season as the undisputed first choice hooker. Another ex-rugby union man, Len Clark, the son of 'Nobby' who played for the club either side of World War II, competed with Taylor and young local forward Eric Palmer for the second row positions. Clark also proved an able goal-kicker in Kellett's absences. Poole had returned from injury to lead the side from his usual loose-forward position.

The Challenge Cup brought a home first round tie with second-division Rochdale that the Robins were expected to win comfortably. However, they came close to defeat and managed only a 12-12 draw. In the replay at the Athletic

Grounds, Rovers turned a 7-3 half-time deficit into a 22-7 victory and, in the second round, there was a straightforward 23-7 win at York, in which the only disappointment was the dismissal of Palmer in an apparent case of mistaken identity.

. The other Craven Park team, Barrow, were the visitors in the third round. The game had been in doubt due to snow and ice up until the day of the match and took place only thanks to the work of club officials and supporters in clearing the pitch and terraces. One of those supporters was Len Beecroft, who remembers returning home for lunch before the game to hear on BBC *Grandstand* that the game was off. He contacted the club, who told the Corporation that the game was definitely on, and they broadcast a correction. Rovers gave a top-class performance that afternoon, with Taylor outstanding scoring a hat-trick of tries.

The semi-final took place four weeks later, with Oldham the opposition at Headingley. In a very tight game, the Robins trailed 3-2 at half-time but a 30-yard break by Palmer led to a Blackmore try that put Rovers ahead early in the second half. It was only a drop-goal by veteran Oldham hooker McIntyre in the dying seconds, the only one of his career, that tied the scores at 5-5. The replay took place three days later at Station Road, Swinton, kicking off at 6.45pm in the absence of floodlights. In a thrilling game, Rovers held an 8-7 half time lead and two more tries increased their advantage to 14-7. With just 10 minutes to go, Oldham pulled a try back and the touchline conversion narrowed the gap to just two points. With the last kick of normal time, Dyson landed a penalty goal to level the scores at 14-14. It should have been all over by then though, as the Robins had scored four tries to Oldham's two but, unusually, Kellett had been successful with only one kick.

By the rules of the competition at the time, the teams then had to play 15 minutes each way of extra time. It was

Above: Sid Atkinson scores Rovers' first try when rugby resumed after World War II on 25 August 1945. Normally a second-rower, Atkinson made his debut that day on the wing, scoring both tries in a 14-5 win over Rochdale Hornets

Paul Fletcher collection

Below: East stand fire 1946. The East stand had to be rebuilt following a spectacular fire in the summer of 1946

Above: Geoff Tullock attempts to brush away a Huddersfield defender in the Yorkshire Cup first round first leg tie at Craven Park on 1 September 1951. Tommy Sutton in support. Rovers won 19-13 but lost 38-24 on aggregate.

Matt Dass collection

Left: Huddersfield's Madden breaks in a first round Yorkshire Cup tie at a packed Fartown on 30 September 1946, with Rovers' Horace Gee in pursuit.

Paul Fletcher collection

Above: The side that beat Keighley 21-7 on 14 February 1959. Back (*left to right*): Ray Jaques, Alvin Ackerley, Jim Jenkin, John Taylor, Peter Key, David Elliott, Doug Holland. *Front*: Bill Coulson, Bill Riley (capt), Ken Grice, Roly Moat, Cyril Kellett, Graham Paul

Below: Cyril Kellett starting a Rovers move against Keighley in the first round of the Challenge Cup on 2 March 1963. Three Kellett goals earned a 6-5 win.

Above: How it used to be. Mike Blackmore brings down St Helens' Goddard at a muddy Craven Park on 9 March 1963. Bob Harris (No 5) and Len Chamberlain (making his Rovers debut) are ready to lend assistance, whilst Bob Coverdale and 'Flash' Flanagan look on. Rovers won the game 3-2

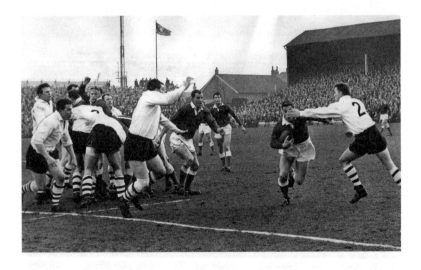

Above: Second leg of the marathon. Arthur Bunting single-handedly takes on the Oldham defence in the first replay of the 1964 Challenge Cup semi-final at Station Road, Swinton. 'Flash' Flanagan pokes his head out of the scrum to find out what is happening, whilst Harry Poole and Alan Burwell prepare to lend their support

Above: Brian Tyson starts a Rovers attack in the 1964 final against Widnes, with Brian Mennell in support and Arthur Bunting looking on

Below: John Moore is tackled in the snow against Castleford at a wintry Craven Park on 28 December 1964. Two Blackmore tries gave Rovers a 10-3 win

Above: Terry Major crosses the line at Derwent Park deep into injury time in a second round Challenge Cup tie on 19 March 1966. Kellett, supporting left, landed the conversion with the last kick of the game to give Rovers a 7-5 win

Below: Mudlarks at Headingley. The Rovers' pack lines up for a scrum in a 3-0 win on 9 April 1966. Front, from the left, are Terry Major, Brian Tyson, Joby Shaw, Frank Fox and Harry Poole (in unrecognisable Leeds colours). Poking between props and hooker are Bill Holliday (left) and Frank Foster

Colin Hutton

Above: Try! Despite the attentions of Leeds's Ray Batten, Geoff Wriglesworth dives over for the well-worked try that decided the third round Challenge Cup-tie 7-2 in Rovers' favour at a sunny but cold Craven Park on 7 March 1970. John Holmes watches on helplessly and behind him Cliff Wallis has peeled away on a dummy run

Above: Cliff Wallis brushes aside Bradford Northern's Drew Broach in a first round Championship play-off game at Craven Park on 19 April 1970. Looking on are 'Flash' Flanagan and Roger Millward. Rovers won 26-13

Above: Yorkshire Cup winners 1971. *Standing (left to right):* Terry Clawson, Ian Markham, Phil Coupland, Johnny Whiteley (coach), John Millington, George Kirkpatrick, Paul Rose. *Kneeling:* Joe Brown, Colin Cooper, Eric Palmer, Roger Millward, Peter Flanagan, Paul Longstaff. *Front:* Paul Daley, Mike Stephenson

Above: The 1980 squad. Standing (*left to right*): Jack Ounsworth (kitman), John Moore, Len Casey, Steve Hubbard, Roy Holdstock, Paul Rose, David Hall, John Millington, Mike Smith, Mick Crane, Phil Lowe, Cliff Wallis (physio). *Seated:* David Watkinson, Clive Sullivan, Steve Hartley, Bernard Watson, Ian Robinson, Phil Hogan, Brian Lockwood. *Kneeling:* Ray Price, Steve Leighton, Roger Millward (capt/coach), Allan Agar, Paul Harkin

already getting gloomy but whilst it was possible to see, referee Dennis Davies had no option other than to continue. After six minutes, Oldham scored a try to lead 17-14 but six minutes later Davies decided that it was impossible to adjudicate what was going on and he abandoned the game.

There followed an anxious wait for the league's ruling on the result. To the surprise of many, and to Rovers' relief, the league decided that as there were still 18 minutes to go and, as the game was so close, there would be a second replay. That took place at Fartown, Huddersfield six days later. A good omen for the Robins was that for this third attempt, the RFL appointed a different referee. Davies had been in charge of the first two games and both their semi-final defeats in the previous two seasons, and it was hoped that the choice of highly-respected Pudsey official, Matt Coates, might change their luck.

Heavy rush-hour traffic caused many Rovers supporters to arrive late for the 6.30pm kick-off at Fartown and they then got soaked in the uncovered area behind the posts. On a quagmire of a pitch that was expected to favour Oldham's big forwards, Rovers elected to play against a strong wind in the first half and were happy to turn around at 2-2. Within five minutes of the restart, Bunting scored a solo try from a scrum and Kellett's conversion gave the Robins a five-point lead. With 12 minutes to go, they wrapped it up when Burwell and Elliott combined to put Blackmore in and Kellett converted to make the final score 12-2. Under the magnificent leadership of Poole, well supported by half-backs Burwell and Bunting and the experienced Drake, the Robins had reached Wembley for the first time. The longest semi-final in rugby league history lasted 252 minutes and over 88,500 people had watched the three games.

There was more drama to come. Eight days before the

final, during a 10-5 home win over Huddersfield, referee Wingfield rather harshly sent off international forward Taylor. The disciplinary committee met two days before the game and Taylor made a personal appearance, supported by Spaven.

Of the six-man committee, only two, the chairman and vice-chairman, from Rochdale and St Helens respectively, were able to consider the case. Two were unavailable whilst Spaven and the Huddersfield representative were interested parties. They found Taylor guilty, and the one-match suspension imposed put him out of the final. Obviously, the Robins were very disappointed by the verdict and they then had a serious problem in filling the number ten jersey.

Of the contenders, Frank Fox, Bath and Drake were all injured and Peter Fox was unavailable. In an effort to get him fit, Drake was given cortisone injections in a Blackpool hospital to clear up his thigh injury before Rovers travelled to London from their base at Cleveleys in Lancashire on the Friday before the game. However, time was against him, Drake was simply unfit to play and the Robins called up 21-year old Brian Mennell from the 'A' team for their biggest game since the halcyon days of the 1920s.

Mennell had played just three times for the first team in two seasons and never at prop. Now he was going to appear at Wembley against one of the biggest and best blind-side props in the business, Frank Collier of Widnes. To be fair to Mennell, who did not even get a mention in the match programme, he did not let the club down and Collier himself commended the young man's performance. Sadly, however, some of the bigger names did not perform as well and Rovers were beaten 13-5.

There had been some unrest in the camp during the season. Peter Fox became frustrated with a lack of first team football and requested to move, Kellett and Taylor asked for transfers after being dropped in mid-season, and Alan Burwell was unhappy about being asked to play at centre.

At the AGM, the club reported that for the first time in memory it had been possible to run affairs on the money received through the gates. Total receipts, including season passes, were £33,700 and the expenses of running the team were £33,100. The £3,900 received from the cup final appearance more than compensated for a loss of £2,500 on transfers.

The board decided to press ahead with the Winchester Avenue ground project, in which they had already invested over £8,000. With Rovers also benefitting from the club lottery proceeds, the overall picture was highly satisfactory – despite the cup final disappointment. It was a stark contrast to Odsal where Bradford Northern, having been so powerful in the early post-war years, ceased to function in mid-season.

Challenge Cup Final, Wembley Stadium, 8 May 1964
Hull Kingston Rovers 5-13 Widnes

The Robins' first Wembley appearance ended in disappointment for the players and their large following. Twelve rail excursions carried over 6,000 red and white supporters, whilst East Yorkshire Motor Services alone ran 31 coaches to the game. Widnes were deserved winners in a match that was undertaken in a spirit that reflected the best of the sport, the Chemics playing with a buoyant assurance that made them look the more likely winners throughout. Their defence was magnificent and was breached only by a brilliant individual try from Alan Burwell. Whilst the Robins were spirited and never gave in, they looked nervous by comparison and their handling suffered accordingly.

Rovers had spent most of the week before the game at Cleveleys in Lancashire, where they trained hard on the beach. Burwell remembers old campaigner Jim Drake remarking as

*they left the town on the Friday, 'I hope you haven't left all
your fitness on that beach.' From Cleveleys they travelled to
their hotel in the west end of London. 'That was a mistake,'
says Burwell. 'I couldn't sleep due to the noise of the traffic.
I remember hearing voices in the middle of the night and got
up to investigate. Some of the lads were playing cards in Jim
Drake's room down the corridor – none of them could sleep
either. It was not ideal preparation for a cup final the next
day.' Perhaps that interrupted night was a factor, certainly
some of the players did not do themselves justice on the day
whilst a 19-10 scrum deficit also took its toll.*

*The only score of the first half was a penalty goal from
Randall for Widnes following a scrum offence after 34
minutes. Widnes scored their first try after 50 minutes when
their magnificent leader, Karalius, combined with Kemel
before giving Briers the ball in what seemed like an impossible
position. Briers, however, beat four Rovers defenders to cross
wide out. Three minutes later, Hurstfield broke out of a weak
tackle and linked with Hughes, whose well-timed pass put
Myler over between the posts. Randall's conversion made it
10-0 with 27 minutes to go and it looked all over.*

*It was a surprise when Rovers won quick and clean
possession from a scrum on the hour and Arthur Bunting
darted through a gap to release Burwell. The stand-off had
it all to do but he raced between two defenders and rounded
Randall without a hand being laid on him. Kellett's
conversion made it 10-5 with a quarter of the game left.
Despite two tremendous breaks by Graham Paul, however,
the Chemics' defence was too strong and the Robins had no
more clear chances. In the final moments, with Widnes
applying pressure to Rovers' line, Kemel sold an outrageous
dummy to send in the big prop Collier for the final score of
the game. Collier had an outstanding game and won the
Lance Todd trophy but there were several contenders
amongst his teammates.*

At the end Collier praised young Brian Mennell, who had

stood up well to the difficult task of playing opposite to a man who had enjoyed the best season of his career. He had not been disgraced and Hutton also commended his efforts. Mennell said that he had expected the old campaigner against him to be up to all sorts of tricks, but that he played absolutely hard and fair. Harry Poole commented that he was: 'Disappointed but not downhearted.' Rovers were beaten by a better team and he had no complaints.

There was conjecture about what might have happened if Taylor had been able to play. He was a destructive runner but with the reputation of flitting in and out of games. Ten minutes of his brilliance might have broken the Widnes defence; equally, Widnes might have tackled him out of the game. No one will ever know and, in Bunting's words, the Robins were second best on the day.

> **Rovers:** C. Kellett; G. Paul, T. Major, D. Elliott, M. Blackmore; A. Burwell, A. Bunting; B. Tyson, P. Flanagan, B. Mennell, E. Palmer, L. Clark, H. Poole (capt).
> **Widnes:** R. Randall; R. Chisnall, A. Briers, F. Myler, W. Thompson; G. Lowe, R. Owen; W. Hurstfield, G. Kemel, F. Collier, J. Measures, A. Hughes, V. Karalius (capt).
> Referee: R.L. Thomas (Oldham)
> Attendance: 84,488 (£44,840)

The Greats – No 14
Graham Paul - *see Hull KR legends gallery*

Of Rovers' recruits from rugby union in the South West of England in the late 1950s and early 1960s, Graham Paul was probably the most successful. Born in 1934, he was an outstanding schoolboy athlete and made his debut for Penzance-Newlyn Colts at the age of 14. He subsequently acquired a big reputation in rugby union as a pacey fly-half, playing for Bedford and Nottingham as well as his home

209

town club and representing both Cornwall and the RAF. Paul spent seven years in the air force, latterly as a Physical Training Instructor at RAF St Mawgan. The Robins persuaded him to try his luck in East Yorkshire in November 1958 at the age of 24. His signing was kept secret to allow him to play in his 100th game for Penzance-Newlyn, which he certainly would not have been allowed to do had his defection become public knowledge.

Whilst not a particularly tall man, his key strengths were his pace off the mark and remarkable acceleration and he became a big attacking threat for the Robins. After making his debut on Boxing Day 1958 at home to York, a game in which his two tries represented all Rovers' points in a 15-6 defeat, he was moved to stand-off for the remainder of the season. For the next three seasons his appearances were divided between there and wing but from August 1962 he played exclusively on the flank.

The 'Cornish Express' as he became known to Rovers' fans, was an ever-present in both 1960-61 and 1962-63, finishing as the club's top try-scorer in three seasons. In 1962-63, he set a then post-war club record of 34 tries for the season becoming, in the process, the first Rovers' player to score tries in ten consecutive club matches. Paul made his final appearance, which he also marked with two tries, in the last match of the 1963-64 season at home to Widnes. He played in 197 games for the Robins and scored an impressive 116 tries.

Johnny Whiteley remembers that he was 'exceptionally fast' and Len Beecroft recalls his trademark dive for the line as he scored. 'He must have taken off five yards from the line, but the fact that he did not achieve any representative honours is a reflection of the quality of the wingmen in the game at the time.'

Retiring at the comparatively early age of 29, Paul and his family returned to Penzance where he and his wife ran the Sportsman's Arms for 21 years. 'He was a fine winger,' *says Alan Burwell. 'It was a bit of a surprise when he retired so early but he wanted to go out at the top.' When eventually the RFU relaxed their regulations on professionalism, Paul returned to his old club, now known as the Cornish Pirates, initially coaching the juniors and then serving as groundsman. He continues to live in the Penzance area.*

Cumbrian reinforcements

In the summer of 1964, Nelson Mandela made his, 'I am prepared to die' speech on the opening day of the Rivonia Trial in South Africa, at which he and seven others were sentenced to life imprisonment on Robben Island. In the UK, twelve of the men who committed the Great Train Robbery the previous August were sentenced to a total of 307 years in prison and Terence Conran opened the first Habitat store on London's Fulham Road. Denis Law was voted European Footballer of the Year and, in August, the first episode of *Match of the Day* was broadcast on BBC2.

For the 1964-65 season, the rugby league clubs voted for a return to a single division at the end of which there was to be an expanded Championship play-off involving the top 16 clubs. Bradford Northern had been reformed so Rovers' fixture list comprised the 15 other Yorkshire clubs plus St Helens and Warrington, home and away. Another significant change was that, for the first time, rugby league allowed substitutes. Each team could make a maximum of two substitutions, for injured players only, up to the beginning of the second half. Rovers made none in the first three games, so reserve full-back Ted McNamara had the distinction of being the club's first replacement when he came on at Leeds on 7 September.

The Robins started well and lost only four league

matches before the turn of the year. In an excellent opening game in front of a 14,642 crowd against the reformed Bradford side at Odsal on 22 August, Rovers took command in the second half. A brace of tries each for winger Young, Palmer and former Hull FC hooker Alan Holdstock turned a 10-7 interval deficit into a 34-20 win. Joint-second in the table with Wigan at the start of January, a loss of form resulted in six defeats in seven games, including a shock first-round Challenge Cup defeat at the hands of Batley. After that, Rovers won six of the last nine league games and finished in eighth place, five above the Airlie Birds, who won 12-10 at the Boulevard on Good Friday to end Rovers' record run of ten successive derby victories.

In the new top 16 Championship play-offs, Rovers were initially at home to the ninth-placed Oldham and won comfortably. As all eight home teams had won, they then travelled to table-toppers St Helens in the second round, where the season ended on a controversial note. With Saints leading 12-2 in the second half, referee Wilson disallowed what appeared a perfectly good try by Elliott and the Saints went on to win 24-6. Halifax won the Championship from seventh place and sparked discussion about the credibility of such a play-off. There was talk of a reversion to a top-four but the RFL retained the format for the time being.

The big transfer news of the season was the capture in January of Cumbrian forwards Bill Holliday from Whitehaven for a new club record £8,000 and Frank Foster from Workington for £6,500. Taylor again requested a transfer claiming that he was fed up of being made a scapegoat, and was sold to Castleford for £6,000, a then record incoming fee. Holdstock provided Flanagan with more competition for the hooking role, whilst Holliday and Foster ended the fight for second row places from mid-March.

With the ever-reliable Kellett at full-back and kicking

141 goals, just one short of his club record, Rovers had a fairly settled back division. Left-centre Moore missed only one of the 39 games whilst Elliott and Alan Burwell competed for the stand-off position. At one point, Elliott asked for a transfer as he was unhappy with being in and out of the side and having to play in different positions but later withdrew his request. The choice was either the steady reliability of Elliott or the match-winning individual brilliance but occasional inconsistency of Burwell. In fact, Elliott shaded it with 19 starts to 17 in the jersey.

Hatch, Coverdale, Drake and Bonner all played their last games for the club during the season. Rovers rewarded Hutton for his work so far by giving him a new four-year contract on improved terms. Unsurprisingly, given the considerable transfer fee deficit and much reduced cup receipts, the club made a £7,800 loss on the season but, in the circumstances, that was not a disaster. A pleasing note during the season was Poole's deserved selection for Great Britain against France, his only GB cap whilst with Rovers.

The 1965-66 season started on a sour note as the players threatened strike action in support of their demand for improved playing terms. They wanted £18 for an away win and £16 for a home win but reluctantly withdrew the demand before the opening game against Swinton, and accepted the same terms as the previous season – £15 for a win and £8 for a defeat. Swinton, Wigan and Workington were included in the fixture list whilst for the first time for 60 years there was no league match against Huddersfield, who played in the Lancashire league that season. A minor change was that clubs could use substitutes for any reason, not just injury, but only until the start of the second half.

Not until April did Rovers put together a decent run of wins by which time they could manage only a twelfth-place league finish. An early season tour game saw the New Zealanders triumph 21-11 in a game that marked the first team debut of a young half-back, Mike Stephenson.

The drama took place in the Challenge Cup. Drawn at lowly Bramley in the first round, a ground on which they had won only two weeks earlier, the Robins were expected to progress without too much difficulty. However, surprises are the fascination of cup football and they were happy in the end to escape with a draw and get Bramley back to Craven Park. Even then it was not straightforward and Rovers were thankful for Mike Blackmore's second half try that saw off a dogged Bramley side.

The second round brought a visit to Workington, rarely a happy hunting ground for the Robins and one on which they had lost 5-0 a fortnight before. It looked as if this game would go the same way as Rovers trailed 5-2 in the dying minutes with the home fans clamouring for the final whistle. In four attempts, the Robins had not won a Challenge Cup tie refereed by Dennis Davies but this time their luck changed. With Workington convinced that the 80 minutes were already up, the Manchester official did not blow his whistle until Terry Major had scored the try that, with Kellett's conversion, put Rovers through to the third round.

Of all the controversies and injustices to befall the club over the years, the third round defeat at St Helens was arguably the worst. After 80 minutes Rovers, led superbly by Frank Foster and the better side throughout, were ahead 10-7 and tackling Saints out of the game. Deep into injury time, Saints' Alex Murphy, unable to find a way through the defence, put up a speculative up-and-under, which bounced over the dead-ball line. Following up, he grabbed the ball as it bounced up and touched it down back inside the in-goal area. After consulting his linesmen, referee Eric Clay awarded a try and when Killeen had kicked the goal to put Saints 12-10 ahead, the official blew for full-time. Tyson remembers the encounter well: 'The game was postponed from the Saturday because of snow and played on a Monday night. We were the better side – Arthur Bunting played a blinder. When the incident occurred, Clay copped out and went to the linesman. I remember Murphy coming to our dressing room afterwards and saying "hard luck". Foster threw something at him!' A well-known Saints player later admitted that the try should not have been awarded. Rovers protested to the RFL about Clay's handling of the game, in particular the extent of the injury time and the legality of the final try, to no avail.

In the end-of-season play-offs, there were wins at Castleford and Wakefield before another defeat at Knowsley Road in the semi-final by 14-6.

On the transfer front, the most significant event was the departure of Harry Poole to Leeds in October. Although he was interested in coaching opportunities as he neared the end of his playing career, Poole did not ask to move. He had been a great player for Rovers and, thankfully, the club had not seen the last of him.

Moore and Blackmore were ever-present, the latter finishing top try-scorer for the second successive season. The club avoided a selection dilemma when Alan Burwell took the season off to concentrate on his studies and Elliott and Bunting formed a regular half-back pairing. Winger Bob Harris lost his place to Blackmore and retired. Harris scored a remarkable 77 tries in 128 games for the Robins. 'He was an excellent winger,' says Burwell. 'He was very fast.'

In the forwards, Frank Fox was the regular number eight with Holliday and Foster, the new skipper, in the second row. Tyson missed the first half of the season due to injury but returned in January to reclaim the open side prop shirt.

Flanagan missed the start of the season and was transfer-listed following a dispute about safeguarding his future in the event of injury. He came off the list again, however, and reclaimed his first team slot in October. Local man Arthur Mullins had a run at loose-forward after Poole's departure but Major took over at the beginning of March. Len Clark retired after sustaining an injury in the second game of the season.

Chairman Wilf Spaven was chosen to be manager of the 1966 Great Britain tour party, captained by former Rovers' skipper Poole and Flanagan was selected for the tour party, subsequently becoming the club's first serving player to play in a Test match in Australia. After his retirement from playing in July 1965, Bob Coverdale took over as 'A' team coach.

A legend arrives

In 1966, Moors murderers Ian Brady and Myra Hindley were sentenced to life imprisonment and, in South Wales, a mining slag heap collapsed on the small village of Aberfan and claimed the lives of 144 people. The first episode of *Star Trek* was broadcast and the mini-skirt was the height of ladies' fashion.

Rugby league introduced a four-tackle rule whereby the team that had the ball was allowed to retain it for only four consecutive tackles before a scrum was formed. The change was a response to the unambitious football played by some teams who, once ahead, practically eliminated passing and kicking in order to deny their opponents possession. The change was trialled in Britain in the 1966 BBC2 Floodlit Trophy, by then in its second season and introduced in all competitions that November.

During the summer of 1966, Rovers decided to abandon the Winchester Avenue ground project and opened negotiations with the greyhound company about a fresh lease on Craven Park. At the same time, they obtained permission to make improvements to the 44-year old stadium. Firstly, the supporters club paid for the Well in front of the best stand to be re-terraced. Then, during the season, the famous Sunday morning volunteer force, led by director Percy Johnson, set to work.

They renewed the turnstiles and re-concreted the Aberdeen Street entrance, replaced the crumbling terracing, barriers and fencing at the Holderness Road end of the ground, refurbished the dressing rooms and concreted the area behind the best stand. All the while, volunteer tea-ladies sustained the workers with mugs of brew from the old supporters club shed. Director Albert Draper paid for a new directors' room in the main stand, enlarging the existing facility. All this unpaid work enabled the club to keep money in the kitty to start work on the installation of floodlights.

Without question though, the Robins' major achievement of the summer of 1966 was the capture of 18-year old Castleford stand-off Roger Millward. Rovers had been aware of the situation at Wheldon Road for some time. Cas had an established pair of quality half-backs in Alan Hardisty and Keith Hepworth when Millward first came onto the scene in 1964 and his appearances for his home town club were either on the wing or filling in if they were unavailable. The situation could not continue.

Chairman Spaven had made an informal approach some time before and was given a promise of a first refusal should they decide to sell. When he received the call from Castleford that summer, Spaven moved quickly to persuade his board to get the deal done. Millward signed for Rovers whilst on holiday in Blackpool in early August. It was the best piece of transfer business the club has ever done. At just five feet four inches tall, Millward may have been short in stature but he was high in talent and commitment and was never afraid to go in where it hurt.

Millward made his debut in the opening match of the 1966-67 season at Hunslet and scored the first of over 200 tries for the club at home to Batley a week later. He remembers his Rovers debut clearly and afterwards going into a pub with his wife-to-be Carol. Emphasising the stark contrast to 2016, he says: 'We had a few drinks and then caught a bus home to Castleford.' The young Millward soon settled in at Craven Park, finding the atmosphere around the club more relaxed.

Hutton believed that he now had the final piece in his jigsaw and the team could make a serious challenge for honours. After defeat in the second game at Workington, the Robins embarked on a 17-match winning run, equalling their 1961-62 best as a professional club. It included a victorious Yorkshire Cup campaign. In the first round Rovers overcame Hull FC 24-20 in a thriller. The Robins then beat Hunslet and Huddersfield before putting on an excellent show to defeat Featherstone Rovers in the final at Headingley.

Just four league games were lost before the turn of the year and the Robins were challenging Leeds at the top of the table. They lost 9-6 at Headingley on Christmas Eve but turned the tables with an 11-9 triumph at Craven Park in the return game three days later. In the end, Rovers record of six defeats and two draws was not enough to give them the top spot but they finished runners-up to Leeds, their highest-placed finish since 1928-29. Honours were even in the derby games, the Black and Whites winning 13-12 at the Boulevard on Good Friday and the Robins turning the tables with a strong second half performance that resulted in a 26-8 home win a week later.

After a 9-9 draw with Castleford at Craven Park in the second round, the Challenge Cup campaign ended in a 13-6 defeat in an uncompromising replay at Wheldon Road. The

4.30 kick-off, necessitated by the absence of floodlights, had to be delayed due to the number of spectators trying to get in. The gates were locked when the ground was full but were reopened to prevent them being broken down. The official attendance was 23,000 but hundreds more climbed over the fences. There was devastating tackling from both sides, and the game turned on a couple of Rovers handling errors in the second half. Hutton said: 'We have never experienced from Castleford such fire and aggression as we got in this game.'

In the play-offs, there were home wins over Barrow and Swinton, the latter featuring one of Rovers' best displays of the season. Wakefield then ended the Championship hopes with an 18-6 semi-final win at Craven Park – the only home defeat of the season.

The club again benefitted from having a settled team. With Alan Burwell returning to the fold and agreeing to play at centre, the regular team was; Kellett; Young, Burwell, Moore and Blackmore; Millward and Bunting; forwards Fox, Flanagan, Tyson, Holliday, Foster and Major. Fox and Young played in every game, Young being the season's top try-scorer with 34 and equalling Paul's post-war Rovers record. Kellett landed 145 goals to extend his own club record, also equalling his club point-scoring record of 290 for a season.

Yorkshire Cup Final, Headingley, Leeds,
15 October 1966
Hull Kingston Rovers 25-12 Featherstone Rovers

The Robins, clear favourites on the day, tore into the Colliers from the start. Negating Featherstone's tactics of making it a forward battle, they moved the ball quickly and utilised their speedy backs.

After five minutes, Roger Millward sent Mike Blackmore in at the corner and Cyril Kellett kicked a magnificent conversion. Featherstone fought back and although Smales kicked a penalty, their handling let them down. The Robins then laid siege to their opponents' line and when Brian Tyson went over, a defender dislodged the ball from his hands and Peter Flanagan was there to touch down the rebound. Kellett's conversion made it 10-2 to give Rovers some breathing space and they took charge of the game. Flanagan and Alan Burwell inter-passed for the latter to score a brilliant try that Kellett again converted. Already 13 points in arrears, Featherstone's chances all but disappeared when referee Baker dismissed Dooler for tripping Frank Foster and Kellett's penalty goal made it 17-2 at half-time.

Arthur Bunting and Johnny Moore combined beautifully to send in Chris Young early in the second half, and, with Kellett's conversion, it looked all over at 22-2. Perhaps Rovers eased off a bit at that point because a Colliers revival narrowed the gap to 22-12 with two converted tries by former Rovers centre Brian Wrigglesworth and big prop Colin Forsyth. The Robins were in no mood to let the game slip though, and tightened up their defence. With three minutes to go, Moore took Burwell's pass to round off a fine handing move and make it 25-12.

The Robins had won with a mixture of excellent teamwork, classy football and tough defence. Kellett, who had scarcely put a foot wrong, won the White Rose trophy as the man-of-the-match, although there were several other candidates in the side, in particular Burwell, who had an outstanding game.

> *Featherstone:* D. Kellett; V. Thomas, K. Greatorex, B. Wrigglesworth, G. Westwood; M. Smith, C. Dooler; M. Dixon (capt), M. Kosanovic, C. Forsyth, A. Morgan, S. Lyons, T. Smales. Subs not used: J. Bell, V. Farrar
>
> *Rovers:* C. Kellett; C. Young, A. Burwell, J. Moore, M. Blackmore; R. Millward, A. Bunting;

F. Fox, P. Flanagan, B. Tyson, W. Holliday, F.
Foster (capt), T. Major. Subs not used: D. Elliott,
E. Palmer
Referee: B. Baker (Horwich)
Attendance: 13,237 (£3,482)

At the end of the season, three regulars bowed out. Mike Blackmore, the powerful three-quarter from Barnstaple, retired after breaking his arm in March. Popular with the fans, Blackmore was a distinctive figure with his shock of black hair. He had played 190 games for the Robins and scored 96 tries, many of them with his familiar trade-mark dive. The final game against Wakefield saw the last appearances of props Frank Fox and Brian Tyson. Fox moved on to Castleford after playing exactly 100 games for Rovers whilst Tyson retired to concentrate on his family business.

Tyson, who won three Great Britain caps, played 231 games for the club in a little over six years. He was a whole-hearted performer in both the scrum and the loose, whose hero was Wigan's international prop Brian McTigue. Sadly, towards the end, Tyson got a bit of unfair barracking from a small section of the crowd who did not appreciate his importance to the team. He was neither the first nor the last Rovers' forward to suffer in this way. It is easy to appreciate the flair players, but there can be no success without hard work. 'I was a grafter,' says Tyson. 'I was always fit and just loved training and playing.'

Rovers were the league's top point scorers with 888 points comprising 178 tries and 177 goals, all club records for a season. They also had the best defensive record in the league for the first time. Whilst there was disappointment that they did not win a second trophy to stand alongside the Yorkshire Cup, it had been a brilliant season. The average attendance was 8,250 and although there were five gates in excess of

The Robins

10,000, there were four around the 5,000 mark. Even when following an entertaining and successful side, spectators choose their games. Despite all this, the Robins lost £3,750 over the year. Kellett and Elliott shared a benefit year and 17-year old former Craven Park Juniors second-rower Phil Lowe made his first team debut at home to Featherstone in March.

49 games

In 1967, the dominance of St George over the Australian domestic game ended when their 'never before and never again' run of eleven consecutive Sydney premierships was ended by Canterbury Bankstown, who beat them 12-11 in the preliminary final, whilst in Britain, the first professional matches took place on Sundays. It was a time of great sadness in the city of Hull when early in 1968 three trawlers, the *St Romanus, Kingston Peridot* and *Ross Cleveland,* disappeared in Icelandic waters, with only one of the 59 members of the crews surviving.

1967-68 was another excellent season for the Robins who played 49 games, including 26 at home, both club records. Although they slipped one league place to third, they retained the Yorkshire Cup and reached the Championship Final. There was also a magnificent win over the Australian tourists in one of the best games ever seen at Craven Park.

The one real disappointment was the first round exit at home to Featherstone Rovers in thick snow in the Challenge Cup. It was the first Sunday game played at Craven Park and it attracted the best home crowd of the season, 15,000. Due to Sunday trading laws, it was illegal to charge at the turnstiles and spectators had to buy a team-sheet that allowed them admittance. Rovers chose to play into the elements in the first half and turned around 7-0 down. The plan backfired because the worsening conditions negated the Robins' attacking style and they were unable to get back into the contest, losing 9-0.

In the league, after losing two of the first three games, the Robins were unbeaten in 17 league and cup matches between 28 August and 11 November, and only three further league games were lost before mid-March. At that point, the Robins were well in contention for top spot but a run of four defeats around Easter meant they had to be content with third place on points difference to Wakefield, who won their last game by a single point.

That run included a very disappointing 19-5 derby defeat at Craven Park and a double conceded to Bradford, for whom Terry Clawson impressed – a performance Rovers' board remembered later. League highlights included nine league doubles, a 15-9 Christmas Day success at the Boulevard where Flanagan's try was decisive and a very first win at Oldham's Watersheddings in 27 attempts.

The club officially switched on its' new floodlights, completed at a cost of £16,000, for the home league game with Wakefield Trinity on 29 September. Rovers entered the BBC2 Floodlit Trophy and won their first round game against Wakefield after a replay, before they lost at home to Warrington in the second. In the Yorkshire Cup, the Robins were drawn away from home in all three early rounds. Having disposed of York comfortably in the first, they beat Wakefield in a home replay, and won the semi-final at Dewsbury 21-0.

In the final at Headingley, the Airlie Birds awaited in a repeat of the 1920 final that saw the Robins earn their first silverware in the then Northern Union. On a damp and dismal autumn day, honours were even 5-5 at half-time and it looked as if Davidson's second half drop-goal was going to

be enough to take the trophy back to the Boulevard, until
Rovers came up with a brilliant handling move with just six
minutes to go. Flanagan started the move on the 25-yard line
and Elliott, Holliday and Major combined before Burwell
crossed in the corner for the try that retained the trophy by a
single point, 8-7.

The end-of-season Championship play-offs saw the
team regain its form after the Easter dip. Straightforward
wins over Swinton and Leigh were followed by a tremendous
semi-final win over St Helens at Craven Park. Saints, who
had finished fourth, were certainly no mugs but the Robins
simply blew them away with a first half performance that
saw them romp into a 20-0 lead. In the second half, they eased
off a bit but they still recorded a comfortable 23-10 win to
reach their first Championship final since 1925. At the end of
this game, the Craven Park faithful gave legendary Saints
winger Tom van Vollenhoven a standing ovation on his
retirement from the sport.

Their opponents in the final were Wakefield, who
were seeking their first win over the Robins in seven attempts
that season; the most Rovers have played against any one
club in a single season, whilst the three drawn games at Belle
Vue are the only instance of three draws in one season against
the same opposition. The game was played at Headingley in
conditions that were perfect for Rovers' attacking style. The
first half was even at 5-5 but in the second half the bounce of
the ball just did not go their way and they went down 17-10.

Roger Millward had a brilliant season, playing in 42
of the 49 games and setting a new rugby league try-scoring
record for a stand-off with 38 touchdowns. He had Burwell
to thank for the try that broke the previous record as the
centre crossed the line himself against York, but passed to the
supporting Millward to give him the landmark. Moore was

ever-present, playing mostly at left-centre but also covering at full-back, wing and number six. The hard-tackling former boxer, Colin Cooper came in at scrum-half when Bunting was injured and retained his place. There was only one major signing, that of Huddersfield's Yorkshire county centre Paul Longstaff for £7,000 in December. He had a tough baptism, making his Rovers' debut in the Christmas Day derby win at the Boulevard. Long-serving full-back Cyril Kellett left in November and went to play for his home town club, Featherstone.

Another stalwart, David Elliott, lost his place in November and, seeing his opportunities further diminished by the arrival of Longstaff, joined York in January. Elliott, who made his debut in October 1956, made 295 appearances at centre and in both half-back positions, scoring 60 tries. Not the flashiest of the backs the club had at the time, he was nonetheless a versatile and reliable member of the first team squad, who always did a good job wherever he played.

In the forwards, then Great Britain captain Bill Holliday moved to the front row in place of the departed Fox, enjoying an uninterrupted run until returning to the second row after the disastrous Featherstone cup-tie. Holliday took over the kicking duties following Kellett's departure, landing 79 goals.

John Taylor had returned to the club from Castleford in the exchange deal that saw Fox move in the opposite direction and played at prop until getting injured in the Australia game. Mennell then seized his chance to claim a regular place and stayed there for the remainder of the season. Lowe also claimed a regular place and started to make a big reputation as a fast and powerful runner.

With an average home crowd of 9,545 and an exciting and successful side containing a good mix of experience, ability and graft, it seemed that the club was in a good position to kick on and bring more silverware to Craven Park. However, it was not to be, and the next few years were a rollercoaster ride.

Tour match, Craven Park, Hull, 7 October 1967
Hull Kingston Rovers 27-15 Australia

Sport survives on widely differing opinions but amongst those fortunate enough to witness this game there is widespread agreement that it was one of Rovers' best-ever performances.

The Robins fielded their strongest possible side, missing only the injured Terry Major and Frank Foster. They started brightly but John Taylor broke his wrist whilst driving powerfully into the tourists defence in the early minutes and had to go off. Undeterred, Rovers continued to attack and when King failed to deal with a loose ball, Roger Millward kicked through to score. Cyril Kellett converted and the Robins were on their way. They continued to press but when the tourists launched their first attack, McDonald scored a try that he converted himself. After McDonald missed a penalty chance to put the visitors ahead, Rovers came back strongly with Bill Holliday to the fore. Using their long kicking game to good effect, Australia created a try-scoring chance that went begging due to a forward pass but McDonald was there to seize on a loose ball and score when a Rovers' move broke down. Kellett's penalty goal pulled it back to 10-7 with 15 minutes of the first half to go. Rovers then put pressure on the tourists' line and it took a thunderous tackle by Sattler and a bad bounce from Millward's kick to keep the Robins at bay. Australia attacked again and only good defence kept the Rovers' line intact. From a penalty, Holliday found touch near the line and followed up by kicking a smart drop-goal to narrow the visitors' lead to one point. Kellett had to be on top form to stop Gleeson and referee Hunt angered the home crowd when he called back Burwell who was clear, and gave Rovers a penalty for offside. The crowd's disapproval quickly turned to rapturous applause as Millward backed up Phil Lowe's break and made a weaving run before firing out a bullet pass to Burwell who crossed in the corner before turning towards the posts to make Kellett's conversion easier. It was 14-10 to the Robins after a breathless forty minutes.

In the second half, Rovers continued where they had left off and Burwell was held on the line. It was end-to-end and when Australia broke, Holliday's powerful run led the Robins' response. With 20 minutes to go, Gleeson's kick gave the tourists field position and he combined with Jones to send in McDonald for a converted try. Australia led 15-14 and McDonald had scored all their points. However, Rovers finished strongly. After another great Holliday run, Millward sidestepped and swerved his way through the visitors' defence to score near the posts and Kellett's conversion edged the Robins 19-15 ahead. Millward was obstructed from following up his own kick when he might have scored and Kellett missed the ensuing penalty. Australia came back strongly again through Goldspink but Rovers intercepted and Holliday charged up field once more, this time linking with John Hickson, Brian Mennell and Johnny Moore, the latter shrugging off two defenders to score. Kellett's conversion attempt hit the upright. With five minutes to go, Millward took the ball almost out of the hands of Raper and raced 45 yards for his hat-trick try, Kellett kicking the conversion to seal a memorable win. There was still time for Gleeson to break away again but Rovers brought him down a yard short.

It was a marvellous team performance by the Robins. In the forwards, Holliday was outstanding and Mennell played the match of his career, whilst in the backs Millward was at his imperious best, closely followed by Burwell. At the after-match reception, tourists' skipper Johnny Raper said: 'This is the best game of football that I have played in, in my four tours of Britain …. this is the finest English club side I have played against.'

> *Rovers: C. Kellett; C. Young, J. Moore (capt), D. Elliott, A. Burwell; R. Millward, C. Cooper; W. Holliday, P. Flanagan, J. Taylor (G. Young), B. Mennell, J. Hickson, P. Lowe. Sub not used: P. Coupland*
> *Australia: L. Johns; J. King, J. Greaves, J. McDonald, L. Hanigan; K. Junee, J. Gleeson: P. Gallagher, N. Gallagher, J. Sattler, K. Goldspink, E. Rassmussen, J. Raper (capt).*
> *Referee: H.G. Hunt (Prestbury)*
> *Attendance: 15,000*

The Greats – No 15
Cyril Kellett - *see Hull KR legends gallery*

Born in the Featherstone area in April 1937, Cyril Kellett joined Rovers at the age of 19 on 28 September 1956 from the Willow Park junior club. In his amateur days, Kellett was a stand-off and he made his debut for Rovers in that position at Salford in November that year. It was not a particularly distinguished start and nothing in his three half-back appearances that season suggested that he would ultimately find a place amongst Rovers' greatest players.

Playing at right-centre against Halifax in September 1957, he kicked his first goals for the club, scored a try for good measure and went on to play 18 matches in that position during the season. However, the arrival of experienced centres Bill Riley and Joe Mageen meant that such opportunities would be limited and Kellett got his first chance in the problem full-back position at Halifax on 18 January 1958. From then onwards, he was Rovers' regular custodian. In his second full season, he kicked 128 goals to beat Bunker Carmichael's 47-year old club record. He broke his own record in 1962-63 and again in 1966-67 when he finished with 145, passing the 100 mark on seven occasions for Rovers. He was the first Rovers player to kick 100 goals before Christmas in 1962-63 and was rugby league's top goal-kicker with 150 in 1964-65.

Kellett played his last game at home to Leeds on 17 November 1967 and left the Robins to join his home town club. His goal-kicking exploits continued there, notably with eight goals at Wembley to help Featherstone win the 1973 Challenge Cup final.

Although not the fastest full-back, Kellett read the game well and had a very good positional sense; he timed his tackles brilliantly and was safe under the high ball. However, it was as a goal-kicker that he really excelled. In 382 games he kicked a remarkable 1,194 goals – easily then a club record – and scored 35 tries. His total of 2,493 points for Rovers was nearly a thousand more than Laurie Osborne's previous career best. 'He was a very reliable full-back, with excellent timing,' says Alan Burwell. 'Very similar to Arthur Keegan at Hull FC.'

After retiring at Featherstone in the summer of 1974 with 3,686 career points, Kellett turned his hand to coaching and had a spell as 'A' team coach at Odsal in the late 1970s. His son Brian played for Featherstone and Mansfield in the 1980s. Sadly, Kellett died at the age of just 55 in March 1993.

*****

8. Turbulent Times

1968-1977

AFTER a sustained period of progress on the field, the Robins entered an unsettled and inconsistent phase, before putting down the foundations for their most successful-ever era.

Anti-climax

In 1968 civil rights campaigner Martin Luther King was assassinated in Memphis, Tennessee, the right-wing MP Enoch Powell gave his controversial 'Rivers of Blood' immigration speech and British Railways took its last steam engines out of service – some ending up in the Hull scrapyard of the Draper family, long connected with the Robins. In sport, Manchester United became the first English club to win football's European Cup and Colin Cowdrey the first cricketer to play in 100 Test matches.

In East Hull, Hull Kingston Rovers failed to live up

to the expectations raised during the previous two seasons. Inconsistent adequately sums up their 1968-69 season. They produced were some good performances and doubles were gained over very good sides like Castleford, Wakefield and Hull FC but there were some very poor away performances, a particularly disappointing losing run in January and first round defeats in the Challenge Cup and Championship. The Robins had to settle for tenth place in the league.

Bill Holliday left to join Swinton in September. In his three-and-a-half years at the club, he probably played the best football of his career, becoming the first serving Rovers' player to captain Great Britain. He appeared in 145 games for the Robins, scoring 18 tries and kicking 139 goals. Holliday's fellow Cumbrian, Foster, moved to Bradford in a part-exchange deal that brought centre Geoff Wriglesworth and forward Terry Clawson to Craven Park at the end of October, with Rovers paying a £5,000 cash adjustment. On Foster's departure, the club captaincy passed to Johnny Moore.

The scrum-half position had been a problem since Arthur Bunting had passed his prime and the directors sought to address this with the £6,000 signing of Carl Dooler from Featherstone Rovers in January. Unfortunately, although he was a very talented player, injuries dogged him and he managed only 18 appearances for the club. At the same time, the Robins signed former Great Britain international centre Peter Small from Castleford for £3,000. The prevalent view was that Rovers had been influenced to sign him after his performances against them in the 1966 Challenge Cup ties. In any event, he was by then in the latter stages of his career and never really realised Rovers' hopes of him.

The big money capture, Paul Longstaff, also disappointed. Signed as a centre, he had ended the previous season on the wing and in 1968-69, he lost his place after the opening three games. He subsequently absented himself from training, later explaining that he was unable to play due to his new job. Returning to the club in November, he was transfer-listed at £8,000. Longstaff regained his place in the side in December but played only five more games before he was left out and then disappeared again.

There was some good news for the fans in October when the Australian test legend Artie Beetson arrived on a short-term contract from Balmain. Beetson, a strong personality on and off the field, quickly became a favourite at Craven Park. Supporter Steve Myers recalls a home game with Huddersfield when a couple of the visiting forwards seemed bent on provoking him. 'He took it for a while, then when he'd had enough, he took them both on, sorted them out and didn't wait for the ref to send him off.'

Disaster struck, however, when Beetson broke his leg in what was to be the very last Christmas Day derby game, won 9-0 by Rovers at Craven Park. Despite the bravest of attempts to play on after the injury, Beetson had to bow to the inevitable and was replaced by fellow Australian Jim Hall. The supporters did not see Beetson in a Rovers jersey again and the Tigers were unhappy to see their star man return home incapacitated.

The Greats – No 16
Frank Foster - *see Hull KR legends gallery*

There have been many players that played more games for Rovers than Frank Foster but few have gained such a formidable reputation in such a relatively short time.

Born in Cockermouth in 1940, he was an integral part of a tough Workington Town pack in their Western Division title-winning side of 1962. When they enquired about Foster's availability at the beginning of 1965, the Robins were told that

233

he did not want to live in Hull and not to waste their time. Undeterred, Wilf Spaven and his vice-chairman Ron Chester made the journey to Cumberland and persuaded Foster to change his mind. After signing for the Robins that January, he made his debut in the second row in the disastrous first round Challenge Cup defeat to Batley on 6 February 1965.

But the Robins had acquired one of the toughest men in the game. Foster made an indelible impression, not just on those who played with him and against him but also on those who watched from the terraces. It was clear that some opposition players were notable by their absence when his name was on the teamsheet. A hard and uncompromising man, he was respected and feared in equal measure.

GB World Cup winner and now pundit Mike 'Stevo' Stephenson remembers Foster as the toughest player he encountered, an opinion shared by Phil Lowe, who recalls Foster looking after him as a young player. In his second game for Rovers, at Bradford, an opposing forward punched the 17-year old Lowe in the tackle. Foster immediately had a word. 'Cut it out, he's only a young 'un,' he said, but the Bradford man unwisely gave Foster a few verbals back. 'Five minutes later there was a fracas,' says Lowe, 'and this forward was lying on the ground spark out. He had to be carried off.'

When the Robins signed diminutive Roger Millward in 1966, Foster made it his personal responsibility to give the little man the protection he deserved. He did not discriminate in his approach either, and Mike Spivey tells of at least one Rovers' player who would watch carefully to see which side Foster was on in training games and quickly ensure that he was on the same one. Kelvin Hannath remembers: 'His huge hands and crushing handshake.' Johnny Whiteley termed him as not only a hard nugget and a destroyer, but also: 'A very good, tenacious player who motivated his team.'

Foster was not just a hard man, he was very good ball-handler and kicker too, an outstanding all-round back-row forward who was good enough to be picked by Great Britain, even if his international career never really blossomed. A strong personality, he was a natural leader who took over as club captain when Poole left in September 1965. According to Roger Millward: 'You always did what Frank said but he was a hell of a footballer who didn't get the recognition he deserved.'

Foster made 130 appearances for the Robins, his final game being at home to Hunslet on 25 October 1968. He subsequently played with Bradford, Barrow and Oldham and before a 10-year stint as coach of Barrow between 1973 and 1983, where it was rumoured that he was sacked several times but no-one dared tell him. He also coached Whitehaven for a couple of seasons but he is now retired and living back in Barrow.

The same side started two consecutive matches only four times during the season and 35 players played in the 39 games. Comfortably the most regular performers were Moore and Lowe, who missed only one match each. Moore ended a run of 102 consecutive appearances when he was injured in the Good Friday win at the Boulevard and was left on the bench for the Halifax game on Easter Monday as a precautionary measure.

Attendances, which were between eight and nine thousand for the first three matches soon dropped off and less than five thousand watched the last five games. The club lost £1,442 on the season.

For the 1969-70 season, the RFL changed the substitutes rule again, Clubs could now use two substitutes at any time and for any reason. At Rovers, long-serving secretary Cyril Williams retired and was replaced by Cumbrian-born accountant Ron Turner, who was chosen from around 50 applicants. For Turner, who was a frequent rugby league spectator, it was a dream job and he was to serve the Robins loyally for 33 years.

The Robins

The season started under a bit of a cloud for the Robins when, after a hammering at home to the Black and Whites in a pre-season friendly, Millward said that he would not play for the club again. He said he had taken a lot of punishment over the previous year behind Rovers' pack, and that the performance against Hull FC had been the last straw. It is impossible not to make the link between Millward's criticisms of the forwards and the departure of Foster. Fortunately, after talks with chairman Spaven, Millward settled his differences, and played in all but seven games during the season.

There was a significant improvement in the Robins' form after the beginning of December and only six more games were lost, two of these being cup-ties. They finished fifth in the league, won at Wigan for the first time since 1929 and reached the semi-finals of two cup competitions and the Championship play-offs. However, there was no derby success, Jim Macklin's late drop-goal settled a try-less game at the Boulevard on 27 December and the Robins fought back from a 10-2 deficit to draw 10-10 at Craven Park.

A run to the semi-final of the Challenge Cup featured wins at Wakefield and at home to Swinton and Leeds, the latter courtesy of a try by Wriglesworth that was the result of a well-worked move. The Robins went to Headingley for the semi-final in good heart having completed a league double over their opponents, Wigan, and with five consecutive wins under their belts. However, on a miserable wet day they never really got going despite taking an early 3-2 lead through Phil Coupland's try, and Wigan's forwards dominated. They built a 14-3 lead before referee Davies, in charge of a fifth unsuccessful Rovers' cup semi-final, gave the Robins a lifeline when he awarded a penalty try after an obstruction on Wriglesworth. Millward's conversion cut the gap to six points but the Robins' defence cracked again and they lost 19-8.

In the Championship play-offs, Rovers played some of their best football of the season to see off Bradford and Salford in the first two rounds but the trip to Headingley for the semi-final, played in perfect conditions this time, turned into a nightmare with Leeds romping to a 47-5 win. Without four of their best defenders in Moore, Millward, Cooper and Gordon Young, it was the Robins' heaviest defeat since January 1961, made worse by the fact that Leeds played with 12 men for nearly all the second half, after Watson had been sent off for a late tackle on Brian Brook.

Locally-born full-back Ian Markham, who had made his debut the previous season, came in for the second game and did not miss a match thereafter. Stephenson, who preferred to play at half-back, was the regular right-winger with Coupland on the left. Burwell emigrated to Australia in November and Canterbury-Bankstown snapped him up, his departure meaning the regular centre pairing was Moore and Wriglesworth. Millward and Cooper formed the half-back partnership. Millward took over the captaincy relinquished by Moore in November and finished top of the try-scoring and goal-kicking charts with 21 and 99 respectively.

Clawson and Flanagan made up the front row with Cliff Wallis until December, when the former Hull and East Riding RUFC prop, Steve Wiley, took over as the regular number ten. Rovers switched Wallis to loose-forward to give him more opportunity to use his ball-handling skills and, along with Markham, he made the most appearances with 45. At the same time, strong-tackling Gordon Young, who had started the season at loose-forward, replaced Small as Lowe's regular second-row partner. Another young second-row forward, Paul Rose, made his first team debut in September at the age of 16 years and nine months – the youngest player to play for the first team since they joined the NU in 1897.

International winger Chris Young made his final appearance in August and joined York. Possessing genuine pace and a safe pair of hands, many believed that he was second only to Graham Paul as the club's best right-winger since the war. Young scored 85 tries in 164 games for Rovers. Major, Small and Wriglesworth all made their last games in the final match at Leeds.

Geoff Wriglesworth, who had enjoyed an excellent season, found that his farm commitments at Dunnington made travelling increasingly difficult for him and although Rovers did not want to lose him, they allowed him to join York. He won international honours whilst with Leeds and was a tough-tackling, no-nonsense centre who had stiffened up the three-quarter line. Terry Major, who first played for Rovers in November 1959, was originally a centre but moved into the back row in 1965-66 and loose-forward was probably his best position. A one-club man who achieved Yorkshire county honours, he played 274 games for the club, scoring 52 tries.

In January 1970, the repurchase of Craven Park was finalised at a cost of £65,000. They also took over the greyhound operation which became a subsidiary of the parent company, Hull Kingston Rovers RFC. The directors sold the land earmarked for the new ground at Winchester Avenue to Stepney Homes for £22,000, offsetting this against the Craven Park purchase, with a further sizeable chunk coming from the Development Fund.

Millward, Flanagan and Lowe were picked for the Great Britain tour of Australasia with Hull FC's Johnny Whiteley as coach and the outstanding Millward played a starring role in what remains Britain's last Ashes series win over Australia.

New leadership

In August 1970, after 13 seasons as coach, Hutton took on a new role as the club's General Manager, with Johnny Whiteley joining as the new coach. Hutton's new role was a direct consequence of the club now owning the stadium and having the responsibility for its running. At the same time, Arthur Bunting took over from Coverdale as 'A' team coach.

Whiteley had a difficult start. Millward again requested a transfer at the start of the season. He emphasised that he had no grouse with the club but he now had to work shifts at the colliery, which made travelling from the West Riding very difficult. The club turned down the request and Millward submitted another. Then, in the fourth league game, at home to Warrington, he sustained a broken leg that was to put him out until February.

The playing strength was nowhere near what it had been three years earlier and Whiteley's resources were dangerously thin. Injuries had sidelined second-rowers Lowe and Young and full-back Markham, and Rovers had not adequately replaced centre Wriglesworth. However, until the derby game on Boxing Day, the Robins managed to win all their home matches and with an away win at Barrow, in which the young second-rower Rose was outstanding, they comfortably sustained a position in the top half of the table. After that, Rovers' form was very patchy and only wins in the last two games secured a top half finish.

It was the first time in ten years that Hull FC had finished above the Robins. They completed a league double as well as knocking Rovers out of the Yorkshire Cup in the first round. The Robins gained a small amount of revenge with a second round victory in the Floodlit Trophy, a feisty game that saw Cooper and Flanagan dismissed in the first half. Leeds then beat the Robins comfortably in the semi-final. For the Challenge Cup first round trip to Keighley, the return of Millward and the signing of former Airlie Bird loose-forward Joe Brown boosted Rovers hopes. Nevertheless, despite Millward's try and Brown's drop-goal, the Robins only drew 9-9 and in the replay Keighley full-back Brian Jefferson dumped them out of the competition with an immaculate kicking display. They suffered a similar fate in the Championship play-off at Leigh, when despite Coupland scoring the only try of the game, the home side won thanks to five penalty goals from Stuart Ferguson.

After Markham's early injury, Coupland took over at full-back and along with Moore missed only two games. Millward's injury restricted him to 12 games and Clawson took over the goal-kicking, becoming only the third Rovers player to kick over 100 goals in a season. Unfortunately though, after an excellent 1969-70 season, Clawson spent much of the time in dispute with the club about his request for a transfer back to the West Riding and his performances dipped. Lowe returned to action in October but a further injury in February put him out for the remainder of the season. Paul Daley arrived from Bradford in exchange for Small and replaced Cooper at scrum-half at the start of December. Longstaff returned to the club and played in the last nine games.

Millward asked to come off the transfer list whilst recovering from his broken leg, recording his appreciation of the way the club had looked after him during his injury, but Flanagan joined his front-row colleague Clawson on the list for a spell during the season. Another front-rower, the reluctant Wembley hero Brian Mennell, played his last game at home to Bradford in September due to the impact of injuries on his family business commitments.

Northern RL, Craven Park, Hull, 12 February 1971
Hull Kingston Rovers 14-9 Wigan

This Friday evening visit of league-leaders Wigan, defending an all-time rugby league record of 31 successive league wins, was arguably the best game seen at Craven Park since the visit of the Australian tourists in 1967. The Hull Daily Mail *reporter said that the game '...was more than a glorious triumph for Rovers, it was a triumph for the game as a spectacle. For this stirring end-to-end battle held the 5,767 fans enthralled from first whistle to last, and after the drab fare served up on so many occasions this year, it was like a breath of spring.'*

After a hard-fought first half, Wigan led 7-4 thanks to a try from their Great Britain back-row forward Laughton whilst Terry Clawson's two penalty goals kept Rovers in the hunt. However, minutes into the second half, Johnny Moore got his winger Geoff Druery away down the right hand flank. The Aussie beat two men for pace and cut inside full-back Tyrer, before winger Jones managed to race across from the opposite flank to pull him down. As he fell in the tackle, Druery managed to release an overhead pass to scrum-half Paul Daley who scored by the posts and Clawson's conversion gave Rovers a 9-7 lead. Wigan were not going to end their winning run without a fight and mounted a series of fierce assaults on Rovers' line. Just as the Robins seemed to have weathered the storm, Wigan's influential second-rower Ashurst, whose kicking in open play had again caused the Robins problems, dropped a magnificent goal from 45 yards to bring Wigan level with five minutes to go. At this stage, Wigan were favourites to snatch the game but Rovers went on the attack. After the visitors halted Phil Coupland's fine break in sight of the line, John Millington drove in hard to the right and Rovers switched the ball quickly to the left where Phil Lowe drew the defence and sent Ian Markham over for a last gasp match-winning try. Clawson added his fourth goal from four attempts before referee Naughton drew the game to a close.

It had been a wonderful team performance. Man-of-the-match Coupland was outstanding in both attack and defence, half-backs Millward and Daley had teased the Wigan defence with their half-breaks and shrewd kicks, and Millington, Lowe and Colin Cooper had led the forwards in returning the fire of the Wigan pack with interest.

> *Rovers: P. Coupland; G. Druery, J. Moore, I. Markham, M. Rooms; R. Millward (capt), P. Daley; T. Clawson, P. Flanagan, J. Millington, P. Lowe, E. Palmer, C. Cooper. Subs not used: D. Wainwright, P. Rose*
> *Wigan: C. Tyrer; K. Jones, W. Francis, K. O'Loughlin, S. Wright (W. Ayres): P. Rowe, F. Parr; B. Hogan, C. Clarke, G. Fletcher, D. Robinson, W. Ashurst, D. Laughton (capt). Sub not used: R. Burdell*
> *Referee: M.J. Naughton (Widnes)*
> *Attendance: 5,767 (£1,110)*

Three notable debuts were those of young stand-off Steve Hartley, centre David Hall and prop-forward John Millington. The trio were to have long careers at the club. They had come up through the 'A' team, playing alongside the likes of Ray Norrie and Mike Spivey. Millington recalls: 'It was very hard. Everyone was fighting for first team places and no one would pass to you – once they got the ball they kept it.'

Spivey has many memories of his 'A' team career. When Halifax turned up three men short on one occasion, Spivey was one of two players loaned to the visitors. Early on, he was crunched in a fearsome tackle by Millington. 'Steady on, John, we're mates.' He told his team-mate. 'Wrong f...ing shirt,' growled Millington. 'I spent the rest of the game trying to avoid him,' says Spivey. He also recalls the primitive dressing rooms at Batley and a very cold night in Leeds. 'A young Australian, Wayne Gapps, literally stepped off the plane and was pitched into a night match at Headingley. It was absolutely freezing, the poor lad ended up with hypothermia.' Spivey's first team career was brief, two substitute appearances a year apart: 'And on the second one, at Castleford, I was knocked out,' he notes.

The summer of 1971 saw peace protests against the war in Vietnam spread across the USA. There was further escalation of the Northern Ireland troubles, with 12,500 troops deployed in the province by August. The controversial British film *Sunday Bloody Sunday* was released, and George Harrison had spent 17 weeks in the charts with 'My Sweet Lord'.

From 1971-72, the earlier rounds of the county cup competitions were regularly played in August as curtain-raisers to the season, allowing the introduction of a new knock-out competition for all clubs, initially known as the John Player No 6 trophy. In the absence of Leeds, who declined to take part in the competition, Rovers reached the final of the Yorkshire Cup against Castleford at Belle Vue, Wakefield. The celebrations after the 25-6 semi-final win over Bramley at Craven Park had near-disastrous consequences as Clawson had an accident on the way home to the West Riding and his injuries put him out for a month. Millington took his place in the final, which was an exciting if low-scoring affair, and a solid team performance resulted in an 11-7 win that brought the trophy back to Craven Park for the third time in six years. Longstaff scored Rovers' only try, Millward kicked four goals and full-back Ian Markham won the White Rose Trophy.

Another early season highlight was the Robins' 12-10 win over the New Zealand tourists. Tour games were played under international rules, under which the value of a drop-goal was then only one point, it was three more seasons before the RFL incorporated this change into the domestic game. The honour of scoring Rovers' first one-point drop-goal thus fell to Stephenson, playing on the wing that day. It was Rovers only score of the second half, during which they withstood a fight-back from the tourists, who had trailed 11-5 at half-time.

Rovers had a fine 17-14 home win over Salford in their first John Player trophy game but were beaten 18-11 at home by a Bill Ashurst-inspired Wigan in the second round, the big second-rower scoring all Wigan's points with six goals and two tries. A 'dropped ball' incident resulted in a redraw of the first round of the Challenge Cup which gave the Robins a visit to the Boulevard. This was the first of five meetings with the Airlie Birds in the competition in nine seasons and ended in a disappointing 7-5 defeat.

In mid-February, with 15 league wins from 24 games, coach Johnny Whiteley left the club. He had been outspoken in his criticism of the club's selection system. As coach he had very little say in the team chosen but he was judged on its performance. Whiteley remembers one occasion when he congratulated forward Cliff Wallis on his display at the end of one game, only for the board to drop him for the following week. 'I had to lie and say that he'd been left out because his replacement was better and I didn't like doing that,' Whiteley acknowledges. Matters came to a head early in 1972, when Whiteley resigned his international coaching role for personal reasons. The board were unhappy about it as they believed there was prestige in having the current Great Britain coach at the club. There was an exchange of words after which it was impossible for Whiteley to continue.

There had always been those within the club hierarchy who did not like Whiteley's strong Hull FC background, and no longer being the Great Britain coach would have further weakened his position. Chairman Spaven recorded his thanks to Whiteley, saying that he was sorry that things had not worked out as anticipated. Rovers promoted 'A' team coach Arthur Bunting on a trial basis, with Daley taking the 'A' team role. Whilst at the club, Whiteley did not have the strongest squad to work with and injuries to key players hampered him further. Nonetheless, he had won a trophy and there were some promising signs for the future.

Bunting's first game was a 5-2 home win over St Helens that had some excellent tackling to compensate for a lack of possession. However, Rovers won only two of the season's remaining ten matches and the final league position of 14th was one place lower than the previous season.

Markham, who appeared in all 43 matches, reclaimed the full-back position whilst Coupland and George Kirkpatrick, a new arrival from Sheffield RUFC, were the regular centres. Another newcomer, former Redcar RUFC flyer, Ged Dunn, claimed a regular spot on the left wing in January. Another scrum-half signing from Featherstone, Terry Hudson, took over from Daley in October.

Terry Clawson moved to Leeds in November. Rovers were the third of the nine clubs he served in his 23-year career. He was a talented ball-handling forward and a great dressing room character who had overcome tuberculosis earlier in his career. In his autobiography *All the Wrong Moves*, Clawson says: 'I was sad to be leaving Hull KR. I'd had some terrific times over on Humberside with some terrific mates …' But his self-confessed liking for a drink or two after the game and the travelling to and from Featherstone did not mix. Understandably, the unfortunate incident after the Yorkshire Cup semi-final caused the club, in Clawson's own words, to 'call time on his Rovers career,' after 111 games. He later landed two goals that helped Great Britain win the World Cup against Australia in 1972.

Clawson's departure left the Robins with a shortage of experience in the front row that they attempted to address by signing former Hull FC veteran Jim Neale in January. Millington had at least benefitted from the situation with a good long run in the team. A promising local hooker, David Heslop, made his debut in February, displacing Flanagan for the remainder of the season.

In addition to Clawson, Eric Palmer and Colin Cooper both played their last games for the club. Palmer, who had been in the second row at Wembley in 1964, perhaps never fully realised his potential and had a short spell at Keighley before returning to Craven Park in 1970. Cooper made 150 appearances at scum-half and loose-forward. His main strengths were his commitment, reliability and robust tackling, the latter of which made him somewhat unpopular with opposing fans. After leaving Craven Park, he played a handful of games for the Airlie Birds. Cliff Wallis also departed for a spell at Castleford in the New Year.

At the end of the season, the hierarchy confirmed Bunting and Daley in their respective coaching roles and made three signings for the forthcoming season. Prop-forward Derek 'Sammy' Windmill joined from Featherstone as a replacement for Clawson and the Leeds pair of prop Ted Barnard and utility man Dave Hick arrived.

1972-73 was the season when the four-tackle rule increased to six, although for a further 11 seasons the game still restarted with a scrum rather than a turnover on the last. In addition, to address concerns about the variable amounts of injury time allowed by referees, the RFL introduced independent timekeepers at games with the now-familiar sound of the hooter to signal the end of each half.

After the disappointing end to the previous one, hopes for the new season were higher, yet home attendances fluctuated between a low of 1,794 and a high of 4,331 for the derby on Boxing Day. However, the final league position of 10th out of 30 was more than respectable and in spells Rovers played some very good rugby, scoring a then club record 196 tries.

Probably the best performance was reserved for high-flying Leeds, who were beaten 26-16 at Craven Park in January, thanks to a first half try hat-trick by Kirkpatrick. Whilst both derby games resulted in wins to the home side by four points, the Airlie Birds sank to 25th place in the league in what was to be the final single division table.

The Robins reached the John Player semi-final, in which they scored three tries to one and were decidedly unlucky to lose 15-13 to Salford at Craven Park. The only instance of a first-team game at the old stadium being abandoned due to the weather occurred in the previous round, when a Friday night game against Swinton was ended by thick fog after 21 minutes. After a second round Challenge Cup defeat in the mud at Odsal, the season ended brightly, with Rovers winning six of the last seven league games.

Full-back Markham was injured in the first match against Halifax and was unable to regain his place, subsequently retiring from the game after refusing to play in the 'A' team. By coincidence, just over a month later, Wainwright was also injured whilst playing at full-back position and did not appear again. An exciting attacking full-back from the Dapto club in Australia, Bob Smithies, arrived for a short spell in October and impressed enough for him to be asked to return the following season. Longstaff had his best season, making 28 appearances, including eight at stand-off in Millward's absence through injury.

None of the three close season signings proved a great

success. Only Windmill won a regular place and missed only five games. Neale retired at the end of the season but in his short Rovers career he made a big impression with fellow players and supporters alike. He was a rugged Cumbrian who Lowe called a 'silent assassin' and adds: 'He was a very good all-round forward and a good man to have around when the going got tough.'

In the second row, Lowe had a prolific season scoring 26 tries to beat Andy Sandham's club record for tries in a season by a forward. The signing of the former Hull FC ball-handling second-rower Terry Kirchin for £1,000 at the end of January proved only a short-term success as his job took him to London after he had made six appearances. In September, another former Airlie Bird, Joe Brown, who had made only 26 appearances in over two and half years, said that he was unable to settle at the club. He was transfer listed and then stayed away, as did Rose. The old stalwart, Moore, took over at loose-forward and remained there for most of the remainder of the season.

Unfortunate circumstances surrounded the Floodlit Trophy game at home to Leigh in October. Top referee Mick Naughton was indisposed and senior touch judge Fred Ellam had to stand in. Ellam's first half performance so incensed the visitors that their officials berated him at half time, when the Robins led 10-4. Unsurprisingly, the marginal calls in the second half went the visitors' way and Rovers went down to a 12-10 defeat. Sadly, still not satisfied, the visitors reported incompetence of the hapless substitute official to the RFL.

In December, the club donated the takings from the home league game against Bramley to the joint testimonial fund for Colin Cooper and Peter Flanagan. The parent company made a then record loss of £20,337 on the season. At this time, the players' pay was around £40 for a win.

Relegation

In 1973, Motorola produced the first hand-held mobile phone. Weighing 1.1kg, it had a talk time life of 30 minutes and took ten hours to recharge. The oil crisis, exacerbated by industrial action by the mineworkers and the high price of imported coal, led to severe power shortages in the UK. The beleaguered Heath government introduced energy-saving measures, culminating in the 'three day week' of early 1974. The main impact on sport was a national ban on the use of floodlights.

1973 also marked the formation of the British Amateur Rugby League Association (BARLA) – a single governing body to oversee the organisation and development of the amateur game. The Hull area has always been an amateur stronghold, with BOCM and Dockers dominating at that time, since when the likes of West Hull and Skirlaugh have enjoyed considerable success.

The season marked the lowest point in Rovers' fortunes since the mid-1950s. The RFL reintroduced a two-division structure that was to remain in place for the next 20 years. Their previous season's league position earned the Robins a place in the First Division but it was to be a long hard season. They were well beaten by the better teams and often struggled against the lesser ones. There were only 17 home games during the season, jointly with 1968-69 the fewest in any season at the old Craven Park stadium but, by some quirk, there were an unprecedented six in succession in November and December.

An early bad omen was an embarrassing 23-8 defeat at Batley in the Yorkshire Cup, after which Bunting remarked that not a single Batley player would have got into the Rovers team, but the opposition was more determined on the day. In an immediate response, an outstanding performance at home to a strong Warrington side six days later earned the Robins a 6-6 draw that did not do justice to their efforts. At that point, Rovers had five points from four league games, but there were only two further league wins before the end of the year.

Due to the floodlight ban, the BBC2 Trophy ties were played on Tuesday afternoons, and the recorded highlights shown on television in the evening. In one of these games, a second round tie against Leeds in November, Rovers produced another of their better showings of the season. Inspired by Millward and Rose, the Robins stormed back from an early deficit to level 10-10 at half-time. They then withstood all Leeds' second half attacks and the only score of the second half, a Millward penalty goal, earned them a memorable 12-10 victory. A crowd of only 1,343 watched the game, perhaps not surprisingly given that Hull City were playing at home to Liverpool in a cup-tie that same afternoon. Sadly, though, that was the only win in a nine-match run and when Widnes came to Craven Park for the semi-final two weeks later, the visitors' superior goal-kicking took them through.

Rovers lost seven successive league games in November and December and were in the relegation zone by the end of the year. The last of those was a 45-5 thumping at Castleford, in which former Robin Cliff Wallis tormented his old colleagues. They responded by bringing in experience in the shape of veteran prop Terry Ramshaw in early January but it was too little, too late and with only nine league wins the Robins were relegated with two games to play, ironically both of which were won comfortably away from home.

A 13-2 first round Challenge Cup win over Hull FC at the Boulevard, the season's only derby as the Airlie Birds were then in the Second Division, was followed by a narrow second round defeat at home to holders Featherstone.

For the Robins though, there was light amidst the

gloom. Paul Rose had returned to training during the close season, explaining that he had been saving to get married and could earn more money in his job than playing. He was outstanding, playing in 31 of the 38 matches and his form earned him a place on the 1974 Great Britain tour to Australia alongside his skipper, Millward. Another to step up in difficult circumstances was Millington. Given the number eight jersey in October, he retained it for much of the remainder of the season. Both he and Rose came of age that season and formed the cornerstone of the pack.

In November, Phil Lowe joined Australian club Manly. After much haggling between the clubs, the Sea Eagles agreed to pay a £15,000 fee for three seasons, after which either Lowe would return to Rovers, or they would pay a further £10,000 to keep him. Aussie Smithies returned to the club but broke his arm in his sixth match, ironically a 25-9 defeat against the Australian touring team, and did not play again that season. One of two other imports that season was loose-forward Allan Fitzgibbon from Dapto, the father of Australia international Craig, later of Hull FC.

The much-maligned Longstaff played his final game in a narrow defeat at Whitehaven at the end of March, moving to Castleford in an exchange deal that brought Cliff Wallis back to Craven Park. Whilst never fully justifying his £7,000 transfer fee, Longstaff overcame his early problems and gave loyal service over his last three seasons with Rovers, playing in all the back positions except scrum-half. In all, he made 127 appearances.

The long-serving Moore earned £3,000 from his benefit year and took over from Daley as 'A' team coach. Daley decided that he wanted to find a club nearer to his West Riding home and left. 'A' team stalwart Spivey, who was later an integral part of the Cawoods (West Hull) team that pulled off a remarkable John Player Trophy win at Halifax, described Daley as the best coach he ever worked with, and said that he would have run through a brick wall for him.

Former coach Colin Hutton was elected to the board, which had already taken steps to deflect some of the criticism that came its way after the poor season. They brought in four experienced players that they hoped would ensure promotion from the Second Division at the first attempt. Wakefield Trinity legend Neil Fox, albeit past his international glory days, true great Hull FC winger Clive Sullivan, former Leeds and Bradford Northern centre Bernard Watson and Wallis from Castleford all joined. These arrivals, along with internationals Millward and Rose, established players like Dunn, Kirkpatrick and Millington and young talents Hall, Hartley and former Rovers Juniors forward Roy Holdstock, made Rovers promotion favourites.

At the end of the season, Hull-born David Oxley, a Dover schoolmaster, beat 49 other applicants including red-hot favourite Bev Risman to replace the retiring Bill Fallowfield as the secretary of the RFL. Later in the summer, the Watergate scandal erupted in the USA. Republican President Richard Nixon became the only serving US President to resign from office, as a result of his party's complicity in a break-in at the Democratic party headquarters. In sport, the 'World Cup of total football' saw West Germany beat Holland 2-1 in the final, and Willie-John McBride's British Lions became the first visiting team to win a major Test series in South Africa.

For the 1974-75 season, the RFL reduced the value of the drop-goal to one point in all domestic football, bringing the British game into line with the international rules. Rovers' promotion quest got off to an unconvincing start with three defeats and a couple of very indifferent performances in the first seven games – a combination of seeking the right blend and some complacency against poorer teams.

However, the Robins were most impressive in the cup competitions. They progressed to the Yorkshire Cup final after a semi-final replay against Bradford. They should have won at the first attempt at Odsal, scoring four tries to two and holding the lead for most of the game, before conceding a late try that gave the home side a 16-all draw. The replay was George Kirkpatrick's finest hour in a Rovers' jersey. Playing on the wing, he gave Rovers the lead in the first half with a well-taken try. Then in the second, with the Robins desperately defending a 5-3 lead, he prevented a certain try when Northern had a three-man overlap. Twice Kirkpatrick somehow managed to pressure the man in possession into passing, before tackling the opposing winger into touch.

The final, against Wakefield at Headingley, was a classic, in which Rovers triumphed 16-13. The win seemed to galvanise the team and set them on an eight-match winning run that included a comprehensive 29-8 win over league-leaders Huddersfield at Fartown. The run was broken on a disastrous night at the Willows, where Rovers played in the semi-final of the Floodlit Trophy. First Millward had to pull out on the eve of the game, then the team bus broke down and the Robins had to run literally straight onto the field to face the free-scoring Salford backs. Flying winger Keith Fielding ran riot, scoring four tries as Rovers went down 27-10. Revenge was both sweet and immediate as Salford came to Craven Park for the third round of the John Player Trophy just four days later. The game was as good as over by half-time, with the Robins racing into a 17-2 half-time lead on their way to an excellent 25-17 win.

Before the semi-final, league derbies resumed after a season's break. Rovers won 19-12 at Craven Park on Boxing

Day and the sides drew 10-all at the Boulevard on New Year's
Day, when Rovers surrendered a 10-0 lead earned through tries
by wingers Dunn and Sullivan, the latter's first against his
former employers. Three days later, in the John Player semi-
final at Widnes, a combination of defensive errors and goal-
kicking misses cost Rovers dear. They more than matched the
First Division side in a highly-entertaining end-to-end
encounter in which the lead changed hands several times. Both
sides scored four tries but there was only one conversion from
the normally reliable Fox and Rovers lost 16-14.

After that, the Robins won seven more games in
succession, including another comprehensive win over
Huddersfield, before Wakefield took revenge for the
Yorkshire Cup defeat with a 27-10 third round Challenge Cup
success. A defeat at Workington then put paid to any hopes
of overhauling Huddersfield for top spot and Rovers had to
settle for second place.

That season, the two promoted clubs competed in the
end-of-season play-offs with the First Division clubs and the
Robins again beat Huddersfield convincingly, this time at
Fartown, before disposing of Keighley in the second round.
They lost 18-8 in the semi-final against Leeds at Headingley
but were far from disgraced in a game that could have gone
either way until the last few minutes.

It had been a brilliant season. Rovers achieved their
main objective of promotion and won 14 of a club record 20
cup-ties, 13 of which against First Division opposition, the
Robins winning nine and drawing one. In addition, they scored
a club record 221 tries and 1,001 points during the season and
Neil Fox created a new individual club point-scoring record
with 333, equalling Cyril Kellett's goals-in-a-season record of
145. It was a very impressive showing that gave them
confidence for the next season's First Division campaign.

Aussie full-back Smithies returned with a characteristic flourish, scoring a hat-trick of tries in the first match and played at full-back until returning home at the end of March. Back in his natural wing position after a season and a half at centre, Dunn played in every game and eclipsed Austin's club record with 42 tries in 45 games, including six in one match against New Hunslet – equalling Sandham's 60-year old club record for a league game. Sullivan recovered from early injuries to give Rovers a very potent scoring threat on both wings, scoring 19 tries in one glorious 14-match spell.

Hall and Watson were the usual centres, with juniors' three-quarter Mike Smith debuting in March. In early season, either Stephenson or Hudson partnered Millward at half-back but both played their last games for the club by December, Hudson moving to Wakefield and Stephenson the Boulevard. Millward then switched to scrum-half and Hartley got his first decent run in his natural position until the signing in February of Welsh rugby union half-back Glyn Turner again restricted his appearances. Millington missed only five games at prop and ex-Wakefield front-rower Steve Lyons took the open side when he arrived from Brisbane club Souths in November. Heslop ousted old campaigner Flanagan from the hooking role until the experienced Clive Dickinson arrived from Castleford in January. After playing a handful of games at centre, Fox moved into the pack, where he competed with Rose, Wallis and Brown for a back row spot.

Smithies, Flanagan, Wiley and Brown all played their last games for the club during the season. With 22 tries in his 55 games, Smithies was almost certainly the best attacking full-back to play for the Robins. When he went back to Dapto at the end of March, Rose joined him on a six-month contract.

After returning to the black during the previous season, the parent company lost £13,294 this time. That was largely due to the much-increased winning bonuses paid and a deficit on transfer activity. An interesting point was the increase in TV fees, prize money and advertising to over £22,000, within £4,000 of the total income from gate receipts and season passes.

Yorkshire Cup Final, Headingley, Leeds, 26 October 1974
Hull Kingston Rovers 16-13 Wakefield Trinity

This was a classic Yorkshire Cup final that was watched on BBC Grandstand by millions more than the 5,639 who defied a West Yorkshire bus strike to get to Headingley. It was Rovers' fourth Yorkshire Cup success in eight seasons and, full of good football and excitement right up to the final whistle, it was the best of them.

Wakefield were gifted a 5-0 lead after eight minutes thanks to a penalty by Crook and an interception try from Hegarty. The Robins hit back quickly, with good work by John Millington, Phil Coupland and Bernard Watson giving George Kirkpatrick an opening to score in the corner. Fox converted from the touchline to make it level. Rovers had the better of the exchanges for the rest of the half but the only score was another Crook penalty to give Wakefield a 7-5 lead at the break.

In an end-to-end second half, Fox's penalty levelled the scores at 7-7 before the Robins took control with tries by Watson and Ged Dunn, the latter from Roger Millward's superb pass. At 13-7 down, Wakefield came back when Smith scored the try of the match after a fine break by Morgan. Bob Smithies then sent in Watson to restore the Robins' six-point lead but Wakefield were still not finished and Bratt scored to ensure that the result was in doubt up to the end.

With Cliff Wallis leading the way, a powerful performance

by Rovers' forwards provided the foundations for the win. They repeatedly drove holes in the Wakefield defence and their strong tackling ensured they won the forward battle. Behind the pack, man-of-the-match Millward put in a faultless performance, providing the link with the lively three-quarters. At the back, full-back Smithies, playing one of his best games for the club, repeatedly caused Wakefield problems with his fast and elusive running. Whilst Rovers' tries were the result of fine teamwork and handling, Wakefield had to rely on individual efforts.

Rovers: *R. Smithies; C. Sullivan (G. Dunn), B. Watson, P. Coupland, G. Kirkpatrick; R. Millward (capt), M. Stephenson; J. Millington, D. Heslop, P. Rose, C. Wallis, N. Fox (I. Madley), J. Brown.* **Wakefield:** *L. Sheard; D. Smith, T. Crook, J. Hegarty, J. Archer; D. Topliss (capt), J. Bonnar; G. Ballantyne, R. Handscombe, R. Bratt, T. Skerrett, A. Tonks (N. Goodwin) (E. Holmes), A. Morgan.* *Referee: M.J. Naughton (Widnes)* *Attendance: 5,639 (£3,337)*

The Greats – No 17
Peter 'Flash' Flanagan - *see Hull KR legends gallery*

Yet another in the line of outstanding hookers to have played for the club, Peter Flanagan was born in East Hull on 22 January 1941. He played for Yorkshire Schools before signing for the Robins from Craven Street Youth Club on 9 May 1960.

At the time, Alvin Ackerley was Rovers' rake and Flanagan had to bide his time and learn from the old pro. Even after Ackerley's retirement, he had to fight off competition from Alan Holdstock and Alan Lockwood before getting his first sustained run in the side in 1963-64, by which time he had already played for Great Britain. Flanagan toured Australia three times, enjoying great popularity there. In total, he won 14 caps for Great Britain and five for England and played in the 1968 World Cup.

'Flash', as he was known, was not in the traditional mould of hookers of his time. Although a competent ball-winner, his strength was his flair and trickery in the loose, rather than the more physical side of the game. Possessing both a remarkable sidestep and turn of pace for a short and stocky man, he provided a dangerous threat in attack, and even played at scrum-half on one occasion. 'He was a terrific player in the loose,' says contemporary Brian Tyson. 'I remember him sidestepping the great Lewis Jones at Leeds once. He didn't like training though!' 'You could not coach him, he was a law unto himself. He had pace and anticipation, and was instinctive – a true free spirit who played without fear,' confirms Johnny Whiteley.

Dave Sherwood recalls a game against Bramley in 1965. 'From a play-the-ball deep in his own half, Flanagan dummied to pass, and scooted away down the touchline before slipping the ball to the supporting Mike Blackmore. As the full-back came across to tackle him, Blackmore turned to look for support. There was Flanagan, legs pumping and head bobbing, ready to take the return ball and scoot away to the posts to score. It was just typical of him.' Former director Chris Draper pinpoints his reading of the game. 'He knew just where the gaps would be.' 'Flash was one of the characters of the game, a real one-off,' adds Ron Turner. He was a distinctive figure with his quiff, sideburns and sunglasses and was noted for his impersonations of his idol, Elvis Presley. Along with his sense of humour, approachability and distinctive playing style, it made him a very popular figure on the rugby league scene.

He was an idol to the younger players like David Hall and John Millington, who often played alongside him in the 'A' team. 'He was great to us,' says Hall. 'Always helping and encouraging. I think he was the best rugby league player ever to be born in Hull.' Millington's verdict is succinct: 'He was my hero – a marvellous player and a match-winner.'

Flanagan had to see off further challenges from Peter Walker and Tony Crosby before competing with David Heslop during his last three years. After losing his place to Heslop in October 1974 he retired and went to play with Hull Dockers. Flanagan played in 415 games for Rovers, scoring 57 tries.

In 1975, Hull FC tempted him briefly out of retirement to cover for the injured Tony Duke. He helped the Black and Whites become the first Second Division club to reach the John Player final, in which he picked up a runners-up medal, finally hanging up his boots at the end of the 1975-76 season.

A docker for most of his working life, Flanagan became the licensee of the King William in the Old Town after retiring from rugby. Whilst there, he was injured in a road accident that affected him in his later life. He remained a familiar figure in the city for many years until he was found dead at his flat near the city centre on 8 January 2007.

Back in the top flight

Hull City supporters will remember the summer of 1975 for the sudden death of chairman and benefactor Harold Needler. The priority for the Robins in 1975-76 was to remain in the First Division, a target that they achieved comfortably despite an ever-increasing injury list, finishing in eighth place out of 16 clubs. They did not repeat the knock-out successes of the previous season, although again they reached the final of the Yorkshire Cup.

Five days before that final, the club was shaken by the abrupt departure of coach Arthur Bunting. He said that he had become increasingly frustrated by what he felt was undue interference from a minority of the board who, he said, wanted to run the show. In a dignified statement, Bunting claimed that he had no bitterness towards the club. He still felt that it was a great one and he had thoroughly enjoyed his 26 years there. However, he was concerned that his feelings would transmit themselves to the players, to the overall detriment of the club and its supporters, and felt that he had no alternative but to resign. After his departure, Millward and Moore took charge of the team for a few weeks.

Rovers again travelled to Headingley for the final but this time to play Leeds. For most of the game, Rovers were the better side with second-rowers Rose and Fox outstanding. Rose's powerful burst had sent Sullivan in for the opening score and Fox scored a brilliant individual try and added a penalty from five yards inside the Leeds half. Ironically though, the pair were ultimately the architects of the defeat. With Rovers holding an 11-9 lead in the last five minutes, Rose was penalised whilst in possession at a play-the-ball and in the ensuing Leeds attack, Fox missed his tackle on dangerous centre Dyl, who scored between the posts for Holmes to convert. Holmes then dropped a goal in the dying seconds and the Loiners had a victory they scarcely deserved.

In December, Rovers appointed former playing favourite Harry Poole to replace Bunting. Poole already had coaching experience with Castleford and had run some training sessions for the club's West Riding players two seasons before. Finally, Rovers addressed Whiteley's bugbear and Poole was their first coach who had full control over team selection. His arrival coincided with some indifferent mid-season form but gradually his ideas and influence began to take effect. A good run in April included a tremendous 17-9 win away to Featherstone that effectively put the Colliers out of the title race and gave hope for the future.

Overshadowing all else, however, was the sudden

death from a heart attack of chairman Wilf Spaven in March. No one had done more than Spaven to lead the club out of the doldrums in the 1950s and he was a widely respected figure throughout the game.

Unfortunate John Cunningham signed from Barrow in the pre-season for £8,000. He was a very talented ball-playing forward but sustained a serious knee injury in his fourth game and his stay at the club was bedevilled with time on the treatment table. Richard Wallace arrived from York in September to fill the full-back vacancy left by Smithies. Sullivan missed only one game and was the leading try-scorer for the only time whilst at Rovers. The arrival of Poole ignited Hartley's career and he ousted Turner to establish himself at stand-off whilst Millward played exclusively at scrum-half. In the front-row, Millington retained his spot but by the end of February, Heslop and Holdstock had replaced the experienced Dickinson and Lyons. Rose returned from his stint in Australia in fine form before two suspensions disrupted the second half of his season. The Robins signed loose-forward Len Casey from neighbours Hull FC for £6,000 to add some steel to the pack and he quickly became a key member of the team. Experienced Alan Ackroyd was signed from Castleford in March to strengthen the pack in the final push to ensure First Division safety.

The season saw the departure of some well-known players as Poole largely pursued a youth policy. Neil Fox played in the first match of his tenure at Warrington but Poole did not pick him again and he moved on to York to join several former Belle Vue colleagues. In his short career with the club, Fox played in just 59 games but scored a remarkable 470 points, including 210 goals and 16 tries. Clive Dickinson played his last game in a 18-4 home defeat by St Helens two weeks later. George Kirkpatrick was injured against

The Robins

Castleford in January and, unable to reclaim his place, moved on to Hunslet whilst Alan Burwell played his last game in March. The under-rated Kirkpatrick had been excellent value over 118 games for the club.

Johnny Moore resigned as 'A' team coach at the start of the season in order to concentrate on his playing career and Cliff Wallis took over and at the end of the season, Poole signed a two-year contract. Millward guested with Cronulla during the summer but Paul Rose decided against returning to Dapto for a second spell. Rovers lost £31,255 over the season which was attributed to a significant outlay on transfers and reduced income from the cup competitions. Under coach John Edson, Rovers Colts were the first winners of the Premiership in the newly-introduced Colts league, beating Wakefield in the final 26-12.

The Greats – No 18
Alan Burwell - *see Hull KR legends gallery*

Alan Burwell was born in Hull in December 1942. As a boy he was a Hull FC supporter but joined Rovers from East Hull ARLC in 1962, following in the footsteps of his elder brother, Brian. 'Rovers were the only club that approached me,' he says, 'so I signed for them.'

Burwell was a mercurial attacking talent whose favourite position was stand-off. He made his debut in that position in a 10-9 win at Featherstone on 4 April 1962. At that time, David Elliott was the first choice and Burwell was asked to play in the three-quarter line. He believed that he was too small for centre and in his early years was prepared to play in the 'A' team to try and gain first team selection in his favoured position.

A chemical technician by trade, Burwell missed the entire 1965-66 season whilst at University but returned to the club in 1966. By then, Rovers had signed Roger Millward and acknowledging that he had lost his chance to claim the playmaking role, Burwell said that he was happy to play wherever the club wanted. After that, he appeared mainly at centre but gained the first of his eight Great Britain caps on the wing the following year.

Burwell took a liking to Australia whilst there for the 1968 World Cup and started to consider the possibilities of emigrating. At the time, the Australian government operated an assisted passage scheme to provide workers for their booming industries and Burwell took advantage, becoming a 'ten pound Pom.' Around a million Britons took part in the scheme over a 27-year period. On arrival in Australia he was, as he puts it, 'put up for auction' and, being a current international, Canterbury Bankstown soon snapped him up to play for them in the 1970 season. They paid Rovers a nominal fee of £4,500, which Wilf Spaven felt was a bargain for, 'the best utility back in the game.'

After a couple of successful seasons with Canterbury, Burwell retired due to a hand tendon injury. Returning to the UK in 1974, then Rovers' coach Arthur Bunting persuaded him to come out of retirement to pass on his experience to the promising young centres David Hall and Mike Smith. Burwell marked his 'second debut' with a try in a 56-5 annihilation of New Hunslet. Over the remainder of that and the following season, he made 38 appearances before finally retiring. His last act in a Rovers jersey was to score his 106th try for the club against Huddersfield at Craven Park on 21 March 1976. 'As I went over I felt something go in my leg and I hobbled back-up the touchline. I told Harry Poole, "I've retired",' he recalls. 'The training under Poole was too hard for me at the age of 33 anyway!'

Burwell made 226 appearances in his two spells with the Robins, playing 124 games at centre, 71 at stand-off, 27 on the wing, and four from the bench. He was a great favourite with teammates and supporters alike and his name is

*revered by those lucky enough to have seen him. Brian
Tyson remembers him as: 'A most stylish player who glided
over the ground – perhaps Sam Tomkins comes closest in
the modern game. He was the fastest I've seen over 25-yards
and was very talented – and he was very laid back.' Hall
believes that he was the best Hull-born rugby league back.
'I remember watching him when he scored two tries at
centre in the Championship play-off game against St Helens
in 1968 – he was outstanding that day.'*

*Burwell continues to live in Hedon to the east of Hull,
where he regularly meets up with several of his old Rovers
teammates.*

The Greats – No 19
Wilf Spaven - *see Hull KR legends gallery*

*Wilf Spaven was the main driving force behind the rise of
Hull Kingston Rovers from being perpetual strugglers in
the 1950s to becoming a genuinely competitive side in the
1960s and 1970s, and laying the foundations for the club's
most successful era.*

*Spaven, a Hull bookmaker, was born in the city in 1911
and was a Rovers director for 26 years, most of which time
he was the chairman. He was first elected to the board in
1949 and served two years at the helm between 1950 and
1952. He then lost his seat on the board, but was re-elected
a year later. Spaven was vice-chairman to A.J. Snelling for
five years and when he died during the 1957-58 season,
Spaven took over as chairman again. He was confirmed in
the role at the 1958 AGM and remained in the job until he
died. As vice-chairman in 1957, Spaven was instrumental
in bringing Colin Hutton in as coach and pushed forward a
policy of bringing in the best players if the price was right.*

*Under his leadership, Rovers recruited Harry Poole, Frank
Foster, Bill Holliday, Clive Sullivan, Len Casey and his best
signing of all, Roger Millward. Spaven's great strength was*

that he listened to the views of those he respected before putting forward his own ideas and coming to the considered decisions that he took for the good of the club as a whole. He hardly ever missed a Rovers game unless unavoidably involved in other rugby league business. On his death, his vice-chairman Percy Johnson referred to him as: 'A great leader – always understanding and never dogmatic.' Ron Turner remembers him simply as being a gentleman.

In addition to all that Spaven did for the Robins, he also worked tirelessly for the game. A longstanding member of the Rugby League Council, serving as chairman in 1962-63, he was at various times chairman of the international and disciplinary committees, chairman of the England and Great Britain selectors and three times Great Britain team manager. RFL secretary David Oxley paid tribute to him, saying: 'Few men have served the game of rugby league so continuously and in so many capacities as Wilf Spaven. Wilf brought to his devoted work for the game a massive sense of proportion and ever-cheerful humour that the fluctuating fortunes of the game never shook.' Wilf Spaven died on 23 March 1976 aged just 65.

Progress overshadowed

The summer of 1976 saw the end of the 'Cod War' but the government's agreement to the Icelandic exclusion zone for British trawlers was a major blow to the already declining fishing industry, and had a serious effect on the economy of the city of Hull. One welcome development, particularly for Rovers' West Riding-based players, was the opening in May of the final section of the M62 motorway from the Ouse Bridge to North Cave and the A63 dual carriageway extension into Hull. In the hottest summer since records began, 90°F temperatures were recorded for 15 consecutive days between June and July. Some parts of the UK had no rain for 45 days at the height and it was the worst drought since the 1720s. A three-day riot by inmates of Hull prison destroyed over two-thirds of the building and caused its closure for repairs for a year.

The 1976-77 season was slow to get going. In the first half of the campaign, Rovers won only half their 14 league games and lost in the first round of the Yorkshire Cup, Floodlit Trophy and John Player Trophy. They conceded a league double to Featherstone and whilst defeats at St Helens and Wigan were understandable, those at Barrow and Rochdale were very disappointing. However, it all came right for Poole's men in the New Year, with a nine-match winning run. That included a comfortable win over Leeds, a 5-3 victory at Widnes which featured the first of Millward's two full-back appearances, a second round Challenge Cup win over Hull FC and culminated in the performance of the season, a brilliant 25-15 third round triumph over Castleford.

Tragically, just two weeks later, coach Harry Poole died suddenly of a heart attack. It was a terrible shock. All indications were that the players were responding to his coaching and he had instilled belief and determination in the side. Two days later, Millward was appointed player-coach until the end of the season. His appointment was a bold move by the directors, he was already the captain and best player and he carried a huge responsibility on his small frame. One former Rovers international thought it was a big mistake and that, on the eve of such an important match, the club should have turned to the man in the director's box with 13 years of coaching experience, Colin Hutton, to take over temporarily.

Millward's first task was certainly a daunting one. He had to lift the team to play in a cup semi-final against Widnes, by that time starting to earn their reputation as the cup kings.

After an even first half, the Chemics took control in the second and Sullivan's try was only consolation in the end. The rest of the season, despite good wins at home to St Helens and at Wakefield, was an anti-climax but it ended in real controversy.

Rovers' highly respectable top-four place in the league earned them a home Premiership tie against Warrington. At this point, a dispute arose about Phil Lowe who had been cleared to play at the end of his three-year stint with Manly and had appeared in 21 games during the season. Manly alleged that they had written to both Rovers and the RFL to say that they wished to take up their option of retaining Lowe's services but neither party had received the letters. Manly took the issue to the Australian Board of Control, who in turn referred it to the International Board. Before the game, the RFL told Rovers not to play Lowe again until the Board had ruled on the matter. The Robins took advice from legal counsel and he was in the side to face Wire. It was an excellent game in which the Robins overturned a 10-5 interval deficit and won 18-13 courtesy of a sensational 70-yard Steve Hartley try in the dying minutes.

The RFL then expelled Rovers for disobeying their instruction. The directors still believed that they were in the right but decided not to cause the RFL any further embarrassment and did not protest. The International Board subsequently ratified Lowe's registration but a season, which had already contained a wide range of emotions and dramas, had now ended in farce.

The experienced Ackroyd and Lyons both played their last games in October, leaving Millington, Heslop and Holdstock as the regular front row. In November, the Robins shrewdly signed former Dewsbury half-back Allan Agar to provide cover for Hartley and Millward. The latter had a benefit year that earned him a then club record £9,000.

Injuries to Wallace and the need for a more reliable goal-kicker led to the acquisition of ex-Wigan full-back Colin Tyrer from Barrow in December. An inspired signing was that of David Watkinson from York amateur club Heworth in January. Watkinson, ever-reliable and tough as teak, made his debut against Leeds at prop less than a week later but thereafter played almost exclusively at hooker.

Dunn was ever-present on the right wing, finishing as top try-scorer for the third time. Smith, now established at right centre, completed the regular three-quarter line with Watson and Sullivan. Lowe, Rose and Hughes were the second-row regulars and Casey missed only two games at loose-forward. Hall was transfer-listed at £8,000 after becoming frustrated at not winning a regular starting place.

Cliff Wallis made the last of his 150 appearances for the first team as an emergency substitute at Leeds on New Year's Day. Wallis made his debut against Swinton in April 1964, was later released and then re-signed in 1967. After becoming a first-team regular in 1969-70, he moved from prop to loose-forward. A clever ball handler who could make a half-break and get his pass away, he played some of his best football in that position. Injured in early 1971, he was unable to regain a regular place in the team and subsequently moved to Castleford. After two successful years at Wheldon Road, he returned to Craven Park in April 1974. A regular throughout the ensuing promotion season, he took over as 'A' team coach in 1976. At the end of the season, he resigned his 'A' team duties to concentrate on physiotherapy, in which capacity he continued to serve the club for a number of years.

Overall, the playing strength was in good shape, with a blend of youth, experience, talent and physical presence, and some of the performances had generated real optimism.

Challenge Cup 3rd round, Wheldon Road, Castleford, 12 March 1977
Castleford 15-25 Hull Kingston Rovers

Everything that Harry Poole had sought to achieve with the Robins came to fruition in this one game. Castleford had won two cups already that season and were favourites for Wembley. They had a good home record and had beaten Rovers twice already that season. However, they were swept aside by a Robins' performance that exuded pace and power. On the way into Castleford, the team coach was delayed by traffic congestion. Len Casey remembers Harry Poole making a rousing speech as they waited in the bus. Rovers took the lead after 12 minutes when Roger Millward's kick bounced awkwardly for Wraith, Clive Sullivan dived over and Colin Tyrer converted to make it 5-0. A Stephens try and Lloyd conversion put Castleford level on the half-hour but that only galvanised the visitors into action. Steve Hartley made a 40-yard break from a scrum deep in Rovers' territory, David Hall took his low pass without breaking stride and found Ged Dunn in support on the inside. As he was tackled by the last defender he lobbed the ball inside to the supporting Sullivan, who raced over for a breath-taking try. Three minutes later Hartley took Millward's short pass to race between the posts, Tyrer converted both and the Robins led 15-5 at half-time.

With John Millington having treatment on a leg injury, Fenton's try and Lloyd's conversion pulled it back to 15-10 after two minutes of the second half and Rovers' defence briefly looked a little shaky. The return of Millington and a Tyrer penalty goal put the Robins back in control, however, and they wrapped the game up in the 73rd minute when Phil Lowe went rampaging through the home defence and gave Hartley a straightforward run to the line, Tyrer goaling. Reilly scored an individual try for the home side with two minutes to go but there was still time for Hall to put the gloss on the win by sending in Lowe in for the final touchdown.

Built on solid teamwork, an aggressive and confident performance combined exciting football with uncompromising defence. In his report in the Hull Daily Mail, *John Sexton rightly commented that it was impossible to pick a man-of-the-match. All 15 did their jobs magnificently and each played a full part in what was the Robins' most impressive performance since the 1967-68 season.*

> **Castleford:** *G. Wraith; S. Fenton, J. Joyner, P. Johnson, R. Newton; B. Burton (J. Kain), G. Stephens; A. Bence, R. Spurr, A. Dickinson, M. Reilly (capt) (P. Orr), S. Lloyd, S. Norton.*
> **Rovers:** *C. Tyrer; G. Dunn, D. Hall, B. Watson, C. Sullivan; S. Hartley, R. Millward (capt) (A. Agar); J. Millington, D. Heslop, P. Rose, P. Lowe, M. Hughes (D. Watkinson), L. Casey.*
> *Referee: M.J. Naughton (Widnes)*
> *Attendance: 10,300*

The Greats – No 20
Harry Poole - *see Hull KR legends gallery*

Harry Poole was born in Castleford in March 1935. He played for the famous Lock Lane amateur club before Hunslet signed him immediately on his return from National Service in 1956. There, he soon became an established member of their famous back row alongside Geoff Gunney and Brian Shaw, which was selected en bloc by Yorkshire in 1958.

Rovers made enquiries about him in the autumn of 1960 and although Hunslet were prepared to let him go and agreed a fee, Poole was happy at Parkside and reluctant to leave. Leeds then made a bid but Rovers persisted and Poole became their then most costly player when he signed on 25 January 1961 for £6,000. Later Poole admitted that: 'The bottom dropped out of my world,' when Hunslet sold him and that he considered quitting the game. He quickly acknowledged, though, that the move was the best thing that

270

could have happened to him and that he had been treated like a Lord by the Robins. A six-foot 14-stone second-row forward, Poole was in his prime when he joined Rovers and it proved an excellent move for both.

Coach Colin Hutton believed that Poole had all the attributes to be a top loose-forward and it was in that position that he played the majority of his matches for the Robins. In his first, club skipper Jim Jenkin broke his leg and Poole took over; a role he held throughout his four and a half seasons. A natural leader through example and inspiration, the responsibility added a further dimension to his game. He added an impetus and authority that helped the Robins make the transition from a mid-table side to one that challenged for the top honours. Poole was a fighter. Over his career he had to overcome a number of serious injuries including breaks to his leg, arm and fingers, a dislocated shoulder and knee ligament damage but on the field, he was always at the heart of the action. He was a strong and determined runner who had a keen eye for a gap and the ability to get away a pass in tight situations, as well as an excellent tackler and useful kicker in open play.

Poole played on numerous occasions for Yorkshire but won just three Great Britain caps, a meagre return for a man with such great talent and a reflection of the enormous loose-forward strength the British game could boast at the time. As at Hunslet, Poole was very happy with Rovers and had not asked to leave when they sold him to Leeds in September 1965. 'He was heartbroken,' says Brian Tyson. 'He didn't want to leave.' Tyson likened him to Rocky Turner on the field. 'Both were very hard men who could do the lot. He was all over the field, always taking the lead. You couldn't fail to be inspired by Harry.' He played 123 games for the Robins, scoring 27 tries.

After retiring at Leeds, he went into coaching having a spell with home town club Castleford before answering the Robins' call in November 1975. The respect he had earned enabled him to handle being Rovers' first coach to select the team. He was hard but fair and expected no less from his players than he himself had given. Poole did not have an easy start but by the beginning of 1977 his ideas and leadership were starting to bear fruit. In John Millington's words: 'He instilled a steel and aggression into the side that had been lacking and he treated everyone the same.' He also addressed the team's regular failing of being a soft touch away from home. Just 15 months after he took over, his tenure was tragically cut short by a fatal heart attack. His legacy was the nucleus of the team that Roger Millward led into the club's most successful era.

According to former director Chris Draper: 'He was a real leader. As a player he was very creative with great passing ability and as a coach he inspired his teams being both feared and respected.'

*****

9. Glory Days

ALL the work done by Wilf Spaven and his directors and staff over the previous 20 years came to fruition in a golden era during parts of which the Robins could justifiably lay claim to being the best team in the country.

Breakthrough

The summer of 1977 saw the celebrations of Queen Elizabeth II's Silver Jubilee, the West Yorkshire police had started the hunt for the notorious Yorkshire Ripper and in the Fourth Test against Australia at Headingley, Geoff Boycott scored his 100th century.

At Craven Park, Roger Millward prepared for his first full season in charge. He had a good squad to work with and there was a mood of confidence. It was certainly a shock when the 1977-78 season opened with a 14-8 defeat at New

Hunslet in the Yorkshire Cup. After that, there were four largely uninspiring league wins, followed by a run of five matches without success including a 20-13 home defeat to the Airlie Birds when league derbies resumed following Hull FC's promotion, after a two-season absence.

Every Rovers fan present at Post Office Road will remember the last game in that winless sequence. It was a first round John Player tie refereed by Ron Campbell of Widnes, who had previously taken charge of nine Rovers games without attracting particular attention. Playing their best football of the season, Rovers romped into a 19-4 lead after 34 minutes with tries by Hall, Sullivan and Hartley. The key moment came when Campbell, seemingly rather harshly, dismissed Featherstone prop Farrar. After that, he appeared, consciously or otherwise, to try to compensate for the decision. The subsequent penalty count was 17-1 to Featherstone, two of the Colliers' three tries were highly contentious and Campbell sent off two Rovers' players, Sullivan and Hartley, after what appeared innocuous incidents. It was the only dismissal in Sullivan's long and distinguished career.

Not surprisingly, Featherstone pulled themselves back into the game and narrowed the gap to 19-13 early in the second half. Cunningham then scored a converted try to put the Robins 24-13 ahead and it looked as if the bizarre officiating might not matter. However, the Colliers cut the deficit to a single point as the game neared the end of normal time. At that point, Agar was penalised whilst in possession at a play-the-ball just inside his own half and Featherstone prop Townend, who had already kicked seven goals, made no mistake. Adding insult to injury, at least two Rovers' players were hit by projectiles whilst standing behind their posts. The mood at Craven Park was of disbelief and outrage but vice-chairman Percy Johnson discounted the possibility of complaint. 'We did that last time,' he said, in reference to St Helens cup-tie. 'But it goes against you in the end.'

In hindsight, this was a turning point in the Robins' fortunes because the team responded magnificently to the setback with eight wins in their next nine games, a run that took them to victory in the BBC Floodlit Trophy. The path to the final included wins over Wigan, Wakefield and Castleford, the latter with a brilliant first half display at Wheldon Road on their way to a convincing 23-5 victory. In the final, they demolished St Helens 26-11, a triumph that had huge significance in that it was the first time for 50 years the Robins had won a trophy in competition with the big Lancashire clubs, not just those in Yorkshire. It was the beginning of a new period of success.

The New Year brought more controversy. The first round of the Challenge Cup saw the Robins drawn at the Boulevard. There was outrage at Craven Park when Rovers found that Ron Campbell was to referee the game and, to no avail, they asked for the appointment to be changed. There were never more than a few points in the game and again Campbell dismissed two Rovers' players in the first half. Lowe was distraught at the only sending-off of his career but Tyrer seemed intent on settling an old score with former Castleford scrum-half Hepworth and there could be no complaint about his dismissal. The man-in-the-middle controversially disallowed a Sullivan try and the Airlie Birds won 9-7 after he upheld Macklin's late score although the winger appeared to have stepped into touch. In fairness, Campbell refereed Rovers several times over the following years without any major incident and he earned a reputation as a capable and respected whistle-blower.

The Robins

Hull Kingston Rovers 26-11 St Helens

*On an unforgettable night, the Robins made a significant
breakthrough and created a springboard for greater things. It
was not just that they won the trophy but the confident and
stylish way in which they did it. It was a magnificent team
performance.*

*Roger Millward and Phil Lowe combined to send in Mike
Smith for an unconverted try in the fifth minute but Glynn
levelled for St Helens soon after. Saints could have taken the
lead but for a knock-on but Rovers came back strongly. After
16 minutes, Len Casey's strong drive and brilliant pass sent
in Clive Sullivan for a try that David Hall could not
convert, but the full-back more than made amends with a
try-saving tackle on Jones shortly after. In the 26th minute,
Paul Rose's powerful charge was halted on the line and he
played the ball to himself to dive over for a characteristic try.
Hall's conversion put Rovers 11-3 ahead and the Robins'
pack was taking control. There was another sweeping move
before half-time involving Casey, Rose, Steve Hartley and
Ged Dunn that failed to produce a try when Sullivan could
not take the final pass.*

*Rovers continued in the same vein after the break. After
52 minutes, an excellent run by Smith drew the cover and
he found Hall on the inside. The full-back was tackled short
of the posts but managed to get his pass away to Hartley to
score. Ten minutes later, Rose sent Smith away again. Smith
passed to the supporting Millward who, despite the
attentions of two defenders, managed to get the ball away
for Dunn to stroll over. Just three minutes later there came
a try that had TV commentator Eddie Waring in raptures.
From deep inside his own half, Millward released a superb
pass round a defender to send Hartley, head back, racing
into open space. He drew the full-back and unselfishly lofted*

a pass to Dunn who outpaced the remnants of the defence to score. 'What a glorious try in rugby league football,' Waring eulogised. Hall converted all the second half touchdowns and the Robins led 26-3 with 15 minutes to go. Saints kept going and Glynn scored a second before Eddie Cunningham went over for the visitors a minute from the end but it was merely for the record books.

John Millington won the man-of-the-match award for his powerful charges and non-stop defence but it was a night when everyone played their part to the full. There was not a weak link anywhere in the team. The crowd invaded the pitch when Millward held the trophy aloft and Hull Daily Mail *reporter John Sexton said: 'On this form, this will not be the last that he collects in the next few years.' Millward reflected afterwards that: 'It was an incredible night – everything we did just fell into place.' Hall recalls: 'To win like that was an unbelievable feeling.'*

> **Rovers:** *D. Hall; G. Dunn, M. Smith, B. Watson, C. Sullivan; S. Hartley, R. Millward (capt); J. Millington, D. Watkinson, J. Cunningham (M. Hughes), P. Lowe, P. Rose, L. Casey. Sub not used: A. Agar*
> **St. Helens:** *G. Pimblett (W. Platt); L. Jones (N. Courtney), D. Noonan, E. Cunningham, P. Glynn; W. Francis, K. Gwilliam; D. Chisnall, G. Liptrot, M. James, M. Hope, A. Karalius, H. Pinner.*
> *Referee: M.J. Naughton (Widnes)*
> *Attendance: 10,099 (£6,580)*

The rest of the season was an anti-climax with only five wins coming from the last eleven league games and the Black and Whites made it a hat-trick when they completed the league double at the Boulevard in March. Despite this, the Airlie Birds finished in 13th place out of 16 and were relegated, along with the other three promoted clubs. The fairness of the four up, four down system in leagues of 16 and 14 was questionable.

Again finishing fourth in the First Division, the Robins qualified for the Premiership semi-final, played that season over two legs. Rovers lost the home leg to Widnes 22-12 and despite missing five key players, the Robins gave the chemics a real fright in the away leg, overturning the first leg deficit before half-time and winning 19-13. However, they eventually lost 35-31 on aggregate.

There were few changes to the squad from the previous season. The most significant was the arrival of former Castleford and Great Britain forward Brian Lockwood, from Wakefield at the beginning of February. Tyrer, Hall and local utility back Steve Leighton all had spells in the rather troublesome full-back position. Tyrer played his last game before retirement at home to Castleford in April, having kicked 108 goals in his 31 games with the Robins. In the centre, Watson missed only one game all season whilst forward Cunningham's 25 games were the most he played in any season in his injury-ravaged career. Burly former Hull & East Riding RUFC goal-kicking winger, Steve Hubbard, made his debut in the latter stages of the season.

Having had the opportunity to observe Millward in action as player-coach over the season, the board awarded him a two-year contract. He had overall charge of coaching, complete responsibility for team selection and shared with the board responsibility for transfers. At the AGM chairman Land expressed delight at the Floodlit Trophy win, but lamented what he referred to as the 'year of the referee'. He said that when referees came to Craven Park they were looked after and treated with respect and he did not know what else the club could do.

Richard Wallace took over as 'A' team coach at the

beginning of the season but when he left in October to resume playing with New Hunslet, Moore resumed the reigns once more. The reserves had a good season, narrowly losing in their Championship play-off final. Casey was transfer-listed at his own request towards the end of the season, saying that he felt that the side had lost its team spirit and that the players were not playing for each other. The club arranged a benefit for the family of late coach Harry Poole.

Champions

In the summer of 1978, Bob Colgrave of top Hull amateur side Ace (formerly BOCM), captained the first ever BARLA tour of the southern hemisphere, when his Great Britain side visited Papua New Guinea, Australia and New Zealand.

Refreshed from the summer break and with a trophy in the cabinet, there was renewed optimism that Rovers could go on to greater honours in 1978-79. After a hard-earned Yorkshire Cup win in the first game at Wakefield, interest in the competition ended at Bradford the following week. However, by the time the Robins went back to Odsal for a second round Challenge cup-tie in early March, they had taken the league by storm, sitting proudly at its summit, with 14 wins from 16 games.

An eleven-match winning run started with a 21-8 home victory over Warrington in the first league game. The run included a 67-11 John Player Trophy win over Oldham on 24 September, the then second-highest score ever recorded by the Robins. The following week Rovers beat Leeds at Headingley for the first time in 17 attempts, the convincing 20-5 win coming despite Millward's absence. Two weeks later there was a dramatic win at Salford when, after Millward's 200th career try had helped to tie up the scores at 14-14,

Hartley produced a thrilling individual kick-and-chase to secure the game 19-14 in the dying minutes.

The Challenge Cup defeat at Odsal enabled Rovers to concentrate on the league. They won nine of the next 12 games, which was enough to bring the First Division title to Craven Park. They included some great performances, none more so than the massive mid-week win at Widnes that gave them one hand on the trophy, whilst the Easter double over Huddersfield included a 57-3 home thrashing, featuring five tries by Hartley in a team lacking five regulars due to a flu epidemic.

Of as much importance, though, were the wins when Rovers did not play particularly well but still came away with the points. Two days after the Bradford cup-tie, they entertained Wakefield and struggled to find their form but Hartley scored two trademark tries to give them a 10-7 win. In the run-in, Rovers ground out a 13-11 win in the gloom at Featherstone without several first-choice players. After losing Agar in the opening 10 minutes, centre Watson had to play at scrum-half but a magnificent pack performance, together with Hartley's 100th career try, saw them home. The RFL fined Rovers £200 for not fulfilling the Featherstone fixture earlier in the season, when they had only three fit first teamers. The title was sealed when nearest challengers Warrington lost whilst Rovers were not in action and the Robins eased up in their last two games, losing for a third time at Odsal.

However, the main objective was achieved and the Robins were First Division champions – the first time they had ended the season at the top of the table since 1921. It was a great achievement for a club that had endured more than its share of dark days over the previous 50 years.

Bad winter weather had interfered with the fixtures with the result that by the time Rovers faced Bradford in the Premiership play-offs, they had played 13 games in 45 days. In their fifth meeting of the season, Rovers played some brilliant football to lead 13-0 at half-time. However, in the second half, Bradford rallied and it seemed that the season had caught up with the Robins. There was no more in the tank and Northern won 18-17.

There were two big transfers during the season. First, Great Britain tourist back-rower Phil Hogan arrived from Barrow in December for a world record £32,000, and in January, international loose-forward Casey was sold to Bradford in an exchange deal valued at £25,000, with Bradford scrum-half Paul Harkin moving to Craven Park. After Casey's departure, Hogan took over at loose-forward. They were two completely different types of player. Casey was as hard as nails and feared no one, a strong tackling, hard-working forward who could slip out a pass in the tackle, whilst Hogan was a pacy and destructive runner who was equally at home in the three-quarters. A less costly but important transfer was the arrival of much-travelled forward Geoff Clarkson from Wakefield. An acolyte of Alex Murphy at Leigh and Warrington, he was hugely experienced and a proven winner and provided invaluable forward cover.

The regular First Division-winning pack was Millington, Watkinson and Lockwood in the front row and behind them, Lowe, Rose and Casey or Hogan, with Clarkson, Hughes and Holdstock providing back-up. In the backs, Millward largely reverted to stand-off with Agar at scrum-half and Hartley at left-centre. It seemed to do Hartley no harm at all and he enjoyed his most prolific season, scoring 35 tries, making him the league's leading poacher. Dunn, Hubbard and Youngman competed for the right-wing spot, whilst Smith and Sullivan were automatic selections at right-centre and left-wing respectively. Hall started the season as the regular full-back and remained there until former Colt Ian Robinson took over in mid-April. Watkinson and Hartley missed only four games each.

The Robins

Paul Rose had a testimonial that earned him £16,000 but he dislocated his shoulder in February and missed the rest of the season, whilst the unfortunate Cunningham had a third knee operation at the start of the season, and only played twice. Hogan, Lockwood, Millward, Smith and Watkinson were all selected for the Great Britain tour of Australasia.

The Annual Report recorded a record overall profit of £49,532, despite a loss of £54,597 on the rugby side – mainly due to a £37,010 transfer deficit and a record £76,858 spent on players and coaches' wages. Nevertheless, the £102,029 lottery profit, now boosted by a £1,000 first prize, ensured that the club was in a very healthy situation. £6,737 ground maintenance costs, up from £1,625 the previous year, included various improvements, and were not yet sounding warning bells. To add to the first team's success, the Colts team, under the continued astute guidance of coach John Edson, again won their league championship.

First Division, Naughton Park, Widnes, 19 April 1979
Widnes 8-15 Hull Kingston Rovers

This game did not mathematically win the First Division title for Rovers, there were still six games to play, but it was the biggest of the run-in. The result put Widnes out of the race and increased pressure on second-placed Warrington.

It was a first-class performance, with two players outstanding. Ian Robinson, playing only his fourth game at full-back, was brilliant in attack and defence and Phil Hogan, back after six weeks out with a rib injury, produced some devastating running that had Widnes in trouble throughout.

In a cut-and-thrust first half, with missed chances for both sides, the scores were level at 2-2 after 37 minutes when Robinson ran onto Bernard Watson's superbly delayed pass, dummied, and raced over at the corner. Moments later, he had to be alert to stop Wright scoring out wide but could do nothing to prevent big Jim Mills forcing his way over after Shaw was held up on the line, and it was 5-5 at half-time.

After 51 minutes, Allan Agar and John Millington combined to send Phil Lowe over and Steve Hubbard's goal made it 10-5. Agar's attempted drop-goal went wide shortly after. However, Widnes did nearly all the attacking in the last 20 minutes and Rovers' defence had to be at its best to stop Shaw again. Moran did score after 68 minutes but the Robins held on to a two-point lead until the sixth minute of injury time, when Ian Madley and Roger Millward sent Hogan on another magnificent run through. As he rounded Myler, he slipped a short pass to the supporting Lowe who scored by the posts. Hubbard's kick made it 15-8 and, despite a further six minutes of added time, Rovers were home.

The win was based on a powerful performance led by Brian Lockwood, backed up by half-backs Millward and Agar and their hard-working back division.

Widnes: *J. Myler; S. Wright, M. Aspey, M. George, M. Burke (D. Moran); E. Hughes (M. O'Neill), R. Bowden; J. Mills, K. Elwell, G. Shaw, D. Hull, A. Dearden, M. Adams (capt).*
Rovers: *I. Robinson; S. Hubbard, M. Smith, B. Watson, G. Dunn: R. Millward (capt), A. Agar; J. Millington, D. Watkinson, B. Lockwood, P. Lowe, G. Clarkson (I. Madley), P. Hogan. Sub not used: S. Hartley*
Referee: R. Moore (Wakefield)
Attendance: 8,270

The road to Wembley

But for the victorious Challenge Cup campaign, 1979-80 might have been a case of after The Lord Mayor's Show. After first round defeats in the Yorkshire and John Player cup competitions, wins over Castleford, Keighley and St Helens took the Robins into the last BBC2 Floodlit Trophy final against the Airlie Birds. In front of a competition record crowd of 18,500 at the Boulevard, Rovers, without Millward, Watkinson and Rose, never looked like winning and went down 13-3. Five league defeats before the turn of the year had made the task of retaining the First Division title difficult, which became impossible after all four January games were lost.

Nevertheless, the Challenge Cup campaign changed the season. Rovers' first round draw at Wigan was never going to be easy as the Central Park side were enduring a miserable season and the cup represented their only hope of glory. They were encouraged by a 23-14 league win at Craven Park in mid-January, in which their international full-back George Fairbairn was outstanding. Rovers gave themselves a boost by beating the transfer deadline to re-sign Len Casey from Bradford for a then world-record fee of £38,000.

Casey went straight back into the side for the visit to the Cherry and Whites and was man-of-the match in the Robins' 18-13 win. The next two rounds brought convincing home successes over Castleford and Warrington, in both games they wore the opposition down in the first half and then asserted their superiority in the second.

Widnes and outsiders Halifax made up the semi-final line-up with the two Hull clubs, and Rovers draw against Halifax appeared to offer the best chance of getting to Wembley. With Watkinson back for his first match of the season, two Sullivan tries inspired a comfortable 20-7 success over the Thrum Hall side. Once again, the first half was tight before Rovers pulled away in the second. The Robins were back at Wembley after 16 years.

There was another derby game beforehand and the

Robins put in one of their best performances of the season a month before the big day to record a 29-14 success. The events of 3 May 1980 will live forever in Rovers folklore and in three consecutive seasons the Robins had brought the BBC Floodlit Trophy, the First Division title and the Challenge Cup to Craven Park.

The team underwent several changes during the season. There were problems at hooker due to a long-term injury to Watkinson. Heslop started the season but after his injury in October, Rovers brought in Graham Tyreman from Castleford. After an injury to Tyreman in January, Rovers paid Dewsbury £4,000 for the under-rated Ray Price. Holdstock staked his claim to the number eight position, and his excellent season won him the league's Young Player of the Year award. At half-back, Millward made only 12 appearances – injured at the Boulevard in October, he sustained a cracked jaw in his comeback game against St Helens in December and then suffered the same injury against Widnes in February. In his absences, Hartley and Agar shouldered most of the half-back duties. Hubbard made the right wing position his own, playing in all but three of the 42 games and scoring a club record 366 points, with 138 goals and 30 tries that saw him joint top of the league's touchdown charts alongside Salford's Keith Fielding. Watson reclaimed his centre position and the versatile Hall played at loose-forward early in the season, followed by a spell at centre, finally moving to full-back to replace Leighton.

Several players made their last appearances for the club. The first was hooker David Heslop, who was unable to get back into the side after his injury and moved to Wakefield. He was a solid all-round performer and a noted dressing room joker who was probably unlucky not to have played more than his 139 games. Geoff Clarkson made the last of his

51 appearances against Bradford on 27 January, just days before he joined them. His strength and experience played a big part in the previous season's First Division title win. John Cunningham, made the last of his 37 appearances in five injury-ravaged seasons against Workington in March, and later signed for them.

In the penultimate game of the season at Widnes, a first round Premiership tie, Rovers put out a scratch side that featured the final games of Steve Leighton, Bernard Watson and Johnny Moore. Watson moved on to Dewsbury to end his career but he had been an excellent servant over six seasons, making 186 appearances and scoring 44 tries. He was a very good and unselfish footballer, nicknamed 'the burglar' due to his knack of ball stealing in the tackle and had an aggressive streak to his game. 'He was as hard as nails but he was a lovely man,' says Millington,

A further four players made their final Rovers appearances at Wembley. Brian Lockwood left to join Oldham for a nominal £2,000 fee after an unfortunate saga during which Rovers reported the Lancashire club to the RFL for making an illegal approach. Lockwood only played in 76 games for the club but he was one of the best. Not the biggest forward, his work-rate, ball-playing ability and textbook defence were first-class. In addition to claiming the game's two biggest domestic trophies, he won two Great Britain caps whilst at Craven Park.

The club offered Allan Agar a place on the coaching staff although not with the contract that he wanted, and he left to join Wakefield. He was an astute footballer, a good organiser and whilst not the fastest or flashiest, a capable operator in either half-back position. Millward notes: 'He was very solid, a good man to have in your side. He could take the pressure off other players.' Agar made 113 appearances, scoring 32 tries and kicking 33 goals, of which 17 were drop-goals – memorably four in the win at Headingley in the 1978-79 championship-winning season. Rovers released Clive Sullivan to join Oldham during the close season and despite an attempted 'A' team comeback, Roger Millward never again appeared in the first team.

There was a tragic end to Rovers' visit to St Ielens in October, when popular referee Joe Jackson collapsed and died in the dressing room after the game.

The Greats – No 21
Clive Sullivan MBE - *see Hull KR legends gallery*

Many players have played for both Hull FC and Hull Kingston Rovers but none has been so loved by the supporters of both clubs as Clive Sullivan. He transcended the often-bitter rivalry to achieve a near unique popularity.

Born in Cardiff in April 1943, Sullivan had a major leg injury at the age of 14 that threatened even his ability to walk. Despite that, he started to play rugby whilst in the army and based at Catterick. Invited for a trial match at the Boulevard in 1961, he scored three tries and signed for Hull FC the following day. Although his early seasons there were interrupted by his military commitments and a serious car accident, Sullivan's exceptional pace and strong cover defence made him an automatic choice once he had left the forces in 1964.

After making 352 appearances and scoring 250 tries for the Airlie Birds, Sullivan joined the Robins for a fee of £3,250 in the summer of 1974. Making his debut at Doncaster on 25 August 1974, he went on to appear in 213 games, scoring 118 tries.

Sullivan played a leading role in Rovers' 1974-75 promotion season and in their later BBC Trophy, First Division championship and Challenge Cup successes. In

Millward's absence, he often skippered the side. After the Wembley success, the Robins released him at his own request to join Oldham. Returning to the Boulevard in 1981, he played in the Challenge Cup final replay at Elland Road in 1982 when Hull FC beat Widnes. He continued to combine playing and coaching duties until ill-health forced his retirement in 1985.

Whilst with the Airlie Birds, Sullivan made 17 appearances for Great Britain, captaining the side to victory in the 1972 World Cup, scoring a spectacular length-of-the-field try and making the crucial break for Mike Stephenson's decisive score in the final at Lyon. Sullivan was the first black captain of any national British sporting team. In the next World Cup, in 1975, he led the Welsh team and in all made 15 appearances for them. His World Cup heroics led to an appearance on the TV programme This Is Your Life *and in January 1974, he was awarded the MBE for his services to the game. His 406 tries put him seventh on rugby league's all-time list.*

'Sully' remains the only man to have played over 200 games and scored over 100 tries for both Hull clubs, and in all he made 640 career appearances in rugby league. As he got older, he lost some of the blistering pace that had launched his great career but he retained his strength both in defence and with ball in hand near the line, and developed an ability to read the game and be in the right place at the right time. 'He really knew the game. I learned a huge amount from him in my younger days just by talking to him in the car on the way to games,' says Len Casey.

Six months after playing in his last game, Clive Sullivan died of liver cancer on 8 October 1985 at the age of 42. In his honour, the main road into Hull from the Humber Bridge is named after him. His son, Anthony, another flying winger, later played for Rovers, St Helens and Great Britain.

Changes

In 1980-81, the RFL welcomed its first new club for 26 years, when Harold Genders launched Fulham RLFC at Craven Cottage, bringing the game back to the capital for the first time since 1934. The First Division was sponsored for the first time and renamed the Slalom Lager Championship. At Craven Park, it is fair to say that following the exodus of so many senior players at the end of the previous season, the supporters were not sure quite what to expect from the new season. Casey was named club captain, Moore as Millward's assistant and Dunn as the new 'A' team coach.

The team for the opening game at Wakefield in the Yorkshire Cup showed six changes from the victorious Wembley side. Two local former rugby union men, Wally Youngman and Gary McHugh, started the season on the wings, Hogan moved to centre to accommodate Hartley's return to his favoured stand-off role and Harkin, after 18 months at the club, finally got the chance to claim the scrum-half position. In the forwards, Millington returned in Lockwood's place and Price deputised for Watkinson, as he continued to do for much of the season. Former Colt Steve Crooks and experienced forward Colin Dixon, signed from Salford to provide cover, came into the side in September.

The Robins got off to an excellent start with an opening run of nine unbeaten matches taking them to the top of the First Division and the Yorkshire Cup final. The only point dropped in the first seven league games was at Workington in the first 1-1 draw in rugby league and the only one in the club's history. On a wild Cumbrian day, it looked for some time as if Price's first half drop-goal might be enough to win the game. The first defeat was to the New

Zealand tourists on 20 October, after which Robinson came in at full-back, and remained there for most of the season.

Going into the Yorkshire Cup final, against Leeds at Fartown, Rovers' confidence was high. But they did not make best use of their opening half opportunities and Leeds dominated the second half scrums to overturn the Robins' 7-2 half-time lead and pull off an unexpected 8-7 win.

After that, the form was inconsistent and indifferent performances were interspersed with some fine wins. Hubbard returned from injury in November to reclaim his wing spot and resume his prolific point-scoring. At Bradford, when Rovers played with 12 men after Rose's seventh-minute dismissal, he scored 20 points with four tries and four goals to lead them to a 26-7 victory. Later, at Headingley, this time with Dixon dismissed in the first half, Hubbard scored three tries and kicked two goals to inspire a Robins recovery from 13-0 down to win 16-13.

In December, Rose received a ten-match ban, the heaviest then inflicted on a Rovers' player, after being sent off at Bradford. It was the 12th dismissal of his career and he was understandably upset, given its rather soft nature and the fact that in same the game a Bradford player deliberately tripped Hubbard in full flight and was not even warned. Rose had been unhappy after his dismissal at Widnes in September and had a transfer request refused but after the second incident he was listed at £60,000.

In January, the club signed a pilot shirt-sponsorship deal with Rank Xerox for the remainder of the season. The players were unhappy about the deal, saying that they felt the club had sold itself short and refused to wear the jerseys, despite being offered half the sponsorship money. They finally agreed to the deal in time to wear them for the first time against St Helens at Craven Park on 11 January.

The talented but somewhat enigmatic loose-forward Mick Crane, who had been signed for £9,000 from Leeds the previous December, returned to his original club at the Boulevard in January. He made only 18 appearances for the Robins, who made a £2,000 profit when they sold him. Two new signings in January were Hunslet winger Peter Muscroft, who took over the left-wing slot from McHugh and second-row forward Chris Burton from Huddersfield for £15,000.

By the end of March, Rovers had lost seven league games but another Challenge Cup campaign was in full swing. Wins over Barrow, York and Salford earned Rovers another Headingley semi-final, this time against St Helens. After an even first half, the Robins produced a powerful display in the second to win 22-5, with five goals from Hubbard and two tries from Hartley.

In the run-up to the cup final against Widnes, Hubbard was again to the fore in a brilliant 34-0 home win over Castleford, with seven goals and three tries. Then, at the Boulevard, Rovers completed a league double in a fine, end-to-end game in which two-try Lowe was outstanding, a performance that was marred by youths throwing bricks and stones into the ground at the Gordon Street end, causing play to be temporarily suspended. The two clubs exchanged their previous season's positions, the Robins this time finishing third and the Airlie Birds seventh. Dixon made the last of his 24 appearances in the last league game at Halifax. Bradford topped the league despite being convincingly beaten by Rovers both home and away,

Wembley was a disappointment. The same side that had beaten St Helens so impressively in the semi-final never got going and Widnes, with scrum-half Gregory and former Rovers' prop Lockwood prominent, took an 11-4 half-time lead. The game was over by the time Chris Burton went over for his first try for the club late on and the final score was 18-9 to the men from Cheshire.

Four days later, the two sides met again at Craven Park in the first round of the Premiership. The kick-off was delayed to give a bumper crowd time to get into the ground and there were over 13,500 people packed in and still more locked out. It was a thrilling game that was played in an electric atmosphere and it was all that the Challenge Cup final had not been. Millward's team changes made all the difference. Hall, not at his best at full-back at Wembley, was moved to loose-forward where he had played some excellent football in the second half of the season. In Robinson's absence through injury, young Paul Proctor came in at full-back. Casey moved into the second row in place of Burton and Millington replaced Crooks in the front row.

The Robins took the game to Widnes from the start and had three try-scoring chances in the first ten minutes. Appearing to weather the storm, Widnes then took the lead with a penalty but Hall, who was having an excellent game and was frequently opening up the Widnes defence with his astute passes, sent Holdstock charging through to put Lowe in for an easy try. Lowe had not been happy with his Wembley display but more than made up for it with some powerful running this time. However, a Wright try then put the Chemics 7-6 up at the break.

After 52 minutes, Holdstock rumbled across for Rovers' second try, Hubbard's goal making it 11-7. There were no more tries but a drop-goal to each side and two Widnes penalties made it 12-12 with five minutes to go. Lowe then went on another tremendous run and when his pass was knocked down by a defender and picked up by a team-mate in an offside position, Hubbard kicked an angled penalty from 30 yards to win the game. The forwards had been outstanding, Hall and Harkin linked effectively with the backs and centres Smith and Hogan had run strongly all game. It was an emotional night and the standing ovation at the end brought tears to the eyes of many. It was the first cup win over Widnes in eight attempts since 1963.

After that, the semi-final against St Helens could have been an anti-climax but Hartley, subdued in the two Widnes games, was back on form with a try hat-trick. Hubbard scored two tries and kicked six goals and Rovers were through to the final at Headingley, where they beat the Airlie Birds to win the Premiership for the first time.

A very sad incident took place at Craven Park in a home match against Batley 'A' in October. Millward, playing in his second 'A' team match as he fought his way back to fitness after his injuries, took another blow to the face in an off-the-ball incident. His jaw was broken once more and he never played again. Hall was playing in that match. 'It was just a cheap shot. As Roger left the field he just said: "That's it." He was a brilliant player, and it was such a sad way for him to go.' In hindsight, it was a great pity that he did not retire after the Wembley win that May but he was then only 32 and felt he had more to give.

A benefit for Hall and Lowe raised £17,000, whilst Hornsea Pottery made 36 special mugs to commemorate the club's Challenge Cup win and after their presentation to players and officials, the mould was destroyed. The club converted the garages on the car park at Craven Park into a player's gym. In the accounts for the year ended April 1981, the parent company announced a £21,674 profit, despite a £69,645 loss on rugby running costs, with players and coaches' wages being more than double what they were two years before – now standing at £170,126. Again, the club lottery provided an invaluable £129,647 profit.

The Robins

The club paid tribute to popular referee Mick
Naughton following the retirement of the top official after a
heart murmur was diagnosed. Sadly, he died at the age of just
46 two years later. Looking back on nearly 60 years of
watching rugby league, Dave Sherwood rates Naughton as
the best referee he has seen. The Widnes-based official had
charge of several memorable Rovers games over the years,
culminating in the 1977 BBC2 trophy final.

Premiership Final, Headingley, Leeds, 16 May 1981
Hull FC 7-11 Hull Kingston Rovers

*This was a better game than the previous year's Wembley final
and, despite the closeness of the scores, a more convincing
performance by the Robins, who scored three tries to one.*

*Using prop-forwards Roy Holdstock and John Millington
to drive gaps in the Airlie Birds' defence, Rovers soon started
to make inroads. Holdstock started a move involving Steve
Hartley, Mike Smith and Peter Muscroft that ended with the
latter being tackled halfway inside the Hull FC half. It was
Holdstock again who drove in hard and when he was brought
down, Phil Hogan scythed through some slack defence
around the play-the-ball to open the scoring after 13 minutes
and Steve Hubbard landed an excellent conversion from near
the touchline to give the Robins a 5-0 lead. Rovers were not
looking secure in defence around the set-pieces either and the
Airlie Birds capitalized by setting up two attacks that ended
with Woods failing with penalty attempts. The Robins still
looked dangerous in attack and Dean foiled them when he
intercepted Smith's pass. The Black and Whites created an
overlap but Hubbard was alert and tackled Prendiville into
touch. In the 34th minute, Paul Proctor snapped up a loose
ball deep in his own half and from the play-the-ball, David
Hall put Phil Lowe into a half-gap. The second-rower fed
Hartley, who raced past the cover and rounded Woods with*

ease to score a glorious 65-yard try. Hubbard was unable to convert but Woods kicked a penalty to make it 8-2 and Prendiville was held just short on the stroke of half-time after the Airlie Birds again broke through from acting half.

The second half started with Rovers covering brilliantly to halt a Hull FC attack. After Hubbard failed with a 45-yard angled kick, the Robins surged forward again through Hartley and Hubbard and they kept the pressure on when the referee penalised Norton for holding down. Rovers' next attack produced a brilliant individual try. There appeared to be little danger when Smith took Len Casey's pass deep in the Hull FC half but he handed off Wileman and raced past Stone to reach the line before the cover could catch him. Hubbard failed with the conversion but at 11-2, the Robins had one hand on the trophy. Lowe then made two tremendous runs, the second of which had the cover defence scrambling desperately to keep him out. However, Rovers were still slack around the play-the-ball and Crane made them pay when he scored after 63 minutes. Woods' conversion narrowed Rovers' lead to 11-7 and made the last 17 minutes tenser than they need have been. The Robins could have sealed it when substitute Chris Burton drove in and passed to Lowe who set up a chance for Hubbard, but the winger slipped and Prendiville made the tackle. Rovers then had to cover well to scramble away Peacham's kick and, in the dying seconds, the Robins' cover had to be at its best to snuff out another Airlie Birds' attack.

Casey lifted the Trophy, his first as skipper, as well as the Harry Sunderland trophy for his powerful display and leadership. It was a brilliant end to the season. In a game that had all the thrills and spills expected of a derby, Rovers' more potent attacking threat the difference. After the trophy was presented, veteran BBC commentator, Eddie Waring, hung up his microphone for the last time.

*   **Hull FC:** P. Woods; G. Peacham, D. Elliott, T. Wilby, P. Prendiville; B. Banks, A. Dean; K.*

The Robins

Tindall, R. Wileman, C. Stone, T. Skerrett (I. Madley), M. Crane, S. Norton (capt). Sub not used: R. Chester
Rovers: *P. Proctor; S. Hubbard, M. Smith, P. Hogan, P. Muscroft; S. Hartley, P. Harkin; R. Holdstock, D. Watkinson, J. Millington, P. Lowe, L. Casey (capt), D. Hall (C. Burton). Sub not used: K. Watson*
Referee: J. Holdsworth (Leeds)
Attendance: 29,448

More controversies

The summer of 1981 will be remembered for riots in many of Britain's major cities that were related to racial tension and inner-city deprivation. The Humber Bridge was opened to traffic on 24 June 1981, whilst in cricket an Ian Botham-inspired England won the Ashes series 3-1.

Meanwhile, the Robins paid a world record £72,500 to secure the services of full-back George Fairbairn from Wigan. Already a Great Britain international, the Scotsman a quality player and it was a surprise that Wigan were prepared to let him go. Since the departure of Cyril Kellett in 1967, the Robins had failed to discover a worthy successor to their long line of last lines and Wigan's loss was definitely Rovers' gain.

Unfortunately, the shirt sponsorship row resurfaced at the start of the season. Rank Xerox reached agreement with the club to renew the previous season's deal. The club gave the players a 25 per cent pay increase, part of which, they later said, to cover wearing the shirts. There was clearly a lack of communication somewhere as the players demanded some of the sponsorship money and threatened not to wear the shirts. Eventually, the dispute was resolved when Rank Xerox agreed to pay an additional substantial amount to the players' pool so that the club could keep all the sponsorship money for ground improvements. The unsatisfactory episode did not reflect particularly well on any of the parties involved.

The 1981-82 campaign was far from a disaster but the club had won trophies in the four previous seasons and there was disappointment that no silverware came to Craven Park. Nevertheless, it was still a season of incident and interest.

In the first game of league campaign, away to newly promoted York, Rovers were staring down the barrel after 30 minutes. They were already 8-0 down to a spirited Wasps side when referee Allatt dismissed prop-forward Holdstock after an incident that degenerated into a free-for-all. Stand-in skipper Hall then followed him immediately for protesting too vigorously. Proving the old adage, 'when the going gets tough, the tough get going', John Millington stepped up. The veteran prop virtually singled-handedly pulled Rovers back into the game. Repeatedly driving into York's defence, it frequently took three and four defenders to bring him down and even then, he managed to slip out passes. With the other ten following his lead, the Robins gradually took control. By half-time, they had cut York's lead to 8-5 and in the end won comfortably 20-10. The supporters ran onto the field at the end and carried 'Millo' off. It was no more than he deserved and the game at York on 30 August 1981 will always be remembered by Rovers' fans as 'Millington's match'.

Another game that will be recalled but for different reasons, was that at Whitehaven on 11 October. In what had been up until then an unremarkable contest, with the scores level at 5-5 after 71 minutes, Whitehaven scrum-half Arnie Walker went to the ground after a two-man tackle involving Millington and Burton. It soon became apparent that there was a serious problem as the player lay motionless whilst the medics worked on him. After over 15 minutes, he was carried from the field and taken straight to hospital. After consulting both sides, referee Mick Beaumont abandoned the game. Fortunately, there was no lasting damage to 'Boxer' and he was playing again later in the season.

Dave Sherwood reminices: 'The mood of the Whitehaven fans near us was really ugly. Millington took Walker by the legs, which was fine, but Burton clattered him, which really upset them. They really thought he was dead. It's the only time I've been concerned for my safety on a rugby league ground.' Under normal circumstances, when a game is abandoned in the last 10 minutes, the result stands but the RFL sought the views of both clubs before reaching a decision. Rovers' board was happy to accept the draw but consulted with Millward who was adamant he wanted a replay. He was sure that his team would win second time around. He was right, the Robins eased home 25-5 on 9 April.

The nearest Rovers got to a trophy was in the John Player campaign, the highlight of which was undoubtedly a tremendous 9-8 third-round win at Widnes. After Rovers lost Fairbairn to injury in the first five minutes, the home side dominated for the opening quarter and led 5-4 at the interval. In the second half, after another 24 minutes of tense cup football, there had been no further score. Then the Chemics produced a superb move that looked to have produced a game-clinching try. However, as Cunningham went over the line, stand-in full-back Proctor not only prevented him from scoring but also managed to steal the ball. Three tackles later, out of nowhere, Hartley took the ball inside his own half and sprinted clear of the cover before dummying full-back Burke to score a brilliant 80-yard try. In the last 15 minutes, lengthened by six minutes of injury time, Rovers had to withstand some ferocious pressure from the Chemics, who were hitherto unbeaten in 20 home ties in the competition and were not going to let that record go easily. Despite almost constant Widnes possession, Rovers' defence cracked only once in the period and they held on for a nail-biting win.

In the final, once again the opposition were Hull FC at Headingley. As expected, the game was high in commitment and uncompromising defence but a crucial injury to Harkin early on, together with a couple of defensive lapses meant a 12-4 win for the Airlie Birds.

In the Challenge Cup, Rovers played Featherstone in a preliminary round game, necessitated that year as the number of professional clubs had increased to 33. However, it was the first round tie at home to Leigh that caused the most controversy. A thrilling game turned on two refereeing decisions. With the Robins holding a narrow lead in what proved to be a try-less second half, Robinson supported a brilliant break by Hartley and was pulled back as he chased the latter's kick to the line. At the very least it appeared a penalty but referee McDonald waved play on. Then, with Rovers leading 16-15 with three minutes to go, he penalised Crooks for not releasing the ball when playing it to himself. Sexton commented in the *Hull Daily Mail* that the decision was undoubtedly correct but reasonably questioned why, given that the same thing had happened on numerous occasions during the game, the referee had waited until that crucial moment to award a penalty.

After that, there were some fine performances in the league. A 25-6 win at Featherstone featured a brilliant hat-trick from Hartley on one of his most productive hunting grounds and a 28-16 success at St Helens was the first on that ground for 50 years, while the 19-13 triumph in a tremendous derby at Craven Park prevented the Airlie Birds from recording a double. Ultimately, the Robins' failure to record an away win against any of their main challengers and a sole home defeat against Barrow, meant they had to settle for fourth position, two points and two places behind Hull FC.

Perhaps the greatest controversy was once again in the Premiership play-off. Rovers played Bradford at Craven Park in the first round. The two teams had met on three previous occasions during the season with Rovers winning twice, and it appeared that there were some old scores to settle. Certainly, there was a lot of niggling from the start of the game. Referee Whitfield, no angel in his own playing days, had a reputation for allowing a bit of give and take. In hindsight he was too slow to take action, particularly after two incidents involving Crooks and Bradford second-row man Parrott, which led to the Northern man having to leave the field. However, when in the 21st minute Millington and van Bellen came to blows after an innocuous tackle, Whitfield decided that he had had enough and dismissed them both. Hartley and Bradford half-back Carroll followed after failing to heed a warning and carrying on their feud after a scrum then, two minutes before half-time, Northern's Ellis was sent off after Harkin had been laid out. At the break, the Robins led 12-5 on the scoreboard and 11-10 in men.

After 16 minutes of the second half, with Rovers leading 17-8, a Bradford player lost the ball in the tackle. When Whitfield ordered a scrum, Northern skipper Jeff Grayshon appeared to throw the ball at the referee, who immediately sent him off. As he left the field, Grayshon signalled the eight remaining Northern players to follow him. After a short delay whilst he left the field to investigate, Whitfield returned and blew his whistle to signal the end of the game. The excellent performances of Hogan for Rovers and Noble for Bradford were overshadowed. The RFL confirmed the award of the game to the Robins.

Five days later, the season ended when a weakened side lost 16-15 at Widnes in the semi-final, the third one-point defeat in cup football of the season.

Fairbairn, as expected, made the full-back spot his own, missing only two games and kicking a new club record of 160 goals in the season. In a season of relatively few comings and goings, 'A' team coach Dunn made his final appearance in the last match at Widnes and Steve Hartley and John Millington enjoyed a joint benefit during the season. Rovers 'A' were again champions of the Yorkshire Senior Competition and the Robins had five players chosen for the first ever Great Britain Colts tour of Australia. The historic pioneers were Asuquo 'Zook' Ema, Malcolm Beall, Stu Wardle, Garry Clark and Tracey Lazenby. All but Wardle progressed to the first team, whilst Clark gained full international status.

Across the City, the Tigers had ended the 1981-82 season in receivership,but on 15 May 1982 the former Rovers 'A' team full-back and professional wrestler Don Robinson came to their rescue. Scarborough-based Robinson had built his fortune in the leisure industry and had built up that town's football club to become the most successful non-league team in the country. In the first season under his stewardship, City were promoted from the fourth division of the football league. Few then would have dreamt that Robinson would come to Rovers' rescue less than 20 years later.

On the eve of the 1982-83 season, Paul Rose moved to Hull FC for £30,000. He had been unsettled at Craven Park for some time and the club had signed Wakefield second-rower Andy Kelly for £60,000 in the close season. Since making his first team debut at the age of 16, Rose had made 270 appearances for the Robins, scoring 43 tries, many using his strength to power over from play-the-balls near the opposition line especially as, in those days, players were allowed to tap ball to themselves. A powerful and direct runner with an ability to slip the ball in the tackle, Rose was also a hard tackler and a perfect foil for Lowe. Their second-row partnership was widely held to be best the club has had. Rose was most destructive when taking a short pass at full speed and bursting through the first line of defence. A gentle giant off the field, Rose's aggressive approach on it sometimes got him into trouble.

Ever alert to opportunities to improve the team's performances, Millward introduced the use of a multi-gym as part of training sessions and devised more sophisticated pre-match warm-up routines. Colin Hutton had taken over as chairman from Bill Land and his first season in charge coincided with the Robins Diamond Jubilee celebrations of 60 years at Craven Park.

In the first match of the season, a comfortable home win over Workington, Kelly and former Colts winger Garry Clark made their first appearances. In the third game, earmarked for the Jubilee celebrations, a highly impressive performance saw Rovers beat St Helens 31-10. A thrilling 16-12 derby success at Craven Park on 22 September marked the debut of the first of three New Zealanders who were to play a huge part in the club's successes over the next few years. Gary Prohm played at loose-forward that day but switched to the left wing in December, where he struck up a partnership with centre Ian Robinson.

October saw the visit of the 1982 Kangaroos, inspired by the mighty Mal Meninga, who created history by going unbeaten throughout the whole tour. Rovers gave them a scare at Craven Park, putting up a real fight and leading 8-5 at half-time. The Robins trailed by only two points after 65 minutes before they ran out of steam and lost 30-10. The sin-bin was introduced for the tour and was retained in domestic rugby thereafter.

A second Kiwi, extremely popular half-back Gordon Smith, made his debut against Leigh on 7 November. Smith then played through to the end of the season at scrum-half, replacing Jamie Walsh, who had been brought in from Castleford as cover for the injured Harkin.

The Robins reached the third round of the John Player trophy where they were beaten 11-10 at Warrington in December. Egged on by the partisan home crowd, an overzealous linesman made their task more difficult by making several incursions into the field of play that all culminated in penalties against Rovers. Even then, a very late try by Hogan would have brought victory had Fairbairn been successful with the difficult conversion.

In the first match of the New Year, at home to Halifax, Prohm was the first Rovers' player to be sin-binned. Despite his lost ten minutes, he still managed to score four tries. The following month's one-point Challenge Cup first round defeat at Hunslet was akin to disaster and Millward made several changes for the following week's trip to Wigan. They brought immediate reward with a 21-5 success which launched a seven-match winning run. Millward moved regular right-centre Mike Smith to stand-off in place of Hartley and Fairbairn from full-back into centre. Former Hull & E.R. back John Lydiat, came in at full-back, Old Hymerian David Laws to the wing and former Colts' loose-forward Lazenby made his debut.

On Good Friday, despite seven league defeats, Rovers were the closest challengers to the Airlie Birds at the top of the table when they visited the Boulevard. However, a 21-3 loss and a home draw against Warrington two days later meant that the Robins had to be content with second place in the league, four points behind their neighbours. In the Premiership, after a comfortable home win at Castleford, the Robins lost 21-10 at home to Widnes in the semis.

By the end of the season, Fairbairn and Mike Smith had resumed their normal roles and Lazenby retained his jersey. Casey remembers Lazenby well. 'He was a natural – one of the best young players I'd seen. When I went to Wakefield he was on Rovers' transfer list and I told Trinity they had to raise the money to sign him.'

Rovers used just 27 players all season, the lowest number since 1966-67. Watkinson led the way, missing only two games. There were three significant departures. In November, goal-kicking winger Steve Hubbard was injured at Bradford and subsequently decided to retire. In a relatively short career with the Robins, he achieved considerable popularity for his powerful wing-play and excellent goal-kicking. Although not the fastest winger the club has had, his strong physique made him a hard man to stop and he put the same force into his goal kicks. Sadly, injuries restricted him to 122 games in which he scored 72 tries and kicked 327 goals – a remarkable tally of 870 points.

The very capable reserve hooker Ray Price, who had twice played in the first three rounds of the Challenge Cup only for Watkinson to return for the semi-finals, made the last of his 52 appearances at home to Bradford in November. The last remaining member of the 1960s team, Phil Lowe, was the highest profile casualty of the cup-tie at Hunslet. He initially decided to retire but when he wanted to resume playing with York, Rovers refused to release his registration.

The financial picture was very much as the previous season. The club lottery made a £180,136 profit but the rugby running costs and transfers deficit amounted to £171,989 and the parent company made an overall £34,537 loss on the season. Players wage costs were £197,680, with first team winning pay having risen to around £250-£300, and losing pay £50.

Record-breakers

For their centenary season, Hull Kingston Rovers had a new look on the field, reverting to their original red jerseys with a wide blue band at chest level. This bore the name of a new sponsor, local company Savoy Tyres who had advertised in the club programme for many years. The RFL introduced two significant rule changes for the new season. The value of a try was increased from three points to four and. after the sixth tackle, instead of a scrum being formed, the ball was handed over to the defending side to restart with a play-the-ball.

Rovers did not make an impressive start to the season, winning only two of the first seven games which included another first round defeat in the Yorkshire Cup at Odsal. The third of the club's New Zealand trio, uncompromising forward Mark Broadhurst, made his debut at home to Oldham on 25 September. However, it was the following game, in the Boulevard derby, which really turned things around. Although not a perfect performance, the 23-8 win was a great improvement on what had gone before. The forwards dominated, and Gordon Smith and Hall provided an effective link to a dangerous back division in which Mike Smith was outstanding.

That was the start of an eight match-winning run. In the following game, a 16-14 home win over Bradford, experienced Australian back John Dorahy made his first appearance. The following week saw another narrow win, a famous 8-6 victory over the Queensland tourists with Broadhurst in the thick of the action. The winning run ended a month later with a second round John Player defeat at Leeds, but the Robins lost only one further league match before a comprehensive 44-16 win at Leigh on 15 April sealed this Championship. Over the period, Rovers won 23 out of 27 games. The single league defeat at Odsal on 3 February coincided with the absence of key players Fairbairn, Broadhurst, Watkinson and Casey and prevented the Robins from equalling the then Championship record of 13 successive wins.

There were impressive league doubles over Widnes and Wigan, more free-flowing rugby in which they passed the 40-points mark eight times and a run of five consecutive away wins that culminated in the title-clinching success at Leigh. The 795 points scored in 30 Championship games was a new record.

The regular Championship-winning team was; Fairbairn; Clark, Mike Smith, Prohm and Laws; Dorahy and Gordon Smith; Broadhurst and Casey or Millington at prop; Watkinson, until he broke his leg in January, when youngster Chris Rudd took over; second row, two from Burton, Kelly and Hogan and Hall at loose-forward. Hartley started the season at stand-off but after his injury against Queensland he was mainly used as a reserve. Winger Clark missed just two games all season.

The Greats – No 22
Phil Lowe - *see Hull KR legends gallery*

Phil Lowe was born in Hull in January 1950, signing for Rovers from Jervis Youth Club on his 16th birthday. A former Hull and Yorkshire schoolboys' captain, he quickly progressed through the Juniors and 'A' team ranks. Lowe made his first team debut in a drawn game at home to Featherstone on 4 March 1967 and although he made only a handful of appearances that season, he earned a regular second-row place the following one when he appeared in 44 of the 49 matches.

Lowe was 6'2", very tall for that time, and he possessed a powerful physique and considerable pace for a forward. He caused havoc to defences with his strong running coupled with a high knee action and a sledgehammer hand-off. He was the club's player of the year in 1968-69, by which time he was attracting comparison with the legendary Cumbrian international forward Dick 'Tiger' Huddart.

He made his international debut the following season and became the youngest member of the victorious 1970 Great Britain tour party to Australasia. Although he did not play in the historic tests against the Aussies, it was a great experience for the young man and he worked one-to-one with coach Johnny Whiteley on his handling during it. Whiteley was a great admirer of the young forward whom he had tried to sign for Hull FC when only 15. "He had physique and speed, he was a natural athlete – you could see that he was destined for success," he notes. In all, Lowe played 12 games for Great Britain and five for England in addition to several Yorkshire County appearances and helped Great Britain to victory in the 1972 World Cup final.

1972-73 was Lowe's most prolific try-scoring season in which he beat William Sandham's 60-year old club record for a forward with 26 tries, including 14 in a spell in which he crossed in eight consecutive games. The following year he decided to take on a new challenge and emigrated to Australia to spend three years with top Aussie club Manly. He scored 25 tries in 72 games for them, none more important than their only score in the 1976 Grand Final success over Parramatta.

In October 1976, still only 26 and at his peak, Lowe made a try-scoring return to Rovers against Workington at Craven Park and he was a regular member of the side until his retirement in 1983. On his return from Australia, in addition to his powerful running, he had developed into a fine cover-tackler. In the championship-winning 1978-79 season he made a huge contribution to the success with 24 tries in 37 appearances.

Lowe's last game was in a Challenge Cup defeat at Hunslet on 13 February 1983 – certainly not the way he would have chosen to end his glorious career. However, there is little doubt that for those who were privileged to see him in a Rovers jersey, he was the finest running second-row forward the club has had. In all, Lowe made 418 appearances for the Robins and scored 179 tries, playing in a record five finals against Hull FC and finishing on the winning side on three occasions.

Since his retirement from playing, Lowe had a short spell coaching at York before two with the Robins as a director, serving both as chairman and football director – the latter a position he still holds. He has also become a very successful businessman through his hostelry and property interests.

16 October 1983, Tour match, Craven Park, Hull
Hull Kingston Rovers 8-6 Queensland

Reigning Australian State of Origin champions Queensland undertook a short tour of Great Britain in October 1983 that included fixtures against Rovers, Leeds and Wigan. The first of these, at Craven Park, is written into Rovers folklore not for the standard of rugby but for the way Rovers stood up to and overcame the over-aggressive approach of the tourists. It was also the first competitive game in which the Robins used more than two substitutes.

The Queenslanders were brutal with a third man continually coming in at the tackle to wreak havoc. Watkinson was led off with a gash to his forehead that required seven stitches, Holdstock was stretchered off following a late tackle and Prohm was lucky to carry on after several unsavoury challenges. The incident that changed the game took place late in the first half when Queensland hooker Shane Bernardin punched Mark Broadhurst in the tackle. He picked the wrong man. Broadhurst, an ex-boxer, got to his feet and unfurled a devastating left hook that felled Bernardin on the spot. It should certainly have earned Broadhurst a sending off but with the crowd cheering wildly, referee Robin Whitfield decided simply to deliver a finger-wagging. After that, the game settled down and the official imposed some authority by sending Queensland's Bernardin and Bryan Niebling, and Rovers' Chris Burton, to the sin bin for separate offences.

6-4 down at half-time, Rovers started to take control through their forwards in the second half. They took the lead in the 43rd minute when Queensland failed to clear Gordon Smith's angled kick and Mike Smith touched down. Apart from occasional touches by Aussie great Wally Lewis, the visitors rarely threatened and Dorahy and Gordon Smith controlled the game at half-back whilst George Fairbairn produced a typically solid and fearless performance at full-back. In the end a magnificent team performance saw the Robins home.

The crowd, who had a new hero in Broadhurst, gave the team a standing ovation. The club, counting the cost of the victory, were not so enthusiastic and castigated Queensland's tactics. Queensland asked for a rematch but Rovers declined saying that they could not fit the fixture into their busy schedule. The two other tour games were totally one-sided with the Maroons scoring over 50 points against both Leeds and Wigan and not conceding a single try in the process.

> **Rovers:** *G. Fairbairn; G. Clark, M. Smith, J. Dorahy, G. Prohm; S. Hartley (D. Laws), G. Smith; R. Holdstock (A. Kelly), D. Watkinson (capt) (T. Lazenby), M. Broadhurst, P. Hogan, C. Burton, D. Hall.*
>
> **Queensland:** *C. Scott; S. Stacey (J. Kilroy), G. Miles, I. French, M. Brennan; W. Lewis, M. Murray (W. Lindenberg); P. Khan (T. Paterson), S. Bernardin, B. Tessman, B. Niebling, C. Phelan, W. Fullerton-Smith (capt). Sub not used: G. Jones*
> *Referee: M.R. Whitfield (Widnes)*
> *Attendance: 6,383 (£9,600)*

The Robins

The Robins then finished the season in real style by becoming the first club to complete a Championship and Premiership double. In the first round of the play-offs, they had a Premiership record 54-0 win over Leeds, who Rovers had failed to beat in their three earlier matches that season. After a hard-fought semi-final win over St Helens, the final against Castleford at Headingley was the classic game of two halves. Castleford held an 8-0 lead at the break before skipper for the day Hall and man of the match Dorahy inspired the Robins and four clinical tries by the backs swept them to an 18-10 success. For Hall it was a dream come true. 'I was a bit jaded in the first half and at half-time Millward told me that he needed more from me. I was able to raise my game and lifting the trophy at the end was a great feeling that I'll never forget.'

It was a really strong and talented squad possessing a tremendous team spirit, that had come together with magnificent support from a very capable backroom and coaching set-up, to produce the greatest season in the club's history.

The only disappointing note was a financial one. For the first time the lottery income reduced, from the previous year's peak of £171,989 to £143,104. Players and coaches' wages, understandably, increased and although there was an increase in gate receipts, worryingly the attendances and season pass sales reduced. A cash deficiency of £23,927 was the subject of legal proceedings.

The summer of 1984 saw the start of the national miners' strike that dominated the news for the next 12 months, Liverpool won their fourth European Cup in eight years, *Crimewatch* first appeared on our TV screens, and Frankie Goes to Hollywood were at number one for nine weeks with 'Two Tribes'.

It was going to be a tall order for the 1984-85 season

to top the achievements of the previous one but the Robins made a fine start with nine consecutive wins. For the opening game at Odsal, there were three changes to the previous season's regular team. Mike Smith moved up to stand-off for Dorahy who did not return that season, Robinson took Smith's centre position and Zook Ema, with only two substitute appearances behind him, filled the number 10 shirt. Harkin returned from his injury as a substitute for Gordon Smith, the two vying for the scrum-half role for the rest of the season. Watkinson came back after his broken leg and took over as captain in the absence of the suspended Casey. In the opening game, Prohm ran strongly on to the astute passes of Mike Smith and Kelly to score four memorable tries in a 34-6 win over Bradford.

In the nine-match winning run that ensued, St Helens were eclipsed 32-6 by a powerful second half performance and in the Craven Park derby, playing with a stiff breeze behind them, the Airlie Birds' stifled Rovers' attacking threat for 30 minutes and an interception try and a defensive lapse gifted the visitors a 16-2 interval lead. However, it was all Rovers in the second half and, with Watkinson controlling the scrums and Gordon Smith pulling the strings behind them, they powered to a 26-17 win. The following week there was a comprehensive 18-4 win at Widnes but then the Robins came down to earth with a three-match wobble. Home league defeats to Wigan and Leeds came either side of a disappointing Yorkshire Cup final defeat by Hull FC in front of 25,243 spectators at Boothferry Park. Rovers took an early 12-0 lead but the noisy neighbours came back strongly to cut the advantage to 12-8 at half-time and ran out comfortable winners 29-12.

After the Leeds game, the Robins travelled to Oldham with Gavin Miller, a relatively unknown Australian loose-forward, replacing the injured Hall. With Miller making an impressive debut, a 31-5 win sparked a 16-match winning run. That included a John Player Trophy final, again at Boothferry Park against the Black and Whites, which Rovers won 12-0. In the New Year, there were successive away wins at Leeds and St Helens, no mean achievement in any era. The Saints game was a classic, hard-fought Challenge Cup tie with some tremendous defence typified by Fairbairn's magnificent try-saving tackle on Meninga. Prohm did brilliantly to carve out an opening for Clark to score in the corner after 72 minutes and Fairbairn's touchline conversion made it 8-3. Even then Saints piled on the pressure and Fairbairn and Miller had to be at their best to tackle Day into touch as he crossed the line in the dying moments. The win partly avenged the controversial defeat in Rovers' previous Challenge Cup tie at Knowsley Road 19 years earlier.

Another wobble, with only one win in four games, followed a contentious defeat at Wigan. The Robins, already without Harkin, Watkinson and Kelly, lost forwards Ema and Burton in the first 20 minutes, by which time they were 8-0 down and fielding two players who had not played a first team match in over three months. However, with Broadhurst, Miller and Hogan taking the lead in the forwards and Fairbairn outstanding at full-back, they fought back to lead 16-14 with 15 minutes to go. There were chances at both ends but in the second minute of injury time, Ford collected Kenny's kick in what appeared to be an offside position and crossed in the corner as Wigan sneaked home.

Three matches later, Wigan beat the Robins for a third time in the season in a thrilling Challenge Cup semi-final at Elland Road, 18-11. The men from Central Park led 4-1 at the end of a tight first half and the game came to life when Rovers brought on Gordon Smith and Hall at half-time. The two substitutes combined to send Miller in for a try soon after the restart, Fairbairn goaling. After the only penalty goal of the game cut Rovers' lead to a single point, Wigan skipper West sent in Stephenson for a converted try to give them a 12-7 lead on only their second incursion into Rovers territory since break. After 63 minutes, brilliant work by Hall and Hogan got Clark in at the corner, just too far out for the conversion. Then, a point down, Clark swooped on a poor pass and appeared to be clear but Scott's despairing fingertip tackle did just enough for the defence to cover and Rovers' last chance had gone. Three minutes from time, the long-striding West created a try for Gill to settle the issue.

After that, the Robins could once again concentrate on the league and a run of nine wins in ten games, including an impressive 22-11 win at Warrington and a record 36-12 win at the Boulevard, culminated in a 30-14 triumph at Barrow that sealed the Championship title for a second consecutive season. Rovers then reached a second successive Premiership final but once again Elland Road proved to be a bogey ground and at the end of a long, hard season, St Helens were just too fast and strong and won 36-16.

John Player Trophy, Boothferry Park, Hull, 26 January 1985
Hull FC 0-12 Hull Kingston Rovers

This was the only time that the Robins won the John Player Trophy and sweet revenge for the earlier Yorkshire Cup final between the sides, when they had taken a 12-0 lead and capitulated badly. The Rovers pack, brilliantly led by skipper David Watkinson, put in a powerful display and the Airlie Birds, despite majority possession, never really threatened.

After a robust start in which the former Rovers' man Paul Rose was lucky to escape with a lecture from veteran referee Stan Wall, the Robins established a grip on the game. George

The Robins

Fairbairn, who had an uncharacteristic off day with his kicking, missed an early penalty attempt but on 13 minutes Gavin Miller's brilliantly delayed pass gave Ian Robinson a chance to put David Laws in. Then, when Evans knocked the pass down, Gary Prohm was there to gather the ball and go over. Soon after, Phil Hogan swept through a gap from Miller's pass and burst through a tackle to score. Fairbairn missed both conversions but Rovers were in control. Man of the match Paul Harkin controlled the game with his astute passing and tactical kicking – in the first half in particular he repeatedly pinned the Black and Whites back in their own half.

The Robins were not as precise in attack in the second half but, with eight minutes to go, Miller's long pass to Robinson saw the centre cut inside and pass to the supporting Hogan, who beat three men before looping out a long ball to the right wing where Garry Clark went in unopposed. As the Robins' fans in the competition-record crowd celebrated at the end of the game, Watkinson lifted the trophy – his first as captain.

The wintry weather in the lead up had resulted in difficult underfoot conditions and Roger Millward was unhappy about the decision that it should go ahead. Nevertheless, by the end he was justifiably proud of his team's performance as well as relieved that there were no major injuries.

Hull FC: G. Kemble (G. Schofield); S. Evans, F. Ah Kuoi, J. Leuluai, D. O'Hara; D. Topliss (capt), P. Sterling; P. Edmonds (A. Dannatt), S. Patrick, P. Rose, L. Crooks, W. Proctor, G. Divorty.
Rovers: G. Fairbairn; G. Clark, I. Robinson, G. Prohm, D. Laws; M. Smith, P. Harkin; M. Broadhurst, D. Watkinson (capt), A. Ema, C. Burton, P. Hogan, G. Miller. Subs not used: J. Lydiat, L. Casey
Referee: S. Wall (Leigh)
Attendance: 25,336 (£69,355)

314

Centre Prohm enjoyed a wonderful season. The only ever-present, he continued as he had started at Bradford, and scored a club record 45 tries in 46 games. Fairbairn assumed full goal-kicking responsibility again and kicked his second century of goals with 135.

A number of club stalwarts played their last games. Former skipper Casey played in only five matches and left to join Wakefield in March. Steve Hartley made his last appearance when he came on as a substitute at home to Rochdale on 2 December, the old warhorses Millington and Holdstock donned the colours for the last time in April and David Hall did likewise in the Premiership Final.

Hall's career possibly suffered due to his versatility. A very talented player, he played at full-back, centre, stand-off and loose-forward at various times. Many supporters felt that it was at loose-forward in the later part of his career that he was at his best. He possibly did not have the pace to be a top-class back but locking the scrum he showed his array of skills, eye for a half-gap and ability to put a man into space. Making his debut at Bradford in April 1971, he played in 383 games for the Robins, kicking 166 goals and scoring 89 tries and won two Great Britain caps in 1984. A particular highlight for Hall was captaining the side that won the Premiership against Castleford that year. 'I'll never forget the feeling of pride at leading up the side to collect the trophy with all those great players behind me,' he recalls.

Roy Holdstock also made his debut at Odsal, at second-row in March 1973. In all, he made 277 appearances, mostly at prop. One of his finest performances was in the win over Hull FC at Wembley in 1980, a tremendous climax to his best-ever season. He won two Great Britain and three England caps and enjoyed a testimonial in his final season.

To add to the first team's two trophies, the 'A' team

won the new Alliance league that amalgamated the previous county competitions, posting a record 106-0 win over Keighley in the process, and the Colts won their Premiership trophy.

The Greats – No 23
Len Casey - *see Hull KR legends gallery*

Len 'Cast Iron' Casey was born in Hull on 28 January 1950. He joined Hull FC from Beverley Juniors in 1970, making his debut at centre in September. After making 102 appearances, during which time he made the switch to loose-forward, he transferred across the city to join the Robins in September 1975. At the time, Rovers had just achieved promotion to the First Division and were looking to add some steel to their pack.

Casey's career with the Airlie Birds was faltering and he needed a change. 'Things were at a low ebb at the Boulevard. Bill Ramsey was at the club then and when Rovers came in for me he told me to get myself there – he said that Rovers were going to be a good side in a couple of years.' Casey had not anticipated the abuse that he and his family would suffer because of his move. 'We lived in Black & White territory then, we were shouted at and things were thrown at the house – I had become a Red and White bastard!'

Casey quickly settled at Craven Park where he became the automatic selection at loose-forward. He had only been there a couple of months when Rovers appointed Harry Poole as coach. Casey credits Poole with setting him on the path to the game's top honours. 'I owe him more than I can say, his advice and encouragement helped me enormously,' he recalls fondly. For his part, Poole appreciated the commitment and aggressive streak shown by his young loose-forward and made him his pack leader.

Casey developed his reputation not only as a player not to be trifled with but as a ball handler who could be relied upon to step up and lead by example in the big matches.

However, by the end of the 1977-78 season, feeling that the team had lost some of its spirit, he asked to leave. He remembers a letter he received from a nine-year old Rovers supporter. 'It had fifty pence in it and it said, "My dad says you are going to leave Rovers – will this help you to stay?" Unfortunately it had no address on it but I still have it.'

In December 1978, he signed for Bradford Northern in a deal valued at £25,000 which also brought Paul Harkin to Craven Park. Profiting from playing with the likes of Jeff Grayshon and Jimmy Thompson at Odsal, Casey played some of his best football there and quickly became a big favourite. But within a month of winning the man of the match award in Bradford's John Player trophy win over Widnes in January 1980, he returned to Craven Park. The Robins had faltered after their 1978-79 First Division championship win and wanting to boost their hopes, they paid Bradford a world record £38,000 to get him back.

Returning an even better player, Casey was instrumental in Rovers' 1980 Challenge Cup success and was rewarded with the club captaincy the following season. During the 1980-81 season he started to appear more regularly in the second row and later at prop. In May 1981, he led Rovers to a trophy for the first time, winning the Harry Sunderland memorial award as best player in their Premiership success over Hull FC. On 3 February 1985, by which time he was appearing mainly as a substitute, he played in his last game for the Robins, at home to Halifax.

'He was a great leader,' says John Millington. 'He was the man you needed when the going was tough, he backed down to no one.' David Hall agrees: 'He was a born winner, insufferable in defeat!'

'He wrote the winning fee on the strapping on his arm,' remembers Mike Smith. 'When we conceded a try, he pointed at it and growled at us, "That's what we're on today."' Chris Draper says: 'When he was skipper, we'd give him the money for the players' post-match drinks but they'd

*have a hell of a job getting it off him! He'd always have been
in my team though, he rose to the big occasion.'*

*In two spells for the Robins, Casey played in 237 games,
scoring 19 tries. At international level, he won 14 Great
Britain caps and five for England, captaining both. After
leaving Rovers, Casey had a successful 18-month stint as
player-coach at Wakefield, earning them promotion in 1986
before leaving to take over from Arthur Bunting at the
Boulevard. After his resignation in 1988, Casey returned to
Craven Park to join Rovers' board. He left in February 1991
to take up the post of manager-coach at new club
Scarborough Pirates, after which he coached Beverley ARLC.*

*As amiable and friendly off the field as he was tough and
uncompromising on it, he will live long in the memories of
Rovers' fans and he looks back with fondness on great days
with Rovers. He pays particular tribute to the work of
coaches Cliff Wallis, Johnny Moore and Ged Dunn for the
tremendous role they played in supporting Roger Millward.
'It was a family club. Everyone was made to feel welcome,
Carol Millward played a huge part in that too.'*

*Len Casey now runs a B&B in the Lake District with his
partner, Sue.*

The Greats – No 24
Steve Hartley - *see Hull KR legends gallery*

*Steve Hartley was born in Hull in 1950. A one club man,
he signed for the Robins from Craven Park Juniors in 1970.*

*After making his debut at stand-off at home to Wakefield
on 2 January 1971, he found opportunities hard to come by
in his early years, mainly due to the presence of Roger
Millward in the jersey.*

*Even in Millward's absence, Hartley was not an
automatic selection and by the time Harry Poole succeeded
Arthur Bunting as coach in late 1975, he had made only 68
appearances, 14 as a substitute, in four-and-a-half seasons.*

Poole saw his potential and quickly made him his first choice pivot, moving Millward to scrum-half. Hartley repaid the faith by developing into one of the most devastating finishers in the game.

Not in the classic mould of half-backs, his great strength was his elusive running. Using his sidestep and change of pace, he scored tries out of nothing and was devastating when put into space by the astute passes of his teammates. As John Millington remarks: 'When you saw his chin go up and his head go back, you knew it was going to be a try. It was a sight for sore eyes when you were knackered from all the graft you'd got through.'

Recalling some of his great tries, David Hall adds: 'When you saw him race through a gap, it made the hair stand up on the back of your neck.' For the supporters of that era, the 'Hartley specials' are a vivid and treasured memory.

The arrival of Allan Agar in the late 1970s meant that he sometimes moved to centre, where he played in the 1980 Wembley final. His appearances there never diminished his try-scoring threat but he was always at his best in the pivotal role, looking for a short pass to run onto at pace and outstrip the defence. He was arguably the best finisher the club has had. One-on-one against any full-back of his era, Hartley was favourite to score every time.

He played his last game for Rovers in the John Player trophy at home to Rochdale on 2 December 1984. Not wanting to play for any other club, he simply retired when he learned that Rovers planned to sell him to Hunslet. In 369 appearances for the Robins, he scored 191 tries, including five against Huddersfield in 1979, making him second only to Roger Millward in the club's all-time list. The First Division championship season of 1978-79 was his most prolific, when he scored 35 tries to become the league's top try scorer that campaign. Hartley won three Great Britain caps.

He shared a testimonial with his old friend and fellow joker Millington in 1979-80. 'They were both real comedians,' says Millward. 'They could always lift the dressing room tension and relax the players.'

After becoming a licensee towards the end of his rugby days, Hartley is now retired and living in Hull.

The Greats – No 25
John Millington - *see Hull KR legends gallery*

Born in East Hull in February 1949, John Millington joined the Robins in 1970 from the local Priestmans RUFC but had already played rugby league at youth club level; his father played for Bramley. The York scout who initially spotted him subsequently joined Rovers, so Millington was invited for a trial at Craven Park. He made his debut for the Robins at home to Swinton on 28 November 1970 and earned a regular place in the side the following season.

In the 1973-74 relegation season, Millington really made his reputation. In a poor side, he stood up resolutely to his task and his powerful forward charges and strong tackling made him one of the few successes of that season.

The following year he earned one of his two England caps but his wholehearted commitment and ability should have earned him more. Millington invariably stood up to be counted when it mattered most, never more so than his man of the match performance in the Floodlit Trophy win over St Helens and in adversity at York in 1981.

A hard grafter, he sustained his powerful drives and determined defence for a full 80 minutes week after week. Between the start of the 1974-75 season until the end of 1977-78, he played in 139 of the club's 166 games, remaining on the field for a full time in 125 of them. 'If I'd only had to play 40 minutes and not have to push in the scrums for 30 games a season, I'd still be playing now!' he jokes.

A stocky figure with a shock of wavy fair hair and an all-action style, he stood out on the field and was a supporters' favourite. Off it, as a dressing-room joker who had a nickname for everyone, he made a big contribution to team spirit. 'He was the first man to welcome me and make me feel at home when I signed in 1976,' says Len Casey. 'He was the life and soul of the dressing room,' remembers George Fairbairn. 'Always laughing and joking.' The dressing room banter often masked his nervousness. 'I used to get nervous to the point of sickness before games,' he says.

Phil Lowe acknowledges: 'He was a very modest man. I remember congratulating him on his performance at the end of one game and he just said he was simply doing his job, and that the only reward he wanted was to see us scoring tries when his head came out of the scrum.'

His aversion to training runs caused much banter between him and Roger Millward when the latter became coach. 'He knew every short-cut in East Hull,' says Millward. 'But I got him back one day when he shot off first to dive into one of his short cuts and I managed to stop the rest of them following. We had a practice game until he got back an hour later. He was furious!'

Millington says he had the last laugh, when Millward was waiting for him half-way through another run and said he'd run along with him. 'I'd got my second wind by then and got up speed. He was lagging behind and asking me to slow down, he was scared of getting left behind, because he didn't know the way!' Millington had a serious point too: 'I worked all day lugging concrete slabs and the like about, the last thing you needed after that was a ten-mile run.'

In 1984-85, a move to Kent Invicta fell through due to their financial difficulties and Millington returned to Rovers' playing register. On the morning of 8 April that season, not having played or trained for over a month, he got a call from Millward asking him to play that afternoon against Workington due to an injury crisis. In his first outing for the first team that season, he turned the clock back with an outstanding performance that earned him the man of the match award. It was not enough to keep him in the team for the next game, however, and he made one more appearance for the Robins at St Helens in April 1985. After 418 games, he joined Casey at Wakefield for a season before retiring.

Still living in East Hull, Millington keeps in touch with many of his old team-mates. 'They were great times and I made some true friends for life,' he says.

The end of an era

For the 1985-86 season, the Robins reverted to the traditional white jerseys with a red band and a new shirt sponsor, Hanson White Print. The season opened with rugby league's first Charity Shield game between champions Rovers and Challenge Cup holders Wigan, played at Douglas on the Isle of Man. Although the Robins fielded a strong side, Wigan seemed to want the game more and they ended up comfortable winners.

With a team unchanged from the previous year, Rovers then put together seven successive wins, a spell that included a thrilling 19-18 win over Wigan at Craven Park, when Kelly won the game with a 40-yard drop-goal in the 79th minute, the first one-pointer of his career. The run ended in a 28-6 defeat at the Boulevard in October.

The next game, a defeat to the New Zealand tourists, saw the debut of Canterbury prop Peter Johnston, who replaced Broadhurst that season. After another defeat, at St Helens in the league, Rovers then faced Castleford in the Yorkshire Cup Final at Headingley. They dominated for the first hour, with Watkinson and Miller to the fore, and led 22-6, as well as missing three golden try-scoring opportunities. However, in the last 20 minutes international prop Ward almost single-handedly pulled Castleford back into the game and the final score was 22-18. Dorahy, who had returned for his second season, kicked five goals and Miller was awarded the White Rose trophy.

A nine-match winning run followed, including wins at Leeds and Widnes, and a fine team performance resulted in a 22-4 John Player semi-final win over St Helens. The winning run ended in the final, where once again a trip to Elland Road resulted in defeat. However, despite missing Fairbairn, Prohm and Hogan, the Robins played a full part in an exciting and hard-fought game. An uncharacteristic first half defensive error allowed Wane to score from a play-the-ball to give Wigan a 7-1 lead and although Rovers dominated the second half, briefly taking the lead through tries by Lydiat and Laws, a well-worked try from Ford gave Wigan an 11-8 victory.

After league defeats against Widnes and Wigan, another unbeaten run took Rovers to the Challenge Cup semi-final. By then the fixtures were starting to pile up and matters got worse when a thrilling tie against Leeds at Elland Road ended in a 24-24 draw. Leeds built up a 12-2 lead shortly before half-time and Rovers were reduced to 12 men when Harkin was dismissed for an attempted trip in the build up to the second Leeds try. However, the Robins came back so strongly with 12 men, Mike Smith and Laws each scoring two tries, that they led 24-14 with 15 minutes to go. Such an effort had taken its toll and twice Leeds exploited gaps to bring the scores level. Former Robins' prop Peter Fox, then coaching at Leeds, was upset that Laws appeared to lose the ball as he crossed for one of his tries but, on the other hand, Lyons' trip on Miller and Wilkinson's obstruction on Laws went unpunished.

Two days after that, Rovers went to Dewsbury where they won 18-14 with only four regular first-teamers in the side and just three days later returned to Elland Road for the semi-final replay. The Robins produced a most professional performance to win 17-0 and reached their third Challenge Cup final in seven years. But by this stage they had lost seven league games and still needed to play nine matches in 17 days. It was clear that they had no chance of retaining the Championship and they took the opportunity to blood a number of second-teamers. Indeed, in three of those games, no regular first-teamers played at all; unsurprisingly Rovers lost all three. Of eleven who made their debuts over this period two, talented half-back Wayne Parker and forward Chris Harrison, both became stalwarts of the side in later years.

Rovers won only three of the last nine league games and they finished seventh. In the week before the cup final, an almost full-strength side went to Wigan for the first round of the Premiership but after a fairly even first half and the sending-off of Aussie prop Johnston, the game petered out as a contest and Wigan romped home.

The season ended in disappointment at Wembley, where the Robins went down to Castleford 15-14. There was speculation that some of the players were not fully fit, a charge that, except in the case of Miller, Millward rejects. What is not in dispute is that it was the 48th match and third cup final of a very long season and perhaps some of the players had little energy left. Only Johnston and Ema in the front row and Laws on the wing played anywhere near their best, and the Robins made too many uncharacteristic errors in both attack and defence. Sandy's try on 62 minutes appeared to have settled the issue at 15-6, but Rovers produced a storming finish with tries from Prohm and Lydiat and Dorahy had the chance to steal it with the last kick of the match. However, it would have been an injustice to

Castleford had the touchline kick gone over – they were the better side on the day.

With the exception of Broadhurst, all the regulars from the previous season were available but a number of minor injuries meant that the team was not as settled as before. Laws and Ema each missed only three games and Prohm was the leading try scorer for the third season running. At the end of the season, Gavin Miller became the only serving Rovers' player to win the coveted Man of Steel award, centre Mike Smith had a well-deserved benefit and assistant coach Johnny Moore announced his retirement.

Ian Robinson made his final appearance in the defeat at Wigan on 19 January. He had been a versatile, solid and reliable performer who did not always get the credit that he deserved. In just over 10 years, he played in 219 games and scored 50 tries. 'He was a very good, hard player and very awkward to play against,' says Fairbairn.

At the AGM, the financial report was far from rosy. An overall loss of £84,016 was carried forward with the increasing lottery, attendance and cost issues, including increased expenditure on maintaining the ground.

The Greats – No 26
Gary Prohm - *see Hull KR legends gallery*

Before joining the Robins, versatile New Zealander Gary Prohm played in the Auckland competition for Otahuhu and Mount Albert, making his debut for New Zealand in 1978. In all, he played in 23 Test matches up until 1986. A strong and fast runner with good hands, he was also a very capable defender.

Prohm joined Rovers in 1982, and made his first appearance at loose-forward at home to Hull FC on 22 September 1982. After playing a few early games there, he claimed the left-wing position for the remainder of that first season. From the start of the 1983-84 season, he became Rovers' regular left-centre, forming a partnership with Mike Smith that was undoubtedly the finest the club has had.

A top-class practitioner, his try-scoring will live long in the memory. Prohm finished top of the poachers in each of his four seasons at the club – the first jointly with Garry Clark and the other three outright. In his time with Rovers, he scored a remarkable 104 tries in 147 appearances. He also created many more for his regular winger David Laws.

In the 1984-85 season, in which he was an ever-present, Prohm rewrote Rovers' record books with 45 tries in 46 games, beating Ged Dunn's previous best of 42 in 1974-75.

That season he scored four tries in a match twice, a feat he accomplished three times in all, and equalled Graham Paul's record of scoring tries in ten successive club games. Prohm made his final appearance for Rovers at Wembley against Castleford on 3 May 1986 but despite crossing twice in a below-par Rovers' performance that day, he was unable to achieve his final ambition of becoming a Wembley winner. Roger Millward speaks for all who had the pleasure of witnessing his prowess when he says: 'He was a great player – a one-off.'

Seeking to fulfil another ambition, he then went to Australia and signed for Eastern Suburbs for two years. Returning home to play for Mount Albert, he later coached the Auckland City Vulcans side. Since 1990, Prohm has run his own motor business in Auckland with his wife Gayle.

The Greats – No 27
'Johnny' Moore - *see Hull KR legends gallery*

John Robert Moore was born in Hull in 1941. He joined the Robins from East Hull ARLC in 1962 and after missing the entire 1962-63 season through injury, made a try-scoring debut at centre at home to Castleford on 31 August 1963.

After playing in 35 games that campaign, Moore missed only seven matches in the next three seasons and played in every game of the long 1967-68 season – making a club record 49 appearances. Between 14 January 1967 and 4 April 1969, he played in 102 consecutive times before injury forced him to miss the home game against Halifax on Easter Monday.

'Gentleman John' as he was known to many, was a popular and respected figure at the club. He was a solid all-round performer with a safe pair of hands and a good rugby brain and a local government officer by occupation. Phil Lowe remembers him always being immaculately dressed in his collar and tie and polished shoes when he turned up for training, in contrast to his colleagues, most of whom were manual workers. John Millington says: 'In the dressing room his clothes were always put on a proper hanger and he was the only man I've known who had creases in his underpants!' Millington christened him 'office legs'.

'He was a very honest and decent man but he would stand his ground,' adds Millington. Lowe tells of an incident in a derby game at the Boulevard in the 1960s when fighting broke out and Moore was the subject of an unprovoked attack by Hull FC centre Dick Gemmell. 'Johnny squared up to him with his fists up in the classic Queensberry boxing pose,' Lowe chuckles. 'Gemmell couldn't get near him.' It would have been one of the very rare occasions that Gentleman John ever raised his fists on the field.

Whilst he played almost exclusively at centre in his earlier days, Moore's versatility subsequently saw him at full-back, wing, stand-off, second row and loose-forward as he lost a yard of pace. Towards the end of his playing career, Moore coached the 'A' team, and started to support Millward on the coaching side. Rovers officially appointed him assistant coach in 1980 after he made his final appearance at Widnes, on 27 April that year. In all, he played 433 games for the Robins, his only professional club, scoring 105 tries. Brian Tyson refers to him simply as 'the life and soul of the club'.

The Robins

Millward recalls the value that he put on Moore's advice and opinions as his assistant, saying that they were very much on the same wavelength. 'I could always rely on him 100 per cent, he was very straight and knew what he was doing. Looking back, I think perhaps I could have given him a bit more responsibility.' For Mike Smith: 'He was a great manager. He looked after people and was a great club man.'

Moore retired from his coaching role in 1986 but continued to be a regular visitor to Craven Park with his wife Pauline. When he sadly died from a rare heart condition at the age of 71 in 2012, Millward paid tribute to him, saying: 'Johnny epitomised what Hull KR is all about. He was a fantastic to work with – a model professional. He was so cool, calm and collected about everything. Nothing ever fazed him.'

Very fit until his illness, he continued to go running with his old teammate Ged Dunn, who succeeded him both as 'A' team and assistant coach. 'He was a hard act to follow, but he was a role model to me,' said Dunn, paying tribute to him in the Hull Daily Mail. *'His contribution to the club is under-rated – he did a lot behind the scenes during its most successful era. As a player, he was a real gentleman off the pitch and a hard man who took no prisoners on it.'*

Challenge Cup semi-final replay, Elland Road, Leeds, 3 April 1986
Hull Kingston Rovers 17-0 Leeds

After the thrills and spills of the first game, no one expected a scoreless first half in the replay. The play was end-to-end, full of good football and excellent defence but the nearest either side got to posting points was when John Dorahy hit a post with a drop-goal attempt. The game was nearly 14 minutes old before the first stoppage, when Lyons knocked-on. There were half-chances for both sides; David Laws, Garry Clark and Paul Harkin all had to be alert to deny Leeds and for Rovers, Andy Kelly was brought down when almost clear, David Watkinson was stopped inches short and Dorahy was just prevented from getting his pass away to the unmarked Fairbairn. However, it was Fairbairn who produced the best moment when Medley broke clear, forcing him wide and tackling him ball and all into touch.

The second half belonged entirely to Rovers. Peter Johnston, Watkinson and 'Zook' Ema got on top in the front row, man of the match Gavin Miller started to become more and more involved, and the punishing runs of Phil Hogan and Kelly started to take their toll. Harkin dropped a goal in the 42nd minute and the Robins were on their way. Harkin and Hogan almost got Dorahy in and then Clark just failed to take Hogan's pass with the line open. Soon after Johnston scored the first try, dummying a pass at the play-the-ball and strolling through a gap. Dorahy kicked a penalty to make it 7-0 and the two score cushion proved decisive. After another near miss, Hogan's magnificent 40-yard break resulted in Laws being tackled short and from the play-the-ball, John Lydiat sent the defence the wrong way to dart over. With two minutes to go, Ema and Mike Smith combined to send Kelly over near the posts. Dorahy converted and Wembley beckoned.

'It was a great performance, everything happened exactly as we had planned it,' coach Millward recalls. On that April evening, on a ground where Rovers had rarely won, a great side reached its peak in one of the most complete all-round team performances the Robins ever produced.

Rovers: *G. Fairbairn; G. Clark, M. Smith, G. Prohm (J. Lydiat), D. Laws; J. Dorahy, P. Harkin (G. Smith); P. Johnston, D. Watkinson (capt), A. Ema, A. Kelly, P. Hogan, G. Miller.*
Leeds: *I. Wilkinson; A. Smith, D. Creasser, A. Currie, C. Gibson; N. Hague, C. Lyons; J. Grayshon, D. Ward (capt), R. Powell, P. Medley (T. Webb), Kevin Rayne (Keith Rayne), D. Heron.*
Referee: M. R. Whitfield (Widnes)
Attendance: 32,485 (£113,000)

The Robins

The Robins had enjoyed nine amazing seasons during which they had won eight trophies and feared no one. It had topped the 1920s as the most successful period in the club's history. Possessing some of the best players in the game, Rovers had served up some wonderful football, the memories of which would be talked about for years to come.

'They were wonderful times,' says David Hall. 'It was a fantastic club, everyone was looked after and we were like one big family – directors, players, wives and backroom staff. On the away trips the directors sat at the front of the bus, sometimes Percy Johnson would sing us a song, and they all had a great time. The physios, Johnny Williams and Cliff Wallis were both great characters as were the kitmen, Cyril Brewer and Jack Ounsworth – you couldn't even get a sock off Jack! And the overseas players all fitted in, they were the best you could meet. I was privileged to have been a part of it all. I just feel lucky, it was a wonderful experience.'

However, all good things come to an end and the depth of the decline that followed emphasised the transient nature of sporting success.

*****

10. Into Decline

1986-1996

FROM winning nine trophies in nine seasons to falling into the third tier of British rugby league ten years later was hard enough, but that was made worse still by the loss of the club's much-loved Craven Park home.

The wane of a great side

The reasons for Hull Kingston Rovers' decline in the late 1980s and early 1990s are complex. By 1986, the 60 plus-year old stadium was costing more and more to maintain, and the forthcoming safety legislation would increase the burden further. The club lottery, which had been so important in providing income for ground and team improvements, had peaked by the mid-1980s and the income it generated started to tail off. The club had also been very lucky with its overseas imports in the early 1980s. The New Zealand trio of

Broadhurst, Prohm and Smith had given brilliant value at relatively little cost, even Miller originally arrived in 1984 for virtually nothing. Then the price of imports rose as demand, led by the big Lancashire clubs, increased and players' wages continued to increase in general. At the same time, Rovers' luck with their signings ran out. Whilst some looked impressive on paper, with a few notable exceptions they proved generally disappointing.

Both George Fairbairn and Wayne Parker also feel that, in hindsight, the club should have moved on older players and brought in younger blood more quickly. Then, as the team became less successful, interest started to dwindle, and the sale of passes and gate receipts reduced, as did sponsorship income. The highest average crowd was 9,840 in season 1980-81 but by 1986-87 it was just 4,974. Like so many before and since, the Robins found that once in a downward spiral, it is very difficult to climb out of it.

The directors had done the obvious things like investing in their Colts set-up and trying to bring through younger players but successful though it was at the time, it did not consistently produce the required quality of players to maintain success. Of the young players given a taste of first team rugby at the end of 1985-86, probably only two would have challenged for a place in the Championship-winning sides, whilst in later seasons the majority of the better young players were attracted to the bigger and more successful clubs.

The club tried to cut back on expenditure but the cost-cutting measures were too little, too late. Perhaps they should have addressed the ground issue earlier, taking forward the Winchester Avenue project and saving the money spent on Craven Park. But professional sport is littered with clubs that have lived up to their means and beyond in the good days and have failed to ensure financial security for the future.

am Morfitt   *Stuart Quinn*   Bunker Carmichael   Frank Bielby   *Stuart Quinn*

The Greats

 ## A Gallery of Hull KR Legends

Photos courtesy of Hull Daily Mail *unless otherwise stated*

nthony Starks and his 1905-06 team   *Stuart Quinn*

Main pic: Arthur Moore, his son and the Yorkshire Cup   *Stuart Quinn*

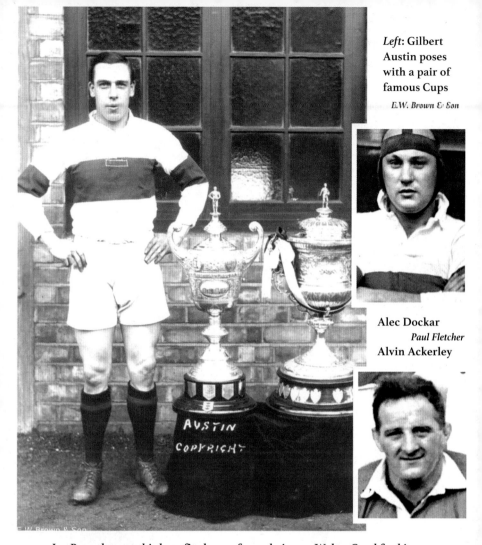

Left: Gilbert Austin poses with a pair of famous Cups

E.W. Brown & Son

Alec Dockar

Paul Fletcher

Alvin Ackerley

Joe Ramsden gets his benefit cheque from chairman Walter Crockford in 1948. His fellow beneficiaries Len 'Nobby' Clark, Wilf McWatt and vice-chairman E. E. Mowforth look on.

Paul Fletcher

Above: Graham Paul, *left*, and Cyril Kellett

Clockwise: Frank Foster, Alan Burwell touches down, and the one and only Flash Flanagan, *left*

Left: Harry Poole

Below: Wilf Spaven

Below: Clive Sullivan

Above: Phil Lowe

Clockwise from top left:
Len Casey,
Steve Hartley,
David Watkinson,
Johnny Moore,
John Millington
and Gary Prohm

Clockwise from top: **Roger Millward, George Fairbairn, Colin Hutton (receiving the Freedom of Hull in 2012) and Mike Smith**

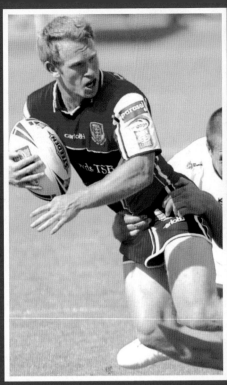

Clockwise from top left: Paul Fletcher, James Webster, Michael Dobson and Stanley Gene

1986 was the year of the Chernobyl nuclear disaster and, in August, estate agent Suzy Lamplugh disappeared in Fulham, never to be found. In the World Cup in Mexico, Maradona's infamous 'Hand of God' goal led to England's quarter-final exit, and the world first saw the 'Mexican Wave'.

'A' team coach Ged Dunn took over from Moore as Millward's assistant for 1986-87. The opening game was a 24-6 defeat at Barrow and by the end of the year, 14 league games had resulted in seven wins and seven defeats. One bright spot had been the October Craven Park derby, which produced a one-sided 29-6 Rovers win based on a powerful forward effort and a sparkling half-back performance by Mike Smith and Parker. There was then a 46-10 thrashing by the Australian tourists and, most worryingly, an 18-14 first round John Player trophy defeat at Doncaster in November.

After Christmas, an upturn in fortunes saw six wins in seven games that included progress to the third round of the Challenge Cup, albeit resulting in a tame 35-7 defeat at Halifax. However, the Robins won five of the last ten league games, including completing a derby double with a 21-8 win at the Boulevard, and finished in sixth position in the league.

Broadhurst returned to the club, without quite being the force he had been before, and made up a familiar front row with skipper Watkinson and Ema. Hogan missed almost the entire season through injury but Kelly missed only one game and was the mainstay of the second row with Burton and Des Harrison, the elder brother of Chris. Miller, in his third season, made only 14 appearances so Gordon Smith and former Colt Paul Speckman covered at loose-forward.

In the backs, former Australia winger Kerry Boustead was the replacement for Prohm. Boustead missed most of the previous season with a broken leg and when Manly released him, he signed for Rovers on a two-year contract. However, injury had taken its toll, and he was a shadow of the player he had been. After he appeared in only half the season's games, the club released him. Fairbairn remained a rock but the rest of the backs were unsettled. Two young local players, Parker and three-quarter Ray Stead, who had both played a handful of games the previous season, started to appear regularly, alongside established names Clark, Laws, Lydiat, Dorahy and the two Smiths.

Parker, the top try-scorer with 15 in his first full season, well remembers those early days in the team. 'Having watched Rovers since I was three, it was an unreal experience to sit in the first team dressing room. You had to be invited in. When I became a part of the first team squad, skipper David Watkinson was brilliant in welcoming and looking after me. I remember he took me to see the secretary to ensure I was on first team wages and I ended up with a pay packet of £1,100 less tax for three wins. I couldn't believe it – I'd only been on £25 a week on the Youth Training Scheme.'

Mark Broadhurst made his final appearance in the home game against Barrow on 25 March. A tough uncompromising forward with a fearsome appearance, Broadhurst made a huge impression in his first two seasons – not least for the infamous left hook in the Queensland game. In his first season, he formed a front row with Watkinson and Casey that was one of the most formidable ever to represent the club. An imposing and reassuring presence who never took a backward step, he was an integral part of the two Championship-winning packs of the 1980s. In all, Broadhurst played 96 games for Rovers before finally hanging up his boots.

In the end-of-season play-off game at Warrington, John Dorahy played his last game for the Robins. 'Joe Cool' added a little extra craft to the back division when he arrived in 1983.

His match winning performance in the 1984 Premiership final was probably his finest hour for the club. He played in 94 games, scoring exactly 600 points with 228 goals and 37 tries. 'I rate him as the best Aussie the club has had,' says Millington. 'He was a fine tackler and goal-kicker and he was always there, feeding on the scraps and making things happen.'

Another to depart was scrum-half Paul Harkin, after eight seasons. For much of that time he faced competition for his place, first from Agar and then Gordon Smith, but he made 185 appearances in which he scored 27 tries and dropped 38 goals, the latter still a club record. At his best, he was a creative livewire scrum-half who took on defences and had a very a good kicking-game.

Over at the Boulevard, the nine-year reign of coach Arthur Bunting ended, and former Rovers skipper Len Casey replaced him. Both clubs mourned the death of rugby league legend Clive Sullivan, who passed away on 8 October and over 1,000 people attended his memorial service in Holy Trinity church in the Market Place.

The Robins started the 1987-88 season with a new shirt sponsor, Mansfield Brewery. There were three new overseas players, Kiwi prop Ross Taylor and two Australians, centre Peter Mortimer from Canterbury and Manly second-rower Glen Ryan. It is fair to say that none of them proved an outstanding success and all three were with the club for just the one season. Young goal-kicking full-back Mike Fletcher, who had found opportunities hard to come by in the previous two seasons due to the presence of Fairbairn, won a place at centre, where he played over 20 games. Rudd was the regular hooker until Christmas, when he sustained a head injury in a motor accident and Watkinson took over again. Watkinson's injury in February resulted in Rudd attempting a comeback but it lasted only one match. Rovers then brought in St Helens reserve hooker David Harrison, initially on loan. With Mike Smith and Parker the regular half-backs, Gordon Smith spent most of the season at loose-forward.

Rovers finished in ninth place in the Championship – now cut from 16 to 14 teams – just five points above relegation. The biggest problem was their away form. They won nine out of 13 home league games, with one draw, but gained only two victories on their travels, one of those being in the Boulevard derby.

There was little cup success and Rovers again lost to Halifax in the third round of the Challenge Cup, this time at Craven Park. Mike Fletcher's two penalty goals gave Rovers a half-time lead but once Halifax got their noses in front in the second half, capitulation was swift and the visitors triumphed 26-4.

In the league, there were fine home wins over St Helens, in Mike Smith's 400th game, and Widnes but without doubt, the performance of the season was the 8-0 win over high-flying Wigan at Craven Park. After a fine defensive effort, Mike Smith and Parker created the opening for Fletcher's match-winning try with eight minutes left. When the Airlie Birds visited for the Easter derby the following week, however, former Welsh rugby union international Gary Pearce was in inspired form for the visitors, who triumphed 21-14 despite a second half Rovers fight back.

Gordon Smith made his final appearance in a depressing 46-4 home defeat to a Paul Harkin-inspired Bradford in the last match of the season. He had been a very loyal and reliable performer over five seasons and was always prepared to play wherever required, but it was at scrum-half where he excelled. Never flashy, always capable and hard-working, he was the type of player that all coaches like to have in their squad. In all, he played in 177 games for the Robins before retiring to his native New Zealand. 'He was such an honest player. He gave everything, every time he came off the field he had to have stitches,' says Millward.

Parker was named as rugby league's outstanding young player. He missed only one game and was the top try-scorer for a second consecutive season, adding a club record 14 drop-goals in the season for good measure. Two new faces were Clive Sullivan's son, Anthony also a winger, who made one appearance and scored with his first touch of the ball in the league win at Swinton and former Eureka second-rower Paul Fletcher, who made his debut in the last match, marking his first appearance with Rovers' only try of the game.

The financial situation continued to cause serious concern. There was a slightly reduced operating loss of £79,162 on the rugby side due to reduced wages as the team was less successful, but there was a continued general decrease in income as attendances and season pass sales continued to fall. The costs of bringing the ground up to safety standards were also looming, and the club owed £217,169 on loans.

Relegation

In 1988, the housing boom was at its peak and it was the year of the Piper Alpha North Sea oil platform tragedy in which 165 workers were killed. Bruce Willis starred in the first *Die Hard* movie. In sport, Wimbledon beat Liverpool in the FA Cup final and Ben Johnson won the 100m gold medal at the Seoul Olympics, only to be stripped of it two days later for steroid abuse.

1988-89 was a season that most Rovers fans would probably rather forget. The Robins finished bottom of the Championship, seven points from safety and were relegated to the Second Division. It was also the last season at the Robins' home of 66 years. A total of 38 players played in the club's 35 matches and not once did the same team play in successive matches. To be fair to Millward, injuries were a big reason as well as trying unsuccessfully to find a winning formula.

Miller returned from Australia for his last and least successful season, bringing with him compatriot prop-forward Michael Porter, who made the most appearances with 28. A third Aussie, back-row forward Chris Close, arrived from Gold Coast and was the leading try-scorer with 14, more than twice as many as anyone else. Like Miller, neither Porter nor Close returned after that season.

Welsh international rugby union scrum-half David Bishop was signed from Pontypool RUFC for a reported £100,000, a club record. He was a big name and undoubtedly had a lot of talent but he was a loose cannon and ultimately his signing proved a big gamble that failed. Other new arrivals were former Leeds winger Richard Pratt, centres Jimmy Irvine from Hunslet and Graeme Hallas from West Riding amateur club Dudley Hill, former Halifax half-back Steve Robinson and Carlisle prop Colin Armstrong. All of them arrived for fees in the region of £20-£25,000 and, in truth, none would have got into the side five years earlier. Probably the most talented was Hallas but he was young and inconsistent and it was a difficult transition from the amateur game. A player-exchange valued at £55,000 saw Burton move to Featherstone and centre or back-row forward Paul Lyman come in the opposite direction.

With only one win in the first six league games, Rovers were in trouble from the start, and they recorded only half a dozen league wins all season. Five successive defeats from 26 February, culminating in a 26-2 reverse in the Good Friday Boulevard derby, made relegation all but certain. Drawn against Second Division opposition in the first two rounds of the John Player Trophy and Challenge Cup, the Robins reached the third round in each, gaining a creditable 16-16 draw at home to Wigan in the former, when Bishop's drop-goal attempt to win the game in the dying moments drifted agonisingly wide. In the replay, Rovers capitulated 30-0 at Central Park, whilst in the Challenge Cup they lost 30-4 at home to Warrington.

Having deputised for Watkinson for much of the previous season, Smith had taken over as club skipper. Des Harrison missed only five games but nearly half of his appearances were from the bench. The final appearances during the season of Laws, Watkinson, Burton, Hogan and Miller severed five more links with the glory years.

Laws, another often under-rated player who won one Great Britain cap in 1986, was a deceptively quick and elusive winger, a strong finisher and a good footballer who could also play stand-off. He played in 194 games for Rovers, scoring 75 tries. Burton, who made 233 appearances for the Robins and nine for Great Britain, was the type of unsung hero that is found in every successful side. He was not a natural athlete, he was all bone and muscle. His strength was his tackling and he hurt the opposition, while his awkward running style made him a difficult opponent. 'He was a very hard man, other teams didn't like playing against him at all,' says Wayne Parker.

Hogan was a flamboyant figure with his wavy blond hair and headband and a snappy dresser off the field but he was a big game player who reserved some of his best performances for the most important matches. He made nine appearances for Great Britain and one for England. A pacy and destructive runner who could also play in the centre, he regularly punished gaps in opposing defences and was a sound tackler. Making 254 appearances, in which he scored

65 tries and kicked 54 goals, he more than repaid the £32,000 the club paid to secure his services from Barrow.

Miller, not at his best in this last spell, undoubtedly galvanised the team when he arrived on the scene in 1984, and he had a big influence in the two trophy successes that season, as well as the near misses in 1985-86. A talented and charismatic figure who was a supporters' favourite with his all-action style, Miller was a strong runner, a fine ball-handler, a useful kicker in the loose and a strong defender. He played in 102 games for the Robins and scored 25 tries. 'He did well in Australia after coming to England,' says Mike Smith. 'It was his time at Rovers that made him.'

The club reported a loss of £375,554 on the rugby side, largely due to the outlay on new players. One encouraging sign was a small increase in receipts from season passes but the lottery was now in steep decline, having realised only £56,933 over the year and the liabilities falling due within the next financial year were £674,890.

Leaving an old home

Whilst Rovers were being given a rugby lesson by St Helens at Elland Road in the 1984-85 Premiership Final, events were unfolding just eleven miles down the road at the Valley Parade home of Bradford City, that were to have a profound impact on the future of the club, in common with much professional sport across the country. At 3.40pm, a media commentator reported a small fire in the main stand. Four minutes later, in windy conditions, it had engulfed the whole stand and 56 people tragically lost their lives.

In the aftermath of the disaster, the Sports Stadiums Act was passed, laying down stringent new safety standards. After a council inspection in 1987, Rovers learned that it would cost at least £700,000 to bring Craven Park up to the necessary requirement and that the investment would guarantee the safety level for only a period of seven years. Strapped for cash, the club simply did not have the money to make the improvements and the board realised that even if they could raise it, that would only be the tip of the iceberg. After seeking alternatives and discussing different ideas, they reluctantly concluded that relocation was the only viable answer.

If they could obtain a good price for the prime site occupied by Craven Park, they could purchase suitable land and build a new ground elsewhere, possibly even with some surplus for team strengthening. The board invited Wright Construction, a builder and redeveloper with experience in supermarket developments, to Craven Park to give a valuation. They eventually agreed it was close to £4 million and the parties reached agreement that Wrights would buy Craven Park and build a new stadium for the club elsewhere. Chairman Hutton was keen that the architect would design a ground that resembled Craven Park as closely as possible.

The search for suitable land alighted first on a site in the Leads Road area, just off the ring road in the east of the city. Ironically, opposition to proposals to build a new stadium there was led by a well-known club shareholder who lived nearby and the council refused planning permission. Coincidentally, however, the council had a former school site on Preston Road, less than two miles from Craven Park, that they would let the club have on a 99-year lease.

Many supporters were unhappy with the proposal. Rovers had been at Craven Park for 66 years. The ground, imperfect in many ways as it was and in need of significant investment, had many happy memories. It had character and it was home. In hindsight, perhaps the club could have done

more to explain their position, even to involve supporters in
the planning and thus engender a sense of ownership of the
new ground. Hutton provided a sweetener by promising that
the bulk of an anticipated profit from the deal of up to £1
million would be available to strengthen the team and thus
enable the club once again to compete for the top honours in
the game.

Perhaps the board had not previously experienced the
escalating costs of major building projects and Hutton was to
regret his promise. 'Through no one's fault, we were hit by a
series of unexpected costs which at the time seemed never-
ending,' explains Ron Turner who was involved in the
negotiations. 'There was unexpected major expenditure to
install a lift in the main stand and to upgrade and widen
Poorhouse Lane, the access road to the stadium, to highway
standards. Both things we were told we would have to do,
along with innumerable other smaller things. The costs just
escalated and ultimately ate into the surplus, which meant
that in the end there was virtually nothing left.'

There was widespread disappointment amongst the
fans that no money would be available after all for team
strengthening and, perhaps inevitably, there were allegations
that funds had been misappropriated. Turner absolutely
refutes them. 'Every penny was accounted for the
accountants went through everything in detail and proper
audited accounts were produced,' he says. Similarly, a
rumour that the club were offered a very significant amount
of money to upgrade Craven Park by a neighbouring
supermarket, who did not want new competition, he
dismisses as: 'A figment of someone's imagination.'

Irrespective of supporters' misgivings, the move went
ahead. The last game on the old ground was a Championship
clash against Widnes on Sunday 9 April 1989, when Rovers

were already relegated. It took place in front of a crowd of 7,844, the second highest of the season after the derby game.

For the thousands of supporters who spent so many happy hours there – and admittedly a few more stressful ones – there are only memories now. Percy Johnson's Sunday morning volunteer force. The wonderful BBC2 Floodlit Trophy win over St Helens. The cushions that were hired out to the main stand patrons to make the bench seats a bit more comfortable – and hurled in the direction of a hapless referee or unpopular visiting player. The three clubhouses from which spectators could watch the game – unique in their time. The old railway carriages that formed the back of the 'popular' stand. The smell of Bovril and liniment that pervaded the Well. The greyhound track and distinctive tote board at the Holderness Road end. The Tuesday afternoon 'floodlit' cup-ties during the three-day week. 'A' team games in front of a few hundred people. The photographs are all that remains.

However, not everyone mourned the demise of the old ground. The Warrington club programme commented that, 'without doubt it is the ground that has the Wires' worst away record – a voodoo since 1927. In that time we have won just three league games, plus three draws, out of 31 games.'

Championship, Craven Park, Hull, 9 April 1989
Hull Kingston Rovers 13-16 Widnes

The last game at Craven Park on Holderness Road saw a classic bottom against top encounter. A spirited young Rovers side did their utmost to give the old ground the best possible send-off against title-chasing Widnes. Despite falling behind to a Currier try and Davies goal as early as the seventh minute, Rovers gave as good as they got for most of the game and for long periods the visitors looked anything but reigning champions. With Widnes increasingly in disarray, the Robins slowly gained confidence, and an excellent pass by Paul Lyman put Mike Fletcher in at the corner after 30 minutes. Seven minutes later, Graeme Hallas gathered Colin Armstrong's pinpoint up-and-under to score and Fletcher's conversion put the Robins 10-6 ahead at the break.

Man of the match Armstrong dropped a goal two minutes into the second half and Fletcher added a penalty eight minutes later to put Rovers 13-6 ahead. However, despite launching waves of attacks, the Robins could not quite crack open the desperate Widnes defence and put the game beyond doubt. Perhaps had skipper Mike Smith not had to leave the field injured in the 12th minute, he might have been able to provide that missing guile. As it was, Widnes' giant Tongan seconder-rower Koloto powered his way over in the 65th minute and, from the re-start, a six-man move resulted in Tait scoring in the corner.

Despite the refusal of the home side to roll over, that was the last try and points on the famous old ground. Rovers were left to reflect on the lack of penetration that stopped them turning all their effort into points and the fact that had they played with the same spirit and commitment throughout the season, they may have gained the wins that would have kept them in the top flight.

After 1,264 competitive first team games over 66 years, the players, officials and supporters left the ground for the last time and twelve months later Craven Park was but a memory. Paul Fletcher will not forget that day. 'It means a lot just to be able to say I played in that game and we put up a good fight. We weren't embarrassed and they were a very good team.'

> **Rovers:** *A. Thompson; G. Hallas, A. Sullivan, M. Fletcher, R. Pratt; M. Smith (capt) (J. Lydiat), S. Robinson; C. Armstrong, L. Richardson, M. Beall, A. Ema, Des Harrison (C. O'Brien), P. Fletcher.*

Widnes: A. Tait; J. Davies, A. Currier, D. Wright,
M. Offiah; D. Hulme, P. Hulme; K. Sorenson
(capt), P. McKenzie (B. Dowd), J. Grima (D.
Pyke), M. O'Neill, E. Koloto, R. Eyres.
Referee: B. Galtress (Bradford)
Attendance: 7,876

A fresh start

The club sold a record £120,000-worth of season passes for the 1989-90 season, for which they had recruited three new overseas players. Kiwi second-rower Tony Botica, who joined the Robins on Gary Prohm's recommendation from his old club, Mount Albert; Queenslander Bryan Niebling, who had played in the second row for the visitors in the infamous 1983 tour game but who rapidly became a favourite at Craven Park at prop; and speedy Australian centre Greg Austin. Early in the season, Rovers signed Cumbrian full-back David Lightfoot to replace Fairbairn, now approaching the veteran stage.

The first game at the new stadium was on 24 September 1989, when the visitors were Trafford Borough for a Second Division match. 8,500 spectators witnessed it, the season's league best. After free-scoring wins in their first two away games, most spectators expected a repeat performance but expectations weighed heavily on Rovers and inspired the visitors for which such an atmosphere was a rare, if once-in-a-lifetime occasion.

After a fairly even first half, in which Rovers took a 6-2 lead, Borough levelled at 8-8 early in the second. However, the Robins' power and class told in the final quarter and they eased to a 48-8 win. The honour of scoring the first try on the new ground went to Mike Fletcher, who also kicked eight goals. The team was:

> G. Fairbairn; G. Clark, M. Fletcher, G. Austin, R. Pratt;
> W. Parker, D. Bishop; C. Armstrong, C. Rudd, A. Ema,
> A. Botica, P. Lyman, M. Smith. Subs: A. Thompson, B.
> Niebling.

The season was not completely without setbacks, but the Robins comfortably achieved their main objective of returning to the Championship at the first attempt. They went up as champions, winning all but three of their 28 games.

They clinched promotion by beating Halifax at home on 4 April, when Mike Fletcher's fourth minute try set them on their way and breaking at the same time Hubbard's record for the most points in a season. Lyman scored a second two minutes later and although Halifax's spoiling tactics prevented Rovers from breaking loose, they scored 12 points in the last three minutes to record a comfortable 29-6 win.

One of the highlights of the campaign was a new club record victory, 92-10, at home to Whitehaven in March. With Niebling and Ema outstanding up front, the Robins were rampant. Mike Fletcher equalled the club record of 14 goals in a match and there were try hat-tricks for Austin, Sullivan, Botica and Bishop – one of whose was a tremendous length-of-the-field effort that brought the house down.

The draws for Challenge Cup and Regal Trophy, as the John Player was renamed, were unkind.

In the first round of the latter, Rovers were sent to St Helens in a Saturday afternoon game that was televised on BBC *Grandstand*. They gave their illustrious opponents an almighty fright taking an early 12-0 lead, and despite being pegged back and having Mike Fletcher controversially sent off, they were ahead 16-12 at the interval. In the second half, although they put up a real fight, St Helens took advantage of the extra man to gain a 40-26 win.

In the Challenge Cup, the Robins were at home to star-studded Wigan. From the beginning of the season the uneven and bumpy pitch had caused problems and by January, it was in a pretty poor and muddy state. It was certainly not suited to the visitors' free-flowing style and again against top opposition, Rovers put up a highly spirited display with Ema and Bishop outstanding. They confined Wigan to just one try in their 6-4 win and only a brilliant Edwards cover tackle in the second half prevented Sullivan from scoring a try that might well have resulted in a remarkable cup upset.

Comfortable wins in the divisional play-offs saw the Robins reach the final against Oldham but the season ended in disappointment, thereby losing for a third time during the season to the Watersheddings side.

There were three ever-presents in the side, the right flank partnership of Garry Clark and Mike Fletcher and hooker Chris Rudd. Fletcher kicked 199 goals and scored 450 points to set new club records. Austin was the leading try-scorer with 38 in 34 games. Andy Thompson, who made his debut in the backs in 1987, moved to loose-forward in October, then settled in the second-row from the St Helens game to the end of the season. Botica's short stay ended in March but he had made a fine impression whilst Fairbairn played his final match for the Robins at York on 13 April

Initially the crowds at the new stadium held up reasonably well but they had dropped to around the 3,500 mark by the end of the season. The new ground was not popular and the club lost some regular supporters when it moved, the location was for many less convenient and the site was generally bleak and windswept.

The Robins

The Greats – No 28
David Watkinson - *see Hull KR legends gallery*

Hooker David Watkinson was born in York in 1954 and was a product of the famous Heworth amateur club. He first came to Rovers' attention in 1976 and was subsequently offered a trial. Making the transition from the amateur game to rugby league's First Division look easy, he made his debut at prop-forward against Leeds at Craven Park on 25 January 1977. Watkinson soon became the first choice hooker and, a couple of long-term injuries apart, kept his place for nearly ten years.

A capable ball-winner, direct and an uncompromising tackler, Watkinson was a tough and respected opponent. In just over 12 years with the Robins, he made 329 appearances. He also made 13 appearances for Great Britain and one for England. When the captaincy of one iron man, Len Casey ended in 1984, Roger Millward turned to another to replace him in Watkinson. Dour and unsmiling on the field, Watkinson led his team by example.

'There was no better hooker,' says Millward. 'He'd get the ball for you and he'd close down the play-the-ball area, nothing would get by him. He was really tough too, there'd be some players looking over their shoulders for him.' For David Hall: 'He was a winner, he was never satisfied – "we might have won," he'd say, "but we were rubbish – we have to be better than that." Like Casey, he was unbearable when we lost.' 'He always came down hard on any of the backs who dropped the ball,' adds Mike Smith with feeling.

Nevertheless, for all his gruff exterior, Watkinson looked after the younger players and Wayne Parker, for one, will never forget that. 'He was great with me. I was very nervous when I moved up into the first team dressing room, but he took me under his wing and looked after me. He was the salt of the earth, just the same off the field as he was on it.'

By 1988-89, his appearances were becoming less regular

and he left the club at the end of the season to finish his career at Dewsbury, subsequently returning to Heworth as coach.

Second Division Premiership Final, Old Trafford, Manchester, 13 May 1990
Hull Kingston Rovers 29-30 Oldham

The Robins made their only appearance at Old Trafford to date in a game played as a curtain-raiser to the 1990 Premiership Final between Bradford Northern and Widnes.

It was a contest they had in the bag but contrived to throw away. The Robins got off to a great start when man of the match Wayne Parker scored a brilliant individual try, dropped a goal, and finished off a move started by Bryan Niebling and Chris Rudd in the first 17 minutes. Mike Fletcher's two conversions put the Robins 13-0 ahead. Lord's converted try got Oldham on the scoreboard but Greg Austin then sent in winger Garry Clark and Paul Lyman intercepted a poor pass to score, and another Fletcher goal put Rovers 23-8 up.

When Des Harrison stormed in two minutes after the break and Fletcher converted to make it 29-8, it looked as if Rovers, playing confident, classy football, would have a perfect ending to their promotion season. However, four minutes later, Ford scored despite an apparent knock-on and ten minutes after that Henderson beat Andy Thompson's desperate cover tackle to bring Oldham within two scores at 29-18. With 18 minutes to go, Irving finished off Clark's superb break and almost straight after Ruane punished some slack defence to score. When Martin dummied his way over to nudge Oldham ahead, they had scored 22 points in 26 minutes. But they were only able to convert one of their five second half tries and with seven minutes to go, Rovers still had a chance. Niebling, standing in as skipper for the injured Mike Smith, urged the Robins forward in the last few minutes and they had two chances to snatch the game back.

The Robins

First Jimmy Irvine lost possession in an excellent position and then David Bishop's long pass was intercepted. Oldham held on for their third win over the Robins that season and Rovers' players slumped dejectedly to the ground.

'We just seemed to ease up a bit,' said Niebling afterwards. 'Oldham came back hard at us, once they'd scored a couple of tries they got a roll on and there was nothing we could do to stop them.' Millward said that whilst the defeat was his worst experience in the game, the club had achieved its main targets for the season and would bounce back.

> **Rovers:** *D. Lightfoot (D. Bishop); G. Clark, M. Fletcher, G. Austin, A. Sullivan; W. Parker, D. Bishop (J. Irvine); B. Niebling (capt), C. Rudd, A. Ema, D. Harrison (C. Armstrong), A. Thompson, P. Lyman.*
> **Oldham:** *D. Platt (T. Martyn); R. Irving, G. Hyde, J. Henderson, P. Lord; B. Clark, M. Ford; L. Casey (K. Newton), A. Ruane, J. Fieldhouse, G. Round, C. McAllister, I. Russell.*
> *Referee: M. R. Whitfield (Widnes)*
> *Attendance: 40,786*

All good things come to an end

On 10 June 1990, county cricket was played in Hull for the very last time, Yorkshire losing a Sunday League game to Surrey at the Anlaby Road Circle. At Italia 90, England were eliminated at the semi-final stage, losing a penalty shoot-out to West Germany – just months before German reunification. In August, Iraq invaded Kuwait leading to the Gulf War and, that autumn, Tim Berners-Lee created the foundation for the worldwide web.

The Daniel Divet affair dominated Rovers' summer in 1990. Local businessman Malcolm West became chairman, succeeding Colin Hutton, who took a new role as football chairman. In a blaze of publicity in May, Hutton signed Divet, a French international second-rower, who then became the subject of an historic court case when the club successfully challenged an RFL ruling that the player would have to be included in their overseas quota. That subsequently opened the way for other English clubs to sign up French stars.

Unfortunately, the week before he was due to arrive at Craven Park on a one-year contract, the player shocked the club by pulling out of the deal ostensibly for personal reasons although he subsequently signed a very lucrative five-year deal with his club, Carcassonne. As Hutton put it: 'We could take the matter through the courts but that would be a long drawn out affair and would be very expensive. And what would be the point? If we were to win – as I am sure we would – we would have a player who does not want to come to Craven Park.'

There were two new faces for the 1990-91 season, Kiwi back David Watson had arrived in place of Botica and former Blackheath RUFC winger Bright Sodje joined. The Robins opened the season with a Yorkshire Cup preliminary round game against the short-lived Nottingham City club at Doncaster, where they eclipsed the previous season's record highest score in a 100-6 win, the highest score by any side away from home. Whilst City were poor, the Robins produced a blistering display of pace and handling. Austin equalled Dunn's post-war record of six tries in a match, Sullivan scored a personal best of five and Armstrong became the third Rovers player to kick 14 goals in a match. Ironically, it was to be Armstrong's last game for the club, whilst Austin played only three more times.

The Robins reached the semi-final of the Yorkshire Cup, which they lost 29-6 at Castleford in what was Austin's last game. At the time, clubs could register only three

The Robins

overseas players and Rovers quota was full. However, they felt they had to increase their forward power for what would undoubtedly be a tough campaign ahead and decided to release Austin to bring in the New Zealand international prop James Goulding. The theory was sound but it did not work out in practice. Goulding had a decent home debut against Warrington in mid-September but after that he struggled for form and the club released him at the end of the season. Halifax quickly snapped up the prolific Austin, who had scored 45 tries in just 38 games for the Robins.

The Regal Trophy and Challenge Cup draws were hard on the Robins, with trips to Leeds and Workington respectively, but again Rovers delivered two of their best performances, failing narrowly in each. The main objective was to stay in the Championship and they got off to a decent start, winning eight and drawing two of their first 16 games.

On 7 October, Rovers visited Oldham for what looked like a 'four-pointer' in the quest for Championship survival. Because of an injury to Lightfoot, Millward moved Bishop to full-back, with Watson and Parker pairing up in the halves. Rovers gained an important 28-25 win and when Lightfoot reported fit for the next game against Widnes, Millward reinstated him and named Bishop as substitute. He reacted badly to being dropped, refused to go on the bench and made some unacceptable personal remarks about Millward, who responded by declaring that Bishop would never again play for the club whilst he was in charge. The Board backed their coach and the player remained out in the cold for the rest of the season. Lightfoot played only twice more at full-back after that and Mike Fletcher took over post-Christmas.

The Robins then turned in a brilliant team display to beat the high-flying Chemics with Thompson putting in a typical non-stop tackling display and Parker orchestrating the attacks. Derby rivalry resumed with Rovers gaining a 20-8 home win on New Years' Day and they comfortably beat Oldham at home but they won only one further game, the last home fixture against Rochdale. It was not widely known at the time, but this was to be Millward's last home match for the little man bowed out at the end of the season after over 14 seasons in charge. He said that after relegation in 1989, he wanted to get the club back into the Championship and keep them there before he called it a day.

The Rochdale win guaranteed that scenario but the next two games were a terrible anti-climax. Rovers' 28-16 Good Friday defeat at the Boulevard was followed by a 62-16 drubbing at Sheffield, the most inept of any under Millward's charge. Only 16-10 down at half-time, Rovers rolled over completely in the second half. Uncharacteristically, Millward afterwards singled out a small handful of players who he felt had actually put some effort into the game, effectively damning the others.

Sullivan and Watson missed only three games each and the regular back row threesome of Des Harrison, Thompson and Lyman clocked up 72 starts between them. The Sheffield debacle marked the final appearances of six players most notably Mike Smith, who was playing in his 489th game for the club. Queensland prop Bryan Niebling, a consummate professional who never gave less than his all in his 56 games, retired to Australia and Watson moved on to join Austin at Halifax. Much under-rated hooker Chris Rudd also retired and he was a talented rake who might well have made a lot more than his 161 appearances if he had not had to understudy Watkinson in the early part of his career. Anthony Sullivan, a winger with genuine pace who was clearly destined for greater things, moved to further his career with St Helens. Prop-forward Goulding returned to

The Robins

New Zealand and another well-known name to leave the club was winger Garry Clark, who made his last appearance at home to Castleford in February before moving to Scarborough Pirates. He played in 255 games for the Robins, scoring 121 tries and won three Great Britain caps and one for England.

On the board, local solicitor Max Gold replaced Malcolm West as chairman.

The Greats – No 29
Roger Millward MBE - *see Hull KR legends gallery*

Roger Millward was a true great, not only of Hull Kingston Rovers but the sport. Although 5'4" and just over 10 stones, he was a giant of the game. Equally at home in both half-back positions, he was born in Castleford in September 1947, coming to prominence as a schoolboy starlet in the then ABC television inter-town junior games in the early 1960s. After making his first team debut as an amateur in October 1964, he signed for his home town club on his 17th birthday for £200. Castleford at the time had two international half-backs in the established partnership of Hardisty and Hepworth.

Despite appearing only as understudy to the duo, making a few appearances on the wing and playing predominantly in the 'A' team, Millward was chosen for Great Britain at just 18 in March 1966. He was clearly too good not to be playing regular first team football and Rovers' chairman Wilf Spaven asked his Castleford opposite number for a first refusal if ever they decided to sell. When he received a call in summer 1966, Spaven wasted no time. He agreed to pay the full £6,000 asking price and Spaven travelled to Blackpool, where Millward was on holiday, to complete the signing. It was without doubt the best investment the club ever made.

Millward made his Rovers debut at Hunslet on 15 August 1966, scoring his first try in his first home game against

Batley a week later. He posted 25 tries that first season and the following campaign's tally of 38 set a new season's record for a stand-off as well as making him the league's top try scorer. Those first two seasons were plain sailing for Millward, with a very good side around him and Frank Foster ensuring that no one took any liberties. However, as the Robins then entered a more unsettled phase, he often had to shoulder the burden of the Robins being seen as a one man team. In those early years, Millward continued to live in Castleford, working as a colliery electrician. During the week, he would typically be up at 5am then after a day's work would set out on the two-hour trip to Hull. There was no M62 then and with detours to pick up other players, he often did not get home until around midnight. Only when appointed coach did rugby become his full-time occupation.

With a total of 29 Great Britain and 17 England caps, Millward enjoyed a glittering international career and its pinnacle was the 1970 summer tour of Australia. He was left out of the first test, which GB lost but returned to the side for the second – scoring 20 points in a 28-7 win. He also scored a crucial try in the decider – still Britain's last series win over the Aussies.

The same year, Millward also took over the Rovers captaincy leading them to a Yorkshire Cup success the next season. After relegation in 1974, he played a big part in the Yorkshire Cup success and promotion that followed and also had a short summer spell with Cronulla in 1976. When Harry Poole died unexpectedly in 1977, the Robins directors appointed Millward as player-coach. In that role he lead them to Floodlit Trophy, First Division championship and Challenge Cup successes, before a fourth broken jaw in 12 months saw his retirement from playing. Fittingly, his last first team appearance was in the 1980 Wembley final, when he achieved a career ambition of lifting the Challenge Cup and a club record fifth trophy as captain. Millward made 406 appearances for Rovers, scoring an all-time club record

207 tries, kicking 607 goals and setting a post-war club record of 31 points in a match against Hunslet in 1972.

At his peak as a player, Millward had everything; pace, sidestep, good hands and a varied kicking game in the loose, as well as being a capable goal-kicker. He had a great ability to read the game, an impeccable textbook defence and, perhaps most important of all, he never shirked anything on the field. 'The best player I've seen in my life,' says Phil Lowe. John Millington agrees, saying: 'He was unbelievable, he had a heart like a lion.'

Having shed the boots, Millward continued as coach for a further eleven years winning six more trophies to become the most successful in the club's history. When he bowed out at the end of the 1990-91 season, he had been with the club for an incredible 25 years. 'As a coach he was brilliant," says David Hall. 'He always looked after us. He will always be loved and respected for what he did for the club.'

After leaving Rovers, he had a short spell in charge of Halifax in 1991-92. Awarded the MBE for his services to rugby league in 1983, Millward was inducted into the Rugby League Hall of Fame in 2000 and Rovers named the main stand at Craven Park in his honour. Looking back at his career with the club, he says: 'It was a great time to be there – a great club, great players around you – and the crowd were something else!'

No longer actively involved in the game, he lives in Kippax with his wife Carol, and has battled against ill health in recent years.

The Greats – No 30
Mike Smith - *see Hull KR legends gallery*

Probably the finest centre ever to pull on a Rovers jersey, Mike Smith was a proud, loyal home club man. Born in Hull in January 1958, he attended the club's summer school and graduated through the 'B' team and Colts, signing as a professional in 1974. The club were well aware of his potential and carefully managed his progression.

Making his debut as a second half substitute for Steve Hartley at Barrow on 28 March 1975, Smith went on to play in 489 games for the Robins – a club record that is unlikely to be beaten. In the process, he scored 140 tries. As a centre, he was a selfless player who created many tries for his wingers – Ged Dunn, Steve Hubbard and Garry Clark profiting most from playing outside him. A classy player and a clever footballer, as the best players do, he always appeared calm and unflustered.

Smith won 11 Great Britain caps and five for England, touring Australasia twice with Great Britain. He was undoubtedly a top-class club centre but perhaps just lacked that extra yard of pace that would have seen him add considerably to his international caps.

Having been a key member of the successful sides throughout the glory years of the 1977-86 period, Smith took over as club captain when Rovers' fortunes were waning in the late 1980s. He increasingly showed his versatility, appearing more regularly at stand-off and loose-forward. He enjoyed a testimonial in 1985-86. After 17 years with the club, Smith made his final appearance for the Robins at Sheffield on 31 March 1991, one of the few to emerge with credit that day.

'He was one of the very best,' says Wayne Parker. 'He had a great rugby brain and was always able to create gaps with his superb passes.' David Hall adds: 'He was a legend in every way, he always kept himself in great shape, a fitness fanatic.' 'He was special,' recalls John Millington. 'He had everything and he was a really good bloke too.'

After his marathon career with Rovers, Smith played for a short spell with Doncaster before retiring from the game. Having worked for BP Chemicals at Saltend for over 30 years, he is now semi-retired and living in one of the villages to the east of Hull, where he maintains regular contact with

The Robins

*many of his old teammates. Quiet and unassuming, he still
looks back fondly on his time at the club. 'The best team I
ever played in was the 1983-84 double-winning side with
the three Kiwis and John Dorahy,' he says.*

A new coach

After winning only two of the last 13 games the previous
season and losing four key players, hopes were greater than
expectations for the 1991-92 season. The Robins had a new
coach and captain, George Fairbairn and Wayne Parker. For
the first time in ten years, the club signed no overseas players.
A young Australian half-back, Troy McCarthy arrived in
September but made only 13 appearances and in January,
Kiwi international Dean Clark joined from Scarborough
Pirates.

The Fairbairn era got off to a good start with opening
wins over Bradford and Halifax and by the end of January,
his charges had won nine out of 15 Championship games.
Although they won only three of the last eleven games, they
had done enough to ensure Championship football for the
following season. A low point was a record-equalling 76-8
defeat at Halifax in a Sunday evening televised game. It was
the highest score conceded by the Robins at that point but in
mitigation they finished with only ten men. Fairbairn and his
team deserved a lot of credit for the way they bounced back
with a 23-4 win over Wakefield in the following game. The
only knockout success was a first round win over Dewsbury
in the Yorkshire Cup.

There was a bit more stability in the side with both
Mike Fletcher and Sodje being ever-presents. Former Hull
Ionians RUFC winger Julian Barkworth, centre Hallas, former
Hull Boys Club hooker Lee Richardson and second-rowers

Thompson and Paul Fletcher also played in most of the games.

Bishop returned to the fold, but made just half a dozen appearances before moving to London Crusaders on loan. John Lydiat made his last appearance in the same game, eleven years to the day since making his debut. He totalled 180 appearances for the Robins, scoring 45 tries and kicking 50 goals from full-back, centre, wing and off the bench. Not the fastest or flashiest back, he was a tough customer. Another of the last remaining links with the glory days of the 1980s was broken when Zook Ema made his final appearance in the season's penultimate game. A very solid and hard-working performer for the Robins, Ema had clocked up 233 appearances since progressing from the Colts in August 1983.

After a gap of five seasons due to his occupation as a fireman, Chris Harrison returned in the second row in the second round Yorkshire Cup defeat at Castleford and Richard 'Tich' Chamberlain first appeared at Swinton in early October, deputising for Richardson at hooker.

Whilst the club remained in significant debt, with £648,433 being due to creditors, they had at least made significant steps to reduce the rugby loss from £180,632 the previous year to £42,846.

In 1992, the signing of the Maastricht Treaty created the European Union and led to the creation of the euro. Prince Charles separated from Princess Diana and the Conservatives under John Major won a fourth consecutive general election. In sport, Nigel Mansell won the Formula One title and Nick Faldo his third and last Open. David Oxley, now the RFL Chief Executive, retired after 18 years' service and was replaced by Wigan's Maurice Lindsay.

For the Robins, the 1992-93 season started with a third new chairman in three years, former international second-row forward, Phil Lowe. It was a difficult start for him, making the blunt decision because of the financial situation that most of the players would no longer receive contract payments and they were to be rewarded on a 'no play, no pay' basis, as they had for most of the club's history. 'It was hard for the players to accept at first, which I can understand and it affected team spirit for a while,' says Fairbairn. Averting potential disaster, he gradually pulled things round and only one player left – Graeme Hallas, who was another to join Halifax.

A 14-6 defeat at the Boulevard on 13 September marked the club's very last Yorkshire Cup tie. The county cup competitions, which had played a big part in the rugby league calendar since 1905 but had been steadily losing their appeal were consigned to history.

Winning only seven of 26 league games, the Robins finished in bottom spot in the Championship. Only the RFL's decision to revert to a 16-club Championship granted them a temporary reprieve from relegation. A 14-10 win at Salford in the first game merely raised false expectations and Rovers won only one more match before 20 December – a period that included heavy defeats at Widnes, Bradford and Wigan.

The final one of that spell was a 31-24 defeat at Leigh, a creditable result given the makeshift side. The contracts issue had come to a head again and eight who had played in the previous game took strike action. The players had not received an additional payment that they believed they were promised when their contracts were ended. However, the dispute lasted just the one week and, with agreement reached, the missing players returned to action to help the Robins to a much-needed win over Warrington.

For the supporters, the highlight of the season was the 8-0 home win over Hull FC in January, whilst the best performance was in a third round Challenge Cup replay defeat at Widnes. On a ground at which Rovers had lost 52-0 five months earlier, they put up a very spirited performance before going down 16-11. The game hinged on an incident late in the first half when former Norland forward Wayne Jackson, who had led the forwards with a tremendous performance, had to leave the field following a bad challenge by Davies. The Welshman was lucky to remain on the field and although he returned later, Jackson was not the force he had been. The Robins had led 11-5 in the second half but Widnes fought back to take the spoils.

After that, only two more wins came in the last seven league games and the season ended depressingly with a 38-6 home defeat to Halifax. The weakness was in the backs, where Parker was the one quality player. In the forwards Paul Fletcher, Andy Thompson, Wayne Jackson, Craig O'Brien, Chris Harrison and either Lee Richardson or Tich Chamberlain at hooker made up a competent pack. O'Brien missed only three games all season. Former Colt Tracy Lazenby, who had made his debut back in 1983, briefly returned from his spell at Wakefield and made substitute appearances in the last two games. He played only 26 times for the Robins, a low return for his undoubted talent.

The club was in no financial position to make big-money signings, losing £60,478 on the rugby side. Two young Australian backs, Troy Goldman and Craig McKeough were given their chance but neither really impressed and it was seasoned back David Liddiard, signed from Manly in December but with considerable experience in England, who made an impression. Then director Barry Lilley remembers the night of the cup replay at Widnes: 'It was a freezing night and we had to persuade Liddiard to come out of the hot shower for the second half, he was a good player though.'

The Robins

Down again

Liddiard remained with Rovers in 1993-94 and was joined by fellow-countryman Dave Hosking, a prop from Liddiard's former club Manly. Neither completed the season, both playing their last games in January.

The campaign started with an encouraging 16-10 home win over St Helens and wins at Wakefield and at home to Bradford gave the Robins six points from the first six games. However, there was only one more win before the Airlie Birds visited on Boxing Day and relegation, fortuitously missed the previous season, was looming. After a 14-6 derby win raised hopes for the New Year, Rovers won only twice more before Wigan came to Craven Park in April with the Robins needing to win their last three games to have a chance of survival. It was a remarkable achievement that they beat a Cherry and Whites side full of household names 21-10, a score-line only made more respectable for the visitors by a late converted try. Unfortunately, the following week Rovers lost away to fellow strugglers Salford 30-12 to confirm the drop. The following week at Widnes, with only pride to play for, the Robins won their final first division game.

The RFL revamped the Challenge Cup that season, with the first two rounds proper contested by amateur clubs, the Second Division teams entering at round three and the First Division clubs thereafter. Victory over Ryedale-York saw the Robins in to the fifth round, only to fall at Featherstone.

Fairbairn had tried to field a settled team. Mike Fletcher missed only one game at full-back and Barkworth and Sodje were the regular wingers. The centre positions were more problematic, with the most regular performers being former East Park junior Mike Bibby and Rob

Hutchinson, who had signed from Halifax the previous season. Skipper Parker at scrum-half had no fewer than six partners. The nucleus of the pack was Chris Harrison, Chamberlain, Jackson and Paul Fletcher, Hosking playing in only 16 games. Rovers scored only 64 tries but Mike Fletcher kicked 90 goals. 'When I was captain and we got a penalty in the opponents' half, I gave the ball to Fletch to go for goal – we were just grateful for the two points,' recalls Parker.

At the end of the season, Hutchinson moved to Sheffield and forward Wayne Jackson to Halifax. Off the field, the financial situation had worsened with the rugby operating loss trebling from the previous year to a record £183,997 and a reduction of over £45,000 in gate receipts. The immediate debt due had risen again to £660,120, with a further £441,722 owing longer term. At the AGM, Phil Lowe stood down as chairman and Barry Lilley, a former police officer and long-time Rovers supporter, took his place.

There was another threat on the horizon; the RFL engaged in planning the introduction of a European Super League for the start of 1996, backed by significant money from BSkyB, greatly encouraged by their viewing figures for televised Championship matches. There were signs that early plans included proposals for a number of club mergers one of which was to be between Hull FC and Hull Kingston Rovers which caused outrage amongst supporters.

The Greats – No 31
George Fairbairn - *see Hull KR legends gallery*

There have been a number of top line full-backs to have worn the oveted colours over the years but arguably the best of them was signed from Wigan for a then world record £72,500 in the summer of 1981.

The Robins

Born in Peebles in the Scottish border country in July 1954, George Fairbairn started his rugby career playing for Kelso RUFC, turning professional with Wigan in 1974. He played over 200 games for them, his last season as player-coach, taking them back to the First Division after unthinkable relegation in 1979-80. In the close season there were changes in the Wigan hierarchy and Fairbairn decided it was time to move on. 'Wigan had been a very good team and I'd enjoyed my time with them but Rovers were at the top and it was a new challenge for me.' In his first two seasons, he made the arduous journey from across the Pennines for matches and training, eventually moving to Hull in 1983.

Full-back had been a problem position for the Robins since the departure of Cyril Kellett 14 years earlier. On hearing of the availability of an international of Fairbairn's proven class and ability, they moved quickly to recruit him. He made his Rovers debut at home to Huddersfield on 14 August 1981, kicking eight goals. That first season proved to be his most prolific, as he posted a new club record 160 goals, breaking Neil Fox's club record and missing only two games in the process.

Qualified by virtue of his grandmother, Fairbairn played 15 times for England, scoring 118 points, a record only beaten by Kevin Sinfield in 2012. He also won 17 Great Britain caps, the last against the great Australian Invincibles of 1982, and captained the side on several occasions.

At the time of his arrival, Rovers had another top goal-kicker in Steve Hubbard but a premature end to his career through injury saw Fairbairn become Rovers' first choice kicker. However, he was much more than that. Strong and fearless, safe under the high ball and a solid tackler, his timed running was always dangerous when he linked up in attack. Rovers' fans who saw him at his best will recall numerous occasions when the opposition broke through and a try looked certain, only for the door to be slammed shut by a crunching tackle at the death from one of the best cover defenders in the game. In April 1990, he made the last of 269 appearances for the Robins, in which he kicked 554 goals, 19 drop-goals and scored 51 tries.

When Roger Millward called it a day in 1991, the directors turned to Fairbairn, with his previous coaching experience, to take over. A fitter by occupation, the coaching role was his first full-time post in rugby league. Despite having no money to operate with despite a threadbare first team squad, in his first season in charge Rovers finished in a respectable ninth place out of 14. 'It was difficult making the transition from player to coach and we had nothing like the playing strength there was when I arrived at the club,' he says. In Fairbairn's third season, Rovers were relegated. Wayne Parker remembers him as someone who played to his strengths. 'He had a straightforward no-nonsense approach, he knew what he wanted but he always gave Ged Dunn and I chance to give input.'

The dire financial situation meant that the club needed to make economies and Fairbairn left in 1994. He then coached Huddersfield and the Scottish national team, remaining as the Bravehearts team manager. He is now one of the team of RFL match commissioners. Looking back over his career, he notes: 'It was hard work, but they were lovely years. The game was less structured then, we had some moves, but there was generally more freedom.' Fairbairn continues to live in the Hull area.

Championship, Naughton Park, Widnes, 17 April 1994
Widnes 10-13 Hull Kingston Rovers

Rovers were already relegated by the time they played their last top flight league game for almost 13 years. Playing without pressure, they produced one of their best performances of the season.

The Robins

Led by talismanic skipper Wayne Parker, the Robins tore into the opposition from the start. Both sides could have scored before Paul Smith put Widnes ahead in the 34th minute but Rovers came back strongly and were in the lead within two minutes. Substitute Nick Halafihi and Sean Hoe drove towards the line and Parker burrowed his way over. Mike Fletcher converted and Parker, who had earlier produced a magnificent tackle to deny Spruce, dropped a goal to put the Robins 7-4 up at the break.

A David Ruane try and Bobby Goulding conversion sent Widnes 10-7 ahead but Rovers kept hammering away at the hosts. It was no more than they deserved when Parker's long pass found Mike Crane who went over for the winning try with just eight minutes to go. Fletcher's conversion made it 13-10 and Rovers held on for a great win.

Parker outplayed his illustrious opposite number Goulding and was behind most of the Robins' best moments. The pack, led by front-row trio Wayne Jackson, Tich Chamberlain and on-loan John Glancy, stood up well to their more experienced and powerful opponents and every Rovers player played his part. As Hull Daily Mail reporter John Fieldhouse put it: 'If only the pride and passion that Rovers showed against Widnes had been in evidence on other occasions .... if only.'

There was praise for George Fairbairn and his team from their opponents but it proved to be his last game in charge and half a generation before the Robins were back amongst the elite.

Widnes: S. Spruce: D. Myers, K. Hammond, D. Ruane, P. Smith; C. Tyrer, R. Goulding (capt); A. Ireland, A. Ruane, D. Smith, E. Faimalo (P. Moriarty), T. Russell, D. Hulme (S. Barrow).
Rovers: M. Fletcher; M. Coult, R. Hutchinson, A. Charlesworth, S. Hadi; M. Crane, W. Parker (capt); W Jackson, R Chamberlain, J Glancy, S. Richardson (C. Hardy), P. Fletcher (N. Halafihi), S. Hoe.
Referee: R. Smith (Castleford)
Attendance: 3,350

In the close season, Fairbairn, who had not agreed a new contract and his assistant Dunn both left the club. Ged Dunn had been at Craven Park since 1971 and in his 11 playing seasons established himself as one of the club's best wingmen. In his 296 appearances for the Robins, Dunn scored 160 tries to put him in fifth place in the clubs' all-time list, three behind Gilbert Austin. 'He was a most under-rated winger, the fastest man at Craven Park in my time,' says Hall, who played alongside him many times. Taking over first as 'A' team coach in 1980 and then as assistant to Millward in 1986, Dunn was a loyal and dedicated clubman, popular with the players and a part of the fabric of the club for many years.

The Robins appointed another former player, Steve Crooks, to succeed Fairbairn as coach and there was genuine hope that 1994-95 would bring the Robins another swift return to the top flight. However, the side was nowhere near as good as that of four years earlier and there were some good teams in the Second Division.

There was big blow early in the season with the departure of Wayne Parker, to Halifax. He recalls that he did not know that he was being sold and did not want to go. 'I got a phone call from a bloke who said he was Mal Reilly – I thought it was a wind up and put the phone down. When he rang back a third time and I realised it really was him, he told me that he had agreed to sign me for Halifax for £50,000. He persuaded me to go over and see them and they offered me ten times what Rovers had and I just couldn't refuse. But I'd been happy at Rovers and was sorry to leave.' Others were sorry to see him go too. 'It was a big loss for us,' says Paul Fletcher.

It all started promisingly with five consecutive wins but when the next four games yielded only one it was clear that the Robins had a fight on their hands. It was in that run that Rovers suffered their infamous 1-0 home defeat to Barrow, the only instance of such a scoreline in their history. An inconsistent spell ensued before Rovers lost their last six games, finishing in eighth spot and losing in the divisional play-off to Keighley. The only cup wins were against amateurs Hensingham, in the Regal Trophy, Thornhill and then fellow Second Division side London Broncos in the Challenge Cup.

Two notable arrivals were those of former York centre Gary Atkins and ex-Castleford and Sheffield winger David Plange. Form and injuries prevented Crooks from playing a settled side but there were outstanding efforts from forwards Chris Harrison, the new skipper, and Paul Fletcher, who both played in every single game. Without Parker, half-back was a headache and nine players played in these two positions, one of them curiously being Stuart Farr, who made his final appearance for the club some eight-and-a-half years after his previous one.

Andy Thompson made his last of his 166 appearances in a heavy home defeat by Batley on 9 April and retired. Thompson, who had made his debut at the end of the 1986-87 season in the backs, was slightly on the small side for a second-rower but his work-rate and defence more than compensated.

Having profited from the RFL's tinkering with the league structure two years earlier, it was Rovers' turn to suffer this time. When the clubs voted for a three-division structure of 11 teams each, the Robins eighth-place finish qualified them for no more than a place in the Centenary Second Division and they now faced a season in the third tier of professional rugby league.

Behind the scenes the planning for Super League continued. Lilley remembers being called to a succession of chairmens' meetings on the subject. 'There was still a lot of talk about mergers but there was never any real chance of them happening. I remember that Jim Mills was the chairman at Widnes at the time and a merger between Warrington and Widnes was first mooted at a meeting when he was on holiday. At the next meeting he went ballistic, which was a frightening sight. It all went on for a while before it was accepted that the idea of mergers was unrealistic and they were dropped from the Super League plans.'

A 'third division' side

In 1995 the first DVDs appeared and Pierce Brosnan brought James Bond back to life in *Goldeneye* after six years in limbo. In football, a legal dispute between a little-known Belgian footballer, Jean-Marc Bosman and Club de Liege changed sport's transfer systems for ever by introducing the concept of a player becoming a free agent at the end of his contract, and Wigan won a record eighth successive Challenge Cup.

New arrivals at Craven Park for 1995-96 included Kiwi international back-rower Sam Stewart, who took over the captaincy, former Hull FC, St Helens and Great Britain prop Andy Dannatt, his former Boulevard teammate Paul Eastwood, and West Hull ARLC centre Rob D'Arcy. Rovers romped through the Second Division in a truncated programme of 20 league games arranged to facilitate the transition to summer rugby in 1996.

The Robins lost only two league matches, at York and at home to Carlisle who they beat 20-14 in the return fixture to all but seal their title in January. Rovers scored 870 points in the 24 games played, with Mike Fletcher kicking 122 goals and Plange finishing as top-try scorer for the second successive season. A narrow home defeat to First Division Rochdale in the last Regal Trophy competition was not totally unexpected but the 24-0 home defeat by Leigh in the Challenge Cup marked a disappointing end to the short season. Again, both Paul Fletcher and Chris Harrison were ever-present as was Mike Fletcher, who returned to his more natural full-back position after the Carlisle defeat in early November.

May 1995 saw the return of speedway to Hull with Craven Park the venue this time. Whilst the addition of a track alongside the greyhounds reduced the playing area further, the club hoped that it would bring in much-needed revenue.

The first season of summer rugby in 1996 coincided with the launch of Super League as BSkyB paid the RFL £87 million for five years of exclusive TV rights. The campaign was again a comparatively short one, opening on 31 March and ending in October. It was also the first time the sport allowed four substitutes and the transition to a 17-man game started.

There had been no promotion or relegation for Centenary First and Second Division sides so despite the previous year's success, it was a second season in the third tier for the Robins in the newly-named National Leagues.

They signed two of the Papua New Guinea team from the '95 World Cup. Initially keen on centre John Okul, half-back Stanley Gene also impressed them and they signed both.

Rovers won all but one of their league games, scoring 1,009 points and conceding only 294 in the process. They topped 50 points in ten out of their 22 league games, including a record-equalling 92-10 win against Chorley in April. The main objective, promotion, was achieved with a thumping 60-16 home win over Leigh in the penultimate league game to secure a consecutive championship. In the National League play-off semi-final, the Robins travelled to play First Division winners Salford and were not disgraced by a 36-16 defeat.

Mike Fletcher missed only one match at full-back and

had his second most prolific season with 145 goals. Scrum-half Gene was one of five ever-presents but had several half-back partners. He quickly became a favourite with his all-action displays but after an early injury, Okul made only 10 appearances in three seasons. Atkins, Stewart, Paul Fletcher and hooker Shaun Hoe and were the others not to miss a game. Rob Wilson signed from Hull FC and was a regular performer in the second row and half-back Mike Crane started 18 of the 23 games from the bench.

A curious occurrence concerned Hull & E.R. RUFC winger Richard Oliver, the son of former Hull FC player 'Nobby' Oliver. He had made a dozen appearances before the 1996 season and was recalled to the side for the visit to Chorley on 21 April, in which he scored five tries, was selected for the following game against Bramley, where he scored three more, but he never played for the club again.

Sam Stewart retired at season's end. An excellent all-round forward, he won many admirers in just 46 appearances and would have graced the team in better times. 'We were very lucky to have had him, he was an unsung player and a very hard man,' says Paul Fletcher. Another to make his last appearance was Chris Harrison. A tall long-striding forward, he made 161 appearances for the Robins, a total that would have been much greater but for his fire service commitments. Paul Eastwood also played his final match for Rovers in June.

The Robins had done as much as could have been expected on the field but off it the situation was dire. The debt now stood at £1.3m and they were losing £3,000 per week. They attracted a crowd of over 2,000 only in the first home game and there were only 1,412 there for the match with South Wales. Storm clouds were gathering.

*****

11. On the Brink

THE situation facing the club at the start of 1997 was bleaker than at any stage of its history to date – put simply, the choice was administration or extinction.

The darkest hours

1997 was the year of the 'New Labour' landslide general election victory, the death of Diana, Princess of Wales, and the birth of text messaging. In rugby league, Brisbane Broncos won the first and only World Club Championship and BARLA trialled a new summer competition.

It had been common knowledge for some time that Rovers were in desperate financial circumstances but the announcement in early January 1997 that the directors were to apply to put the club into administration was a sickening blow. There was bitter criticism of chairman Lilley and his board but they had little choice, the stark reality was that the alternative was to wind the company up. Despite having only the club at heart, their resources were limited and there was no wealthy benefactor.

The major problem was the debt owing to the Inland Revenue, who had previously agreed to several arrangements for its clearing but unfortunately they had not been adhered to. Their patience having run out, the tax men were now ready to serve a winding-up order. The Robins were duly put under the stewardship of administrators appointed by Coopers & Lybrand, who operated on a strict 'cash in, cash out' basis. There would be no money for investment in players but at least the club could continue to function.

The administrator, Edward Klempka, was to play a huge part in safeguarding the future of the club. Not long after he took up his role he turned down 'a derisory bid' from former Hull FC player Tim Wilby, who then turned his attentions to the Black and Whites, purchasing the Boulevard club with the aim of getting them into Super League. Wilby made clear his view that there was room for only one professional club in Hull. He believed that a Super League franchise would be granted to a single 'super club' and that the two Hull set-ups should merge.

Klempka then received a bid from a consortium representing an unnamed 'well-known sports personality.' Whilst it was acceptable financially, the administrator was suspicious and demanded guarantees about the future of the Robins. He never received those assurances and when Hull FC subsequently achieved promotion in their own right, the mystery bidders withdrew the offer – further fuelling the local rumour mill as to their actual identity.

On the field, Halifax knocked Rovers out of the Challenge Cup in the fourth round but, bizarrely, the Robins made Wembley by qualifing for the inaugural Challenge Cup Plate, contested by clubs who had been knocked out of the main competition early. By beating Doncaster, Lancashire Lynx and Leigh Centurions, they faced Hunslet Hawks as a curtain raiser to the Bradford Bulls versus St Helens Challenge Cup final on 3 May. Rovers did more than their bit to provide entertainment for the 78,000 crowd, hammering the Hawks 60-14 – the highest score by a rugby league team at the national stadium. The plate was never played for again.

However, the league was a more difficult matter and by the time of that final, the Robins had won just three out of ten National League First Division games. Two fixtures later Crooks resigned as coach, saying that he had 'run out of motivation to fight any more fires,' further claiming that he had achieved the targets set when he took over against a very difficult financial background. He added there were a number of reasons for his decision but denied that they included the abuse directed at him by fans who perceived that he had favoured the proposed merger. Crooks said that he believed the club did have a future, provided the board and administrators were committed to it. Rovers appointed assistant coach Dave Harrison in his place, but on a part-time basis.

In June, with five games left, and relegation a distinct possibility, Lowe persuaded Wayne Parker to return to the club. Parker became Harrison's assistant and took over at scrum-half, whilst Gene moved to stand-off. Parker took over the captaincy too. 'It was great when he came back and I could hand the captain's armband back to someone that knew what he was doing!' says Paul Fletcher, who had inherited the captaincy from namesake Mike in mid-season. Parker's influence immediately paid dividends and the Robins won four of their last five league games to ensure eighth place and survival.

The Robins

The improved form was carried into the Divisional Play-off (East) competition, in which Rovers won five consecutive games before the season tailed away with three more defeats. The promotion to Super League of Hull FC, or Hull Sharks as they had been renamed, meant that there would be no competitive derby games for ten years. Former Skirlaugh winger Paul Rouse was an ever-present and ex-Hull Boys Club loose-forward Chris Charles took advantage of Sam Stewart's departure to claim that position. Hooker Sean Hoe was the most notable of several players who left the club during the year. He made his final appearance in the last match of the season, having played 135 games for the Robins at half-back, loose-forward and as an impact player from the bench. He was talented and versatile and gave one of his best displays in the win at Widnes at the end of the 1993-94 season.

Encouragingly, under the administrators' strict control, the club made a small profit of £50,000 over the season, albeit nowhere near enough to reduce the debt. In the desperate financial situation, players and supporters worked together to raise money and Parker remembers fundraising in the pubs and clubs with Rovers diehard, the Reverend John Leeman, Vicar of nearby Sacred Heart church on Southcoates Lane. 'The situation was dire,' Parker says. 'It was a struggle just to keep going and the chairman couldn't spend any money without the administrators' approval.'

At this time, died-in-the-wool supporters Adge Cutler and Keith Lyon set up the Rovers Supporters Group, whose objective was to raise money for new players. So successful was the RSG that when it eventually wound up ten years later, it had raised over £200,000. The money had enabled the club to remain competitive on the field, whatever the troubles off it. Lyon looks back now in appreciation of the support they received. 'There were people who contributed generously

however often we went to them, they never refused.' Colin
McNicol, who joined the board the following year, speaks
highly of the RSG's efforts, commenting: 'Without them, it is
very doubtful that the club would have survived.'

**Challenge Cup Plate Final, Wembley Stadium,
3 May 1997**
Hull Kingston Rovers 60-14 Hunslet Hawks

*Rovers rewarded their 4,000 fans who made the trip to a
sun-drenched Wembley with a brilliant display that crushed
the Hawks. However, before the game, a security alert
sparked fears that the match would not take place, and it
eventually started 45 minutes late.*

*The Robins made an edgy start and Hunslet soon took
the lead when Southernwood forced his way over from a
play-the-ball. However, Rovers started to get into the game
and in the 14th minute Rob D'Arcy took Rob Wilson's
inside ball and rounded former Rovers' man Coult to score
from 15 metres out. Mike Fletcher converted to nose Rovers
ahead. Five minutes later Chris Charles and Jon Adams
combined to send Paul Fletcher over but Hunslet came back
after 25 minutes when Mansson got through the defence all
too easily to cross and a minute later Booth's penalty levelled
the scores at 10-10. It was a 13-minute spell either side of
half-time that swung the game irrevocably in the Robins'
favour. In the 34th minute, a mistake by Coult gave Rovers
a scrum in a good position and after a break by Stanley
Gene, Darren Hutchinson picked up a loose ball to send
Adams over. Three minutes later, Gene, Wilson and D'Arcy
combined to release Gary Atkins and with Mike Fletcher
converting both tries, the Robins had a 22-10 half-time lead.*

*Within seven minutes of the restart, they extended it to
34-10. Charles sent Gene in and, after Andy Dannatt had
made good yards to field a Hunslet kick, Adams broke down*

the touchline and Atkins scored from Wilson's pass. Mike Fletcher converted both tries. Although Hunslet scored from a rare attack in the 53rd minute, Adams cut back inside to finish off a fine move four minutes later and the Robins led 38-14. The last 20 minutes were all Rovers and some devastating finishing led to four more tries. Dannatt drove in hard and popped a short pass to Gene, who crossed for his second; Paul Fletcher stormed over after good work by Mike Crane; Andy Dearlove provided the pass for Gene to sprint 50 metres for his hat-trick; and, two minutes from time, Dearlove, Adams and Paul Fletcher combined to send Charles romping across. Mike Fletcher landed three more conversions for a final tally of eight.

It was a tremendous team performance. Rovers played some brilliant football that would have seen off better sides than the Hawks. Gene was a deserving man-of-the match winner, but the Robins had the upper hand in all departments. 'Playing at Wembley was an unforgettable experience and to produce a performance like that was the icing on the cake,' says Paul Fletcher.

To win some silverware at such a difficult time was a real fillip and the resulting £50,000 prize money a more than welcome boost to the finances.

> **Rovers:** *M. Fletcher (capt); J. Adams, D. Hutchinson, R. D'Arcy, P. Rouse; G. Atkins, S. Gene; A. Dannatt, R. Chamberlain, C. Hardy, R. Wilson, P. Fletcher, C. Charles. Reps: M. Crane, A. Dearlove, S. Hoe, D. Harrison*
> **Hunslet:** *M. Coult; R. Baker, M. Pechey, G. Boothroyd, P. White; P. Mansson, T. Murphy; S. Pryce, G. Southernwood, S. Tuffs, G. Cochrane, S. Flowers, C. Booth. Reps: M. Coyle, B. Hill, D. Brook, N. Rushton*
> *Referee: R. Connolly (Wigan)*
> *Attendance: 78,000*

False hopes

For all the troubles off the field, 1998 represented a significant improvement in the club's fortunes on it. Rovers made three signings; centre Rob Danby, hooker Mike Dixon and second-rower Andrew Smith from Hull Sharks and Howard Hill arrived from Oldham. In 1998, the eleven National League First Division clubs played each other three times and the Robins finished runners-up to Wakefield Trinity, whom they beat in all three league encounters. Winning their first six fixtures, including a convincing 36-6 home win over Trinity, they moved to the top of the table by the end of March. The first defeat of the season, 46-18 at London Broncos in the sixth round of the Challenge Cup, ended a four-match knock-out run.

A spell of just two wins in seven games ultimately cost the Robins the First Division title but they then picked up again. A one-point defeat in the penultimate match at Hunslet, after letting slip a 16-4 interval lead, cost the Robins a chance of pipping Wakefield for top spot.

In the end-of-season play-offs, the Robins followed victory over third-placed Dewsbury with a narrow semi-final defeat at Wakefield, who thereby gained some measure of revenge for the earlier defeats. The season then ended on a very disappointing note when Rovers were thrashed 54-6 by Featherstone in the final eliminator at Craven Park. It was academic, as even if the Robins had won the play-offs they would not have been accepted into Super League whilst in administration.

Further arrivals during the season were second-rower Jamie Kennedy and winger Keith Beauchamp from St George-Illawarra, scrum-half or hooker Daniel Brown from Parramatta and Bradford winger Richard Smith. Wayne

Jackson returned to the club after his stint at Halifax but after failing to regain a regular place he joined Doncaster. Danby and prop Alex Thompson, who had arrived from Sheffield Eagles the previous season, played in all the games, crowd favourites Gene – the top try-scorer for the second time – and Paul Fletcher missing only one match each.

The three Australians left at the end of the season along with Hill, but the biggest departures were those of Mike Fletcher and Gary Atkins. Fletcher, the club's all-time leading point-scorer and goal-kicker, made his last appearance in the play-off defeat to Featherstone at the end of the season. He played 360 times for the Robins, scoring 2,759 points, with 1,267 goals, 56 tries and one drop-goal. Whilst the majority of his games were at full-back, he also made 124 starts at centre and six at stand-off. Never the fastest player, what he lacked in pace and guile he made up for with his honest commitment, fearlessness and his remarkable goal-kicking. After ending his Rovers career, he had a short spell with Hunslet.

Gary Atkins, who started his career with Castleford, made his last Rovers appearance as a substitute in the final league game at home to Keighley. He returned to York, from whom he had joined the Robins, after making 121 appearances in which he scored 79 tries. A pacy and skilful back who was equally adept at centre or number six, he proved a stalwart of the Rovers back division over the four years that he served.

Nearly two years after the club went into administration, there was a flicker of false hope for Rovers' fans in late November. The administrator announced that the owner of Leeds Rhinos, Paul Caddick (Holdings) PLC, had made an official bid to take the club out of administration. The company said the Robins would be run by an independent board, a clear effort to satisfy RFL regulations about the ownership of more than one club. The crux of the Caddick plan was to build a new stadium that could house Rovers, Hull City and, possibly, Hull Sharks and to redevelop the Craven Park stadium as a community facility as part of the Preston Road redevelopment project. However, three weeks later, Caddick Holdings pulled out. Hull City Council told them that they would have to pay £400,000 to lift the restrictive covenant on Craven Park and they felt that without the support of the City Council they could not proceed.

Colin McNicol, whose wife Lesley had supported the Robins since 1955, had at the time recently retired from his position as a senior officer in the Fire Service. Lilley approached McNicol to pull together a group of business people who would help raise money for the club. McNicol involved the then Lord Mayor Councillor Brian Petch, and the 'Lord Mayor's Fighting Fund' as it became known, ultimately raised more crucial money for the club. Paul Fletcher had a testimonial season that earned him £10,000, a figure that would have been several times greater in better times.

In 1999, the Scottish Parliament and the Welsh Assembly were formed. Manchester United won the Champions League, beating Bayern Munich in Barcelona to add to their domestic double, and manager Alex Ferguson was knighted.

For a third season running, 1999 opened with the club in administration. Lilley had pledged that after the Caddick setback, it would be business as usual. The league structure altered yet again and the two National League divisions were amalgamated under the name Northern Ford Premiership. Amongst a clutch of new arrivals was experienced former Sheffield Eagles and New Zealand centre Whetu Taewa, who was to prove a shrewd capture. Other significant signings were former Castleford winger Jon Wray, Australian forward

The Robins

David Luckwell, who arrived from Canterbury, and former Hull Sharks utility back Chris Kitching, who had joined the club on loan the previous season.

For a second successive season, the only loss in the first ten games was a Challenge Cup defeat by London Broncos, this time by a narrow 6-0 margin in the mud at Craven Park. By the time the Robins entered the final six games of the season, they were well in the running for the championship, having lost only three times. However, talisman Gene was injured and, with a couple of others missing, the team lost form and won only once on the run-in.

On the eve of the final game, which the Robins needed to win to reach the end-of-season play-offs, the news broke that fans' favourite Gene had signed to play in Super League for Gateshead Thunder. He said that he had always been happy at the club but when Gateshead came in with an offer to play in the top flight he could not turn it down. He hoped the fans would understand and said that he planned to return one day. The timing was not good and coach Harrison asked Gene to stay away from training. The Robins went down 23-10 at Featherstone and missed the play-offs.

As it transpired, Gene never played for his new club. In their one and only Super League season in 1999, Thunder finished sixth but struggled financially. At the end of the season, the league was to be reduced to 12 clubs from 14, and they accepted a £1.25million payment from Super League to merge with Hull Sharks who had finished joint bottom and were in financial difficulty themselves. The 'merged' club would be based in Hull and would benefit from the cash injection and the best players from both clubs. Gene, therefore, effectively joined the Black and Whites, who somewhat fortuitously avoided relegation as a result.

Richard Smith, Wray, Taewa and Kitching were back

division stalwarts, but injuries disrupted the pack. Andrew Smith and Thompson were both ever-present, as was Paul Fletcher. The latter, however, played half his games at centre whilst Danby was out, and he was the top try-scorer with 14. Des Harrison and former Academy prop Craig Hardy were regular starters from the bench. Hardy made his debut in 1992 but injuries had disrupted his career.

In addition to Gene, a number of other well-known faces left the club. Andy Dannatt was having increasing trouble with injuries and retired at the end of the season. He had spent four years with Rovers, playing in 93 games and despite being in the latter stages of his career, did a very good job, providing on-field leadership and experience at a difficult time.

Wayne Parker was another at the end of a very distinguished career, making his final appearance in the last league game at Featherstone. He spent ten years with the Robins either side of a three-year stint at Halifax, playing in 245 games, during which he scored 62 tries and dropped 33 goals including equalling Agar's record of four in a match. Parker was a very talented half back who played in a difficult era and was one of very few who played between 1986 and 2006 who would have held his own in the great teams before that. Paul Fletcher claims: 'Wayne was the perfect leader, with a great rugby brain and if he'd been with a more fashionable team at the time I'm sure he would have played for Great Britain.' Taewa assumed the captaincy in Parker's place.

Veteran prop Des Harrison retired after 15 years, also making his final appearance, as a substitute, in the last league game. A strong and rugged forward, he played in 295 games for the Robins, including 104 as a substitute, making him the first Rovers' player to clock up a century of appearances from the bench. Lively hooker Richard 'Tich' Chamberlain played his last game, at Bramley in July, after being at the club for eight years and making 142 appearances, in which he scored 44 tries. Others to leave at the end of the season included full-back or winger Richard Smith, centre Danby and winger Paul Rouse.

As a cost-cutting measure, Klempka had advised Lilley to trim the board during the season. He believed that only three directors were necessary, and six left, leaving Lilley, Draper and Johnson. One to go was Colin Hutton, who was made the club's life President in recognition of his service of over 40 years.

It had been a disappointing end of the season but there were soon rumours of positive developments.

The Greats – No 32
Colin Hutton - *see Hull KR legends gallery*

Colin Hutton was born in Widnes in May 1926, learning to play rugby league at primary school with future Great Britain captain Alan Prescott. "All I wanted to do was to play rugby league," he says. At grammar school, he played rugby union but after leaving at 14 following the outbreak of war, he joined Farnworth ARLC.

When Widnes reformed after the war, Hutton joined them and earned a place in the side at centre, playing in the team that beat Wigan in the 1945 Lancashire Cup final.

National Service interrupted his Widnes career and he missed two seasons in which he served as a Lance Corporal in the Royal Engineers in Egypt. Returning to the Widnes side, he won two Lancashire caps and played in the Challenge Cup final against Warrington at Wembley in 1950. Losing his place the following season, Hutton asked for a transfer. Legendary broadcaster Eddie Waring had a friend on the Hull FC board and arranged a move for him. Hutton soon settled in Hull, conveniently finding a suitable house in the Boulevard. He remembers feeling a warmth of welcome and he quickly developed a sense of affinity with the city. 'There was still plenty of evidence of the dreadful bomb damage it had suffered but it was a privilege to witness the rebirth of the great city that I have grown to love.'

The following season, he moved to full-back, in which position he made the majority of his 262 appearances for the Black and Whites. Long-time Airlie Birds supporter Mike Smith remembers him as: 'A very sound full-back – a good tackler who read the game well – and, above all, an excellent goal-kicker. You were glad to have him in your side.' Hutton kicked 628 goals in six-and-a-half years at the Boulevard.

By the autumn of 1957, however, Hull FC had signed a new full-back in Peter Bateson and Hutton was not getting a regular game. 'I even played three games in the second row, one of which was in the 1957 derby at Boothferry Park.' By then, he was the landlord at the Avenue pub on Chanterlands Avenue in Hull and he remembers getting a visit shortly afterwards from three men in suits. By then Hutton had done his coaching qualifications and they offered the Rovers coaching job at just the right time.

Recalling his early days at Craven Park, Hutton says: 'It was chaotic, there was no organisation at all. And the training was so repetitive that the players were bored.' He changed all that and gradually his approach bore fruit. In the process, he had to make it clear to one director that he would not tolerate his interference in the dressing room. One of the board Hutton did have a high regard for was vice-chairman Ron Chester. 'He was the main man for me,' Hutton notes. 'If I had any problems he sorted them out.' But on team selection and player transfers: 'I had no input at all. I was just told, "We've signed Poole" or whoever, and what the team would be after the directors picked it. Later when I was on the board I helped to change all that.'

After 13 seasons, in which Rovers were once more established as a force in the game, and with three trophies and two final defeats, Hutton stepped up to the role of general manager in 1970. Amongst his most important achievements were the summer and weekend coaching courses he set up for prospective young rugby league players in the town, developing new talent has always been a passion.

The RFL had already recognised his coaching and he toured with Great Britain in 1962 and 1968. 'I felt I'd gone as far as I could and I recommended Johnny Whiteley for the role. The club had just bought the stadium back and they needed someone to be responsible for it.' It was typical of Hutton that he took on a role for the good of the club for minimal reward. By then, he was the landlord of the Zetland Arms in Portobello Street, where he took many new Rovers' imports into his family over the years. In 1975 he was elected to the game's governing body, the Rugby League Council, upon which he served for over 20 years, and in 1997 he was appointed a life Vice-President of the RFL.

In 1982, after a spell as vice-chairman to Bill Land, Hutton took over as chairman. After overseeing on-field success in his four years, it was Hutton and his board who regretfully made the decision to leave the old Craven Park in 1989. 'We had no choice, the main stand roof and the woodwork all needed replacing to bring the stadium up to safety standards, we simply could not afford to stay there.'

After the club had safely moved into his new home, Hutton stood down as chairman, remaining on the board until 1997, when he was made president. He remains closely involved in an ambassadorial role and current chairman Neil Hudgell says: 'His presence is great for the club, he is welcomed by everyone, he gets instant respect from the players for all he has achieved.'

There will always be those who disagree with some of the decisions of those in authority but no one can deny all the time and effort that Hutton has given to the club he loves. He considered it his greatest honour when, joining a small and select band of people, he was awarded the Freedom of the City of Hull in February 2013. In June 2014, Rovers named the new North Stand at Craven Park in his honour.

Rescue

The Queen opened the Millennium Dome in Greenwich, number one in the charts was West Life with 'I Have a Dream' and Leeds United topped the FA Premier League. The predicted 'Millennium Bug' was a damp squib with the anticipated computer failures and malfunctions not materialising.

A major step towards securing the club's long-term future was taken in December 1999 when a deal was drawn up involving Hull City Council and Gaingroup, now known as Kingston Community Development Ltd. The council agreed to purchase the ground for £450,000 and lease it back to Gaingroup, who would rent it to the club. Gaingroup would purchase an interest in the club for £200,000 that would bring the total rescue package to £650,000. That would finance a CVA (Creditors Voluntary Agreement) which would fully pay off Rovers secured creditors and 80 per cent to preferential creditors. Gaingroup, whose directors included former Hull City chairman Don Robinson and local businessmen Keith Brown and Jack Brignall, would be represented on the club's board by Robinson, who would be the chairman.

Even after reaching agreement in principle, there was a long period of financial wrangling, during which time the future of the club remained in doubt until everything was finally signed and sealed. Robinson took over before the Keighley game in mid-May, meeting supporters at the turnstiles to usher in a new era for the club. The new board consisted of Robinson, accountant Mark Jackson, who was the interim chief executive, Wayne Smith, Ron Curzon and coach David Harrison, with Robinson later inviting Colin McNicol to join the board. The ground rent was set at £30,000 per year for five years and was subject to five-yearly review. The future

of the club was secure in the immediate term at least and
Rovers finally waved goodbye to the administrators in July.

The three members of the old board that had helped
steer the club through some of its darkest moments slipped
quietly away but to this day they remain passionately
committed. Chairman Barry Lilley's links go back to his
father and grandfather who had worked on the turnstiles at
Craven Park. He remembers them taking him to the ground
and leaving him in the stands at just seven years of age. After
his retirement from the police force, he had served on several
benefit committees before then chairman Phil Lowe had
asked him to become a director. Since leaving the board, he
has continued to serve on the RFL disciplinary committee and
is currently a match commissioner.

Lilley has no regrets about the decision to put the club
into administration. 'It was the only way the club could
survive. It was administration or extinction by then. The
financial decline had started long before I came onto the
board and finally someone had to grasp the nettle. But I will
always be proud of the fact that we managed to bring the club
back out of administration and ensure its survival.'

Chris Draper originally served on the board between
1981 and 1986 and Lowe persuaded him to return and help
raise funds in 1992. He agrees with Lilley about the decision
to enter administration and both men pay tribute to Klempka
and his assistant David Thornhill, who managed the club's
day-to-day affairs. 'David kept a tight rein on the finances
and I looked after everything else,' Lilley continues. 'We had
a close working relationship. I had to ask him before
spending any money that hadn't already been agreed but he
helped us if he possibly could. When we went to Wembley
in 1997, he ensured that we had the money to do it properly.'

'My second spell on the board coincided with very

difficult times,' Draper adds. 'But despite that, I wouldn't change a thing. I look back to the 1980s, which were the finest times of our lives. Money couldn't buy the experience of being a part of all that.' The third retiring director was Peter Johnson, whose family was represented on the board for nearly 40 years first through his uncle, Percy. Peter's father Jack was also a very significant, although reticent, benefactor to the club.

New signings for the 2000 season included centre Rob Nolan from Hull Sharks, Whitehaven stand-off Leroy Joe, scrum-half Mark Hewitt from Widnes, and Featherstone loose-forward Richard Slater. Amongst several new local faces were winger Dean Andrews from Hull Dockers, prop Jon Aston from Bransholme ARLC, East Hull's Jamie Bovill and Ian Kirke via Rovers Juniors, whilst former Academy full-back Bob Everitt, who played 26 times between 1995 and 1997, returned to the fold after overseas missionary work.

Despite the new off-the field optimism, the new millennium campaign was a disappointment on the field. After a slow start, when the the side struggled to build attacking fluency, a run of eleven wins in twelve league games saw Rovers competing at the top of the table by early April. Seven defeats in eight games then saw them slip down it again, ironically, the one win in the spell a 20-12 success over champions-to-be Dewsbury. Despite a late-season revival, they finished in only seventh place and lost 22-14 to Oldham in the elimination play-off semi-final. There was a change of opposition in the Challenge Cup from the previous two seasons, Rovers losing to Halifax, who were now playing in Super League as the Blue Sox and sharing the Shay with the football club.

Ever-present skipper Whetu Taewa led a fairly settled team with Everitt at full-back; Andrews, Nolan, Taewa and Wray in the three-quarters; Joe and Hewitt at half-back; and

The Robins

Fletcher, Dixon, Hardy, Andrew Smith, Charles and Slater the forwards. Bovill and Kirke were regular starters off the bench. Hewitt took over the goal-kicking and landed 108 goals. Former Hull FC prop Richard Wilson made his debut in May and claimed a regular place thereafter.

At the end of the season, coach Dave Harrison left the club, as did Nolan, Joe and Hewitt. Craig Hardy called it a day after making 116 appearances for the Robins and Ian Kirke made what was to be his last appearance in a heavy defeat at Whitehaven near the end of the season. A stress fracture put him out for the following season, and when he subsequently returned to fitness, Rovers released him. He then started his circuitous journey to the Leeds Rhinos via Hull FC, York, Dewsbury and London Broncos. Another future international forward, Jon Wilkin, started his professional career on 26 May that year, as one of Rovers' substitutes at Sheffield.

The 2001 National League season actually started on 3 December 2000, and finished as early as July. It was a low-key start for new Rovers' coach Gary Wilkinson, previously Harrison's assistant, with no major signings and just three wins from the first eight league games. French opposition came to Craven Park for the first time when the Toulouse Spacers were beaten 44-0 in the Challenge Cup, only for Rovers to lose at Oldham in the next round. The Robins continued to be inconsistent but six wins in the last seven games secured them a play-off place. Sadly, once again it was to no avail, as after a 19-6 away win in the elimination semi-final against reigning champions Dewsbury, the season came to another disappointing end at Rochdale in the next round.

Skipper Taewa and Fletcher did not miss a game and prop Richie Hayes, signed from York during the previous season, was the player-of-the-season. In a brief return to the club, Bright Sodje played in just 12 games after leaving

Sheffield. Former Driffield RUFC speedster, Alasdair McClarron, took over the left-wing spot after making a try-scoring debut at Chorley in March. Rob Wilson returned to the club in May, to make up a solid back three with Slater and Charles and, later that month, Rovers signed half-back Craig Murdock from Salford. He made his debut at stand-off in a heavy defeat at Leigh, switching to scrum-half in the following game and remaining there for the rest of the season. Only Kitching and Slater left at the end of the season, both making their final appearances in the play-off game at Rochdale.

The financial situation at the club was worse than Robinson had thought and when it came to light during the season that there were still debts of around £250,000 in addition to those covered by the CVAs, he resigned as chairman. Wayne Smith took over and invited former director David Wilkinson back onto the board. The club appointed ex-player Nick Halafihi as the new chief executive and charged him with developing the commercial side of the club's activities.

'For a while there was a strong possibility of the club going back into administration,' says McNicol. 'It was a very difficult time. One of the problems was the lack of security at the ground at the time, there were constant break-ins and the club was losing money hand-over-fist.'

Two debutants in the opening games of 2002 were three-quarter Craig Farrell from Hull FC and the former Sheffield Eagles goal-kicking utility-back Lynton Stott, who signed from Workington. There was an improvement in results but another mid-season wobble cost the Robins the chance of the runners-up spot to runaway champions Huddersfield Giants. The Giants almost emulated Hull FC's 1978-79 feat of winning all their league games, but dropped one point. The Robins won 17 of their first 22 games losing just twice in the league, at Rochdale and at home to Huddersfield, both by four points. A third league game, at home to Leigh, was abandoned due to floodlight failure after 51 minutes, somewhat fortuitously as Leigh led 14-2 at the time, and Rovers won the rescheduled fixture at the end of the season, 18-12.

That successful run also saw the Robins progress to the final of the new National League cup which included a very impressive 38-18 win at Leigh in the quarter-final. In the final at Post Office Road the Giants convincingly beat Rovers 32-6, starting the mid-season dip.

The following week Rovers returned to Featherstone for a league game, where they were beaten 46-40 – the first time they had ever scored 40 points and lost. They won only four out of nine games in June and July but then picked up again, and a heavy defeat at Huddersfield was the only loss in the last eight league games. A fourth-placed finish was their best for five years but once again, there was to be no play-off joy, as the Robins fell at home to Oldham at the first hurdle.

Former Wakefield half-back Dane Dorahy, son of 1980s import John, made his debut in February and claimed a regular place whilst another former Sheffield Eagle, three-quarter Nick Pinkney, joined in July. Taewa missed one game, his first in three seasons. Charles, who had taken over the captaincy from Taewa, had his most prolific goal-kicking season, finishing with 138. For the first time since his debut, Paul Fletcher did not feature in the starting 13 but made 38 appearances off the bench.

Coach Gary Wilkinson also left the club at the end of the season. Paul Fletcher pays tribute to both Wilkinson and his predecessor Dave Harrison. 'They were both very good coaches but they didn't really have much to work with – if they'd had the resources that later coaches had, I'm sure they'd have done at least as well.'

Whetu Taewa, by then 32, retired at the end of the

season and the club appointed him as assistant to new coach Steve Linnane for the 2003 season. A former Kiwi international who had enjoyed a successful career in Australia and Super League, he was undoubtedly one of Rovers best overseas imports since the glory years. He made the last of his 131 appearances, in which he scored 59 tries, in the play-off defeat to Oldham. A good footballer, Taewa was a strong runner and tackler and a consistent and reassuring presence. Remarkably, he missed only four matches in his four seasons. 'He was very strong and led by example, we were lucky to have him,' Fletcher adds.

A number of players ended their Rovers careers in the last match of the season, including Everitt, Hayes, Dixon, Wilkin and Charles. Former Academy product Bob Everitt retired after making exactly 100 appearances, in which he scored 37 tries, and had arguably been the club's best full-back since Fairbairn. Despite Rovers' efforts to keep him, the powerful Premiership prop-of-the-year Richie Hayes returned to former club York, after playing in 66 matches. Hooker Mike Dixon retired having given good service to both Hull clubs and winning three caps for Scotland. A clever and elusive player, he played in 146 games for the Robins, scoring 39 tries. After playing in 39 times, Jon Wilkin left to pursue a brilliant career with St Helens.

Salford signed Chris Charles after their relegation from Super League at the end of the season as part of their rebuilding for an immediate return. He spent four years with them during which he won one England cap, before joining Castleford and ending his playing days in France. A former cricketer with the old BR North club in Hull, Charles played in 231 games for Rovers, kicking 304 goals and scoring 41 tries. A strong and clever player, as well as a more than capable goal-kicker, he remains arguably the best loose-forward since Gavin Miller. "We knew he was special when we first saw him," notes Fletcher.

Other to leave included former Black and White second-rowers Rob Wilson and Matt Schultz, and Australian forward, Luckwell.

Early in the season, loyal and hard-working company secretary Ron Turner left. Having held the position for over 32 years, he was the longest-serving secretary in Rovers' history. Since his arrival from Cumbria in August 1969, he had overseen many momentous events from the heady days of the early 1980s to administration. In those latter days, Turner had the almost impossible job of keeping the creditors at bay and the administration of the club ticking over. His memories include the wonderful experience of Wembley 1980 and the never-ending expense of the move to a new stadium.

Change, change and more change

In December 2002, the KC Stadium was opened on the site of the old Anlaby Road Circle, the home of Hull Cricket Club since 1898. Hull City played their first competitive game on the new ground on 26 December, when they beat Hartlepool 2-0. Hull FC vacated the Boulevard home that they had occupied since gazumping the Robins 107 years earlier and moved into the KC on a ground-share basis for the start of the 2003 Super League season.

At Craven Park, Colin McNicol took over as chairman from Wayne Smith, who stood down due to his business commitments. McNicol quickly set about restoring the credentials of Craven Park as a rugby stadium first and foremost. Greyhound racing photographs in the West Stand were replaced by historic club rugby images and memorabilia. The upstairs bars were renamed after Harry

Poole and Peter Flanagan and the West Stand was dedicated to Roger Millward. Despite some reservations at the time, Flanagan's bar was successfully converted into the 10-5 Restaurant. Three years later both greyhounds and speedway had gone and one of McNicol's aims had been realised.

Meanwhile the Robins prepared for the new season under their first overseas coach and the first full-time appointment since Crooks. Steve Linnane had made his name as a half-back with St George and, after moving into coaching, had been in charge at Halifax until his sacking the previous August. His assistant, Taewa, left early in the season due to the illness of a close friend at home.

There were four new signings for the start of the season. Kiwi scrum-half Latham Tawhai, who was signed from Rochdale, the former Hull FC pair of full-back Craig Poucher and centre Paul Parker and former Embassy hooker Paul Pickering. The RFL split the National League into two divisions again and the Robins competed in a ten-team First Division, in which they finished fourth. Disappointing though this might have been, it was probably a fair reflection of the club's playing strength.

The season started with the Challenge and National League cups, Rovers losing to Salford in the former in round five and progressing to the quarter-final of the latter. However, they then lost four of the first five league games and in such a short competition, the poor start left them with too much to do. Despite winning their last five matches, Rovers finished behind Salford, Leigh and Rochdale. The Robins had gained only one win from their fixtures against these three, coming against Salford in the last game, which they won 18-16 – but the visitors still claimed first place on points difference.

The winning run extended into the play-offs and after a relatively comfortable home success over Oldham, Rovers came from behind to claim a thrilling 30-26 win at Rochdale. With the scores level at 26-26, Rovers charged down a Rochdale drop-goal attempt and broke away for Paul Parker to score the match-winning try with the last play of the game. That set up an elimination semi-final at Leigh, where the home side were far too good for the Robins, leading 32-4 at half-time and going on to win 42-12.

It was difficult for Linnane to establish a settled side. Missing as many as seven regulars from the previous season, his four new signings from the start were augmented by further arrivals as the season progressed. Much-travelled international prop Harvey Howard signed from Wigan and he made his debut at home to York in March. Howard, with seven international caps and a Grand Final winner with Brisbane, had a reputation as a powerful and aggressive forward, but by the time he joined the Robins he was 34 years old and, sadly, injury forced his retirement after just 17 appearances.

Probably the most influential signing was that of Australian forward Anthony Seibold from Ipswich Jets. He had played with Brisbane Broncos and Canberra Raiders before coming to England to play in Super League with London Broncos. He'd sustained a career-threatening knee injury in the capital and returned to Australia but eventually worked his way back and proved his fitness by playing in Queensland Cup rugby. Seibold made his debut against Sheffield in April and took over as club captain from Pinkney, who had replaced Charles.

Later in the season, Papua New Guinea prop Makali Aizue arrived and made his first appearance off the bench at home to Oldham in June. Tawhai had six different half-back partners before the arrival of Kiwi Paul Mansson from Hunslet in July. Former Cottingham Tigers hooker Andy Ellis made his debut in the win against Salford at the end of the season. Forwards Richard Wilson, Jon Aston and Paul Fletcher were all ever-present – all but one of Fletcher's appearances coming from the bench. At the end of the season, Tawhai was the only one of the regulars to leave the club. He moved to Hunslet, who offered him a player-coach role.

McNicol remembers the effect that Linnane and Seibold had on the side. 'They brought in up-to-date ideas of coaching, fitness and diet that the players bought into. They were also real motivators and could work the players up to fever pitch before they went out on the park. Gradually there was improvement and for the first time we started to think that getting into Super League was a real possibility.' McNicol recalls the spirit of kinship that existed between the players at the club and the fans in those days. 'We did not have the money for pre-season training camps like today but Linnane was keen to forge bonds between players and on Sunday nights after matches, all the players, the coaching staff and the directors would have a night out in the 'Old Town'. Only the injured players did not come and there were always very few of them. The fans got to know about this, and some came along too. They enjoyed the close and easy contact with the players and the players always responded well and professionally. Johnny Aston called it the 'win or lose, we're on the booze' night. It built up a great positivity and camaraderie at the club and re-created the family atmosphere that had disappeared whilst we were in the doldrums.' 'We played it hard,' says Fletcher, 'but we had some laughs and always had a few beers after the game. I remember one game that got rather nasty, but both teams ended up in the bath together drinking cans of lager.'

Unfortunately, to the disappointment of many, Linnane had to resign in November due to personal problems. 'Linnane was the best coach I played under,' says

Paul Fletcher. 'He started to turn us into a professional outfit. I was gutted when he left.'

The Robins took the opportunity to overhaul their coaching set-up. Phil Lowe returned to the club as football director; Rovers appointed experienced Mal Reilly, who had left his assistant coach role at Leeds at the end of the season, as team manager; and Martin Hall, who won the National League coach-of-the-year at Rochdale in 2003, as head coach.

There was disappointment that the team's playing record in 2004 was no better than the previous year. The squad was augmented by ex-Featherstone centre Matt Calland, Mansson's former Hunslet half-back colleague, Phil Hasty, forward Dale Holdstock, son of former favourite Roy, Scott Thorburn, East Coast Tigers half-back and captain, who arrived on a six month loan and Kiwi Frank 'the tank' Watene.

Interest in the Challenge Cup lasted only one game, a third round home tie against Union Trieste Catalan that Rovers lost 23-22. The Robins reached the final of the National League cup for the second time in three years but they lost heavily to eventual league winners Leigh Centurions in the final at Rochdale. In the league, the Robins finished third but with an identical playing record to the year before and at no stage won more than two matches in succession. The team struggled to find any consistency, with 33 players used in the 32 matches.

Widnes loose-forward Tommy Gallagher, who had Super League experience with London Broncos, had a short spell with the club midway through the season before moving on to Toulouse. Mansson was ever-present, with either Hasty or Thorburn as his half-back partner. McClarron was the leading try-scorer for the third year running, with Parker, Pinkney and Poucher the other regular members of the back division. Skipper Seibold formed the backbone of the pack with Aizue, Bovill and Andrew Smith, whilst Pickering and Ellis fought a private battle for the hooking position. Fletcher was regularly joined on the bench by Watene, who moved on to Castleford at the end of the season. Other end-of-season departures included Pinkney, Smith and skipper Seibold. Reilly, never popular with the players, left his post as team manager during the season and Hall, a good coach who was perhaps at the club at the wrong time, left at the end of it.

It was all change again in the boardroom at the end of the season. Local compensation solicitor and long-time supporter Neil Hudgell, who had come onto the board to replace David Wilkinson the previous year, took over as chairman. McNicol notes: 'Neil was keen to invest but he wanted to have control of his investment and I was happy to stand down for the good of the club. During my time on the board, it often seemed as if we were walking on a tightrope and were working under constant financial pressure, but they were still fantastic times. I didn't know a lot about rugby but I was a good administrator and that was what was needed then.' McNicol pays tribute to major shareholders Peter May and Dave Stanley, who invested heavily in the club, to Adge Cutler and Keith Lyon and their Rovers Supporters Group and to the various businesses and supporters who contributed to the cause. 'Without their generosity, the club would not exist today.' By the time McNicol stepped down, the club had paid off nearly 90 per cent of its' old debt.

Hudgell brought fellow businessman and supporter Rob Crossland on board, Paul Lakin replaced Halafihi as CEO and Harvey Howard returned to the club, this time as head coach. With the promise of investment, a new chapter was opening for the Robins at last.

*****

12. Phoenix from the Ashes

2005-2015

IT was clear that Neil Hudgell and Rob Crossland had ambitions beyond National League but even with their investment, getting into Super League was only the start, staying there would be an equal challenge.

Silverware again

In mid-December 2004, Brendan Cole and Natasha Kaplinsky won the first series of *Strictly Come Dancing*, Kelly Holmes was the Sports Personality of the Year and Band Aid 20 re-recorded 'Do They Know It's Christmas?' On Boxing Day, the world was shocked by the biggest earthquake for 40 years, resulting in tsunamis in the Indian Ocean that took over 230,000 lives – £45 million was raised in 48 hours as a result of donations to appeals by British charities alone.

Meanwhile, the promised investment at Craven Park

was bearing fruit. Rovers were strengthened for the 2005 season by the arrival of Australian scrum-half James Webster from Parramatta. Also came wingers Jon Steel from Scottish borders rugby union and little-heralded Aussie Byron Ford; Samoan centre Kane Epati from Cook Islands side Tupapa Panthers; and much-travelled prop Neil Harmon, who had been out of the game for 18 months. Another Australian, prop David Tangata-Toa, was signed along with Huddersfield-born second-rower Andy Raleigh from Sheffield. Then, two months into the season, the Robins added Castleford's talented Kiwi Michael Smith.

The Robins had a fine start. By the beginning of May they had won 11 out of 13 games and they had a perfect league record. That disappeared when they lost successive games to the two clubs that were to finish above them, Whitehaven and Castleford. An emphatic 62-0 league cup quarter-final win over Swinton put Hull KR back in the winning enclosure.

After the Swinton game, coach Howard was asked to trim the size of the playing squad. The following week, he dispensed with the services of Harmon, Paul Fletcher, Mark Blanchard and Craig Poucher in what was effectively his last act at the club. By then, Fletcher had made more appearances than anyone except Mike Smith and it was an inappropriate way for his distinguished career to end, a point that chairman Hudgell fully acknowledged. Concerned by the coach's increasingly eccentric behaviour, Hudgell called him to a meeting. When Howard did not attend, he was suspended and subsequently sacked. Of the four players who left, Blanchard alone returned after Howard's departure and played on to the end of the season.

Rovers put skipper James Webster in temporary charge whilst a new coach was found and he led the team during a nine-match winning run that saw the Robins reach the now

Northern Rail Cup final for the second year running. Tony Smith, then at Leeds, recommended young Australian coach Justin Morgan and, liking what they saw, Rovers persuaded him to join them. Morgan, a former prop-forward with Parramatta, Canberra and New Zealand Warriors, had risen to prominence as coach of French club Toulouse Olympique, who he had taken to the 2005 Challenge Cup semi-final against the Rhinos. Morgan watched from the sidelines as the Robins beat Castleford to win the NR cup decider.

He took over after that game but the early signs were inauspicious. Rovers won only five of the last nine games to finish third for the second successive year. The final match was a disappointing 36-22 home defeat to fourth-placed Halifax in the play-off elimination semi-final. However, the new coach had taken the opportunity to assess the strength of his playing squad and there would be many changes for the following season.

Gareth Morton, a former colleague of Steel's, had joined during the season and claimed one of the centre positions, after initially marking his debut with 22 points from loose-forward against Swinton in May. In just 15 matches, Morton registered 200 points, kicking 90 goals. Morgan also brought with him from Toulouse goal-kicking centre Damien Couturier and loose-forward Tommy Gallagher, the latter having played 10 games for the Robins the previous season. Paul Mansson missed only two matches and again made the most appearances. A classy player who was a favourite with the fans, he left the club at the end of the season and retired to his native New Zealand. In 71 appearances, Mansson scored 35 tries. Raleigh made an excellent impression in his only season at the club and there was disappointment when he left to try his luck in Super League with home town-club Huddersfield. Others to bow out during the season included Kane Epati, Jamie Bovill, Phil Hasty, Dale Holdstock, Paul Pickering and flying wingman Alastair McClarron, who scored 67 tries in 105 appearances.

After a wonderful 2004, in which they won three trophies including the Premier League title, the speedway team again fell on hard times and disbanded after the 2005 season. For the first time since before WWII, the Robins' home was exclusively a rugby stadium.

Northern Rail Cup Final, Bloomfield Road, Blackpool, 17 July, 2005
Castleford 16-18 Hull Kingston Rovers

On the Bloomfield Road ground once graced by football legends Sir Stanley Matthews and Jimmy Armfield, the Robins' lifted their first trophy in eight years in a thrilling Northern Rail cup final against the National League leaders. The victory was seen as heralding greater things to come, as all the previous winners had gone on to take their places in Super League.

On a scorchingly hot day in front of the Sky TV cameras, the Robins were underdogs on the field but their fans, outnumbered on the terraces, witnessed a classic triumph. There was little in the game until, with half an hour gone and the scores level at 2-2, Rovers had a Dwayne Barker try controversially ruled out due to an accidental offside. Immediately Castleford struck with a Platt try and two Huby goals to make the half-time score 10-2.

Rovers came out strongly in the second half and after Jason Netherton had gone close, Andy Raleigh took Barker's pass to beat three men and score. Gareth Morton's conversion and two penalties, one from inside his own half, gave Rovers a 12-10 lead. The crucial score then came with 15 minutes to go when Byron Ford leaped high to intercept a long pass from Davis and raced the length of the field to score. Morton's conversion, his fifth successful kick from five attempts, gave Rovers some breathing space, and Hepworth's try, converted by Huby, was no more than consolation for Castleford.

Stand-in coach James Webster, for whom this was a sixth consecutive win, was delighted: 'It's been a pleasure, and the boys have been great. They've shown the true professionalism you'd expect from a team of a higher standard.' New coach Justin Morgan, who had arrived the week before, was keen to praise Webster and his players. 'The full credit is to James and everyone else involved this week,' he said. Raleigh was man-of-the-match but, in truth, the award could have gone to any one of several Rovers heroes on the day.

Netherton feels that the win changed the mind-set of people at the club: 'It was a taster of what could be achieved and we wanted to be involved in more of these types of game.'

> **Castleford:** M. Platt; W. Price, D. Bird, J. Hepworth, M. Shenton; P. Handforth, B. Davis; A. Watene, A. Henderson (capt), A. Bailey, T. Haughey, C. Huby, C. Crouch. Reps: A. Kain, R. Fletcher, B. Smith, F. Watene.
> **Rovers:** L. Rivett; J. Steel, K. Epati, G. Morton, B. Ford; P. Mansson, J. Webster (capt); J. Garmston, A. Ellis, D. Tangata-Toa, A. Raleigh, J. Netherton, D. Holdstock. Reps: P. Pickering, D. Barker, J. Bovill, M. Aizue
> Referee: B. Thaler (Wakefield)
> Attendance: 9,400

The Greats – No 33
Paul Fletcher - *see Hull KR legends gallery*

Paul Fletcher was born in West Hull in March 1970. In his early years at Paisley Street School, pressed to declare his allegiance to either the Airlie Birds or Robins, he chose

Rovers because he liked the name better – despite his parents being Hull FC supporters. From school rugby, Fletcher joined Eureka youth club and from there progressed to Rovers' Colts in 1986. He made his Colts debut in August 1986 against a Wigan team that included a young Denis Betts, after which he played for two seasons in the Colts and 'A' teams, often playing for both teams on the same weekend.

Fletcher made a try-scoring first team debut against Bradford at the old Craven Park stadium on the last day of the 1987-88 season and signed for the senior side on 23 May 1988. Over the next couple of seasons, he only had a handful of first team chances and it was not until George Fairbairn took over as coach in 1991 that he made his real breakthrough. Fletcher's powerful performances earned him a regular place and he started every game of the season, winning the Supporters Club Player of the Year award in the process. From then, he retained a regular starting place, usually in his favoured second-row spot but occasionally at centre or loose-forward.

Between 15 November 1993 and 6 July 1997, he played in 131 consecutive games, covering three seasons, and was ever-present again between 6 September 1998 and 30 January 2002 – a run of 105 games. During that first spell, he played a huge part in the two Second Division championship wins that rescued Rovers from the third tier of domestic rugby.

From 2001-02, Rovers used Fletcher more as an impact player off the bench, from which he made all of his appearances that season and he was in the starting 13 on only one more occasion – at home to Sheffield on 23 February 2003. He made the last of his 464 appearances at home to Batley on 15 June 2005. Only Mike Smith made more appearances for the Robins and Phil Lowe is the only forward to have scored more tries than his 99. 'He was a natural,' says George Fairbairn. 'A very strong runner and tackler, who just played because he loved the game.'

At 6'2" and over 17st, he was a very powerful and physical player who had an aggressive streak to his game. His ability to break the line and off-load the ball made him a constant threat to opposition defences. At his peak, Fletcher gained the reputation of being the best English forward outside Super League. That he remained at Craven Park was of his own choice as he had several offers from Super League clubs including the then powerful Bradford Bulls. 'I just wanted to play for Rovers, they were my team. I have no regrets, except perhaps the way it ended. I'd like to have been able to say goodbye to the supporters in a final home match.' His loyalty and commitment to the cause along with his outstanding performances made him a huge favourite with the club's supporters. 'He was a very wholehearted player who always put in 100 per cent,' says Dave Sherwood. 'That and the fact that he remained loyal to the club during one of the most difficult periods in its' history, made him very popular.'

Fletcher acknowledges the part played by veteran Colts coach John Edson at the start of his career. 'He was, without a doubt, the biggest influence as I'm sure he was for so many of the young local players of the mid-1970s through to the early 1990s. He was a real inspiration, who always got the best out of the young lads.' After a short injury-ruined spell with Sheffield, Fletcher retired in 2006. He continues to live in Hull and supports the Robins home and away.

An historic season

The Robins started the 2006 season as a full-time outfit for the first time in their history. Newcomers included full-back Ben Cockayne, who signed from Doncaster, Oldham centre Jon Goddard, stand-off Scott Murrell from Leeds, Australian hooker Ben Fisher, who arrived from Halifax, and Huddersfield second-rower Iain Morrison.

Seven players made their debuts in the opening 32-2 Northern Rail cup triumph at York, which started a club record 24-match winning run. By the time Rovers returned to Blackpool for another cup final they were top of National League one and had reached the semi-final of the Challenge Cup, beating in-form Super League side Warrington in a memorable quarter final at Craven Park.

Defeat at Blackpool, where Leigh triumphed 22-18, brought to an end the victory run. Early on, the Robins made light of the absence of Webster by racing into a 16-2 lead inside 25 minutes but the underdog Centurions came back strongly to level at 16-16 at the break. After Morton's early second half penalty, Wilson's try mid-way through the second half won the game for Leigh. The players and fans were devastated at the final whistle but Morgan was careful afterwards not to blame either the absence of Webster or a couple of very close calls that went against the Robins – he knew that more important business lay ahead.

Six days later at Craven Park, the Robins faced nearest challengers Widnes in a vital league game with skipper Webster back at the helm. It was a perfect opportunity for them to bounce back in style and they did so brilliantly, having all but won the game when they led 28-8 at half-time. Despite a more even second half, Rovers won comfortably 49-24.

The following week, St Helens lay in wait at Huddersfield's Galpharm Stadium in the Challenge Cup semi-final. There were no complaints or excuses after the Saints' 50-0 win. Morgan admitted that good as St Helens were, his side had been poor on the day. With just six league games to go, he knew that four wins would secure top spot for the Robins.

Two of them were difficult away games at Leigh and Whitehaven, so he made full use of his squad by playing fringe players and introducing new blood. The Welham brothers started in the three-quarter line at Leigh, the only instance in the club's history of two brothers making their debuts together. Both the games were lost, but on 3

September, Rovers fought back from an 18-12 half-time deficit to win 28-24 at Batley to clinch the minor premiership.

In order to secure a place in Super League, they now had to reach and win the National League Grand Final. Widnes were the visitors again for the Robins' qualifying semi-final. In a game fit for the denouement itself, Rovers beat the Vikings for the third time that season. The crucial part of the game was the five minutes before half-time, when with the scores level at 12-12, Cockayne first capitalised on a Widnes error to score, then fielded a Widnes drop-out and ran to within inches of the line, from where Fisher dived over. Morton's conversions gave the Robins a 24-12 half-time lead and his two early second half penalties provided the cushion to withstand a strong Widnes comeback. At 28-22 with 10 minutes to go, the Vikings spurned several scoring chances before Murrell's drop-goal settled matters in the dying minutes. Rovers had reached the Grand Final, and had a perfect home record for only the second season in their history.

When Widnes beat Whitehaven 24-20 in their elimination semi-final the following week, the stage was set for the two clubs to meet again. At Warrington's Halliwell Jones Stadium on 8 October 2006, the Robins beat the Vikings for a fourth time that season to secure a place in Super League XII.

After the game, Morgan told a packed press room how proud he was of his team and their determination to succeed and that it was a privilege to coach them. He said that planning for the following season would now start in earnest and he was looking forward to seeing how his players would cope in Super League. On Sky TV, Mike Stephenson saw the other side of the coin. He spoke of the reality that Rovers would have to spend more money and get bigger players and that many of the ones celebrating that night would not be there the following season. However, of the 17 players who featured that night, only two would not get their chance with the Robins in Super League.

Challenge Cup 6th round, Craven Park, Hull, 4 June 2006
Hull Kingston Rovers 40-36 Warrington Wolves

There can be no doubt that this Challenge Cup quarter-final win, for many the match of the season, turned Rovers into genuine Super League contenders in the eyes of the rugby league world. It provided the players with belief that they could compete at the highest level. Beforehand, few outside Craven Park would have shared coach Justin Morgan's pre-match confidence.

The tie had captured the imagination of the Craven Park faithful and in front of the BBC TV cameras on a sun-drenched day, over 7,000 noisy fans turned out to see arguably the biggest game then hosted at the stadium. The Robins, who were at full strength, were given an early boost when Wolves' lost linchpin Lee Briers in the warm-up.

It did not start well for Rovers when Swann scored twice in the first 12 minutes and a Bridge conversion gave the visitors a 10-0 lead. However, after forcing a drop-out from James Webster's kick, a set move saw Ben Fisher and Scott Murrell send Ben Cockayne in for a try that Gareth Morton converted on 15 minutes. Five minutes later, Morton's conversion put the Robins ahead after Murrell's kick through had rebounded off the post and Mikali Aizue had touched down. Converted tries by Reardon and Martin Gleeson restored Wolves' ten-point lead after 30 minutes but the Robins came storming back again. First, a Morton penalty after a foul on Michael Smith narrowed the gap, then Webster's long pass sent Jon Steel in at the corner. Within two minutes of the break, Webster's high kick was gathered by Jon Goddard, who sent Byron Ford across. Morton's magnificent touchline conversion gave Rovers a 24-22 lead after a breathtaking first half.

There was no let-up in the second. After Fisher had carved out a try for Morton to give Rovers a six-point advantage on 43 minutes, first Fa'afili out-jumped Ford to cross and five minutes later Ford returned the compliment from Murrell's kick to make it 32-26 after 52 minutes. The Robins made it three tries in five minutes when Ford completed his hat-trick from Smith's long pass and David Tangata-Toa and Fisher created the opportunity for Jason Netherton to force his way over for what proved the match-winning try after 57 minutes. Morton unfortunately was unable to add either of the conversions but Rovers led 40-26 with 23 minutes left. The Wolves responded again when Fa'afili scored his second, before Michael Sullivan's converted try made it 40-36 with still 13 minutes to go. In a nail-biting finale, both sides had their chances, but the Robins held out to secure a famous win.

Rovers were only the second National League One side to reach the cup semi-final since the inception of Super League. Skipper and play-maker, Webster, with his brilliant kicking and astute passing won the man-of-the-match. He spoke of how the Robins really believed they could win, how they had planned for it, knowing they would need to post a decent score to do so and how they believed in themselves. 'We played really well,' says Netherton. 'And it gave us confidence that we could compete in Super League.'

> ***Rovers:*** *B. Cockayne; J. Steel, G. Morton, J. Goddard, B. Ford; S. Murrell, J. Webster (capt); M. Aizue, B. Fisher, D. Tangata-Toa, I. Morrison, M. Smith, T. Gallagher. Reps: G. Price, S. Martins, J. Netherton, D. Barker*
> ***Warrington:*** *S. Reardon; H. Fa'afili, Martin Gleeson, B. Grohse, R. Barnett; C. Bridge, M. Sullivan; C. Leikvoll, J. Clarke, P. Wood, M. Wainwright, L. Swann, S. Grix. Reps: Mark Gleeson, M. Hilton, T. Kohe-Love, B. Westwood*
> *Referee: S. Ganson (St Helens)*
> *Attendance: 7,012*

The Robins

National League Grand Final, Halliwell Jones Stadium, Warrington, 8 October 2006
Hull Kingston Rovers 29-16 Widnes Vikings

Roared on by five-and-a-half thousand of their enthusiastic and noisy fans in the stadium, Rovers got away to the kind of blistering start that had been a hallmark of their season.

After only five minutes, Ben Fisher darted through from the play-the-ball and linked with Jon Goddard, who sent Byron Ford in at the corner. Gareth Morton hit the post with his attempted conversion from wide out. After Mikali Aizue had gone close, Rovers increased their advantage when Ford returned the compliment to his centre, flicking the ball back inside from Webster's pinpoint kick to allow Goddard to score. This time Morton converted to put the Robins 10-0 up after 17 minutes. Murrell then went over for a try from a play-the-ball after Cockayne was stopped just short and Morton made it 16-0 just six minutes later. On the half-hour, Widnes responded with a try when Moran and Cassidy sent Dodd across despite Cockayne's attempted tackle. The Robins were undeterred and although Dwayne Barker lost possession inside the Widnes half, Cockayne picked up the loose ball and made good metres before flighting the ball into the path of Goddard, who scored his second try. Morton's conversion made the half-time score 22-4, and on TV Mike Stephenson described Rovers' first half performance as being as near to perfect as it gets.

Two minutes into the second half, a brilliant break from Murrell led to James Webster sending in Pat Weisner and it seemed that the only danger might be complacency. Nine minutes later, Weisner was bundled into touch just short of the Widnes line. This time the Vikings replied with one of their best spells of the game, resulting in a try for Tandy near the posts. Dodd's conversion cut Rovers' lead to 16 points. The Robins went close again when Goddard was denied his hat-trick by the corner flag but, soon after, Murrell dropped

412

a goal to give Rovers a 27-10 lead with 17 minutes to go. Goddard had another chance to get his hat-trick but could not take Ford's inside ball. Gleeson gave Widnes hope when he put Blanch in and the Vikings had another chance in the 72nd minute when Blanch miscued his kick ahead and the ball hit the corner flag. The Robins then survived one more frenzied Widnes attack before Webster broke up field. When he was obstructed, referee Bentham, who had an excellent game, awarded the penalty. Morton was successful with the straightforward kick on the stroke of the final hooter.

The Rovers fans went wild and the team celebrated as Webster lifted the Trophy and Cockayne took the man-of-the-match award. The pundits praised the Rovers' performance and Morgan faced the press with a quiet satisfaction. 'It was a fantastic night,' says Jason Netherton. 'Having beaten them three times already that season, we were favourites to win and were under a bit of pressure, but everything just went to plan."

> **Rovers:** B. Cockayne; L. Rivett, G. Morton, J. Goddard, B. Ford; S. Murrell, J. Webster (capt); M. Aizue, B. Fisher, D. Tangata-Toa, I. Morrison, M. Smith, T. Gallagher. Reps: P. Weisner, D. Barker, J. Netherton, D. Wilson
>
> **Widnes:** G. Dodd; D. Blanch, S. Gleeson, D. Cardiss, J. Kirkpatrick; D. Moran, I. Watson; T. O'Connor, M. Smith, B. McDermott, M. Cassidy, D. Allen, R. Beswick. Reps: A. Summers, O. Wilkes, J. James, R. Tandy
>
> Referee: P. Bentham (Warrington)
> Attendance: 13,024

The nucleus of the 2006 team was Cockayne at full-back; Steel, Ford and former Leeds Rhinos Wembley hero Leroy Rivett on the wings; Goddard and Damien Couturier at centre; Murrell and Webster the half-backs; Aizue, Fisher and

The Robins

Tangata-Toa in the front row; Michael Smith or former Leeds Academy forward Jason Netherton with Morrison in the second row and Tommy Gallagher at loose-forward. Morton featured in 23 games at centre, second-row or on the bench and surpassed his previous season's points tally with 252, from 96 goals and 15 tries.

Even after such a successful season, there were a number of departures as the Robins made space on their roster to strengthen their playing staff for the challenge ahead. The longest-serving of these, centre Paul Parker, had made 78 appearances for the Robins but only appeared twice, as a substitute, in 2006. Of those who appeared in the Grand Final, Rivett and substitute Barker left and Damien Couturier made his final appearance in the final National League game against Doncaster.

There were only four months before the 2007 Super League season was to start. It was an alarmingly short timescale for Hudgell, Morgan and their staff at Craven Park.

Into a new era

Whilst 2007 will be remembered in Hull for the damage sustained to its housing in the July floods and the opening of the £160 million St Stephens transport interchange and shopping centre. For the Robins, it marked their long-awaited debut in Super League.

As expected, they brought in a number of new players in an effort to make them competitive in the top flight. They were headed by former New South Wales and Australia prop Michael Vella and former Wests Tigers Grand Final winner Mark O'Neill. Old favourite Stanley Gene, by then at Huddersfield Giants, negotiated a release from his contract to enable him to return to Craven Park to be part of it all.

Further additions to the forward strength were Chris Chester from Hull FC, Castleford's Danny Ward and Gene's former Giants teammate Jim Gannon. Australian-born Welsh international three-quarter Luke Dyer also arrived from the Tigers. Amongst a handful of additional reinforcements that arrived during the course of the season was former St George-Illawarra centre or back-rower Rhys Lovegrove.

The 2007 fixtures were kind to the Robins in presenting them with a winnable opening game and they marked their Super League debut by snatching a dramatic morale-boosting home success over Wakefield in the dying minutes. The following week they followed up with a 17-10 win at Huddersfield that had Morgan enthusing about their completion rate, reflecting the importance of valuing possession and being disciplined.

Super League XII, Craven Park, Hull,
10 February 2007
Hull Kingston Rovers 14-9 Wakefield Trinity Wildcats

The Robins' long-awaited Super League debut took place on a cold, wet Saturday evening in front of the Sky TV cameras. Nine of the previous season's Grand Final-winning team took their places in the starting line-up alongside debutants Luke Dyer, Michael Vella, Danny Ward and Chris Chester. Coach Justin Morgan told his players before the game that he had the faith in them to do the job.

They could hardly have had a better start. Within three minutes of the kick-off, Chester's dummy opened up the visitors' defence and Scott Murrell scored Rovers' first try in Super League. Gareth Morton stroked over the conversion from wide out to give them a 6-0 lead. Clearly fired up for the occasion, the Robins dominated the opening quarter but Wakefield punished them for a lapse in

415

concentration in the 15th minute, Obst capitalising on Ben Cockayne's fumble and sneaking over from a play-the-ball. Morton's penalty goal nudged Rovers ahead again in the 22nd minute but they had to defend stoutly as the visitors applied pressure in the second quarter. Tempers became frayed and referee Klein showed three yellow cards before half-time, one to Cockayne. However, Rovers' defence held firm, and they led 8-6 at the break.

Shortly after half-time, Jon Goddard, covering for Cockayne at full-back, made a tremendous try-saving tackle to deny Jeffries and did brilliantly to deal capably with several testing high kicks. The visitors then levelled with a Rooney penalty in the 48th minute and three minutes later Dyer went close for Rovers, but two Wakefield men prevented him getting the ball down. With defences on top and time ticking away, the visitors started to look for drop-goal opportunities. Chester did well to charge down Rooney's first effort midway through the half but when a mistake by Cockayne gave Wakefield good field position, Rooney made no mistake from 35 metres. Wakefield led 9-8 as the game entered the last minute with the Robins in the visitors' half and seemingly in a good position to level the scores. However, using a move practiced many times in training, Webster dummied to go for the drop and slipped the ball to Chester who sent Cockayne over for the winning score. Morton added the goal, the hooter sounded immediately after Rooney's restart and the crowd celebrated as if their team had won the Grand Final.

Morgan praised his men for their defence which restricted the visitors to just one try, saying that he felt that had been the decisive factor. 'There was a huge amount of pressure on us that night, in front of a full house of our own supporters it was really important to get off to a winning start, it gave us confidence that we could play at that level,' says Jason Netherton. 'The way the game ended was brilliant too – it was a night I'll never forget.'

Rovers: B. Cockayne; L. Dyer, J. Goddard, G.
Morton, B. Ford; S. Murrell, J. Webster (capt); D.
Ward, B. Fisher, M. Vella, I. Morrison, J.
Netherton, C. Chester. Reps: M. Aizue, J. Gannon,
T. Gallagher, P. Weisner.
Wakefield: M. Field; P. Fox, J. Demetriou, R.
Atkins, S. Tadulala; J. Rooney, B. Jeffries; A. Watene,
S. Obst, R. Moore, O. Elima, J. Golden, B. Ferres.
Reps: P. March, T. Leo-Latu, N. Catic, D. Lima
Referee: A. Klein (Keighley)
Attendance: 7,154

For the Robins, in a season in which every point was going to
be vital, winning the first two was a huge boost. However,
Super League can be unforgiving and if a team's attitude is
not right or they are not quite on their game they can be facing
a mountain before they get going. The Robins found that out
in the third game at home to Harlequins; 22-4 down at half-
time, they did well to limit the damage to 26-10.

The following Friday night, the faithful supporters
who made the trek to Wigan were well rewarded. This time
it was Wigan who started slowly and everything came off for
the Robins, who took an unbelievable 26-0 interval lead with
two tries from Ford. The inevitable Wigan second half
comeback duly materialised, but despite some scares, Rovers'
defence was up to the job and the ecstatic visiting fans had a
famous 26-16 victory to celebrate. This was not the best-ever
Wigan side but it was still a great result. The following
Saturday, in front of the Sky cameras, a thrilling game against
Leeds just went Rovers' way, 22-20, and the Robins were
riding high in the table with four wins from five. That was as
good as it got in terms of league position but those eight
points proved invaluable later on.

Reality now kicked in, and an eight-match losing run

saw them eliminated from the Challenge Cup and slide down the league table. It included heavy defeats at St Helens and Bradford, a very disappointing four-point home loss against one of their potential relegation rivals, Salford, and a 22-14 setback on the Robins' visit to the KC Stadium for the first competitive derby since 1997.

However, it was off the field that the big headlines were made towards the end of April. Hull FC's talented play-maker Paul Cooke, a long-time Rovers supporter, walked out on the Black and Whites and signed for Rovers, claiming that he was a free agent as he had not signed a new contract with the Airlie Birds, who threatened legal action. The RFL, however, accepted the player's registration with Rovers and he was free to play. Their neighbours' loss was definitely the Robins' gain, Cooke added some much-needed class and physical presence to the now ailing back division. The management, quite reasonably, had focused their close season recruitment on forwards, and in the main, they had held their own but the gulf between National League and Super League was evident behind the scrum.

Cooke marked his debut with four goals and some neat touches against Huddersfield but it was not enough to stop the Giants exacting revenge and they triumphed 28-16. In the following game, Rovers' debut at the Super League 'Magic Weekend,' the losing run was broken. Cardiff's Millennium Stadium was the scene of the Robins' first Super League win over Hull FC. Aizue and Cockayne crossed for tries, whilst Cooke kicked four goals and generally ran the show but it was still rather close for comfort at 14-10.

Even closer was the following Friday's visit to the JJB stadium, Wigan, one of four sides played three times to make up 27 rounds. The second trip to Wigan was effectively a lower scoring version of the first. Tries by Ian Hardman and

Dyer gave the Robins a 10-0 interval lead and they then had to withstand severe second half pressure from the home side before Cooke's penalty goal gave them a 12-10 win. With 14 of the fixtures gone, Rovers had 12 points and they had given themselves a chance of survival.

But a five-match losing streak ensued, with a home defeat to Leeds at a sodden Craven Park, a disappointing loss at Wakefield, where Rovers led 9-2 before a rush of blood saw Aizue dismissed in the first half, a 40-0 home thrashing by St Helens and defeats at Harlequins and in the home derby. A hard-fought 22-20 victory in France, where the Robins had to withstand Catalans Dragons' fightback after a 22-6 half-time lead, was followed by another heavy home loss to Warrington, where the damage again was done in the first half.

The next game was a potential relegation decider against Salford at the Willows in front of the Sky TV cameras. It was a cut and thrust encounter in which the scrappiness of the play exemplified the nervous importance of the game to both sides. After the lead had changed hands several times, Rovers came away with a 30-24 win with decisive contributions from the experienced pair of Cooke, with a try and five goals, and O'Neill, with two touchdowns, the first after he lost his footing and somehow stumbled over the line.

Defeats to Bradford and Leeds followed but on 2 September, the Robins ensured their survival at the KC Stadium with their most comprehensive win of the season. The last two home games resulted in Wigan taking revenge for their two home defeats, triumphing 40-24 after another first half collapse and Cooke's drop goal won the final match, at home to Huddersfield, 25-24. The Robins finished in eleventh spot, seven points clear of relegated Salford.

Rovers succeeded in their main objective and in many ways, the achievement was greater than the season before.

The Robins

They had lived to fight another day amongst the game's elite and learned valuable lessons. Craven Park had been far from the fortress that they had hoped for, only three of the ten wins had come at home, and four of the defeats were the result slow starts. After the season, there was a wholesale clear-out unprecedented in the history of the club. Half of the 34 players who played during the campaign never pulled on the shirt again and the Robins retained only seven of the 17 who featured at the Halliwell Jones just a year earlier.

As Morgan had sought to find his best combination for the arduous campaign, there had been frequent team changes. Only in the second game did he field the same starting 13 as in the previous match. Dyer missed only one game and finished the leading try-scorer with 12, twice as many as anyone else. Often under-rated, his tries were crucial in the fight for survival and it was a surprise to many when he was allowed to leave at the end of the campaign.

Other stalwarts in the backs were Cockayne, Goddard and Webster. In the forwards, Vella led the pack magnificently, with great support from hooker Fisher, who topped the Super League tackling chart with 841, Gannon and Netherton. The ubiquitous Murrell appeared in every game, starting 12 at stand-off, two at scrum-half, two at hooker and four at loose-forward plus four from the bench.

There was an early blow when Michael Smith failed to regain full fitness and was released by mutual consent after appearing in only three games. In his two years with the club, Smith appeared 43 times and scored 20 tries. When fit he was a real asset, both on the field and off it, a true larger-than-life character. Another to struggle with fitness was the Queenslander, O'Neill, who announced his retirement at the end of the season. When fit, he started 17 games and made some telling contributions, none more so than in the crucial game at Salford. In addition to Dyer, who signed for the Celtic Crusaders along with Tangata-Toa, others to leave included Gallagher, Gannon, Goddard, Morrison, Morton and Ward.

Super League XII, KC Stadium, Hull, 2 September 2007
Hull FC 6-42 Hull Kingston Rovers

The Robins visited a packed KC Stadium for the second time in 2007, needing two points to ensure their Super League safety. They came away with a record derby win that sent their fans home in ecstasy.

Considering there was so much at stake, Rovers started unexpectedly confidently, taking a deserved lead inside 15 minutes. Cooke set up the position by racing through a gap and Andreas Bauer tapped back his superb kick to the corner for Jason Netherton to score. Cooke added the conversion from the touchline. The Robins' forwards were keeping the Airlie Birds quiet and when Head, Tony and Horne did put a move together, referee Ganson spotted an infringement. When Yeaman lost the ball, Scott Murrell swooped onto it, passed it on to Luke Dyer and the pacy centre raced away from the cover to score Rovers second try. In the closing minutes of the half, Dyer was alert to a poor off-load by Maiava, which he snapped up and raced the length of the field to score his second. Cooke added the goal to send the Robins in 16-0 ahead at the break.

The Airlie Birds began the second half with more determination but Dyer typified Rovers' commitment when he tackled Yeaman into touch as he looked set to score in the corner. Cooke's kicking was causing the Black and Whites problems and one to the corner eluded Briscoe, allowing Mark Lennon to score unopposed. Cooke converted from the touchline and at 22-0 the Robins were firmly in control. Hull FC came back briefly when Rovers were unable to halt

The Robins

Washbrook's strong run to the line and Tickle converted. Rhys Lovegrove then finished off a handling move by breaking through Briscoe's challenge to score and Cooke added the extras to a solo effort by captain James Webster to make it 32-6 with only 15 minutes to go. When Stanley Gene raced over for his 100th Rovers try, the visiting fans were delirious. Cooke converted, and appropriately, then had the final say with a looping pass to Lovegrove who scored wide out.

It had been a brilliant display. Orchestrated by Cooke, the forwards had subdued the opposing pack and the backs had taken their chances clinically. Jason Netherton notes: 'It was vital we stayed in Super League – if we were relegated it would have been a long hard way back. That, added to who we were playing and where we were playing, made it very special. We totally outplayed them over the full 80 minutes.'

Hull FC: *M. Tony; S. Briscoe, C. Hall, K. Yeaman, G. Raynor; R. Horne, M. Head; E. Dowes, W. Godwin, P. King, L. Radford (capt), W. Manu, D. Tickle. Reps: R. Whiting, H. Maiava, S. Wheeldon, D. Washbrook.*
Rovers: *I. Hardman; A. Bauer, L. Dyer, R. Lovegrove, M. Lennon; P. Cooke, J. Webster (capt); M. Vella, B. Fisher, R. Tandy, C. Chester, M. O'Neill, S. Murrell. Reps: J. Netherton, S. Gene, J. Gannon, D. Tangata-Toa*
Referee: S. Ganson (St Helens)
Attendance: 23,004

New faces

There were a whole host of new signings for 2008. In the backs, Shaun Briscoe moved across the city to claim the full-back role, winger Peter Fox joined from Wakefield, former Leeds centre Chev Walker returned to the 13-a-side code from his ill-fated sojourn in rugby union with Bath and New Zealand test three-quarter Jake Webster arrived from Gold Coast, along with versatile Aussie Dan Fitzhenry. NRL Grand Final winning second-rowers Ben Galea from Wests Tigers and Clint Newton ex-Melbourne Storm arrived, the latter bringing with him prop Garrett Crossman, whilst prop David Mills, the son of legend Jim, was recruited from Harlequins. Cooke was given a six-match ban from the start of the season for his part in his controversial move across the city, but the Robins were cleared of any wrong-doing. Another former Hull FC legend, Lee Crooks, joined the coaching staff as Morgan's assistant.

Rovers had a record nine debutants in their line-up for the first match of the season at a rain-swept Headingley, including an entire new three-quarter line, and a new captain in Vella. For three-quarters of an hour no neutral would have known that the team had not played together before. They more than matched star-studded Leeds and as the game went into the last quarter, they held a 12-6 lead thanks to two Jake Webster tries, the second a thrilling long-distance effort. Only then did a combination of errors, lack of match fitness and a few tough refereeing calls mean that Rovers ended up playing virtually without the ball in the last 20 minutes. The pressure finally told and they lost 20-12.

A thrilling 24-22 win at home to St Helens followed, then a second consecutive win in France, coming back from a 14-6 interval deficit to edge home 24-20 with a late try from Gene. The old failing of slow starts resurfaced and Warrington did much as they pleased in building up a 28-4 half-time lead at Craven Park in the fourth game. The Wolves may have thought it was all over but the Robins had different ideas and came storming back with four second half tries. A Briers drop-goal, Warrington's only second half score, was all that separated the teams in the end. In the next game, at Wakefield, Rovers were always playing catch-up but referee Thaler upset the Robins by awarding a controversial penalty try that proved crucial as the home side held on for a 22-20 win.

After beating Castleford, the Robins had three wins from six games and welcomed back Cooke for the season's first derby game. Jake Webster and Fitzhenry gave Rovers a 10-0 lead before the Airlie Birds levelled as the weather deteriorated. In the end, Rovers were indebted to James Webster's drop goal into the wind to give them an 11-10 win. The game ended with a sheet of hailstones being driven fiercely down the ground by a mounting gale and the players protecting their faces as they trudged into the teeth of the storm.

Rovers then entered a patchy period and, although they progressed to the sixth round of the Challenge Cup, they won only three out of the next 13 league games, one of which was a second derby success at the Magic Weekend. On the weekend before the trip to the Millennium, though, there was a considerable blow when James Webster sustained a serious injury and the side was left without an experienced specialist scrum-half. The ever-willing Murrell stepped into the breach as the Robins beat the Airlie Birds 22-17 in Cardiff.

Amidst rumours that Webster would be out for the remainder of the season, the club clearly had to find a replacement. Even so, it seemed with almost indecent haste that Webster was struck off the playing register in order that Rovers could bring in Canberra Raiders reserve scrum-half Michael Dobson. Dobson was known to Super League followers through his successful loan spells at Wigan and Catalans and was a target for Hull FC. The Robins acted quickly and decisively and got their man – it was to prove an inspired signing. Unfortunately, for Dobson though, his arrival coincided with the worst run of the season. He made a two-try debut in a 22-8 win over Harlequins the day after Hull City's historic play-off win over Bristol City had earned them a place in English football's elite for the first time ever. But after that, Rovers lost six consecutive games, including a 24-18 home cup defeat against St Helens.

The Robins won four of the last seven games in a roller-coaster end to the season. In a remarkable 39-22 win over Wigan, Dobson became the first Rovers' player to register a Super League try hat-trick, finishing with four. At the KC stadium, the Robins endured a pointless second half as an 18-16 lead turned into a 44-18 defeat. A strong second half performance produced a 30-16 home win over Catalans but 10 days later it was followed by a shocker as Harlequins ran up a 28-0 half-time lead at Craven Park and won 40-16. After that came a remarkable performance when they triumphed 36-34 at Warrington, the only side that they had not previously beaten in Super League. Next up at Bradford, skipper Vella inspired them to an early 18-0 lead that they squandered by conceding 42 unanswered points. Finally, the Black and Whites returned to Craven Park for the fourth derby of the season and the Robins sent their fans home happily for the winter with a comprehensive 36-8 triumph.

After a promising start, Rovers had gained only three more points than the previous season but that left them in seventh position in the table, four places up and just one place outside the play-offs. The Robins were able to field a more settled team than in the previous season with Fox, the top try scorer, claiming 15. Walker was unlucky with injuries, but his absence gave the promising Kris Welham an extended run in the centre at the end of the season. In the pack, Vella again led by example, missing only the cup tie at Workington, and the other regulars were Mills, who played in every game, Fisher, Newton, Galea and Gene.

Steel, another member of the promotion-winning outfit, Crossman and Chester all played their last games for

The Robins

the club during the season. Chester, a cultured ball-playing forward had made 36 appearances in his two seasons with the Robins but ultimately his injuries forced his retirement. After a brief spell on the coaching staff at Castleford, he returned to Rovers and took over from Lee Crooks as assistant coach. In June, Chief Executive Paul Lakin left to take on a new role at Wolverhampton Wanderers FC and in his place came Paul Blanchard, a former sales and marketing director at Surrey County Cricket Club.

The Greats – No 34
James Webster - *see Hull KR legends gallery*

The Robins' signing of half-back James Webster from Parramatta in December 2004 was both a real coup and a significant statement of ambition by a National League side.

Born in Sydney in July 1979, he started his professional career with Balmain Tigers.

Finding opportunities limited, he moved on to the Eels where he made 22 appearances between 2002 and 2004 but was still unable to win a regular place. Webster came to Rovers' attention and the promise of regular first team football enticed him to England.

Installed immediately as captain, he made a two-try debut for the Robins on the first day of the 2005 season in a 27-26 win at Keighley. Although he played a handful of matches at stand-off in the early part that first season, by early June his performances established him as the first choice scrum-half. He was a natural leader and when coach Harvey Howard left the club in July, Rovers asked Webster to act as captain-coach on an interim basis.

In the role, he led the side to success over favourites Castleford in the Northern Rail Cup final. It was a first success in that competition for the Robins, after final

426

disappointments in two of the three previous seasons and their first silverware for seven years.

Although that season ended disappointingly, when new coach Justin Morgan rebuilt the side for a serious crack at promotion to Super League the following year, Webster was the linchpin. Scott Murrell arrived from Leeds to become his half-back partner and the two quickly forged a pairing that no other National League side could match.

Webster played in 30 of the 35 matches in that glorious season, leading, prompting, organising, and chipping in with 15 tries and four drop-goals. When he was named National League Player of the Year, it was fully merited. The main achievement though was promotion and Webster's performances were integral.

Continuing to skipper the side in 2007, he missed only four matches in the inaugural Super League campaign and played a key role in ensuring that the Robins maintained their top-flight status. The following year he sustained a serious shoulder injury against Leeds on 25 April. When it looked as if he would miss most of the season, the Robins quickly signed a replacement in fellow Aussie Michael Dobson and released Webster in early May.

Short and lithe, Webster was an intelligent player who read the play well. He had an excellent kicking game and was dangerous with ball in hand, both darting through gaps and creating space for his teammates.

In his 94 appearances for the Robins, he scored 33 tries and dropped nine goals. According to Jason Netherton: 'He was a fine all round player who was very highly thought of at the club. He was very professional in his outlook, and he played a very big part in instilling a more professional approach in the players.'

After his release by the Robins, Webster moved across the city, where his only appearance was against Rovers in the last game of the season in 2008. He subsequently moved to Widnes Vikings, where he played until then Hull FC *coach Richard Agar brought him back there as assistant coach. He followed Agar to Wakefield, taking over as coach when Agar moved on in June 2014 but lost his position early on in 2015 after the Wildcats made a poor start and relegation was on the agenda.*

He was appointed first coach to the merged City of Hull Academy side in 2015, taking over the reins of the first team on an interim basis after the sacking of Chris Chester in 2016.

Super League best

Further restructuring took place in Super League in 2009. No team was relegated at the end of 2008 but the promotion of National Grand Final winners Salford and the awarding of a Super League franchise to Welsh side Celtic Crusaders brought the number of clubs to 14. A straightforward fixture list was then adopted, with the teams playing each other home and away and the Magic Weekend fixture making up 27 games. At the same time, the end-of-season play-offs were extended to the top eight clubs.

After the flurry of activity in the last four close seasons, the Robins were quiet in the transfer market. Just three men came in; experienced former Leeds, Warrington and St Helens prop Nick Fozzard, Wigan winger Liam Colbon, and prop Scott Wheeldon from Hull FC. Paul Blanchard quit after six months and Neil Hudgell combined the role with his chairman's duties, alongside new commercial manager Mike Smith.

There was a blow in the first match at Bradford, when skipper Vella, outstanding in his first two seasons, was carried off with a serious knee injury. Fox scored two tries in a game in which having led for most it, the Robins had to thank a late Dobson drop-goal for rescuing them a point. A rousing contest at home to Leeds in the next match saw Rovers take a 10-4 half-time lead but the Rhinos dominated the second half to earn a 19-10 win.

The third game produced a remarkable performance at St Helens. Saints went ahead three times only for Rovers to pull back and level each time. The hosts appeared to have won it with a late drop-goal but Dobson's penalty at the death brought the points back to Craven Park. It had been a performance of real character, often with backs to the wall against waves of Saints pressure, but it gave the Robins confidence and belief and they then won 12 out of 14 games, including Challenge Cup wins over Crusaders and Sheffield Eagles.

In the middle of this run, there was a hard-fought 18-14 Good Friday derby win at the KC, in which the Robins had to withstand a strong second half fight-back by the Airlie Birds.

Three days later, on a glorious afternoon, Huddersfield visited Craven Park. After a blistering start in which Welham and Colbon scored tries, the Giants came back into the game. In the 1960s, the *Hull Daily Mail* dubbed Dennis Davies as the ref 'the fans love to hate.' Forty plus years on, Ben Thaler seemed to carry that mantle. Huddersfield, who had led 10-8 at the break, took complete control and Morgan's outburst about the Wakefield official earned him a fine. Although it went down well with the supporters, it probably did more harm than good in the long term. Morgan also made the point that the gruelling derby games on Good Friday took a lot out of his players, putting them at a disadvantage when playing Easter Monday against opponents who may have had less testing matches over the period.

The Robins

After that, six consecutive wins included the return from injury of skipper Vella in a 44-10 hammering of the Dragons, a magnificent 36-28 win over Warrington in a seesaw Magic Weekend battle at Murrayfield – Rovers' first ever competitive game on Scottish soil – while the following league game produced an excellent 20-12 victory at Wigan, with Dobson to the fore.

The excellent run ended in brilliant May sunshine at Craven Park, when Warrington were the visitors in the sixth round of the Challenge Cup. It was another tremendous game in which the lead changed hands several times, with the Wolves fighting back from ten points down in the last quarter as Rovers tired. With the score tied at 24-all at the end of 80 minutes, the Robins experienced sudden-death extra time for the first time. But by then they were struggling even to get out of their own half and after four abortive attempts a Briers' drop-goal finally sneaked over and Rovers were left to rue their failure to take chances when in control early on.

That reverse sparked a run of only two wins in eight games, which ended when the Black and Whites were beaten 24-18 at Craven Park at the end of July. That set the Robins off on another winning spell, which included the completion of a double over Saints with a 26-10 home win that was then arguably their best Super League performance. Despite an uncharacteristically tame defeat at Wakefield in the last match, the Robins had earned a very creditable fourth spot behind leaders Leeds, St Helens and Huddersfield. It was their highest finish to date and an excellent achievement in their third Super League season.

Sadly, Rovers' first experience of the Super League play-offs was an unhappy one. In the first game at Leeds, they were without Briscoe, Murrell and Galea, who were carrying injuries, and then lost Walker with a badly broken leg in the first half. Walker, who had never really won over the Craven Park faithful but had been a real favourite at Headingley, was given a very touching ovation by the Leeds fans as he was carried off in front of the South Stand. Just 10-8 down at half time, Rovers were well in the game but Leeds pulled away in the second half with 34 unanswered points.

By virtue of their fourth placed-finish, Rovers got another bite of the cherry and faced Wigan in an elimination game at Craven Park. Missing only Fisher from their first choice line up, the Robins again made a slow start and the game was as good as lost in the first half, when the Warriors led 18-0. Wigan dashed a second half Rovers' fight-back and substitute Sam Tomkins gave the home crowd a glimpse of his burgeoning talent as they won 30-16.

The season might have ended disappointingly but there had been much to savour. Rovers won nine of the 13 home games in the regular season and there were six away wins in addition to the Murrayfield success. In a largely settled team, Welham earned a regular centre place and Colbon displaced Fitzhenry on the wing. Cooke and Dobson formed an effective half-back partnership and Fozzard came into the front row, where Wheeldon deputised in Vella's absences. Dobson, Newton and Welham played in every game. Dobson kicked 115 goals and scored eleven tries and was Super League's top points scorer with 238. Rovers had four players named in the 2009 Super League Dream Team; Fox, Dobson, Newton and Galea.

Papua New Guinea pair Makali Aizue and Stanley Gene played their final games for the club and both moved on to Halifax. Aussie utility man Daniel Fitzhenry made the last of his 53 appearances in the play-off defeat by Wigan and Nick Fozzard ended his one-season stay in the same game. Chev Walker, whose two seasons were disrupted by a

The Robins

number of injuries that prevented him from showing his best form, did not play again and eventually moved to Bradford for the 2011 season.

Anti-climax

There were again three main signings for the 2010 season. Australian international prop Joel Clinton arrived from Brisbane Broncos, promising young hooker Josh Hodgson crossed the city from Hull FC and second-rower Matt Cook signed from Bradford Bulls.

Rovers struggled from the outset to repeat the successes of 2009 and by the time Harlequins arrived at Craven Park for their league game on 20 June, they had won only eight out of their 17 Super League fixtures. Good home wins over St Helens, Warrington and Catalans and an excellent first Super League victory at a rain-swept Headingley were offset by heavy defeats at Bradford, St Helens, twice – the second during the Magic weekend, Huddersfield in the cup, and at home to neighbours Hull FC.

However, the 42-6 win over Harlequins sparked a run of six wins and a draw in eight games. A 16-all tie at Huddersfield, when the Robins were deprived of victory by a last minute touch-line penalty goal from Brett Hodgson, was followed by a first Super League win at Belle Vue, Wakefield, when props Vella and Wheeldon combined for a memorable length of field score in a 46-14 success. Rovers then completed a rare double over Leeds with a 25-6 home win. After that, a 20-16 derby defeat at the KC was followed by three more wins and, despite losing the last two games, the Robins finished the season in seventh place. They were three points behind their neighbours, whom they would now meet in the play-offs.

That game produced a memorable performance as the Robins convincingly beat their old enemy on their own ground. However, the season ended at Wigan the next week, when, despite Rovers taking an early 14-6 lead, the home side proved too strong, and gained a convincing 42-18 success.

Super League elimination play-off, KC Stadium, Hull, 11 September 2010
Hull FC 4-21 Hull Kingston Rovers

The most high-profile local derby since the 1985 John Player Trophy final saw the Robins gain their first ever Super League play-off victory. Having won both derbies in the regular season and finishing above their neighbours, the Black and Whites were favourites in the eyes of most neutrals. No one told Justin Morgan's men that, however, and they earned a comprehensive and satisfying win.

It was a disastrous start for Hull FC who lost full-back Hall, making his final appearance before crossing the city, after just six minutes. Matters got worse for the home side when Scott Murrell, kicking early in the tackle count, produced a pinpoint chip to the right corner where Peter Fox beat Briscoe to the ball to score the opening try. Michael Dobson kicked the conversion from the touchline. Dobson kept up the pressure with two kicks that forced the Airlie Birds to concede possession and the Robins exemplified their greater intensity in one tremendous tackle by Murrell on Horne that left the stand-in custodian shaken. It was no surprise when the Robins increased their lead after 28 minutes. Shaun Briscoe supported Ben Fisher's darting run through the home defence, the two exchanged passes and Fisher dived over for a try. Dobson's conversion gave Rovers a well-deserved 12-0 lead. In the closing ten minutes of the half, the home side manufactured several chances, but Briscoe's determined tackling halted both Radford and Long

The Robins

on the line, whilst Fox and Ben Cockayne combined brilliantly to deny Turner on the stroke of half-time.

The second half started shakily for the Robins, with Tickle's kick-off forcing them to drop out from between their own posts. As the Airlie Birds sought to capitalise, Rovers were grateful for Washbrook's pass into touch. A heavy shower had made ball handling more difficult, and it was an error that brought the home side back into the game. When Matt Cook lost the ball, Hull FC winger Tom Briscoe gathered it and raced away towards the corner-flag to score, Tickle missing with the difficult conversion. Rovers kept the Black and Whites pinned back, helped by two thunderous tackles on Lyne and Fitzgibbon by the outstanding Murrell. The Robins got the next score when Manu was penalised for a late challenge on Cockayne and Dobson's kick made it 14-4. With five minutes to go, Kris Welham settled it when he followed up his own kick to score and Dobson again added the conversion. With the home fans already streaming out, perhaps it was appropriate that Murrell then had the last say with a drop-goal two minutes from time.

Jason Netherton reflects: 'It was one of the most physical and intense games I've ever played in. They'd beaten us narrowly in the two derbies that season so our game plan was to dominate them from the start and we executed it perfectly.' It was a tremendous all round performance by the Robins, who took their chances and produced a magnificent defensive effort. After giving their heroes a long-lasting standing ovation, the visiting faithful dispersed happily into the night.

Hull FC: *C. Hall; R. Lyne, J. Turner, S. Berrigan, T. Briscoe; R. Horne, S. Long; L. Radford, D. Houghton, M. O'Meley, W. Manu, D. Tickle, C. Fitzgibbon (capt). Reps: D. Washbrook, E. Lauaki, P. Cusack, S. Moa*
Rovers: *S. Briscoe; P. Fox, B. Cockayne, K. Welham, L. Colbon; S. Murrell, M. Dobson; M.*

Vella (capt), B. Fisher, J. Clinton, C. Newton, B.
Galea, J. Netherton. Reps: R. Lovegrove, S.
Wheeldon, M. Cook, J. Hodgson
Referee: P. Bentham
Attendance: 17,699

For the third season running, winger Peter Fox was the leading try-scorer whilst Dobson, remarkably, finished only one point short of his 2009 tally of 276, kicking 114 goals and scoring 11 tries. Again named as scrum-half in the Super League Dream Team of the season, his run of 76 consecutive appearances stretched back to his debut in May 2008. Fox, Murrell, Newton and Lovegrove were also ever-presents whilst Vella shook off the injuries that affected him the previous season and formed the cornerstone of the pack alongside compatriots Newton and Galea. Young prop Liam Watts, with his big physique and off-loading ability, was named Young Player of the Year and looked a real prospect.

Injuries caused significant disruption to the side, however. In the backs, Webster missed the last three months of the season, Welham most of July and August and Colbon was out from April to mid-August. Supporters' favourite Cockayne filled in as required at full-back, centre and wing, whilst another whole-hearted performer, Murrell, partnered Dobson at half-back for most of the season. Young Wigan three-quarter Josh Charnley spent five matches on loan in the latter stages of the season and made a fine impression, scoring five tries, including a hat-trick against Castleford.

Paul Cooke's spell at the club ended when he moved on to Wakefield after playing in just the first three games of the season. In all, Cooke played in 61 matches for the Robins, kicking 92 goals, two drop-goals and scoring nine tries. His added class and experience had undoubtedly been a big factor in the club's survival in Super League in 2007.

The Robins

At the end of the season, Hudgell stood down as chief executive, although continuing as chairman, and he appointed Mike Smith in the role.

An unhappy saga

All the regular players from the previous season were available for 2011 and they were joined by Canterbury Bulldogs stand-off Blake Green and Hull FC utility back Craig Hall. Rovers also announced the signing of controversial New Zealand-born New South Wales and Australia second-rower Willie Mason.

Whilst the intentions behind the Mason signing were undoubtedly of the best, the resulting saga ultimately did not reflect well on either the club or the player. The issue of player quotas had become a highly complex one and Rovers had no available space for another import. They had been assured that, by virtue of his heritage, Mason could obtain a Tongan passport, which would resolve the problem, but he had still had not received it by the time he arrived in the UK. By then, Dobson's run of consecutive appearances had ended at 78 when he was injured in the second match at Warrington and the Robins took the unusual step of de-registering him in order to accomodate Mason.

It is fair to say that this unorthodox move caused many eyebrows to be raised in the rugby league world but the RFL indicated that they were content and it bought more time for the passport situation to be resolved. Mason duly made his long-awaited debut against the Crusaders in the fifth match and showed a few good touches, including a fine off-load to send Watts over for a try in a 40-22 win, but he was clearly not match fit.

Mason played a further five matches without

justifying the hype that surrounded his arrival, scoring his only try in his last appearance against Wigan. By now, no one would have risked any hard-earned cash on the arrival of the Tongan passport and when Dobson was fit again for the next game at the KC, he was re-registered in place of Mason. The following week, it came to Rovers' attention that Mason was engaged in clandestine negotiations with a French rugby union club and they acted decisively to terminate his contract immediately.

The Mason saga deflected interest from the bigger picture, that of Rovers' Super League performances, but perhaps that was no bad thing because they won only three of their first eleven games. The season had opened brightly with a comfortable 34-22 derby win in the Magic Weekend at the Millennium stadium in Cardiff. They led for most of the next game at Warrington only to concede a late try that resulted in a 24-22 defeat. After that, a poor run included a demoralising 36-18 defeat in the away derby.

From early May, helped on their way by a couple of Challenge Cup wins, Rovers won 13 of their 19 games up to the end of the regular season. In that spell, there were heavy defeats against the five top sides but the Robins recorded a 17-10 success in the return derby clash and dispatched all the lower teams. They recorded their biggest Super League win, 70-14 at home to Wakefield, with hat-tricks for Fox, Welham and Colbon and 18 points from Dobson. Rovers then qualified for the play-offs for the third year running by finishing in seventh place.

Coach Justin Morgan had announced in August that he would be moving on at the end of the season and it was a sad and inappropriate end to his Rovers career when Catalans hammered the Robins 56-6 in the play-off game. It was a disappointing end to the season and to the Rovers' careers of four excellent servants in Briscoe, Vella, Fisher and Newton, who made their last appearances in that game.

Welham played in every game and scored 26 tries, almost twice as many as anyone else and the most by any Rovers player in a Super League season. Always a potent attacking threat, it seemed that he just needed to rectify occasional defensive lapses to become a top-class centre. Galea and Hodgson were also ever-present and those three formed the nucleus of the side with Briscoe, Fox, Webster, Green, Dobson, Vella, Newton and Murrell.

Rovers' fans will always respect Justin Morgan not only for getting them into Super League but also for achieving the considerable feat of keeping them there.

Only in the first season did the Robins finish in the bottom four and their fourth-placed finish in 2009 was a real highlight. 'Perhaps at the time we didn't fully appreciate how big an achievement that was,' says Neil Hudgell. Only in that season and the promotion year did the team achieve the level of consistency that Morgan strove for, but there were plenty of other excellent performances. 'He was a big man who had presence,' says Netherton. 'He knew the game but was still keen to learn and he knew how to motivate his players and get the best out of them.'

Skipper Mick Vella retired at the end of the season after playing in 121 games for the Robins, and returned to Australia. The strong running and tackling ex-Parramatta, NSW Origin and Australia prop had led the side by example for four seasons. A tall and distinctive figure of Maltese background, he had done more than any other to ensure that the Robins stayed in Super League in their first season and was named Players' Player of the Year. 'He was a leader on the field, and a character off it,' says Michael Dobson. 'The sort of man you'd want in the trenches with you.'

Shaun Briscoe moved on to Widnes Vikings for the final stop in an illustrious career in which he played exactly 100 games for the Robins, scoring 30 tries. Although he was coming towards the end in his time with Rovers, he was still a courageous defender and dangerous runner who always gave his all. He later returned to Craven Park in a dual coaching and partnerships role.

Ben Fisher spent six seasons with the Robins in which he played in 165 games, moving on to Catalans in 2012. He was one of the stalwarts of the promotion campaign and the side that consolidated a place in Super League, a fine tackler and constant threat around the play-the-ball. Clint Newton finished just one short of 100 appearances and scored 40 tries in his four years with the Robins. A whole-hearted player who regularly played the full 80 minutes, he was a clever ball handler, strong runner and a good tackler. Newton returned to Australia to play with Penrith Panthers, later taking up a lead role with the Players' Association.

Fans' favourite Ben Cockayne moved to Wakefield Trinity Wildcats in search of a fresh start and greater opportunity. His commitment and enthusiasm had endeared him to the fans, who willingly forgave him his occasional failings. His departure, along with that of Fisher, meant that just five years on, only Murrell, Netherton and Welham had survived from the National League days. However, after two seasons at Wakefield, Cockayne too was welcomed back to Craven Park.

A new regime

Neil Hudgell, Rob Crossland and Mike Smith went to Australia in the close season to interview candidates for the vacant coaching job. They came back with the signature of little-known Craig Sandercock, an assistant at Newcastle Knights.

On the playing side, new arrivals were powerful former Canterbury and Tonga prop Micky Paea, Knights pair Shannon McDonnell and Con Mika and three former Huddersfield men in Hull-born prolific try-scoring winger David Hodgson, former Hull FC utility man Graeme Horne and young hooker Keal Carlile. Following Crusaders' withdrawal from Super League, two of their Aussie forwards, prop Ryan O'Hara and hooker Lincoln Withers also arrived at Craven Park. The popular Galea took over as captain from Vella.

The 2012 fixture list gave the Robins a difficult start with a trip to Headingley to play Grand Final winners Leeds. The new-look team gave their illustrious hosts a fright with a spirited performance before tiring in the last quarter and the 34-16 score line was harsh on the Robins. That was followed by a 22-10 win at Wakefield in dismal muddy conditions reminiscent of a bygone era and a thrilling 36-36 draw at home to St Helens, in which winger Foster kicked a touch line conversion in the dying seconds to deny the Robins a win. After that, Rovers managed only two wins in eight games, a run that culminated in a shocking second half performance at the KC that resulted in an embarrassing 36-6 defeat at the hands of the Airlie Birds.

The response to that capitulation was six wins in the next seven league games, including a new club record Super League triumph, 70-12 over Castleford, with four tries from David Hodgson and eleven goals for Dobson. The next game produced a sensational win over the Airlie Birds at the Ethihad stadium in Manchester during Magic Weekend when Rovers were 30-16 in arrears with less than 15 minutes to go. The Robins hit back with converted tries by Latus and

Dobson that narrowed the gap to two points. In the last minute, a fine handling move gave David Hodgson a half-chance and the veteran winger wrote his name into Robins' folklore by beating two men in a 60-metre sprint to the line to seal a 32-30 win.

In another thriller next up at home to Warrington, a 22-6 half-time deficit was overturned with 17 unanswered points, Dobson again to the fore with three conversions, a try and the crucial drop-goal. When the Robins won 44-26 at Huddersfield on 11 June, hopes were high of at least a top-six finish. However, it was not to be and the season turned on a foul night at Craven Park when the four-match winning run ended in a 13-10 defeat to Catalans.

With the elements in their favour in the first half, Rovers had chances to establish a winning lead but their 6-4 advantage was not enough and the Dragons' forward power won the game in the last quarter. That was the start of a run of nine defeats in the last ten games, although in only one game, the return derby, did the Robins lose by more than six points. For the first time in four years, there was no interest in the end-of-season play-offs as Rovers finished in tenth place, having lost more league games than they won for the first time since 2008.

In a rather unsettled team, key players Dobson and hooker Josh Hodgson missed only one game each but Blake Green managed only 10 appearances due to injury. Of the new signings, Paea was ever-present and made the biggest impression whilst David Hodgson finished top try-scorer with 16 from just 18 games. Former Academy player Scott Taylor, who had started to appear regularly the previous season, showed more promise and missed only two matches. Dobson kicked 104 goals to pass the century for the third time in four seasons.

The Robins

In August, the Robins announced that they would not offer Ben Galea a new contract. He had wanted another year with the club but, when they decided to release him, he took up an offer from the Airlie Birds instead. Supporters invariably have mixed emotions when a player moves across the city, especially one they really want to stay. There is a mixture of disappointment at his departure and anger that he has joined the enemy. Galea had been popular during his time with the Robins, but he was now clearly nearing the end of his career and there were good wishes rather than rancour. He had formed an excellent partnership with Newton in the five years they had played together – arguably the best second-row pairing for the club since Lowe and Rose in the 1970s. A strong tackler and a deceptive runner, he had always been a consummate professional. In all he played in 126 games for the club, scoring 36 tries.

Rovers also released the ever-reliable and highly popular Scott Murrell after seven seasons of loyal service. A willing and adaptable member of the squad, Murrell at various stages of his career played at full-back, both half-back positions, hooker and loose-forward and he was a useful goal-kicker and kicker in open play. Murrell played 177 games for the Robins, scoring 240 points. At the same time, Jason Netherton left to take up an opportunity to play in Australia.

Three Australian imports left the club, the most significant being Green's departure to Wigan. After a successful first season, he had endured a disappointing 2012, in which he had struggled for form and fitness. The disappointing three-year stay of prop Joel Clinton ended when he returned to Australia, whilst the departure of full-back Shannon McDonnell, who had agreed to join the Black and Whites in mid-season, aroused little emotion. Local forward Scott Taylor left to join Wigan and Liam Watts, who failed to reproduce his 2011 form, fell out of favour and also moved across the city during the season.

December 2012 saw the formation of an independent Rovers Supporters' Trust, established to encourage fan involvement in the club through working in the local community, improving lines of communication and raising funds to purchase shares in the Robins. The RST became a member of Supporters Direct, a national organisation that promotes sustainable spectator sports clubs through supporter involvement and community ownership, and quickly achieved a membership of over 200.

There was more recruitment for 2013 as the Robins brought in a further three former Huddersfield players; full-back Greg Eden, winger Alex Brown and prop Adam Walker. Other arrivals were Penrith Panthers half-back Travis Burns, second-rower Cory Paterson from North Queensland Cowboys, Newcastle's Kiwi prop Evarn Tuimavave, London winger Omari Caro and Salford centre Sean Gleeson.

Dobson took over the captaincy but he was without his new half-back partner Burns for the first month of the season as the latter served a ban imposed back in Australia. Rovers made a disappointing start with defeats at home to Catalans and at Wakefield, followed by a comfortable win over a poor Widnes side and then a Jekyll-and-Hyde performance in defeat at Salford. This game in many ways summed up the season. Capable of brilliance in attack, the Robins led 34-14 with a little under half an hour to play but then a series of handling and defensive errors allowed Salford to score four tries without reply to gain a 38-34 win.

Burns' debut sparked a March improvement and four wins from five games culminated in a fine 23-10 win over the Black and Whites at the KC Stadium on Good Friday. The point previously made by Morgan was brutally underlined as the hard derby game again took its toll and three days later a weakened side was simply blown away by a rampant Wigan at Craven Park. The visitors employed the simple but effective tactic of moving the ball wide at every opportunity and using their superior pace against the home side's increasingly tired defence. The 84-6 defeat suffered was the heaviest in the club's history.

It caused Hudgell and his vice-chairman Rob Crossland to reflect on the money they had pumped into the club over the previous eight-and-a-half seasons. The shortfall between income and expenditure was reputed to be running at around £500,000 per season and they had been making up the deficit. Hudgell indicated that this could not carry on indefinitely, the club was no longer making the progress he wanted, and that he and Crossland were considering their future. At the very least, new investment was needed to enable the club to compete and move forward.

On the field, following the example of Fairbairn's side in 1991, the Robins showed character and came back from their thrashing in the best possible way with a 22-14 win over St Helens six days later. A lively first half performance had put the Robins 10-0 up after half an hour, with tries by the two Hodgsons, but they let Saints back into the game in the dying minutes of the half and the sides went in level at 10-10. In a well-contested second half, Rovers took the lead with a converted try by Paterson after 50 minutes. Saints cut the Robins' lead to 16-14 when Swift picked up a loose ball to race 90 metres but after more Rovers pressure, Hall and Josh Hodgson combined from Dobson's kick to give Brown the chance to finish strongly in the corner. The defence had to be at its best to withstand heavy pressure from the visitors before Hall sealed the win with a penalty goal in the last minute.

Sadly, the Robins were unable to sustain such form and won only two of the next seven games. After a repeat win against the Saints in the Challenge Cup, Wigan returned for fifth-round tie. There was no repeat of the earlier embarrassment and after Rovers had dominated the first half, the Warriors were very fortunate to snatch a 12-4 lead just before the break. Wigan restarted at a blistering pace and three tries in ten minutes gave them an unassailable 28-4 lead and a comfortable 46-14 win.

The last game in this poor spell was the Magic Weekend derby at the Etihad. With Jason Netherton back in the ranks after cutting short his spell in Australia, the Robins definitely had much the better of a tense struggle until the final ten minutes. Then, tiring and with only two fit men on the bench, their 16-6 lead was cut to four points when Lineham crossed out wide and the conversion went in off the post with seven minutes to go. Two controversial decisions by video referee Steve Ganson were then blamed for Rovers losing the game.

First, he ruled that Yeaman had touched the ball down on the line to score before it squirted out of his control, levelling the scores at 16-16. Then he allowed a try when Green followed up a hopeful high kick by Houghton and capitalised on Eden's hesitancy to score, despite claims that he was several metres offside. Holdsworth's conversion in the last minute completed a 22-16 Hull FC win and the RFL later apologised for the second decision, such was the outcry.

The Robins again reacted positively to adversity and June was easily the best month of the season with four wins, including a fine home triumph over high-flying Huddersfield and successive away victories against Catalans and St Helens. The winning run stretched to five with a home success over Salford but that was as good as it got. Rovers then lost at

Warrington and Wigan, the latter by only five points following a valiant performance and, most disappointingly, 38-20 in the home derby. A remarkable win at Leeds in the next game appeared a mere flash in the pan.

Despite the poor spells, the Robins made it back into the play-offs in eighth place which took them to Langtree Park to face Saints, whom they had beaten on three occasions in a season for the first time. There was never any chance of Rovers making it four, however, as the Saints responded to Salter's early score with three of their own, and by half-time were out of sight at 34-4. A more determined second half performance by Rovers restricted the final margin to 46-10 but it was an inappropriate finale for the departing skipper Dobson, who returned to Australia.

The problems were clear for all to see. Defence, particularly wide out, was an increasing problem – the number of points conceded had gradually increased each season since 2009, discipline was a major issue with the Robins repeatedly being on the wrong end of the penalty count and handing errors often ruined their best work, gifting the ball and points to the opposition.

Of the new acquisitions, 22-year old prop Walker made the biggest impression and he won the Young Player of the Year award. Tall and powerfully built, he showed a great appetite for work, driving and tackling strongly, and his greatest attribute was his ability to get the ball away in the tackle. After finding his feet at the club, he soon showed his worth with some fine try-creating off-loads. Burns took some time to settle and find his form and fitness but by the end of the season, his commitment and character had won over the supporters. Cory Paterson missed only three of the first 16 games but found it difficult to settle and the club released him from his contract to return to Australia and join Wests Tigers. Other departures included Paea, who moved across to the KC after two fine seasons at Craven Park, Tuimavave, who never fulfilled the club's hopes for him, Con Mika, whose two-season stay was also generally disappointing, and Withers and O'Hara – the latter having played in only 15 games in two seasons due to injuries. Young prop Richard Beaumont signed for St Helens.

During the season, ground improvements had started in earnest with the construction of a new North Stand. On the financial side, despite increasing merchandising and sponsorship income, there was still a regular shortfall in the income required to balance the expenditure. However, Hudgell and Crossland had succeeded in finding additional investment and decided to continue their tenure at the club.

At the end of the season, Crossland posted a personal view on the club website. He said that following an internal financial review, the budgets for 2014 would allow the club to be competitive. They would be managed more stringently but improvements to the football support would be better than before, if modest in comparison to other clubs. Crossland admitted to being frustrated sometimes at the lack of understanding about what is a very delicate balancing act that was taking longer than anticipated to deliver. He believed that there was a lot to be positive about and although there were areas where the club still needed to do better, there were planned improvements in areas like marketing, merchandising and the match-day offering.

The Greats – No 35
Michael Dobson - see *Hull KR legends gallery*

Born in Junee, New South Wales in May 1986, scrum-half Michael Dobson was an Australia schoolboy international before joining Canberra Raiders.

447

The Robins

Whilst playing in junior football in the capital, he was given a chance to impress when loaned out to Catalans Dragons to replace injured Stacey Jones in 2006. He took his opportunity so well that the following season Wigan, then six points adrift at the bottom of Super League, signed him for the remainder of the campaign to resolve their half-back crisis. In 14 appearances for Wigan, Dobson scored six tries and kicked 61 goals at a success rate of 84 per cent. That made him the most consistent kicker in the game at the time, as well as kick-starting a revival at Wigan, who finished in eighth place that season.

The following season he broke through into the Raiders first team and in 18 games was their top point-scorer with 124. In 2008, however, Todd Carney and Terry Campese established themselves as the first choice half-backs and Dobson was left on the sidelines. Canberra agreed to release him and, seeking a replacement for the injured James Webster, Rovers beat Harlequins and Hull FC to his signature.

In five-and-a-half seasons with the Robins, Dobson played 153 games, kicking 537 goals, plus 12 drop-goals and scoring 53 tries. He kicked over 100 goals in a season on three occasions, being most prolific in 2010, with 275 points from 114 goals, three drop-goals and 11 tries. In 2009, he won the Rugby Leaguer & League Express *Albert Goldthorpe medal for the best and fairest player in Super League. From his debut on 25 May 2008 at home to Harlequins, he played in 78 consecutive games before being injured in the second game of the 2011 season.*

But the statistics do not fully reflect and do justice to Dobson's importance to the team. His organisation and kicking in the loose, whether for field position or creating try-scoring chances, his ability to take on the defence with ball in hand and his remarkable goal-kicking ability, made him the fulcrum of the side. Whilst it might be over-simplifying to say that when Dobson played well, Rovers played well, he was certainly their most influential player during his time at the club and in 2013, he took on the additional responsibility of being club captain.

Despite still having another year to run on his contract, Dobson exercised an option to return home and have another crack at the NRL. "I think I'm a better player now, I feel as if I'm at the peak of my career – it's now or never," he said. He signed a one-year deal with Newcastle Knights and played his last game for the Robins in an inappropriately low-key and disappointing 46-10 play-off defeat at St Helens on 14 September.

As his last season ended, Dobson reflected on his years at Craven Park. 'I've loved it over here, some great teammates, and a fantastic crowd – they are so vocal, they stay to the end whatever and drown out the opposition.' He singled out the 2010 play-off derby win at the KC as being his most memorable game and Ben Galea as the player who had the most influence on his Rovers career.

'There was a lot of pressure on him when he arrived at Rovers,' says Jason Netherton. 'He was only 22 at the time and had to take charge and organise on the field and he had to deal with some very experienced players. But he coped well and became very important to the team.'

Sadly, his return to the NRL did not work out as Dobson had hoped, and he accepted an offer from Salford to return to Super League in 2015.

Super League XVIII, Headingley Carnegie Stadium, Leeds, 16 August 2013
Leeds Rhinos 12-16 Hull Kingston Rovers

The Robins bounced back from their disappointing home derby reverse in the previous game with an impressive win that boosted their Super League play-off hopes. Any win over Leeds at Headingley is special but this one was the result of a tremendous defensive performance that rivalled anything that Rovers have produced in recent years. Both teams lacked the services of half a dozen regulars due to injury.

On an emotional night, talismanic Leeds captain Kevin Sinfield reached the 3,000 Super League points barrier but the champions were disappointed not to pay a more fitting tribute to their recently deceased Challenge Cup final winning coach Graham Murray, to whom the match was dedicated. It was their first defeat in five matches.

Leeds started in typical vein and it was no surprise when Sutcliffe burst through Rhys Lovegrove and Michael Dobson to put Watkins over for the first try in the 19th minute. Sinfield gave the Rhinos a 6-0 lead with the conversion that brought up his landmark point. The Robins, however, seemed inspired by the reverse and, in the 25th minute, Jordan Cox gathered the ball from Dobson's high kick to touch down. The score seemed to give the Robins confidence and Withers sent Dobson racing into some space. His pass sent Lovegrove charging down the touchline but with Jones-Bishop covering, there seemed little on. Nevertheless, the Aussie showed great strength to shrug off the tackle and remain in play and he held off the remnants of the defence to score. Dobson's conversion from the touchline gave the Robins a 12-6 interval lead.

Three minutes into the second half, Dobson increased Rovers' lead with a penalty when Hardaker was ruled offside after Dobson's high kick. The Rhinos then came back strongly and had their best spell of the game. They laid siege to the Robins' line and gave the defence, which had leaked 93 points in the previous three matches, a severe test. However, Rovers rose magnificently to the occasion, with Josh Hodgson leading the way with a remarkable 47 tackles. There were scares when Watkins failed to gather the ball from Sinfield's high kick, and when the Rhinos' captain placed a grubber kick to the corner, it eluded Omari Caro and Ryan Hall touched down, only for video referee Ian Smith to disallow the score. As they tried to chase the game, Leeds' error rate increased and just before the hour, Dobson increased Rovers' advantage to 16-6 when Sinfield put a goal-line drop out straight into touch.

Leeds came back again and when Hall collected Sinfield's cross-field kick to get Hardaker haring for the line, Travis Burns made a tremendous last-ditch tackle to keep it intact. Eight minutes from time, the pressure finally told. After Rovers tackled Hall on the left, right-winger Duckworth gathered Sinfield's cross-field kick and his inside pass sent in Watkins for his second try. Sinfield's goal cut the gap to four points and the visiting supporters' hearts were in their mouths when, immediately afterwards, Hall burst down his wing and passed inside to the supporting Sinfield, who was in the clear, but he failed to take it, and the Robins held on for a remarkable win.

With Dobson pulling the strings, and Hodgson leading the forward effort, it had been an excellent performance.

Leeds: B. Jones-Bishop; J. Duckworth, K. Watkins, Z. Hardaker, R. Hall; K. Sinfield (capt), R. Burrow; K. Leuluai, P. McShane, J. Peacock, C. Ablett, C. Clarkson, L. Sutcliffe. Reps: J. Moon, I. Kirke, B. Singleton, R. Moore

Rovers: C. Hall; O. Caro, S. Gleeson, L. Salter, D. Hodgson; T. Burns, M. Dobson (capt); E. Tuimavave, J. Hodgson, A. Walker, R. Lovegrove, J. Cox, C. Mika. Reps: L. Withers, J. Netherton, A. Ollett, J. Green

Referee: R. Silverwood (Mirfield)

Attendance: 14,868

In January 2014, the Rovers Supporters Trust made its first investment of £5,000 in the club, purchasing 10,000 shares through their fundraising activity. 'This is a huge step forward that helps to give the Trust and its members not just a moral stake in the club, but a legal stake as well,' said RST chairman Peter Walker. 'We have a good relationship with the club and more people at the club are starting to understand the concept of the Trust. I think that coming seasons will see us working more closely on more events and initiatives.'

Rovers opened the new North Stand for the start of the 2014 season. This significantly improved not only the amenities, particularly for visiting fans which had been very poor, but the aspect and character of the ground itself. Even though there are still stands on just the three sides, the trees at the south end have matured, and the ground now has a much more closed-in feel to it.

The eight additions to the playing strength for the season included three prop-forwards, St George-Illawarra and New South Wales prop Mick Weyman, compatriot Justin Poore, signed from Wakefield, and Adam Walker's twin brother Jonathan, who was at Castleford. They were joined by Newcastle Knights and Queensland back-rower Neville Costigan and Canterbury Bulldogs scrum-half Kris Keating, who had the unenviable job of filling Michael Dobson's boots. Former favourite Ben Cockayne returned after two successful seasons at Wakefield, long-serving back-rower Jamie Langley came from Bradford and Catalans second-rower Kevin Larroyer crossed the Channel on a season-long loan. In appointing a new skipper, Sandercock departed with club tradition by installing Travis Burns and Josh Hodgson as co-captains.

The club did its utmost to start the 2014 season on a high. With the North Stand open, a 'bring a friend' scheme offered season pass holders the opportunity to buy additional reduced price tickets and a partnership with the local Archbishop Sentamu Academy saw staff and pupils given free tickets. A gate of over 11,000 – a record for the stadium – saw the Robins match Leeds in the first half, only to fall away badly in the second and the visitors' pace out wide saw them record a 32–6 win.

The next game produced a sensational finish. In the first half hour at Huddersfield, it had looked merely a question of how many the Giants would score. However, with the home side leading 18–0, Adam Walker's fine off-load gave Eden the chance to put Caro over. In the dying minutes of the half Josh Hodgson lost the ball as he dived over the line after more good work from Walker and, to add insult to injury, in a 12-point turnaround the Giants broke away and scored on the stroke of the hooter to make the half-time score 24–6.

Respectability looked the limit of Rovers' second half ambitions but with Burns to the fore they fought back. Josh Hodgson put Cox over and Burns made it 24–12 midway through the half but the Giants defence prevented any further breakthrough until the 77th minute. Then Hodgson scored from Eden's high kick and Burns' third conversion took the score to 24–18. The Giants kicked deep with the aim of holding the Robins in their own half, but on the third tackle, Rovers moved the ball wide, Eden accelerated through a gap and drew the full-back before passing on to Caro, who raced half the length of the field to score. With no time left to restart the game, Burns had a real pressure kick from near the touchline to level the scores. The pugnacious Aussie struck the ball perfectly and sparked delirious celebrations by the players and the army of travelling fans.

After that, the Robins came down to earth with three further defeats and it was not until Bradford visited Craven Park on a dismal March afternoon that they gained their first win. Rovers, with Burns and Josh Hodgson again pulling the strings, were too strong for a spirited Bradford side and won 16–0. The following week, visitors Wakefield were made to look second-rate, the Red and Whites scoring eight tries to win 44–6. The Robins then fell at the first hurdle in the Challenge Cup at home to Warrington, a game they should have won. They proved that point the following Friday night with a comfortable 25–12 league win against the same opposition at the Halliwell Jones that saw Weyman play his best game for the club, but was marred by a serious leg injury to Adam Walker.

The next game was the home derby. Rankin scored first for the Black and Whites but Burns followed up his own 40/20 by putting in Larroyer to level the scores. Shortly before half-time, Weyman managed to score from Hodgson's long pass despite the attentions of four defenders. The Airlie Birds quickly levelled in the second half, but as the game moved in to the last quarter, Horne scored twice in three minutes and Rovers led 20–10.

It could have been more when Rovers broke away again for Welham to cross but the video referee, called into action for the fifth time, ruled that there had been an offside in the build-up and the Black and Whites escaped. They took full advantage when Houghton immediately burrowed over to make it 20–16. Rovers missed a chance to wrap the game up when they dropped the ball with the line open and it looked as if they would pay the price when the Airlie Birds scored with five minutes to go. Fortunately, Whiting's touchline conversion attempt failed, and the sides were level at 20–20. The Robins drove downfield to set up position for a drop-goal but although Burns' attempt was wide, the referee ruled a Hull FC hand had touched the ball and from the drop out Weyman's drive gave Hall the position to drop the decisive goal. It was a well-deserved win for the Robins, who were inspired by the outstanding Burns.

Graeme Horne has played for both sides in derby games. 'The crowds are so passionate, it means so much to them. That makes it special for the players even the ones who aren't from Hull. The crowd at Craven Park really gets behind the team but especially in derby games. You are really buzzing and you want to win it for them. When you do, you know you've made a lot of people very happy.'

The next nine games produced only three wins, the highlight of which was a 38–24 Magic Weekend win over the Black and Whites. The week after the last of them, a 26–22 home defeat to Huddersfield, Rovers sacked coach Craig Sandercock. The decision to part company received mixed reaction from the supporters. He had been in charge for a little over two and a half seasons, during which the Robins had played 77 games, winning 31, drawing three, and losing 43. There had been little improvement in the regular failings of brittle defence, particularly on the flanks, ill-discipline and poor individual errors in possession. Considering the level of investment in the team – Rovers paid out not far short of the salary cap in 2014 – the directors and supporters were entitled to expect a better return.

The club promoted assistant coach Chris Chester on an interim basis until the end of the season. He had immediate success when league leaders St Helens visited Craven Park a few days later and his team dominated throughout with their best performance of the season. They won 40–10 with hat-tricks from Hall and Caro in probably their first full 80-minute performance of the season. Had Burns been on form with his goal-kicking, the score would have been nearer to 50.

However, the old failings soon returned and the remaining matches followed a depressingly familiar pattern. A 30–6 defeat at Headingley was the result of a failure to make best use of possession and poor defence. A club record Super League away win, 62–10 in London, was sandwiched between disappointing defeats against top-eight rivals Salford and Widnes, both largely the result of error-strewn second half performances. Then a much-improved performance at home to Wigan yielded a 14–14 draw after the Robins had led by 10 points with only seven minutes to go. Following the Wigan game, Rovers confirmed Chester as coach on a three-year contract.

Chester's players let him down badly in the next match, a 28–0 loss at the KC Stadium that meant that the Robins could not qualify for the play-offs. Dave Sherwood described the performance as: 'The worst by Rovers in the 110 derby games I have seen.' After another disappointing home loss to Catalans, who again out-muscled the Robins in the second half, there was the consolation of a 42-18 win at Wakefield.

Chairman Hudgell was forthright in expressing his disappointment about the season. He termed it a dismal effort, apportioning 90 per cent of the blame with the players and spoke of the need for a better attitude and discipline. 'But with a new coach, backroom staff, full salary cap, and a new competition structure, I am confident we can re-ignite the passion of the fans and move our club forward again,' he said. At a celebratory dinner in June, Rovers named the new North Stand after club president Colin Hutton, in a tribute to his 57 years dedicated and distinguished service. At the same time, a presentation was made to Neil Hudgell to mark his 10 years as chairman.

A number of players left the club at the end of the season, the highest profile of which were co-captains Travis Burns and Josh Hodgson. While still not the finished article, Hodgson had matured into a top player in his five years with the Robins and had been the player of the season. He was one of the side's best tacklers and always dangerous with ball in hand. After making 134 appearances and scoring 35 tries, he joined NRL side Canberra Raiders to further his career.

Travis Burns, who had a slow start with the Robins in 2013, responded well to the captaincy and goal-kicking responsibilities taken on in the wake of Dobson's departure. Although sometimes too individualistic, he was a committed and enthusiastic performer who could be a match-winner. After a rather drawn out saga, he left to join St Helens in the close season.

Winger David Hodgson retired after a fine career in which he scored 184 tries in 366 Super League appearances with five different clubs. Rovers released long-serving forward Rhys Lovegrove after eight years and 160 games and he joined London Broncos, versatile Craig Hall moved to Wakefield in search of a settled place and unlucky Jamie Langley, whose season was ruined by injuries, signed for Sheffield. Talented but inconsistent full-back Greg Eden moved to the NRL to join Brisbane Broncos, Neville Costigan and Kris Keating were released early from their contracts to return to Australia and former London speedster Omari Caro was also let go. Centre Sean Gleeson retired from the game in June following an eye injury sustained in a nightclub incident while he was attempting to regain fitness. In two costly seasons he managed only six games.

At the end of the season, the club released assistant coach Stanley Gene who took up a full-time coaching role at Gateshead. Long-serving forward Jason Netherton enjoyed a benefit and retired after his testimonial match in January 2015. He was an often-unsung player who was always willing to do the hard graft and who had played some of the best football of his career during the season. Since making his Rovers debut in 2004, Netherton played in 194 games and scored 13 tries.

The Robins

The Greats – No 36
Stanley Gene - *see Hull KR legends gallery*

Interested in signing Papua New Guinea centre John Okul, Rovers watched the Kumuls in the 1995 World Cup and their attention was also caught by half-back Stanley Gene. Acting on the advice of Sam Stewart, they signed Gene to ensure that Okul had familiar company in a strange country.

Gene recalls his early days in the city in his frank autobiography Daydream Believer. *The move from Papua New Guinea to Hull was a huge culture shock – in fairness, it would have been the same in any English city. His flat above a launderette might now look very modest but with its electricity, cooker, washing machine and inside toilet, it was then the height of luxury for the boys from PNG. Gene's first spell at the club started with a two-try debut against ill-fated South Wales at Bridgend in March 1996, and ended with a try-scoring appearance at Batley in July 1999.*

By then, he had played 111 games for the Robins and scored an amazing 95 tries. Rovers had already refused a reported £60,000 offer from St Helens for him but he wanted to test himself in Super League. With the club's blessing, Gene signed for Gateshead Thunder for 2000. However, they were in serious financial trouble at the time, as were Hull Sharks, and in November agreement was reached that the two clubs would merge. In his book, Gene recalls the sinking feeling when he learned he would be playing at the Boulevard. 'I was now going to hurt the supporters who had loved me, and who I had loved for four years.'

After two less than enjoyable seasons with Hull FC, Gene moved to Huddersfield in 2002 where he had four very happy years, crediting coach Tony Smith's massive influence in making him a better player. Smith was delighted with his acquisition: 'Everyone sees how explosive he can be,' he said. 'But he is a very intelligent player who reads the game better than most.' Gene then moved to Bradford for the 2006 season, scoring a try in the Bulls' World Club Challenge win over Wests Tigers.

Later that year, when the Robins qualified to play in Super League 2007, Gene recalled a conversation with Neil Hudgell years before. 'When we get into Super League, Stanley, you will be my first signing.' Gene knew he had to return and made his comeback at Wigan on 2 March 2007 when Rovers gained a brilliant 26–16 win on an amazing night. Gene scored his 100th try for the club in the 42–6 win at the KC Stadium that guaranteed Super League survival that season. He recalls that moment, which put the Robins 32-6 ahead with 15 minutes to go. 'Four thousand Rovers fans went completely crazy ..... I ran towards them, screwed up my face, clenched my fists and let out a mighty yell. The fans could see the passion and my love for the club. We'd done it ... and here of all places.'

That passion and whole-hearted effort made Gene a real favourite with both players and supporters. Wayne Parker says: 'I loved playing with Stanley in my second spell at the club. He was so fit and enthusiastic and willing to learn.' Michael Dobson remembers that keenness in his latter playing days. 'He was always on my sleeve demanding the ball and he was a really hard man.' For Jason Netherton: 'He was really tough, there were times when he shouldn't have played, but he did. It was a great boost when he came back in 2007.'

Primarily a half-back, he also played in the back-row in his later seasons. The last of Gene's 171 appearances for the Robins was at Leeds in September 2009. He scored 105 tries, including 19 in 10 games in 1998 to equal Graham Paul and Gary Prohm's record of scoring in 10 consecutive games.

After two seasons with Halifax, Gene joined Rovers' coaching staff in 2012 and for three years was a familiar figure at matches, carrying on the kicking tees or water bottles, geeing up the players and urging them to greater *efforts. Gene moved to Gateshead as coach for 2015 but remains a much-loved figure at Craven Park.*

Nor has he ever forgotten his roots, providing classroom equipment for youngsters in isolated communities in Papua New Guinea through his charity, the Stanley Gene Foundation.

For 2015, the RFL announced a new structure with 12 teams in both Super League and the Championship, and 14 in League One. Each Super League and Championship club were to play every other club in their division home and away in the regular season, with their league positions determining their involvement in Super 8s mini-leagues that followed. The top eight finishers in Super League would play in a competition to determine the Grand Finalists and the bottom four would form a qualifying competition with the top four in the Championship to determine promotion and relegation. The top three middle 8 Qualifiers would be in the following season's Super League, and the fourth and fifth place clubs would play off for the final place. The aim of the changes were to ensure that, according to the accompanying slogan, 'every minute mattered.' 'The 2015 changes should help us,' said Neil Hudgell at the time. 'The reduction in Super League clubs will increase the size of the player pool and that should keep players' wages down, and the extra £400,000 television money will be very welcome.'

'Neil is the biggest single part of what has happened at the club in the last ten years,' says Netherton. There will always be those who are not satisfied or want quicker progress and Hudgell feels that frustration more than anyone. 'We seem to have hit a bit of a glass ceiling,' he says. 'We get to seventh or eighth but struggle to get higher. We struggle to get that consistency on the field. When we put in half a million a year, that enables the club to keep going, whereas at Wigan, for example, if their chairman puts that amount in, it enables them to develop and strengthen further.' He also believes that the RFL need to do more to market the game nationally. Recognising that their present level of funding cannot continue forever, Rob Crossland emphasised that the accent at Craven Park in the future will be on sustainability across the whole of the club's operations.

Thrills and spills

The 2015 season started with another wave of optimism. There was a whole host of new signings, whilst Chester appointed two new coaching assistants in Willie Poching, the former number two to Tony Smith at Warrington and David Hodgson, after his retirement from playing.

There were a club record eleven debuts, spearheaded by former Canberra Raiders half-back Terry Campese, in front of a ground record 11,811 spectators for the first game against Leeds at Craven Park on 8 February. In a revamped back division, new skipper Campese was joined by former Gold Coast scrum-half Albert Kelly, ex-London speedster Kieran Dixon, Italian international Josh Mantellato and highly-rated Parramatta flyer, Ken Sio, on the wings and experienced former Wigan centre Darryl Goulding. Rovers' signing of Sio on a two-year contract had amazed some Aussie commentators, who obviously thought he could have done better for himself. Only Welham remained in the back-line from the previous season.

Up front, another former Parramatta man, Mitch Allgood, came in at prop and in the back row, Warrington-born Tyrone McCarthy, back in the UK after a season with Queensland club Northern Pride, joined up with Greg Burke, a season-long loanee from Wigan Warriors. The remaining three debutants were on the bench, utility Maurice Blair, signed with Kelly from Gold Coast, young French hooker John Boudebza and back-rower James Donaldson, signed from Bradford Bulls, who had lost their Super League status at the end of 2014.

Two notable absentees were popular Aussie prop Mick Weyman, due to knee trouble, and another new signing, former Leeds Rhinos prop Ryan Bailey. Like another front rower from the West Riding over 100 years before, Bailey had in the past hardly endeared himself to the Rovers faithful with his somewhat rumbustious style of play but, unlike Alfred Mann, he was beset by personal problems from the start and only appeared in Rovers' colours once before leaving to join Castleford later in the season.

The Robins started well enough against the Rhinos, with Campese and Kelly to the fore, but the old defensive frailties re-emerged as they squandered an early second half 30-16 lead to lose 40-30. After a very disappointing 44-24 defeat at Belle Vue, one of only three games the Wildcats managed to win during the regular season, the Robins then fell into a 'win at home, lose away' sequence in Super League. It was broken only by the derby games, both of which resulted in away wins. Three home wins raised hopes of a top eight finish, but defeats in the last four games saw the Robins finish in tenth place and needing to redeem themselves in the Super 8s Qualifiers to retain their Super League status.

The Robins were certainly unlucky at prop and half-back. At the start of the season, with Allgood and Bailey to add to Weyman, Walker and Green, front row looked to be one of their strongest areas. However, in addition to Bailey's troubles, Weyman never recovered from his injury and rather than sit out his contract, he did the honourable thing and retired. His emotional farewell before the Catalans game in March was an eloquent testimony to his popularity at Craven Park and his powerful running was sadly missed. After making just eight appearances, Allgood suffered a serious shoulder injury and missed the remainder of the regular season. Thankfully, both Walker and Green remained relatively injury free but there were times when the Robins were able to call on just two recognised props. They responded to the injury to Allgood by signing Campese's former Canberra colleague, 6' 7" prop Dane Tilse. When he was then injured after just two games, the Robins brought in Salford's experienced Kiwi Tony Puletua and threw him in at the deep end away to the Leeds Rhinos in May. Although he had not played a first team game that season, Puletua soon started to show his worth.

Perhaps the most significant injury though, was the ruptured knee ligament sustained by skipper Campese in the disastrous Castleford home game, lost 30-22. He had become the Robins most influential player, the genesis of the best of their attacking play. He was quickly ruled out for the rest of the season and his creativity and leadership were missed. Blair teamed up with Kelly at half-back whilst to provide additional cover, Canterbury Bulldogs' Dane Chisholm was brought in on loan towards the end of the regular season. The Robins were also unfortunate that former Wigan centre Goulding was another who had to call time on his career after playing only eight games for the club. The fans never had the chance to see him at his best, but, as with Weyman, they recognised his commitment and honesty.

In April, the Robins announced the loan signing of Huddersfield international hooker Shaun Lunt. He had won a Grand Final with Leeds and was linked with Rovers in the close season as a possible replacement for Josh Hodgson. The

Giants had not then wanted to release a valuable asset, so his arrival was a very welcome surprise.

What partly redeemed an otherwise very disappointing season was the Challenge Cup campaign. It started inauspiciously with a 50-30 win at Bradford that was by no means as comfortable as the score suggests. Rovers started slowly, conceding 12 points, and although they then asserted their superiority and took the lead, they were unable to dominate and four tries in the last 15 minutes gave the score-line a flattering look. The most notable feature of the game was the finishing of Mantellato who showed strength, speed, determination and dexterity in scoring four tries.

The next round took the Robins to Leigh Sports Village to play Wigan, whose DW Stadium was unavailable due to ground work. The Warriors had two weeks earlier inflicted an embarrassing 60-0 thrashing on Rovers, and few gave the visitors any chance this time. Both games were screened live on Sky Sports, whose pundits were scratching their heads about how the Robins could produce such a turnaround in such a short timescale. Missing Kelly in the backs and with just two recognised props in the absence of Walker, they made light of the handicaps with some outstanding defence. They so effectively repelled Wigan's best efforts that the home side were reduced to kicking a penalty goal after 15 minutes to take the lead. Minutes later, Campese started a move that was continued by Blair and Cockayne, with Blair taking a great return pass to power his way over wide out and Mantellato added a fine conversion. After both sides had again gone close, Joel Tomkins levelled for Wigan just before half-time. In worsening conditions, there were only three more penalty goals to show as the game entered its final quarter. Burgess then squeezed over in the corner to edge Wigan ahead 12-10, before two outstanding plays won the game for the Robins.

First, with just eight minutes left, Blair's big hit on Sarginson resulted in the Wigan man losing the ball near his own line. Sio picked up and somehow managed to force his way over to touch down. Mantellato's conversion gave Rovers a 16-12 lead and, as the Warriors threw everything at them in a last desperate assault, Cockayne just managed to force Tomkins' foot into touch as he powered over the line. It was undoubtedly Rovers' best defensive performance since their win at Headingley two years before.

In the quarter-final, Rovers faced Catalans at Craven Park. Inspired by the words of former club great Mike Smith in the dressing room before the game, they produced their best all-round first-half performance for many a year. Their 26-4 lead was no more than they deserved after a brilliant team effort in both attack and defence. Unfortunately, appearing to believe that the job was done, Rovers eased off in the second half, and the visitors mounted a comeback. In the end, it was only Sio's brilliant finish after good work by Kelly and Salter, which enabled the home side to hold off a determined Dragons' assault to win 32-26.

The semi-final was another nail-biter. The Robins got off to the worst possible start when Warrington's huge kick-off was allowed to bounce dead and, from the drop-out, they created the opportunity for Ryan Atkins to score. From 6-0 down and looking rather shaky, Rovers began to fight their way back and turned the game around with two tries in five minutes in the second quarter. First, Kelly, Blair and Dixon combined brilliantly to create a chance for Mantellato, who again demonstrated his great finishing power. Sio then plucked Kelly's towering kick from Ormsby's grasp to score the Robins' try of the season. Mantellato's kick put the Robins 10-6 ahead with ten minutes of the half to go and he increased the lead to six before the break with a penalty.

The Robins

After a Wolves effort was ruled out due to a knock-on, Rovers struck again through French second-rower Larroyer who, seemingly tackled near the line, somehow managed to find the strength to reach out and touch down despite the attentions of several defenders. Mantellato's conversion and subsequent penalty gave the Robins a fourteen point lead as the half moved towards its' midway point. Wolves narrowed the gap to two points with ten minutes to go. Then, with four minutes left, Walker drove for the line and slipped the ball to Lunt, who seemed to have nowhere to go. However, he managed to twist himself over the line and when the video referee confirmed the score, it was the cue for wild celebrations from the 6,000 plus Rovers' fans at Headingley. The celebrations continued long after Mantellato's conversion and the final hooter had sounded. After 29 long years, the Robins were back at Wembley.

Before the final, there was the important business of the Qualifiers to negotiate. In their first game, at Leigh, the Robins started shakily and a poor first half left them facing a 24-6 half-time deficit. Then their extra pace and fitness started to show and they pulled their way back into the game, eventually running out 34-26 winners.

After a very scratchy 34-14 home victory over Halifax, the Robins then faced a very difficult game on the artificial surface at Widnes, upon which they had previously only registered one win in five attempts, just six days before Wembley. Before the game, Chester said that places in the cup final squad were still up for grabs. He rested what he clearly saw as his first-choice starting pack. As it transpired, the game produced one of the season's most spirited defensive performances and against the expectations of many, the Robins triumphed 12-8. Perhaps most encouragingly, youngsters like half-back Matty Marsh and back-rower

George Lawler, the U19s Player of the Year, showed up well in a hard game.

Over 15,000 Rovers supporters made the trip to Wembley on August Bank Holiday Saturday. Despite their impressive run to the final, the Robins were rank outsiders against cup-holders Leeds. Just three Rovers players had played in a Wembley final before – Puletua, Lunt and McCarthy – and only McCarthy had been a winner. Dave Sherwood summed up the feelings of most of the Rovers' faithful: "I'm just hoping we give them a decent game," he said. "We don't want to be embarrassed."

In the main, the team selected itself for the final. There was a big boost when Kelly, who had sustained ligament damage in the semi-final, was deemed fit enough to play. Amongst supporters, there was some debate about whether Cockayne or Dixon should play at full-back – Dixon was a potential match-winner with his electric pace and elusive running but even his greatest fans conceded that he was prone to costly mistakes. The more experienced Cockayne might have been a safer option, but even his game was hardly error-free. Chester went with Dixon's pace, an understandable decision at the time. What appeared less understandable was his decision on the prop-forwards. Allgood's return for the Qualifiers meant that there were five fit props for four places. Puletua and Walker were clearly going to start, but who would miss out? Of the contenders, the big 24 year-old local man, James Green, had been one of the most improved players of the season. Playing mainly off the bench, he had made a real impact with his strong, whole-hearted running and tackling particularly in the semi-final and in the crunch Qualifier at Widnes. Chester's assertion that good performances in that game would be rewarded was not consistent with his selection, and he went instead for the two Aussies on the bench; Tilse, whose form had been largely disappointing and Allgood, who was desperately short of match practice. It was impossible not to feel for Green, and his physical presence would have beefed up a Rovers pack that was somewhat on the lightweight side.

Before the kick-off, Lizzie Jones, the widow of Keighley Cougars' Danny Jones, sang the traditional Wembley hymn, 'Abide with Me'. Jones had died from an undetected heart condition after becoming unwell during a game in May. The spontaneous ovation she earned from the 80,000 crowd brought tears to many eyes – it was a most touching display of all that is good in rugby league. TV presenter Mark Chapman remarked that whatever followed, nothing would match the bravery of Lizzie Jones. For Rovers fans especially it will be the abiding memory of an otherwise forgettable occasion.

The Robins simply failed to pose a serious threat at any stage. As early as the seventh minute, the Rhinos took the lead albeit in slightly fortuitous fashion when Larroyer stripped the ball from Peacock's hands as he dived for the line and Delaney touched down the loose ball for the opening try. Leeds were restricted to two more tries in the first half but even at 16-0, the writing was very clearly on the wall. Leeds posed much the greater threat, whilst Rovers' forwards struggled to make much headway and full-back Dixon was their most dangerous player. Sadly though, Dixon gave Leeds the initiative at the start of the second half with the first of a series of errors. The full-back never shirked or hid and was determined to atone for his mistakes but unfortunately everything he tried to do went wrong. The Rhinos capitalised ruthlessly, adding six more tries without reply. It was not a lack of effort on Rovers part, they were just not good enough on the day. Kelly, although obviously not fully fit, tried everything he knew, and amongst some hard-working forward performances, Donaldson caught the eye. For Leeds, former Hull FC winger Tom Briscoe took the headlines and the Lance Todd Trophy with a five-try display in record-breaking 50-0 triumph – or humiliation depending on which side of the ground you sat.

Having had their hopes so raised by being on the national stage, it was difficult not to feel most of all for chairman Hudgell, whose big day ended in disappointment. Graeme Horne speaks for the players. 'I was angry because I knew that we are better than that. There were a number of reasons; it was not ideal that our preparation had to be crammed into the five days after the Widnes game; we were disrupted by the injuries at half-back; it is a very daunting atmosphere for the players who haven't been there before; and Leeds were a very good and experienced side – their completion rate was over 90 per cent. We were all really gutted, particularly for the fans and the owners.'

After that, it was a return to the more important business of preserving Super League status. Wakefield Trinity Wildcats visited Craven Park eight days after the final and although not putting on a vintage performance, the Robins showed character and determination to bounce back with a 20-18 win. Sio took over at full-back and Dixon moved to the wing where he scored two tries, following that up with four more in a 48-4 demolition of Bradford Bulls the following week. No one with a touch of humanity could fail to be pleased for Dixon, who was in tears after his Wembley nightmare, as again he showed his character and resilience. He was later deservedly named Young Player of the Year.

The Robins' Super League status was confirmed the day after the Bulls game, when Wakefield's defeat meant that they could not be caught by the fourth-placed club. Rovers duly completed their season with fairly low-key wins at Sheffield and at home to Salford to complete the Qualifiers with a 100 per cent record. It was the first time since the introduction of the one point drop goal just over 41 years earlier that the Robins had not recorded a single one during the season.

Rovers had certainly served up some exciting football. Overall, their strength lay in what was their strongest back division since the halcyon days of the 1980s; the creativity and organisation of Campese, unpredictable brilliance of Kelly, deadly finishing of wingers Sio and Mantellato – the former with pace and the latter with power and strength reminiscent of 1980s favourite Steve Hubbard, speed and flair from Dixon, whilst at centre Welham had his best season since 2011 but was somewhat surprisingly released at the end of it. The mercurial and popular Kelly swept the board with three Rovers' Player of the Year awards.

There had been some fine performances, particularly in the Cup, but there was too much inconsistency and far too often the Robins played for only 40 minutes. Defence was a weakness and a relative lack of physicality in the forwards, particularly in the back row, meant that too often the backs did not have a platform to show their talents.

Chief Executive Mike Smith commented in September that the Challenge Cup final appearance masked a disappointing season, and that it was a disaster that Rovers had not made the top eight. 'We can't afford to be [just] seventh, eighth, ninth or tenth,' he said. 'It's just not acceptable. It's not going to keep this club sustainable.'

Certainly, Hudgell and Crossland deserved a far better return on their investment. Coach Chester acknowledged his responsibility, saying that he had to be a better coach next year, but only three games into the new campaign he was gone and James Webster was put in interim charge until the end of the 2016 season.

Off the field, the biggest news was the announcement in March that Leeds Rhinos' veteran international forward Jamie Peacock was to join the Robins as their football manager. One of the most respected and dedicated men in the game, Peacock had seen it and done it all as a player. At the end of his illustrious career, he was seeking a new challenge. Talking to the national media, he said: 'I was drawn by the passion of Rovers' fans; it's their life. To bring success to people who haven't had it for a long time would mean more to me than anything else I've done in the game. I want them to go from being a club that makes up the numbers to one challenging consistently for honours. I am nervous – it's a massive challenge. I have a very good idea of what will work, but putting it into practice? I've not done that. Sometimes I lie awake thinking about it.'

Everyone in and around the club hoped that Peacock would be able to harness all his experience and expertise to the benefit of his new employers, while meeting the challenge in as full-on and uncompromising a manner as he was famous for on the field – while inspiring the players and staff around him to do the same. There were also high hopes that he would have a positive influence on recruitment, an area widely perceived as being hit and miss for some time.

In August, the two Hull clubs announced plans for a new shared 'Super Academy'. The idea was to bring together their youth development systems, with the aim of increasing the quality and quantity of Hull-based players and have more of them in both first teams. Many fans of both clubs were not immediately sold on the concept, but Hudgell was convinced that it was the right way forward. 'A pooled academy will enable us to improve facilities, up-skill the coaches, and attract more specialist talent,' he told the *Hull Daily Mail*. 'I just ask fans to view developments with an open mind.' The colours of the new academy, based at Bishop Burton College, were to be black and red, with the progression of players to the senior clubs decided by a draft system. Successful or not, it was a development that would have been unthinkable even 20 years earlier and it was only made possible through the respect and friendship shared by the two chairmen.

Also in August, Craven Park hosted an official eliminator for the WBC World Lightweight boxing title between two local men, Luke Campbell MBE and Tommy Coyle. Televised live on Sky Sports and attended by a capacity audience, it was another example of the club maximising the revenue from its stadium.

The community spirit that was evidenced so much in the club's early years and had played such a big part in its survival in the dark ones, remains strongly in evidence. Twenty years after their link with Papua New Guinea began, the Robins produced a special limited edition shirt, part of the profit from which went to the Stanley Gene Foundation. The first team squad teamed up with pop group Erasure to record a charity version of the group's song 'A Little Respect', after social media coverage of the fans singing it at the cup semi-final had come to the attention of lead singer Andy Bell. The Robins' version reached 93 in the official singles sales chart. Members of the West Hull Rovers Walking Group completed the Lyke Wake Walk to raise money for the Steve Prescott Foundation, whilst Rovers added the name of 14-year-old supporter Connor Lynes to their squad and presented him with a jersey with his name and number when the teenager recovered from a near fatal brain blood clot after playing for local team Lambwath Lions. At the end-of-year player awards, Connor was presented with a special bravery award. After leaving Craven Park on their journey to Wembley, the team coach stopped at the nearby Elm Tree Court nursing home, where players chatted to and had photos taken with the residents. After the last game of the season, the club held a party on the field at which players and supporters mixed freely and, bringing back memories of Tom van Vollenhoven's last match at Craven Park in 1968, the Robins' fans gave Salford's international prop Adrian Morley a very generous and moving ovation at the end of his 20-year career in professional rugby league.

Club President Colin Hutton celebrated 70 years in rugby league in August 2015 and was presented with a Lifetime Achievement award at the annual dinner. During the season, the newly-formed Heritage Group started to host a series of events aimed at celebrating the proud history of the Robins. 'It is a people's club,' says Horne. 'That is why I've really enjoyed every one of my years here.'

At the time of writing, recruitment for the club's tenth year in Super League had started. Centres Iain Thornley, from Wigan Warriors and Leeds Rhinos Academy product Thomas Minns came in, along with another Rhinos Academy man, Ireland international Robbie Mulhern, and back-rower Chris Clarkson from Leeds, via Widnes. Hooker Shaun Lunt and back-rower Kevin Larroyer also became permanent members of the Robins' squad, both signing long-term contracts.

Long-serving centre Kris Welham moved to Bradford, converting the final try of the 2015 season to record only his second goal for the club. He played in 192 games, in which he scored 102 tries. Welham was a fine attacking centre on his day but, mainly due to injuries, did not quite fulfil his early promise. Back-rower Tyrone McCarthy, who took over as club captain after Campese's injury, announced that he would cut short his stay to play in the NRL with St George Illawarra.

The Robins

Prop Tony Puletua, who had become a popular and valuable member of the squad despite making only 14 appearances for the Robins, retired after the penultimate game at Sheffield.

*****

This then, is the story of our great club so far. I hope that reading it has given you as much pleasure as writing it has given me.

Since that momentous decision to join the Northern Union in 1899, up to the end of 2015, Hull Kingston Rovers have played 4,128 games in fully-recognised first team competitions and tour games, winning 2,167. They have scored 64,721 points and 1,190 players have represented them. There have been times, in the 1920s and in the years between 1978 and 1986, when the club has stood proudly at the summit of the game, fearing no-one. Equally, its very existence has been under real threat, but it has been pulled through thanks to the efforts of those committed to the cause.

Now, the club stands at something of a crossroads.

Does it continue, in Jamie Peacock's words, 'to make up the numbers' in Super League, or can it again take its place amongst the elite?

Nothing would give me greater pleasure in ten years' time than to be able to update this history with an account of another era of success. It would be no more than those who helped it out of the dark years deserve, no more than Neil Hudgell and Rob Crossland deserve, and no more than its faithful supporters deserve.

Post-war Dream Team

TO close the book, Len Beecroft, Dave Sherwood and I selected a XIII from the best players, at their peak, to play for the Robins since the war. Rather than simply the best players for each position, it is a team that we think will complement each other. We did not agree on every selection, and there are compromises. We restricted it to post war players because we do not have enough knowledge of those who played before then to make fair comparisons. We select four substitutes, in the expectation that all 17 would play a part in the game.

These are our opinions; there will be disagreement with some of them but it is certain is that this team has a very talented back division and a powerful pack that would be second to no one. With the advantage of being full-time professionals, and modern diet, fitness and training methods, we believe this team would be a match for any club side.

Our choice at full-back is George Fairbairn, whose all round defensive strength and attacking threat give him an edge over the fine positional play and excellent goal-kicking of Cyril Kellett.

The Robins

Right wing is a difficult choice, but we have chosen 'the Cornish Express,' Graham Paul, for his pace and finishing ability. Other candidates included immediate post-war favourite Geoff Tullock, 1960s flyer Chris Young, the former RU speedster, Ged Dunn, and the powerful goal-kicker, Steve Hubbard. At left wing, we chose the legendary Clive Sullivan. A strong and elusive finisher with the pace to go the length of the field, and a brilliant defender, he would have been an outstanding wingman in any era. He wins the vote over 1960s hero Bob Harris.

At right centre we go for Mike Smith, a complete all-round centre, strong in defence and dangerous in attack, and a shrewd judge of when to use his winger. At left centre we have fellow 80s hero Gary Prohm. More than just a scorer of tries, Prohm was a tough customer, strong in defence and a hard, fast runner who troubled opposing defences. Other notables included the talented Alan Burwell and Whetu Taewa, a strong and professional performer in an average side.

At off-half is Roger Millward. We picked him in that position rather than scrum-half because that is the position he graced whilst at the peak of his powers. His pace, sidestep, anticipation, play-making, kicking game and immaculate defence made him arguably the most complete off-half the game has ever seen. If Millward were unavailable, we could choose between Alan Burwell and that great finisher, Steve Hartley.

Amongst a number of scrum-half contenders, our choice is the rugged Gordon Smith; a fine all-round footballer whose indefatigable commitment and reliability make him a perfect partner for Millward. Other contenders were 1960s star Arthur Bunting, the talented Wayne Parker, the under-sung Allan Agar, Australian tactician James Webster and top kicker and play-maker Michael Dobson.

In the pack, at open-side prop we go for the uncompromising Mark Broadhurst, a big, rugged and mobile prop who never took a backward step and was a key member of the great 80s sides. Other distinguished contenders for the No 8 jersey are John Millington, Bryan Niebling and Michael Vella. On the blind-side we chose the physical presence and graft of Len Casey, a man for the big occasion, over the textbook defence and ball-handling of Brian Lockwood.

Hooker is the most difficult choice of all. Amongst a number of outstanding contenders, three stand out. The all-round ability and professionalism of Alvin Ackerley, the attacking threat of Peter Flanagan, or the strength and defensive ability of David Watkinson. Watkinson just edges it by a majority vote.

In the second row, Phil Lowe was the finest running second row forward the club has had, and he is an automatic selection – but the choice of his partner is more difficult one. We went for Frank Foster, a fine all round footballer and an uncompromising player that opposing team hated to play against, and who would be the perfect foil for Lowe. Other worthy contenders included Paul Rose, Paul Fletcher and Ben Galea.

At loose-forward we go for Harry Poole - a complete all-round footballer with an insatiable appetite for work and the ultimate leader. He is also our captain. Poole wins the vote ahead of Alec Dockar and Gavin Miller.

On the bench, Alan Burwell's brilliance could unlock the defence in a tight game, and as a second hooker Peter Flanagan could inject fresh impetus and take advantage of tiring defences. They are joined by John Millington and Paul Fletcher, two committed warriors who would run strongly, tackle hard, and would always give their all for the cause.

The Robins

Hull Kingston Rovers
Post-War Dream Team

Full-back	1. George Fairbairn
Right wing	2. Graham Paul
Right centre	3. Mike Smith
Left centre	4. Gary Prohm
Left wing	5. Clive Sullivan
Stand-off	6. Roger Millward
Scrum-half	7. Gordon Smith
Open side prop	8. Mark Broadhurst
Hooker	9. David Watkinson
Blind-side prop	10. Len Casey
Second row	11. Phil Lowe
Second row	12. Frank Foster
Loose forward	13. Harry Poole (*captain*)

Replacements

14. Alan Burswell	16. John Millington
15. Peter Flanagan	17. Paul Fletcher

Craven Park on Holderness Road, seen in a 1980s aerial view, was the club's spiritual home for over 66 years.

Above: Len Casey on the charge in the 1980 final, with Watkinson and Agar in support against Hull FC

Above: A Hartley special. Steve Hartley races majestically through the Hull defence on his way to a glorious 65-yard try in the 11-7 Premiership final win over the Black and Whites at Headingley, Leeds, on 16 May 1981

Above: Leaving them for dead. David Hall races away to score against Halifax in January 1983 with the defence nowhere to be seen. John Millington and Gordon Smith have decided their support will not be needed

Matt Dass Collection

Above: Evil eye. John Millington takes on Widnes at Naughton Park in March 1984. In support (*left to right*): Garry Clark, Chris Rudd and Mark Broadhurst

Above: Rovers' players celebrate their 1983-84 Championship and Premiership double in the dressing room at Headingley after beating Castleford 18-10 in the Premiership final. Back row (*left to right*) Paul Harkin, David Laws, John Lydiat, Mike Smith, George Fairbairn, Geoff Plummer (physio). *Front*: John Dorahy, Chris Burton, John Millington, David Hall, Ian Robinson, Gary Prohm

Below: Spot the ball. The game comes to a momentary standstill while the players and referee Ron Campbell watch Andy Kelly's 79th-minute drop-goal beat Wigan 19-18 at Craven Park on 29 September 1985

Matt Dass Collection

Above: Talented half-back Wayne Parker in action at the Boulevard on 17 April 1987. His try and drop-goal helped the Robins to a 21-8 win. Parker played for the Robins in a declining team, but would have graced the side in any era

Below: It's dirty work. Whetu Taewa battles with Featherstone and the Craven Park mud as the Robins graft to a 2-2 draw on day one of the 1999/2000 season

Above: Blackpool 2005, where Rovers beat Castleford 18-16 to win the Northern Rail Cup. Back (*left to right*): Mikali Aizue, Byron Ford, Jon Steel, Gareth Morton, Andy Raleigh, Jimmy Walker, Dale Holdstock, Andy Ellis, Kane Epati, Paul Pickering, Paul Parker. *Front*: Phil Hasty, Jamie Bovill, Jason Netherton, Nick Pinkney, James Webster, Leroy Rivett, David Tangata-Toa, Alan Fellowes (kitman), Paul Mansson, Dwayne Barker. *Inset*: Chairman Neil Hudgell and coach Justin Morgan celebrate clinching a Super League place after the 2006 National League Grand Final win over Widnes

Right: Luke Dyer outstrips the Airlie Birds' defence to score Rovers' third try at the KC Stadium on 2 September 2007. The 42-6 win ensured the Robins' Super League survival

Above: Leading by example. Skipper Michael Vella takes on the Cas defence at the Jungle in Rovers' 46-28 win on 2 August 2009. Vella was instrumental in establishing the Robins in Super League in their first three seasons

Above: That try! David Hodgson speeds away down the touchline to score the dramatic last minute match-winning try in Rovers' 32-30 win in Magic Weekend at the Etihad on 26 May 2012

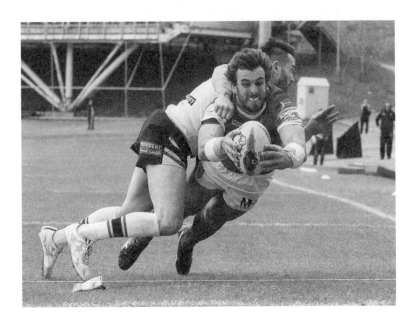

Above: Italian international Josh Mantellato goes for the line against Bradford at Odsal during a 50-30 Challenge Cup win on 19 April 2015. Mantellato bagged 338 points in the season, the most by a Rovers player since Mike Fletcher in 1990

Below: Differing designs in an assortment of Hull Kingston Rovers' matchday programmes, collected since the early post-World War II years

Appendices

Club Honours & Records

Club honours

Championship:	Winners 1922-23, 1924-25, 1978-79, 1983-84, 1984-85; runners-up 1920-21, 1967-68, 1982-83
Premiership:	Winners 1980-81, 1983-84; runners-up 1984-85
Challenge Cup:	Winners 1979-80; runners-up 1904-05, 1924-25, 1963-64, 1980-81, 1985-86
Challenge Cup Plate:	Winners 1997
Divisional Premiership:	Runners-up 1989-90
Minor Premiership:	Winners 2006
National League One:	Winners 2006
Division Two Championship:	Winners 1989-90, 1996
Centenary Second Division:	Winners 1995-96
John Player Special Trophy:	Winners 1984-85; runners-up 1981-82; 1985-86
Eastern Division Championship:	Winners 1962-63
Yorkshire Cup:	Winners 1920-21, 1929-30, 1966-67, 1967-68, 1971-72, 1974-75, 1985-86; runners-up 1906-07, 1911-12, 1933-34, 1962-63, 1975-76, 1980-81, 1984/85
Yorkshire League:	Winners 1924-25, 1925-26; runners-up 1911-12, 1912-13, 1966-67, 1967-68
BBC2 Floodlit Trophy:	Winners 1977-78; runners-up 1979-80
Northern Rail Cup:	Winners 2005; runners-up 2002, 2004, 2006
Yorkshire Cup (rugby union):	Winners 1896-97
Hull Times Cup:	Winners 1887-88, 1889-90, 1890-91

The Robins

Team records

Highest score:	100-6	v Nottingham City (away), 19.8.1990
Highest victory margin:	92-10	v Whitehaven (home), 18.3.1990 (*record for league game*)
Highest score against:	84-6	v Wigan (home), 1.4.2013 (*also highest margin of defeat*)
Consecutive wins:	24	12.2.2006-9.7.2006 (*also most consecutive games unbeaten*)
Consecutive defeats:	14	8.10.1953-26.12.1953 (*also most consecutive games without a win*)

Individual records

Career

Appearances:	489	Mike Smith, 1975-91
Consecutive appearances:	190	Gilbert Austin, 1919-23
International Appearances:	46	Roger Millward, 1966-78
Points:	2,759	Mike Fletcher, 1986-98
Goals:	1,267	Mike Fletcher, 1986-98
Drop-goals:	38	Paul Harkin, 1980-87
Tries:	207	Roger Millward, 1966-80
Highest goals to appearances ratio:	4.773	Gareth Morton, 2005-07
Highest tries to appearances ratio:	1.333	Greg Austin, 1989/90

Season

Appearances:	49	John R Moore, 1967/68
Points:	450	Mike Fletcher, 1989/90
Goals:	199	Mike Fletcher, 1989/90
Drop-goals:	14	Wayne Parker, 1987/88
Tries:	45	Gary Prohm, 1984/85

Consecutive seasons in which tries were scored:

16 Paul Fletcher, 1989-2004

Match

Points:	53	GH 'Tich' West v Brooklands Rovers, 4.3.1905 (11 tries, 10 goals);
	36	Damien Couturier v Halifax, 23.4.2006 (14 goals, 2 tries);
	31	Roger Millward v Hunslet 28.8.1972 (11 goals, 3 tries)
Goals:	14	Alf 'Bunker' Carmichael v Merthyr Tydfil, 8.10.1910; Mike Fletcher v Whitehaven, 18.3.1990; Colin Armstrong v Nottingham City, 19.8.1990; Damien Couturier v Halifax, 23.4.2006
Drop-goals:	4	Allan Agar v Leeds (away), 30.9.1978 Wayne Parker v Salford (home), 10.1.88
Tries:	11	GH 'Tich' West v Brooklands Rovers (home), 4.3.1905
	6	William Sandham v Coventry (home), 1.3.1913; Ged Dunn v New Hunslet (home), 2.2.1975; Greg Austin v Nottingham City (away), 19.8.1990
Scoring in consecutive games:	41	Mike Fletcher, 15.3.89-13.5.90
Scoring tries in consecutive games:	10	Graham Paul, 25.8.1962-6.10.1962 (17 in 10); Gary Prohm, 3.4.85-28.4.85 (13 in 10); Stanley Gene, 21.6.98-9.8.98 (19 in 10)

Attendance Records

Any game involving Hull KR:	95,000	v Hull FC (Wembley), 3.5.1980
Any home game:	27,670	v Hull FC (Boothferry Park), 3.4.1953
Craven Park, Holderness Road	22,282	v Hull FC, 7.10.1922
	16,084	v Hull FC, 20.4.1984 - post-war record
Craven Park, Preston Road	11,811	v Leeds, 8.2.2015
Craven Street	18,000	v Hull FC, 11.3.1922

The Robins

'The Top Tens'

Appearances

	Starts	Subs	Total
Mike Smith	481	8	489
Paul Fletcher	316	148	464
Jack Spamer	445	0	445
Johnny Moore	395	38	433
Laurie Osborne	431	0	431
Phil Lowe	386	32	418
John Millington	371	47	418
Peter Flanagan	411	4	415
Roger Millward	399	7	406
David Hall	333	50	383

Goals

	Goals	Drop-goals*	Total
Mike Fletcher	1267	1	1268
Cyril Kellett	1194	0	1194
Alf Carmichael	723	0	723
Laurie Osborne	718	0	718
Roger Millward	597	10	607
George Fairbairn	554	19	573
Michael Dobson	537	12	549
Wilf McWatt	431	0	431
Steve Hubbard	327	0	327
Chris Charles	301	3	304

	Tries		Points
Roger Millward	207	Mike Fletcher	2759
Steve Hartley	191	Cyril Kellett	2493
Phil Lowe	179	Roger Millward	1825
Gilbert Austin	163	Laurie Osborne	1496
Ged Dunn	160	Alf Carmichael	1482
Jack Spamer	145	George Fairbairn	1308
Mike Smith	140	Michael Dobson	1294
Garry Clark	121	Wilf McWatt	949
Clive Sullivan	118	Steve Hubbard	870
Jim Cook	116	Chris Charles	769
Graham Paul	116		

*since 'one point' drop-goal was introduced in domestic RL in 1974/75

Club officers

Season	Chairman 1	Secretary/ Chief Executive	Trainer/coach	Captain
1897/98		C. Savage		S. Morfitt
1898/99		C. Savage		S. Morfitt
1899/1900		C. Savage		A. Kemp
1900/01		C. Savage		A. Starks
1901/02		C. Savage		A. Starks
1902/03		C. Savage		A. Starks
1903/04		C. Savage	H. Shann 2	A Starks/ J. Gordon
1904/05	F. Langley	C. H. Duggleby	H. Shann	A. Starks
1905/06	F. Langley	G. Johnson	H. Shann	A. Starks
1906/07	E. Ombler	G. Johnson	H. Shann	G. H. West
1907/08	E. Ombler	G. Johnson	H. Shann	Alf Carmichael
1908/09	E. Ombler/J. Moore	G. Johnson	H. Shann	Alf Carmichael/ T. Taylor
1909/10	J. Moore	G. Johnson	H. Shann	Alf Carmichael
1910/11	J. Moore	G. Johnson	E. H. Gill	Alf Carmichael
1911/12	J. Moore	G. Johnson	E. H. Gill	Alf Carmichael
1912/13	J. Moore/E. Ombler	G. Johnson	E. H. Gill	Alf Carmichael
1913/14	E. Ombler	G. Johnson	E. H. Gill	Alf Carmichael
1914/15	J. T. Collier	G. Johnson	E. H. Gill	A. Carmichael / A. Mann
1918/19	J. T. Collier	G. Johnson	E. H. Gill	A. Mann
1919/20	E. W. Brown	T. Williams	W. Jacques	A. Moore
1920/21	E. W. Brown	T. Williams	W. Jacques	A. Moore
1921/22	E. W. Brown	T. Williams	W. Jacques	A. Moore
1922/23	E. W. Brown	T. Williams	W. Jacques	A. Moore
1923/24	E. W. Brown	T. Williams	W. Jacques	A. Moore
1924/25	E. W. Brown	T. Williams	W. Jacques	A. Moore / L. Osborne
1925/26	E. W. Brown	T. Williams	W. Jacques	L. Osborne
1926/27	E. W. Brown	T. Williams	W. Jacques	L. Osborne
1927/28	E. W. Brown	T. Williams	W. Jacques	Andrew Carmichael
1928/29	E. W. Brown	T. Williams	W. Jacques	A.Carmichael / C.Westerdale
1929/30	E. W. Brown	T. Williams	W. Jacques	C. W. Westerdale
1930/31	E. W. Brown	T. Williams	W. Jacques	C. W. Westerdale
1931/32	E. W. Brown	T. Williams	W. Jacques	J. Parkin
1932/33	E. W. Brown	T. Williams	W. Jacques	H. Binks
1933/34	W. A. Crockford	T. Williams	J. Gordon	H. Binks
1934/35	W. A. Crockford	E. E. Haysom	J. Gordon	E. Tattersfield
1935/36	W. A. Crockford	E. E. Haysom	C. W. Westerdale	E. Tattersfield
1936/37	W.Crockford /E. Mowforth	E. E. Haysom	C. W. Westerdale	E. Tattersfield / W. McWatt
1937/38	E. E. Mowforth	E. E. Haysom	C. W. Westerdale	W...McWatt
1938/39	E. E. Mowforth	E. E. Haysom	C. W. Westerdale	J. Oliver
1939/40	E. E. Mowforth	E. E. Haysom	C. W. Westerdale	J. Naylor
1945/46	E. E. Mowforth	E. E. Haysom	S. Adams	W. McWatt
1946/47	E. E. Mowforth	E. E. Haysom	J. Oliver	W. McWatt
1947/48	E. E. Mowforth	A. J. Harper (acting)	J. Oliver	A. Dockar
1948/49	T. C. Williams	S. Pleasants	E. Jacobs	W. Jackson / J. Ramsden

The Robins

Season	Chairman	Secretary/Chief Executive	Trainer/coach	Captain
1949/50	F. Robinson	H. W. Bentley	E. Jacobs	J. Ramsden
1950/51	W. Spaven	A. Shaw / T. C. Williams	E. Jacobs / W. McWatt	A. Dockar / R. Mills
1951/52	W. Spaven	T. C. Williams	W.McWatt / B.Knowleden	A. Dockar / B.Knowleden
1952/53	J. R. Rawson	T. C. Williams	B. Knowleden	B. Knowleden
1953/54	A. J. Snelling	T. C. Williams	B. Knowleden / J.Feetham	B. Knowleden
1954/55	A. J. Snelling	T. C. Williams	J. Feetham	B. Knowleden / J. Tong
1955/56	A. J. Snelling	T. C. Williams	J. Feetham	J. Tong
1956/57	A. J. Snelling	T. C. Williams	J. Ramsden	J. Tong / H. Ellerby
1957/58	A. J. Snelling / W. Spaven	T. C. Williams	J. Ramsden / C. Hutton	H. Ellerby / D. Holland
1958/59	W. Spaven	T. C. Williams	C. Hutton	J. Mageen / W. Riley
1959/60	W. Spaven	T. C. Williams	C. Hutton	A. Ackerley
1960/61	W. Spaven	T. C. Williams	C. Hutton	J. Jenkin / H. Poole
1961/62	W. Spaven	T. C. Williams	C. Hutton	H. Poole
1962/63	W. Spaven	T. C. Williams	C. Hutton	H. Poole / C. Kellett
1963/64	W. Spaven	T. C. Williams	C. Hutton	H. Poole
1964/65	W. Spaven	T. C. Williams	C. Hutton	H. Poole
1965/66	W. Spaven	T. C. Williams	C. Hutton	H. Poole / F. Foster
1966/67	W. Spaven	T. C. Williams	C. Hutton	F. Foster
1967/68	W. Spaven	T. C. Williams	C. Hutton	F. Foster
1968/69	W. Spaven	T. C. Williams	C. Hutton	F. Foster / J. Moore
1969/70	W. Spaven	R. Turner	C. Hutton	J. Moore / R. Millward
1970/71	W. Spaven	R. Turner	J. Whiteley	R. Millward
1971/72	W. Spaven	R. Turner	J. Whiteley / A. Bunting	R. Millward
1972/73	W. Spaven	R. Turner	A. Bunting	R. Millward
1973/74	W. Spaven	R. Turner	A. Bunting	R. Millward
1974/75	W. Spaven	R. Turner	A. Bunting	R. Millward
1975/76	W. Spaven	R. Turner	A. Bunting / H. Poole	R. Millward
1976/77	W. Land	R. Turner	H. Poole / R. Millward	R. Millward
1977/78	W. Land	R. Turner	R. Millward	R. Millward
1978/79	W. Land	R. Turner	R. Millward	R. Millward
1979/80	W. Land	R. Turner	R. Millward	R. Millward
1980/81	W. Land	R. Turner	R. Millward	L. Casey
1981/82	W. Land	R. Turner	R. Millward	L. Casey
1982/83	W. Land	R. Turner	R. Millward	L. Casey
1983/84	C. Hutton	R. Turner	R. Millward	L. Casey
1984/85	C. Hutton	R. Turner	R. Millward	D. Watkinson
1985/86	C. Hutton	R. Turner	R. Millward	D. Watkinson
1986/87	C. Hutton	R. Turner	R. Millward	D. Watkinson
1987/88	C. Hutton	R. Turner	R. Millward	D. Watkinson / M. Smith

Appendices

Season	Chairman	Secretary/ Chief Executive	Trainer/coach	Captain
1988/89	C. Hutton	R. Turner	R. Millward	M. Smith
1989/90	C. Hutton	R. Turner	R. Millward	M. Smith
1990/91	M. West	R. Turner	R. Millward	M. Smith
1991/92	M. Gold	R. Turner	G. Fairbairn	W. Parker
1992/93	P. T. Lowe	R. Turner	G. Fairbairn	W. Parker
1993/94	P. T. Lowe	R. Turner	G. Fairbairn	W. Parker
1994/95	B. Lilley	R. Turner	S. Crooks	C. Harrison
1995/96	B. Lilley	R. Turner	S. Crooks	S. Stewart
1996	B. Lilley	R. Turner	S. Crooks	S. Stewart
1997	B. Lilley	R. Turner	S. Crooks /D. Harrison	M. Fletcher /W. Parker
1998	B. Lilley	R. Turner	D. Harrison	W. Parker
1999	B. Lilley	R. Turner	D. Harrison	W. Taewa
2000	B. Lilley/D. Robinson	R. Turner 3	D. Harrison	W. Taewa
2001	D. Robinson/W. Smith	N.Halafihi 4	G. Wilkinson	W. Taewa
2002	W. Smith	N.Halafihi 4	G. Wilkinson	C. Charles
2003	C. McNicol	N.Halafihi 4	S. Linnane	N. Pinkney /A. Seibold
2004	C. McNicol	N.Halafihi 4	M. Reilly/M. Hall	A. Seibold
2005	N. Hudgell	P. Lakin	H. Howard/J. Morgan	J. Webster
2006	N. Hudgell	P. Lakin	J. Morgan	J. Webster
2007	N. Hudgell	P. Lakin	J. Morgan	J. Webster
2008	N. Hudgell	P. Lakin/M. Blanchard	J. Morgan	M. Vella
2009	N. Hudgell	N. Hudgell	J. Morgan	M. Vella
2010	N. Hudgell	N. Hudgell	J. Morgan	M. Vella
2011	N. Hudgell	M. Smith	J. Morgan	M. Vella
2012	N. Hudgell	M. Smith	C. Sandercock	B. Galea
2013	N. Hudgell	M. Smith	C. Sandercock	M. Dobson
2014	N. Hudgell	M. Smith	C. Sandercock /C. Chester	T. Burns /J. Hodgson
2015	N. Hudgell	M. Smith	C. Chester	T. Campese
2016	N. Hudgell	M. Smith	C.Chester /J. Webster	T. Campese

Notes

1 the position of chairman was introduced in 1904; prior to that the President was in day-to-day charge of the club

2 Harry Shann is generally recognised as the clubs first official trainer, as the role was then known

3 Ron Turner continued in his role as Company Secretary until early in the 2001/02 season

4 the role of Chief Executive was introduced in 2000, Mark Jackson acting on an interim basis until Nick Halafihi was appointed

Club-by-Club

Opponents	Home P	W	D	L	Ab	For	Agst	Neutral P	W	D	L	Ab	For	Agst	Away P	W	D	L	Ab	For	Agst	Total P	W	D	L	Ab	For	Agst
International opponents																												
Australia	11	3	0	8	0	113	236															11	3	0	8	0	113	236
New Zealand	7	3	0	4	0	81	99															7	3	0	4	0	81	99
Queensland	1	1	0	0	0	8	6															1	1	0	0	0	8	6
Professional clubs																												
Actor & Willesden	1	1	0	0	0	4	2								1	1	0	0	0	10	8	2	2	0	0	0	14	10
Altrincham	1	1	0	0	0	43	0								1	1	0	0	0	13	0	2	2	0	0	0	56	0
Barrow (Raiders)	33	26	0	7	0	729	353								31	12	2	17	0	424	535	64	38	2	24	0	1153	888
Batley (Bulldogs)	74	51	7	15	1	1160	530								75	25	5	45	0	792	986	149	76	12	60	1	1952	1516
Birkenhead Wanderers	1	1	0	0	0	16	7								1	0	1	0	0	3	3	2	1	1	0	0	19	10
Blackpool[1]	9	9	0	0	0	288	69								9	6	0	3	0	164	142	18	15	0	3	0	452	211
Bradford (1899-1906)	8	6	0	2	0	65	52	1	0	0	1	0	5	8	7	0	0	7	0	15	64	16	6	0	10	0	85	124
Bradford Northern (Bulls)	90	67	1	22	0	1789	999								88	34	5	49	0	1144	1531	178	101	6	71	0	2933	2530
Bramley	73	65	1	7	0	1774	481								69	40	3	26	0	985	704	142	105	4	33	0	2759	1185
Brighouse Rangers	4	4	0	0	0	80	2								5	2	1	2	0	20	19	9	6	1	2	0	100	21
Broughton, Belle Vue	20	13	1	6	0	236	142	1	1	0	0	0	10	6	23	5	0	18	0	134	363	44	19	1	24	0	380	511
Cardiff	1	1	0	0	0	39	13								1	1	0	0	0	10	7	2	2	0	0	0	49	20
Carlisle	5	4	0	1	0	146	35								4	4	0	0	0	102	80	9	8	0	1	0	248	115
Castleford (1896-1906)	3	2	0	1	0	25	10								3	1	0	2	0	16	7	6	3	0	3	0	41	17
Catalan, inc UTC	81	58	2	21	0	1572	961	5	4	0	1	0	83	66	81	24	6	51	0	1072	1554	167	86	8	73	0	2727	2581
Castleford	12	5	0	7	0	306	263								11	4	0	7	0	204	305	23	9	0	14	0	510	568
Celtic Crusaders	4	4	0	0	0	174	56								3	2	0	1	0	94	58	7	6	0	1	0	268	114
Chorley[2]	5	5	0	0	0	248	46								6	6	0	0	0	340	95	11	11	0	0	0	588	141
Coventry	1	1	0	0	0	53	3								1	0	1	0	0	16	16	2	1	1	0	0	69	19
Dewsbury (Rams)	76	63	3	10	0	1446	581								74	27	4	43	0	712	902	150	90	7	53	0	2158	1483
Doncaster	37	32	1	4	0	1050	349								36	26	1	9	0	852	556	73	58	2	13	0	1902	905
Ebbw Vale	3	3	0	0	0	78	24								3	2	0	1	0	27	21	6	5	0	1	0	105	45
Featherstone Rovers	90	60	6	24	0	1571	1029	1	1	0	0	0	25	12	90	40	2	48	0	1285	1497	181	101	8	72	0	2881	2538
Fulham[3]	15	10	0	5	0	435	239								14	9	0	5	0	493	305	29	19	0	10	0	928	544
Gateshead Thunder	2	2	0	0	0	88	24								3	3	0	0	0	84	14	5	5	0	0	0	172	38
Halifax	78	53	1	24	0	1276	778	2	2	0	0	0	34	15	79	21	4	54	0	773	1484	159	76	5	78	0	2083	2277
Holbeck	2	2	0	0	0	22	2								2	2	0	0	0	20	7	4	4	0	0	0	42	9
Huddersfield (Giants)	88	50	8	30	0	1366	1099	5	2	0	3	0	44	75	87	17	3	66	0	885	1932	180	69	11	99	1	2295	3106
Hull F.C.	105	56	2	47	0	1340	1271	15	10	0	5	0	249	247	104	37	8	59	0	1013	1309	224	103	10	111	0	2602	2827
Hunslet, New Hunslet	86	62	2	21	0	1485	754	3	2	0	1	0	75	33	93	35	2	56	0	1252	1408	182	99	4	78	1	2812	2195
Keighley (Cougars)	87	69	0	18	0	1727	633								79	35	2	42	0	943	978	166	104	2	60	0	2670	1611
Lancaster	1	1	0	0	0	12	3								1	1	0	0	0	8	5	2	2	0	0	0	20	8
Leeds Parish Church	2	2	0	0	0	11	2								2	1	1	0	0	8	4	4	3	1	0	0	19	6
Leeds (Rhinos)	99	47	2	50	0	1274	1306	5	2	1	2	0	55	88	108	17	0	89	0	909	2284	212	66	3	141	2	2238	3678
Leigh (Centurions)	61	42	0	18	1	1234	725	2	0	0	2	0	32	64	60	21	1	38	0	834	1123	123	63	2	58	1	2100	1912

Appendices

Opponents	Home P	W	D	L	Ab	For	Agst	Neutral P	W	D	L	Ab	For	Agst	Away P	W	D	L	Ab	For	Agst	Total P	W	D	L	Ab	For	Agst
Liverpool City (1906-07)	1	1	0	0	0	41	9								1	1	0	0	0	53	2	2	2	0	0	0	94	11
Liversedge	2	2	0	0	0	23	4								2	1	0	1	0	17	4	4	3	0	1	0	40	8
London Skolars	3	3	0	0	0	222	26								3	3	0	0	0	130	20	6	6	0	0	0	352	46
Manningham	3	2	0	1	0	29	14								2	1	0	1	0	21	8	5	3	0	2	0	50	22
Merthyr Tydfil	2	2	0	0	0	105	20								1	1	0	0	0	8	3	3	3	0	0	0	113	23
Millom	3	3	0	0	0	75	2								1	1	0	0	0	9	7	4	4	0	0	0	84	9
Morecambe	1	1	0	0	0	18	0								1	0	0	1	0	4	11	2	1	0	1	0	22	11
Newcastle	2	2	0	0	0	75	10								2	1	0	1	0	15	2	4	3	0	1	0	90	12
Nottingham City	1	1	0	0	0	54	4								2	2	0	0	0	158	6	3	3	0	0	0	212	10
Oldham (Roughyeds)	54	31	5	18	0	968	657	4	1	1	1	1	60	54	52	13	0	39	0	577	905	110	45	6	58	1	1605	1616
Pontefract	2	2	0	0	0	66	8								1	0	0	1	0	3	7	3	2	0	1	0	69	15
Radcliffe	1	1	0	0	0	71	0								1	1	0	0	0	16	0	2	2	0	0	0	87	0
Rochdale Hornets	38	30	1	7	0	850	368								41	18	2	21	0	708	658	79	48	3	28	0	1558	1026
Runcorn (1897-1918)	3	2	0	1	0	26	20								3	1	0	2	0	14	32	6	3	0	3	0	40	52
St Helens	64	42	2	20	0	1072	857	5	2	0	3	0	60	149	63	7	0	56	0	640	1577	132	51	2	79	0	1772	2583
St Helens Recs	13	10	0	3	0	198	106								12	4	0	8	0	79	165	25	14	0	11	0	277	271
Salford (Red Devils)	59	38	4	17	0	957	738								53	15	2	36	0	685	995	112	53	6	53	0	1642	1733
Sheffield Eagles	11	7	1	3	0	269	174								9	4	0	5	0	195	242	20	11	1	8	0	464	416
South Wales	1	1	0	0	0	40	16								1	1	0	0	0	70	8	2	2	0	0	0	110	24
Stockport	1	0	1	0	0	18	0								1	0	1	0	0			2	0	2	0	0	2	2
Streatham & Mitcham	2	0	0	2	0	18	36								2	0	0	2	0	3	33	4	0	0	3	0	21	69
Swinton (Lions)	43	36	0	6	1	901	359	2	2	0	0	0	32	19	35	15	1	19	0	368	439	80	53	1	25	1	1301	817
Toulouse Spacers	1	1	0	0	0	44	0								1	0	0	0	0			2	1	0	0	0	44	0
Treherbert															1	1	0	0	0	22	10	1	1	0	0	0	22	10
Wakefield Trinity (Wildcats)	101	66	3	32	0	1682	1049	2	1	0	1	0	29	30	105	32	7	66	0	1306	1901	208	99	10	99	0	3017	2980
Warrington (Wolves)	62	41	4	17	0	1048	814	3	2	0	1	0	62	52	62	11	2	51	1	698	1304	127	54	6	69	1	1808	2170
Whitehaven	30	20	2	8	0	843	380								27	6	0	20	1	326	602	57	26	2	28	1	1169	982
Widnes (Vikings)	72	43	6	23	0	1142	769	4	1	0	3	0	48	61	70	22	0	48	0	738	1164	146	66	6	74	0	1928	1994
Wigan (Warriors)	66	33	4	29	0	890	1049	5	0	0	5	0	37	100	63	11	2	50	0	636	1615	134	44	6	84	0	1563	2764
Wigan Highfield[4]	16	13	1	2	0	402	117	1	1	0	0	0	4	10	15	8	0	7	0	388	168	32	22	1	9	0	790	285
Workington Town	24	18	0	6	0	503	267								28	9	0	18	0	389	441	52	27	0	24	0	892	708
York (City Knights)	81	66	2	13	0	1518	632								81	51	2	27	0	1268	934	162	117	4	41	0	2790	1576
Junior clubs	21	21	0	0	0	836	90								6	6	0	0	0	225	53	27	27	0	0	0	1061	143
Totals	2050	1424	79	554	4	38350	21779	66	33	2	30	1	944	1089	2001	710	75	1214	2	25427	33624	4128	2167	156	1798	7	64721	56492

1 Blackpool Borough/Springfield Borough/Chorley Borough/Trafford Borough/Blackpool Gladiators

2 Chorley Borough/Chorley Chieftains/Lancashire Lynx/Chorley Lynx

3 Fulham / London Crusaders/London Broncos/Harlequins/London

4 Wigan Highfield/London Highfield/Liverpool Stanley/Liverpool City/Huyton/Runcorn Highfield/Highfield/Prescott Panthers

Barnsley Utd, Beverley, Brookland Rowers, Dewsbury Celtic, Dudley Hill, Eastmoor, Ellenborough Rangers, Featherstone Lions, Fleetwood, Hensingham, Hull Marlborough, Ideal Iöberg, Langworthy Juniors, Leigh Miners Rangers, Maryport, Mayfield, Morley, Outwood Church, Pilkington Recs, Queens, Siddal, Thornhill, Wath Brow Hornets, Wigan Rangers, York Acorn

The Robins

Players' directory - 1897-98 to 2015

Player's name	Position	First	Last	Start	Sub	Total	Goals	D/g	Tries	Pts	Notes
Ablett	Forward	12/30/22	*	1	0	1	0	0	0	0	
Ackerley, Alvin	Hooker	1/24/59	4/23/62	100	0	100	0	0	3	9	Eng/GB intl
Ackrill	Forward	2/15/19	5/10/19	8	0	8	0	0	1	3	
Ackroyd, Alan	Forward	3/3/76	10/10/76	22	0	22	15	0	2	36	
Adams, Jonathan	Three-quarter	8/21/94	9/7/97	45	7	52	0	0	25	100	
Adamson, J.N 'Fred'	Forward	9/27/02	*	1	0	1	0	0	0	0	
Agar, Allan	Half-back	11/28/76	5/3/80	100	13	113	16	17	32	145	
Aitchison, Mike	Centre	4/7/74	4/10/74	0	2	2	0	0	0	0	
Aizue, Mikali	Prop-forward	6/1/03	8/21/09	78	81	159	0	0	29	116	PNG intl
Allen, Kieran	Stand-off	7/21/96	9/1/96	7	0	7	0	0	3	12	Loan from W'field only
Allen, W	Half-back	12/6/13	4/21/19	2	0	2	0	0	0	0	
Allgood, Mitch	Prop-forward	2/8/15	current	11	2	13	0	0	2	8	Australian
Allinson, C.W	Forward	1/25/08	10/24/08	13	0	13	0	0	0	0	
Anchors, Tim	2nd row	4/27/80	*	1	0	1	0	0	0	0	USA gridiron player
Anderson, Chris	Wing	11/4/84	11/25/84	1	1	2	0	0	0	0	Australian intl
Anderson, Matt	2nd row	8/29/51	2/6/54	60	0	60	0	0	4	12	
Anderson, Peter	2nd row	9/25/91	10/20/91	0	2	2	0	0	0	0	Australian
Anderson, Richard	Wing	4/16/01	4/29/01	2	1	3	0	0	1	4	
Andrews, Barry	Full-back	10/24/76	12/10/76	1	3	4	4	0	0	8	Australian
Andrews, Dean	Wing/2nd row	12/27/99	9/11/05	48	49	97	0	0	15	60	
Annetts, Walter	2nd row	11/18/50	4/28/51	15	0	15	0	0	2	6	Welsh
Ansell, H	Three-quarter	10/12/05	10/11/06	4	0	4	0	0	1	3	
Anson, C	Scrum-half	3/16/46	3/23/46	2	0	2	0	0	0	0	
Archer, J	Centre	1/17/53	*	1	0	1	0	0	0	0	
Armitage, Ron	Half-back	9/22/51	3/7/53	37	0	37	3	0	7	27	
Armstrong, Colin	Prop-forward	1/8/89	8/19/90	41	12	53	24	2	6	74	
Ascott, B.S 'Dicky'	Wing	1/13/12	4/20/12	13	0	13	0	0	4	12	
Asquith, C.W	Forward	4/10/02	4/19/02	3	0	3	0	0	0	0	
Aston, Jon	Prop-forward	12/27/99	8/22/04	75	25	100	0	0	13	52	Welsh intl
Atkins, Gary	Centre/half-back	9/4/94	8/30/98	113	6	119	0	1	79	317	
Atkinson, Sid	Back-row fwd	8/25/45	9/18/49	86	0	86	0	0	6	18	
Atkinson, T	Loose-forward	10/16/37	*	1	0	1	0	0	0	0	
Austin, Gilbert	Wing	1/25/19	1/7/28	347	0	347	29	0	163	547	
Austin, G.P 'Pat'	Three-quarter	4/8/50	4/23/56	75	0	75	0	0	20	60	Nephew - Gilbert
Austin, Greg	Centre	9/17/89	9/12/90	38	0	38	0	0	45	180	Australian
Bailey, Ryan	Prop-forward	2/15/15	*	0	1	1	0	0	1	4	Eng/GB intl
Ball, Damian	Centre/loose-fwd	8/1/04	9/26/04	8	0	8	0	0	2	8	
Ballantyne, Greg	Wing	8/19/67	5/2/70	36	3	39	0	0	12	36	Scottish
Bangs, Peter	Back-row fwd	9/21/57	9/2/59	20	0	20	0	0	0	0	
Banks, G	Centre	1/31/53	3/7/53	2	0	2	0	0	0	0	
Banks, R	Forward	11/23/07	12/7/07	3	0	3	0	0	0	0	
Barber, Graham	Three-quarter	2/18/01	4/8/01	1	1	2	0	0	0	0	
Barker, Dwayne	Utility player	7/25/04	10/8/06	28	20	48	0	0	8	32	
Barker, George	Forward	10/4/47	4/11/52	60	0	60	14	0	10	58	
Barkworth, Julian	Three-quarter	9/22/91	4/17/94	76	4	80	4	0	20	88	
Barlow, R H	Forward	4/8/08	12/26/08	8	0	8	0	0	0	0	
Barnard, Ted	Prop-forward	10/20/72	2/17/74	25	7	32	0	0	3	9	
Barraclough, Alf	Centre	11/23/46	9/19/53	45	0	45	1	0	5	17	Brother of Jim
Barraclough, Jim	Centre/2nd row	8/21/48	10/30/54	161	0	161	0	0	31	93	Eng intl
Barraclough, Lee J	Three-quarter	12/26/73	2/17/74	1	2	3	0	0	0	0	Son of Jim

Appendices

Player's name	Position	First	Last	Start	Sub	Total	Goals	D/g	Tries	Pts	Notes
			KR Appearances				**Scoring**				
Barron, Fred	Wing	3/21/08	12/27/09	33	0	33	0	0	16	48	
Barry, Jim	Half-back	9/14/01	11/20/09	208	0	208	9	0	41	141	Welsh
Bartliffe, Alan	Centre	9/17/55	11/24/56	19	0	19	2	0	3	13	
Barwick, A	Wing	11/3/23	2/9/29	10	0	10	0	0	0	0	
Bateman, George W	Wing	8/29/25	4/21/30	145	0	145	0	0	65	195	
Bateman, Karl	Prop-forward	7/21/96	4/20/97	0	9	9	0	0	0	0	
Bateman, T	Half-back	12/6/13	10/16/20	12	0	12	0	0	1	3	
Bath, John	Prop-forward	2/1/64	12/11/65	43	0	43	0	0	2	6	
Batten, William (jnr)	Three-quarter	1/31/31	2/2/35	95	0	95	0	0	23	69	Son of GB intl Billy
Batty, Chris	Hooker	9/10/95	9/24/95	3	0	3	0	0	0	0	
Bauer, Andreas	Utility back	3/9/07	9/15/07	11	2	13	0	0	6	24	Samoan intl
Bays, B.E 'Sid'	Forward	4/3/56	*	1	0	1	0	0	0	0	
Beadle, T	Forward	21/10/1899	1/20/00	3	0	3	0	0	0	0	
Beal, A	Wing	11/17/00	1/19/01	5	0	5	0	0	2	6	
Beall, Malcolm	Prop-forward	3/31/86	10/29/89	57	13	70	0	0	5	20	
Bean, G E	Wing	1/28/33	*	1	0	1	0	0	0	0	
Beauchamp, Keith	Wing	7/15/98	9/20/98	10	0	10	0	0	5	20	Australian
Beaumont, Harry	Half-back/wing	11/4/33	1/26/46	91	0	91	9	0	21	81	Brother - Louis
Beaumont, Louis	3-qtr/2nd row	9/23/33	4/24/46	202	0	202	0	0	15	45	
Beaumont, Richard	Prop-forward	4/25/11	9/8/13	1	17	18	0	0	1	4	
Beaumont, W 'Bill'	Three-quarter	3/4/39	4/24/48	75	0	75	2	0	29	91	Brother - Louis
Beck, Brian	Centre/half-back	8/29/53	4/22/57	74	0	74	28	0	9	83	
Bedford, Arthur	Back-row fwd	1/5/57	4/12/57	10	0	10	0	0	0	0	
Bedford, Ernie	Back-row fwd	1/14/39	10/5/47	43	0	43	0	0	9	27	
Bedworth, M	Forward	12/30/05	1/6/06	3	0	3	0	0	0	0	
Beetson, Arthur	Forward	10/11/68	12/25/68	12	0	12	0	0	1	3	Australian intl
Beharrell, Matt	Scrum-half	4/1/13	*	1	0	1	0	0	0	0	
Bell, George	Wing	11/8/02	1/2/04	9	0	9	0	0	2	6	
Bell, Ian	Three-quarter	3/23/03	4/18/03	4	0	4	0	0	3	12	
Bell, Steve	Stand-off	4/27/80	*	0	1	1	0	0	0	0	
Bennett, Scott	Stand-off	2/6/00	*	0	1	1	0	0	0	0	
Bent, W	Forward	10/12/05	4/16/06	23	0	23	0	0	0	0	
Bibb, Kyle	Prop-forward	7/12/09	8/2/09	0	2	2	0	0	0	0	Loan from Castleford only
Bibby, Mike	Three-quarter	4/20/92	6/6/99	81	19	100	0	0	30	120	
Bielby, Frank	2nd row	1/25/19	2/18/28	276	0	276	0	0	78	234	
Biggs, W	Forward	12/21/07	4/24/09	40	0	40	1	0	0	2	
Bilton, H	Prop-forward	1/1/47	3/22/47	4	0	4	0	0	0	0	
Binks, Harold	Forward	12/8/23	3/31/34	332	0	332	0	0	21	63	
Birrell, Ross	Centre	9/1/73	1/13/74	18	0	18	14	0	2	34	Australian
Bishop, David	Half-back/lse-fwd	8/28/88	12/26/91	60	4	64	1	1	24	99	Welsh RU & RL intl
Blackburn, John	Forward	4/7/51	4/19/54	10	0	10	0	0	1	3	
Blackmore, J	Forward	9/3/10	3/18/12	62	0	62	0	0	6	18	
Blackmore, Mike	Three-quarter	9/9/61	3/4/67	190	0	190	6	0	96	300	
Blair, Maurice	Utility	2/8/15	current	30	2	32	0	0	5	20	Australian
Blake, Matthew	Prop-forward	8/15/04	9/5/04	1	1	2	0	0	0	0	
Blakey, G	Wing	11/2/57	11/9/57	2	0	2	0	0	0	0	
Blanchard, L	Forward	3/12/32	9/1/45	63	0	63	1	0	12	38	
Blanchard, Mark	Three-quarter	7/4/99	9/25/05	38	36	74	0	0	17	68	
Blazier, J	Wing	10/25/30	10/31/31	8	0	8	0	0	1	3	
Bloodworth, C F	Three-quarter	4/13/03	1/28/05	2	0	2	0	0	0	0	
Blossom, Frank	Front row fwd	1/23/32	3/31/34	76	0	76	0	0	7	21	

The Robins

Player's name	Position	First	KR Appearances Last	Start	Sub	Total	Goals	Scoring D/g	Tries	Pts	Notes
Boagey, Frank	Forward	9/25/20	11/3/27	218	0	218	0	0	24	72	
Boagey, R 'Bob'	Forward	11/29/19	5/7/21	56	0	56	2	0	2	10	Brother - Frank
Boltman, Pierre	Forward	11/30/11	4/8/13	37	0	37	0	0	7	21	South African
Bonner, Ted	Back-row fwd	8/19/61	9/19/64	70	2	72	0	0	5	15	
Booth, Arthur	Half-back	9/7/07	10/23/09	70	0	70	2	0	31	97	
Booth, Simon	2nd row	1/2/00	3/5/00	1	7	8	0	0	0	0	
Botica, Tony	2nd row	9/3/89	3/25/90	26	0	26	0	0	17	68	New Zealander
Boudebza, John	Hooker	2/15/15	current	16	11	27	0	0	3	12	French
Bourton, Tom	2nd row	10/29/55	12/14/57	34	0	34	0	0	2	6	
Boustead, Kerry	Winger	9/21/86	4/26/87	19	1	20	0	0	7	28	Australian intl
Bovill, Jamie	Prop-forward	8/22/99	9/18/05	66	50	116	0	0	22	88	
Bowering, H	Wing/back-row	11/9/46	4/18/53	13	0	13	0	0	2	6	
Boxall	2nd row	8/26/39	*	1	0	1	0	0	0	0	
Boyd, A	Wing	10/30/09	2/12/10	3	0	3	0	0	1	3	
Boylen, Frank 'Patsy'	Forward	4/10/14	12/27/19	38	0	38	0	0	1	3	
Bradley, Aaron	Forward	8/20/06	*	0	1	1	0	0	0	0	
Bradshaw, Bill	Hooker	3/26/49	10/29/49	10	0	10	0	0	0	0	
Bradshaw, W 'Billy'	Wing	9/26/14	3/22/22	84	0	84	94	0	20	248	
Brady, H	Hooker	9/17/49	*	1	0	1	0	0	0	0	
Brain, J.C 'Slasher'	Wing/forward	10/19/07	5/3/19	180	0	180	3	0	74	228	WW1 PoW
Bratley, H	Centre	9/3/45	4/20/46	22	0	22	0	0	7	21	
Brear, S	Half-back	11/18/11	*	1	0	1	0	0	0	0	
Brett, E	Full-back/3-qtr	10/22/21	4/11/25	18	0	18	3	0	3	15	
Brien, H	Utility back	10/18/30	4/1/33	32	0	32	0	0	1	3	
Briggs, Dennis	Utility back	9/5/51	4/19/54	26	0	26	29	0	3	67	
Brigham, W	Half-back	3/18/26	11/26/27	7	0	7	0	0	1	3	
Brindle, Fred	Loose-forward	1/19/29	12/31/32	109	0	109	6	0	12	48	
Briscoe, Shaun	Full-back	2/2/08	9/17/11	100	0	100	0	0	30	120	England intl
Britton, Ben	Forward	1/19/24	12/9/33	331	0	331	3	0	17	57	
Broadhurst, Mark	Prop-forward	9/25/83	3/25/87	96	0	96	0	0	14	56	NZ intl
Broderick, R	Half-back	10/15/21	4/27/22	14	0	14	0	0	1	3	
Bromham, A	3-qtr/half-back	10/25/19	11/22/19	5	0	5	0	0	0	0	
Brook, Brian	Stand-off/wing	10/3/67	10/20/72	46	4	50	0	0	10	30	
Brookfield, Laurie	Front row fwd	12/26/51	12/26/58	69	0	69	0	0	8	24	
Brooks, Matty	Half-back	8/2/06	3/31/07	3	2	5	1	0	1	6	
Brosnan	Centre	1/31/48	*	1	0	1	0	0	0	0	
Brown, Alex	Winger	3/3/13	9/14/13	16	0	16	0	0	9	36	
Brown, Charlie	Forward	4/18/31	3/4/39	65	0	65	0	0	2	6	
Brown, Colin	Half-back	9/3/95	11/26/95	11	0	11	0	1	4	17	
Brown, Daniel	Half-back	3/1/98	9/20/98	15	15	30	1	0	4	18	Australian
Brown, E W	Three-quarter	9/14/07	10/5/07	3	0	3	0	0	1	3	KR chairman 1919-34
Brown, Gary	Utility-back	12/13/92	7/21/96	67	7	74	0	0	51	204	
Brown, J	Winger	11/10/45	4/24/46	6	0	6	0	0	0	0	
Brown, Joe	Loose-forward	1/24/71	4/27/75	57	2	59	17	1	9	62	
Brown, Sam	Stand-off	8/21/48	8/29/49	8	0	8	0	0	2	6	
Brown, T 'Harry'	Utility player	12/25/13	10/8/21	27	0	27	0	0	5	15	
Broxholme, H	Three-qtr/Stand-off	2/7/14	4/25/14	9	0	9	0	0	1	3	
Buckle, Terry	Full-back	9/5/53	1/11/58	82	0	82	144	0	2	294	
Bullock, H	Forward	11/15/19	4/3/20	14	0	14	0	0	3	9	
Bunting, Arthur	Scrum-half	9/19/59	9/23/73	231	6	237	1	0	68	206	KR coach 1972-74
Burke, Ernest	Three-quarter	8/21/48	4/27/49	19	0	19	1	0	5	17	
Burke, Greg	Back row fwd	2/8/15	9/27/15	13	9	22	0	0	0	0	Loan from Wigan only

Appendices

Player's name	Position	First	Last	Start	Sub	Total	Goals	D/g	Tries	Pts	Notes
			KR Appearances				Scoring				
Burns, Travis	Stand-off	3/3/13	9/14/14	49	0	49	85	2	8	204	Australian
Burr, G	Scrum-half/wing	9/17/49	3/10/51	5	0	5	0	0	0	0	
Burton, Chris	2nd row	2/14/81	1/2/89	207	26	233	0	0	25	89	GB intl
Burwell, Alan	3-qtr/Stand-off	4/7/62	3/21/76	222	4	226	2	0	106	322	GB intl
Burwell, Brian B	Three-quarter	3/14/59	10/23/65	100	0	100	4	0	10	38	Elder brother of Alan
Busby, David	2nd row	9/7/86	10/26/86	5	2	7	0	0	2	8	
Busby, Dean	Back-row fwd	5/4/03	9/28/03	6	4	10	0	0	1	4	
Butler, E	Stand-off	9/5/51	*	1	0	1	0	0	0	0	
Cain, Mark	Half-back	3/24/02	9/15/02	17	9	26	0	7	8	39	
Cairns, J	Winger	9/29/34	10/6/34	2	0	2	0	0	0	0	
Callaghan, Darren	Half-back	12/3/00	2/13/01	6	1	7	0	0	1	4	
Calland, Matthew	Centre	2/1/04	7/18/04	12	2	14	0	0	6	24	England intl
Calvert, C	Wing	9/1/06	12/8/06	3	0	3	0	0	0	0	
Campese, Terry	Half-back	2/8/15	current	17	0	17	0	0	2	8	Australian intl
Carde, W J	Half-back	9/6/02	4/18/03	22	0	22	1	0	1	5	
Cardy, Ray	2nd row	3/31/72	4/3/72	2	0	2	0	0	0	0	
Carlile, Keal	Hooker	2/26/12	2/15/15	6	31	37	0	0	1	4	
Carmichael, Alf 'Bunker'	Full-b'k	4/20/01	1/25/19	338	0	338	723	0	12	1482	Eng intl
Carmichael, Andrew	Loose-fwd	12/30/22	10/13/28	76	0	76	1	0	12	38	Nephew of Alf
Carmichael, George	Full-back	9/26/29	12/8/34	180	0	180	288	0	17	627	England intl; son of Alf
Caro, Omari	Wing	3/3/13	9/14/14	23	0	23	0	0	22	88	
Carr, Albert H	Centre	2/1/19	3/1/24	13	0	13	0	0	0	0	
Carter, Colin	Scrum-half	3/4/01	5/27/01	9	0	9	0	0	3	12	
Casey, Len	Forward	9/28/75	2/3/85	227	10	237	0	1	19	62	Eng/GB intl
Cator, Mike	Prop-forward	4/18/86	*	0	1	1	0	0	0	0	
Cavill, R.W	Scrum-half	12/14/07	1/2/09	13	0	13	0	0	1	3	
Cayzer, Jack	Loose-forward	8/29/36	9/2/39	114	0	114	0	0	29	87	
Chadburn, J	Centre	1/30/15	*	1	0	1	0	0	0	0	
Chalkley, Barry	Back-row fwd	4/15/53	4/18/55	8	0	8	0	0	1	3	Cousin - Dennis
Chalkley, Dennis	Full-back	1/24/53	4/30/53	17	0	17	24	0	1	51	
Chamberlain, Les	Loose-forward	3/9/63	11/30/63	22	0	22	0	0	2	6	
Chamberlain, Richard	Hooker	10/6/91	7/25/99	111	31	142	0	0	44	176	
Chambers, Anthony	Halfb'k/wing	4/5/99	1/23/01	13	7	20	0	0	3	12	
Chambers, Joe	Half-back	5/5/02	*	0	1	1	0	0	0	0	Brother of Anthony
Chambers, Joseph	Centre	12/15/34	1/5/35	3	0	3	0	0	0	0	
Chambers, O	Half-back/centre	9/3/04	1/1/06	25	0	25	1	0	1	5	
Chan, J	Forward	7/20/14	9/7/14	5	1	6	0	0	3	12	Loan from Hud'fld only
Chant, J	Centre	9/6/02	11/8/02	6	0	6	0	0	0	0	
Chapman, H	Half-back	3/18/22	4/18/22	7	0	7	1	0	0	2	
Chapman, Herbert	Centre/full-back	1/29/49	8/20/49	12	0	12	3	0	3	15	
Chapman, J	Wing	10/1/56	4/22/57	5	0	5	0	0	0	0	
Charles, Chris	Loose-forward	4/4/94	9/15/02	199	32	231	301	3	41	769	England intl
Charlesworth, Adam	Three-qtr	10/24/93	11/1/95	37	5	42	0	0	8	32	
Charlton, Gary	Loose-forward	10/2/88	12/7/88	1	2	3	0	0	0	0	
Charnley, Josh	Three-quarter	7/9/10	8/15/10	5	0	5	0	0	5	20	Loan from Wigan only
Chatfield, Gary	Scum-half	8/26/90	3/12/95	63	9	72	19	7	11	89	
Chester, Chris	Back-row fwd	2/10/07	8/1/08	28	8	36	0	0	5	20	KR coach 2014-2016
Chisholm, Dave	Half-back	7/24/15	9/27/15	7	0	7	0	0	3	12	Australian loan signing

The Robins

Player's name	Position	First	Last	Start	Sub	Total	Goals	D/g	Tries	Pts	Notes
Clark, Dean	Stand-off/lse-fwd	1/19/92	2/6/94	36	6	42	0	0	12	48	NZ intl
Clark, Garry	Winger	8/22/82	2/24/91	255	0	255	4	0	121	475	Eng/GB intl
Clark, Len 'Nobby'	2nd row	9/29/34	4/7/50	117	0	117	3	0	6	24	
Clark, Len A	Centre/back-row	12/26/59	8/28/65	81	2	83	69	0	12	174	
Clark, Peter	Centre	3/13/48	8/19/50	25	0	25	0	0	3	9	
Clark, W 'Mucker'	Utility player	9/6/13	4/10/26	163	0	163	5	0	66	208	
Clarkson, Geoff	Forward	9/3/78	1/27/80	43	8	51	0	0	3	9	
Clawson, Terry	Prop-forward	11/9/68	11/21/71	110	1	111	204	0	9	435	GB intl
Clinton, Joel	Prop-forward	2/27/10	8/5/12	44	15	59	0	0	2	8	Australian intl
Close, Chris	Centre/back-row	9/4/88	2/26/89	24	0	24	0	0	14	56	Australian intl
Cochrane, Steve	Hooker	5/29/00	5/25/03	19	10	29	0	0	4	16	
Cockayne, Ben	Full-back/wing	2/12/06	current	150	33	183	2	0	69	280	Also had spell with W'fld
Codd, A	Three-quarter	2/18/33	9/19/34	5	0	5	0	0	0	0	
Coggles, G.H	Forward	12/19/25	10/5/29	4	0	4	0	0	0	0	
Colbon, Liam	Wing	2/15/09	7/24/11	54	0	54	0	0	21	84	
Cole, Joseph	Forward	18/3/1899	11/15/02	35	0	35	0	0	4	12	
Collins, Andrew	Second-row	2/24/69	8/23/69	2	1	3	0	0	0	0	
Collinson, F	Back-row fwd	12/8/45	9/14/46	7	0	7	0	0	2	6	
Connell, J	Forward	12/7/01	2/27/02	10	0	10	0	0	1	3	
Conyers, Harry	Forward	9/7/07	9/10/10	34	0	34	0	0	0	0	
Cook, Graham	Full-back/wing	9/16/90	8/28/94	23	4	27	0	0	3	12	
Cook, J	Full-back/wing	1/26/07	1/1/08	5	0	5	0	0	0	0	
Cook, Jim	Centre	1/25/19	1/18/30	362	0	362	2	0	116	352	
Cook, Matt	2nd row	2/7/10	7/17/11	10	18	28	0	0	8	32	
Cooke, Paul	Stand-off	4/27/07	2/21/10	60	1	61	92	2	9	222	England intl
Cooke, Shaun	Stand-off	5/18/03	7/20/03	8	0	8	2	0	2	12	
Cooper, Barrie	Full-back	11/24/67	2/23/68	13	1	14	2	0	0	4	
Cooper, Colin	Half-back/l-fwd	9/2/61	4/14/72	136	14	150	3	0	41	129	
Cooper, D	Centre	3/13/20	1/7/22	9	0	9	0	0	1	3	
Cooper, H	Forward	1/7/22	2/4/22	2	0	2	0	0	0	0	
Cork, A	Half-back	4/9/04	2/11/05	4	0	4	0	0	0	0	
Cornforth, Bill	Wing	12/2/50	9/12/53	29	0	29	0	0	6	18	
Costigan, Neville	Back-row fwd	2/16/14	9/14/14	25	0	25	0	0	3	12	PNG intl
Coulman, Bill	Wing	11/21/59	4/29/60	22	0	22	0	0	10	30	
Coulson, Brian	Three-quarter	4/14/56	4/18/62	142	0	142	1	0	73	221	
Coulson, Gordon	Full-back/s-half	12/15/56	1/4/58	33	0	33	0	0	1	3	Brother - Brain
Coulson, T	Three-quarter	11/1/19	12/26/19	2	0	2	0	0	0	0	
Coult, Mick	3-qtr/2nd row	2/13/94	8/27/95	24	2	26	0	0	8	32	
Coupland, Phil	Utility back	10/9/65	10/28/77	205	9	214	26	0	69	259	
Couturier, Damien	Centre	8/21/05	9/10/06	26	2	28	86	0	9	208	French intl
Coverdale, Bob	Prop-forward	12/28/57	1/9/65	161	0	161	0	0	5	15	GB intl
Coverley, Bob	Hooker	11/9/68	2/24/69	9	0	9	0	0	0	0	
Cox, Jordan	2nd row	5/8/11	current	18	46	64	0	0	6	24	
Coyne, Charlie	Half-back/fwd	30/03/1898	3/3/00	2	0	2	0	0	0	0	
Crane, Mick	Loose-forward	12/16/79	12/6/80	15	3	18	0	0	4	12	
Crane, Mike	Stand-off	9/1/91	4/13/01	87	64	151	0	2	42	170	
Craven, B 'Bruce'	Half-back	12/17/10	3/16/12	45	0	45	1	0	15	47	
Creer, A	Forward	10/17/25	12/3/27	3	0	3	0	0	0	0	
Croft, Barry	Prop-forward	1/21/56	10/19/57	30	0	30	0	0	0	0	
Crooks, Steve	Prop-forward	4/2/78	2/3/84	96	13	109	0	0	4	13	KR coach 1994-97
Crosby, Tony	Hooker	11/28/70	1/27/71	7	0	7	0	0	1	3	
Crossman, Garret	Prop-forward	2/2/08	9/7/08	10	19	29	0	0	1	4	Australian

Appendices

Player's name	Position	First	Last	Start	Sub	Total	Goals	D/g	Tries	Pts	Notes
			KR Appearances				Scoring				
Cudmore, H	Wing	12/29/06	3/2/07	7	0	7	0	0	1	3	
Cunningham, John	Forward	8/16/75	3/2/80	32	5	37	0	3	7	24	England intl
Daddy, Maurice	Half-back	10/6/45	4/30/53	133	0	133	5	0	21	73	
Dakin, R.W	Three-quarter	10/23/09	3/5/10	14	0	14	0	0	2	6	
Dale, Harry 'Scrubber'	Scrum-h'f	3/27/26	9/3/38	306	0	306	11	0	88	286	
Daley, Paul	Scrum-half	11/28/70	3/28/73	49	10	59	1	0	7	23	
Danby, Bob	Wing	8/18/51	8/29/51	4	0	4	0	0	1	3	
Danby, R	Forward	1/25/19	2/8/19	3	0	3	0	0	0	0	
Danby, Rob	Three-quarter	2/1/98	8/22/99	53	1	54	0	0	21	84	
Daniels, J	Prop-forward	4/13/57	*	1	0	1	0	0	1	3	
Dannatt, Andy	Prop-forward	8/20/95	8/22/99	90	3	93	0	0	2	8	Eng/GB intl
Danter, Tommy	Prop-forward	12/22/56	12/29/56	4	0	4	0	0	0	0	Loan from Hull FC only
D'Arcy, Rob	Centre	9/3/95	7/30/97	61	1	62	0	0	38	152	
Davison, R C	Centre	10/2/09	11/12/10	3	0	3	0	0	1	3	
Dawson, J	Forward	4/26/05	11/18/05	10	0	10	0	0	1	3	
Dawson, Neil	Prop-forward	8/27/71	9/23/75	52	5	57	29	0	0	58	
Dean, Idris L	Half-back	1/27/12	1/23/15	72	0	72	5	0	6	28	Welsh
Dean, T	Forward	8/27/21	3/4/22	3	0	3	0	0	0	0	
Dearlove, Andrew	Half-back/l-fwd	10/30/94	9/7/97	19	16	35	0	0	4	16	
Debney, J	Forward	26/02/1898	12/14/01	60	0	60	0	0	1	3	
Deeley, F Gordon	Wing	11/30/33	12/8/34	36	0	36	0	0	6	18	
Devanney, Terry	Half-back	10/12/57	12/27/58	3	0	3	0	0	0	0	
Dewsbury, Terry	Prop-forward	9/2/59	11/14/59	4	0	4	0	0	1	3	
Dickinson, A	Full-back	12/22/00	*	1	0	1	0	0	0	0	
Dickinson, Clive	Hooker	1/19/75	12/28/75	34	0	34	0	0	2	6	
Dilcock, W H	Wing	1/26/07	4/19/13	118	0	118	0	0	62	186	
Dixon, Colin	Forward	9/14/80	4/20/81	15	9	24	0	0	1	3	Welsh/GB intl
Dixon, Henry	Wing	9/23/22	*	1	0	1	0	0	0	0	
Dixon, Kieran	Full-back/wing	2/8/15	current	26	2	28	10	0	22	108	
Dixon, Mike	Hooker	2/1/98	9/15/02	134	12	146	0	0	39	156	Scottish intl
Dobson, Michael	Scrum-half	5/25/08	9/14/13	153	0	153	537	12	52	1294	Australian
Dobson, Steve	Scrum-half	4/22/84	*	1	0	1	0	0	0	0	
Dockar, Alec	Loose-forward	8/25/45	4/20/53	255	0	255	133	0	53	425	GB intl
Dodd	Wing	12/6/47	*	1	0	1	0	0	0	0	
Donaldson, James	Back-row fwd	2/8/15	current	4	22	26	0	0	0	0	
Donohue, Jason	Scrum-half	4/25/99	8/15/99	9	2	11	0	2	0	2	
Dooler, Carl	Scrum-half	1/25/69	11/24/69	18	0	18	3	0	1	9	
Dooley, Mark	Forward	1/16/00	*	0	1	1	0	0	0	0	
Dorahy, Dane	Half-back	2/3/02	8/25/02	22	1	23	9	4	2	30	Australian; son of John
Dorahy, John	Centre/Stand-off	10/9/83	4/26/87	92	2	94	224	4	37	600	Australian intl
Douglas, Graham	Forward	5/10/79	1/31/82	4	8	12	0	0	0	0	
Downing, J	Scrum-half	1/12/01	1/26/01	2	0	2	0	0	0	0	
Downing, Ken	Second row	12/6/47	*	1	0	1	0	0	0	0	
Downing, Ken	Wing	9/1/70	1/29/71	13	0	13	0	0	5	15	
Drake, Jim	Prop-forward	11/25/61	2/6/65	64	0	64	0	0	3	9	
Drake, Joe	Centre	2/20/60	1/21/61	14	0	14	0	0	5	15	Brother of Jim
Druery, Geoff	Utility back	1/29/71	4/12/71	9	0	9	0	0	1	3	Australian
Duff, A	Forward	05/03/1898	25/03/1899	6	0	6	0	0	2	6	
Duffy, James	Centre/Stand-off	9/21/12	2/28/14	2	0	2	0	0	3	9	
Dunham, Allan	Hooker/2nd row	8/22/99	5/5/02	7	28	35	0	0	2	8	
Dunn, Dennis	Wing	2/24/23	3/17/23	2	0	2	0	0	0	0	
Dunn, Ged	Wing	10/31/71	5/8/82	277	19	296	0	0	160	480	England intl; asst coach

The Robins

Player's name	Position	KR Appearances					Scoring				Notes
		First	Last	Start	Sub	Total	Goals	D/g	Tries	Pts	
Dutton, C	Wing	1/24/14	4/4/14	8	0	8	0	0	1	3	
Dyer, Luke	Three-quarter	2/10/07	9/15/07	27	0	27	0	0	12	48	Australian; Welsh intl
Dyson, J	Forward	9/15/45	1/26/46	4	0	4	0	0	0	0	
East, E	Scrum-half	2/8/19	*	1	0	1	0	0	0	0	
Eastwood, John 'Mick'	Three-qtr	12/16/33	1/12/46	205	0	205	0	0	65	195	
Eastwood, Paul	Wing	10/1/95	6/9/96	26	0	26	14	0	14	84	Eng/GB intl
Eddoms, W.H.	Forward	1/9/32	11/14/36	145	0	145	0	0	7	21	
Eden, Greg	Full-back	2/17/13	9/14/14	39	0	39	0	0	24	96	
Edmond, Jas	Wing	12/17/32	4/23/46	28	0	28	0	0	8	24	
Edmonds, Phil	Prop-forward	3/21/76	4/14/82	8	6	14	0	0	3	9	
Edwards, B	Full-back	12/13/52	10/17/53	4	0	4	0	0	0	0	
Egan, Billy	Forward/wing	1/1/48	1/16/54	34	0	34	0	0	4	12	
Ellenor, George	Half-back	2/6/54	3/3/56	32	0	32	13	0	4	38	
Ellerby, David	Hooker	1/2/60	*	1	0	1	0	0	0	0	Brother - Harold
Ellerby, Harold	Centre	4/20/53	12/26/57	36	0	36	0	0	3	9	
Ellerington, G	Forward	12/6/06	*	1	0	1	0	0	0	0	
Elliott, David	Centre/Stand-off	10/6/56	11/24/67	286	9	295	0	0	60	180	
Ellis, Andy	Hooker	9/7/03	8/20/06	40	11	51	0	0	18	72	
Ellis, H O	Forward	2/9/29	9/13/30	6	0	6	0	0	0	0	
Ellis, John G	Forward	1/13/00	4/2/10	201	0	201	0	0	6	18	
Ema, Asuquo 'Zook'	Prop	8/21/83	4/17/92	216	17	233	0	0	18	72	
Emerson, Matt	Forward	3/9/03	*	0	1	1	0	0	0	0	
Epati, Kane	Three-quarter	2/13/05	9/25/05	26	4	30	0	0	16	64	Cook Islander
Esders, Ryan	Forward	3/5/06	4/13/09	0	2	2	0	0	0	0	
Esslemont, Sonny	Forward	9/7/14	current	0	6	6	0	0	0	0	
Evans, H	2nd row	11/14/53	11/28/53	3	0	3	0	0	0	0	
Evans, J	Loose-forward	10/12/35	3/21/36	18	0	18	0	0	2	6	
Evans, Ray	Scrum-half	9/28/57	4/7/58	29	0	29	0	0	8	24	
Evans, Sam	Prop-forward	4/6/53	12/26/57	96	0	96	80	0	4	172	
Evans, T	Wing	11/16/35	11/30/35	3	0	3	0	0	0	0	
Everitt, Christian 'Bob'	Full-back	3/26/95	9/15/02	96	4	100	69	0	37	286	
Eyre, R	Half-back	4/21/30	10/18/30	4	0	4	0	0	0	0	
Fairbairn, George	Full-back	8/14/81	4/13/90	267	2	269	554	19	51	1308	GB intl; Coach 1991-94
Fairburn, F	Wing	9/14/01	9/19/01	2	0	2	0	0	1	3	
Fallon, Jon	Prop-forward	3/5/06	8/20/06	1	5	6	0	0	0	0	
Farley, A.F. 'Charlie'	Back-rower	1/15/38	12/10/38	5	0	5	2	0	0	4	
Farnhill, Keith	Back-rower	9/13/58	10/29/60	15	0	15	0	0	1	3	
Farr, Stuart	Scrum-half	4/16/86	10/16/94	4	0	4	0	0	1	4	
Farrell, Craig	Three-quarter	12/9/01	7/25/04	52	12	64	0	0	13	52	
Faulkner, Peter	Forward	12/3/55	4/23/56	2	0	2	0	0	0	0	
Fawcett, G	Centre	26/02/1898	30/03/1898	5	0	5	2	0	1	7	
Fazackerley, T	Forward	3/25/22	9/16/22	4	0	4	0	0	0	0	
Feetham, A	Stand-off	1/21/22	9/16/22	6	0	6	0	0	0	0	
Feetham, Jack	Loose-forward	10/30/26	10/12/29	103	0	103	0	0	30	90	GB intl
Feetham, W	Forward	9/6/02	4/13/03	25	0	25	0	0	1	3	
Fenton, Jesse	Half-back	4/26/05	12/25/08	13	0	13	0	0	2	6	
Ferguson, Archie	Centre	11/19/49	3/4/50	14	0	14	0	0	3	9	Scottish
Ferguson, Dale	Back-row forward	2/9/13	3/3/13	3	1	4	0	0	1	4	Loan from Hud'fld only
Ferney, R H	Forward	9/17/10	11/25/11	8	0	8	0	0	0	0	
Field, H	Centre	12/20/52	*	1	0	1	0	0	1	3	
Fieldhouse, S	Wing	9/15/45	*	1	0	1	0	0	0	0	

Appendices

Player's name	Position	KR Appearances First	Last	Start	Sub	Total	Goals	D/g	Tries	Pts	Notes
Finan, Joe P	Centre	10/17/53	12/3/55	2	0	2	0	0	1	3	
Fish, G	Forward	9/10/04	3/25/05	4	0	4	0	0	0	0	
Fisher, Ben	Hooker	2/12/06	9/17/11	115	50	165	0	0	33	132	Scotland intl
Fishwick, Gordon	Full-back/centre	10/27/56	8/23/58	21	0	21	32	0	2	70	
Fitzgibbon, Allan	Back-rower	10/14/73	2/24/74	20	0	20	0	0	3	9	Australian
Fitzhenry, Daniel	Utility player	2/2/08	9/26/09	40	13	53	0	0	19	76	Australian
Flanagan, Peter 'Flash'	Hooker	10/15/60	10/11/74	411	4	415	13	0	57	197	Eng/GB intl
Flannery, Stan	Winger	3/11/67	3/24/67	3	0	3	0	0	1	3	Loan from Keighley only
Fletcher, George	Forward	26/02/1898	11/26/04	130	0	130	0	0	15	45	
Fletcher, Mike	Full-back/centre	4/23/85	9/20/98	332	28	360	1267	1	56	2759	
Fletcher, Paul	Forward	4/17/88	6/5/05	316	148	464	0	0	99	396	
Ford, Byron	Winger	2/20/05	6/3/07	67	0	67	0	0	58	232	Cook Is intl
Forth, George	2nd row	9/1/51	12/25/51	14	0	14	0	0	0	0	
Foss	Half-back	3/8/00	3/10/00	2	0	2	0	0	0	0	
Foster, Frank	Back-row forward	2/6/65	10/25/68	129	1	130	7	0	7	35	GB intl
Foster, J W	Forward	1/5/24	1/19/24	2	0	2	0	0	0	0	
Foster, Les	Prop-forward	8/28/67	9/26/70	29	3	32	1	0	3	11	
Foster, N	Centre	11/21/36	3/27/37	19	0	19	0	0	2	6	
Foster, T	Forward	10/19/01	4/5/02	6	0	6	0	0	0	0	
Fountain, W	Wing	12/1/21	*	1	0	1	0	0	0	0	
Fox, Frank	Prop-forward	12/7/63	4/29/67	100	0	100	0	0	2	6	
Fox, Neil	Centre/back-row	8/25/74	12/14/75	59	0	59	210	2	16	470	Eng/GB intl
Fox, Peter	Wing	2/2/08	8/14/11	105	0	105	0	0	56	224	England intl
Fox, Peter G	Prop-forward	12/8/62	4/22/64	28	0	28	1	0	3	11	Brother of Neil
Fozzard, Nick	Prop-forward	2/15/09	9/26/09	20	4	24	0	0	1	4	GB intl
Freeman, F	Hooker	3/26/55	*	1	0	1	0	0	0	0	
Freeman, G	Half-back	9/8/00	12/26/00	11	0	11	0	0	1	3	
Fridlington, Robert	Utility back	9/7/32	9/8/45	23	0	23	0	0	1	3	
Fussey, L	Three-quarter	4/10/14	2/21/20	59	0	59	0	0	13	39	
Galbraith, R H	Scrum-half	12/6/06	1/19/07	3	0	3	0	0	0	0	
Gale, J	Wing	4/13/31	4/18/31	2	0	2	0	0	0	0	
Galea, Ben	Back-rower	2/2/08	9/8/12	123	3	126	0	0	36	144	Australian
Gallagher, Tommy	Back-rower	5/30/04	4/15/07	46	10	56	0	0	20	80	Ireland intl
Gannon, Jim	Prop-forward	2/10/07	9/15/07	8	16	24	0	0	1	4	Australian
Gardner, Ade	Wing	3/14/14	8/29/14	19	0	19	0	0	8	32	Loan from St Helens only
Garmston, James	Prop-forward	2/20/05	8/6/06	11	17	28	0	0	2	8	
Garry, Arthur	Wing	9/21/53	9/7/57	137	0	137	0	0	39	117	
Garton, George	Three-quarter	10/7/57	11/14/59	11	0	11	0	0	1	3	
Garvin, G	Three-quarter	4/17/11	*	1	0	1	0	0	1	3	
Gath, Jim	Forward	9/19/01	4/13/08	114	0	114	2	0	18	58	
Gay, Roy	Half-back	12/10/66	11/28/70	12	7	19	0	0	2	6	
Gee, H	Wing	9/15/45	11/2/46	23	0	23	0	0	6	18	
Geenty, J	Forward	26/02/1898	4/19/02	29	0	29	0	0	0	0	
Gene, Stanley	Half-back/l-fwd	3/31/96	8/18/09	150	21	171	1	3	105	425	PNG intl; two KR spells
George, Luke	Three-quarter	4/28/13	5/25/13	4	0	4	0	0	2	8	Loan from Hud'fld only
Giblin, Peter	Half-back	9/13/13	*	1	0	1	0	0	0	0	
Gibson, F 'Sandy'	Forward	1/4/13	9/9/22	123	0	123	23	0	8	70	
Gibson, L	Half-back	4/7/34	10/27/34	10	0	10	0	0	2	6	
Gill, J.W	Centre/Stand-off	04/11/1899	1/25/00	2	0	2	0	0	0	0	
Gillard, Norman	Scrum-half	8/26/61	11/20/65	17	3	20	0	0	5	15	
Gillie, C.L	Stand-off	9/27/13	10/18/13	3	0	3	0	0	0	0	

The Robins

Player's name	Position	First	Last	Start	Sub	Total	Goals	D/g	Tries	Pts	Notes
			KR Appearances				Scoring				
Gillings, T	Scrum-half	10/4/02	10/11/02	2	0	2	0	0	0	0	
Gilmore, James	Centre	11/7/14	3/20/15	17	0	17	0	0	6	18	
Glancy, John	Prop-forward	3/6/94	4/24/94	7	1	8	0	0	0	0	Loan from York only
Gledhill, M	Forward	1/28/05	2/4/05	2	0	2	0	0	0	0	
Gleeson, Sean	Centre	6/22/13	9/1/13	6	0	6	0	0	0	0	
Goddard, Jon	Full-back/centre	2/12/06	8/17/07	53	0	53	0	0	24	96	
Godfrey, Alex	Wing	5/9/01	8/25/02	43	0	43	0	1	25	101	
Golden, Marvin	Three-quarter	6/6/04	7/18/04	5	0	5	0	0	0	0	
Golder, Bernard	Wing	12/4/54	4/3/56	39	0	39	0	0	11	33	
Golding, J	Back-row forward	4/5/48	11/6/48	8	0	8	0	0	0	0	
Goldman, Troy	Stand-off	10/28/92	11/22/92	2	3	5	0	0	2	8	Australian
Goldswain, Bryn	Back-row forward	11/17/45	3/12/49	121	0	121	9	0	18	72	Wales intl
Gommersall, Lee	Three-quarter	8/6/06	7/6/08	1	2	3	0	0	0	0	
Goodin, R H	Forward	25/03/1899	4/8/01	6	0	6	0	0	0	0	
Gordon, Jimmy	Centre/scr-half	10/25/02	2/26/10	149	0	149	20	0	21	103	
Gorman, F	Forward	10/11/02	9/16/05	81	0	81	0	0	2	6	
Gotts, Andy	2nd row	9/22/91	3/9/93	1	2	3	0	0	0	0	
Goulborne, Alfie	Winger	6/30/96	6/29/97	15	10	25	0	0	15	60	
Goulding, D	Winger	11/1/47	*	1	0	1	0	0	0	0	
Goulding, Darryl	Centre	2/8/15	4/11/15	8	0	8	0	0	1	4	England intl
Goulding, James	Prop-forward	9/16/90	3/31/91	18	4	22	0	0	3	12	NZ intl
Goulding, Keith	Centre/full-back	12/11/54	12/3/55	21	0	21	12	0	2	30	
Goulding, R	Forward	10/25/02	3/26/04	44	0	44	0	0	0	0	
Gowan, C	Forward	9/14/01	*	1	0	1	0	0	0	0	
Gowan, G H	Hooker	10/20/34	*	1	0	1	0	0	0	0	
Gradwell, L	Centre	11/26/27	*	1	0	1	0	0	0	0	
Grant, D	Half-back	9/9/50	3/3/51	7	0	7	0	0	1	3	
Grantham, A	Three-quarter	1/25/00	3/24/00	9	0	9	0	0	1	3	
Gray, E	Wing	1/21/33	4/22/33	7	0	7	0	0	0	0	
Gray, Kevin	Utility back	1/31/99	7/18/99	11	6	17	28	1	6	81	
Greaves, George	Back-row forward	9/14/35	10/9/37	8	0	8	0	0	0	0	
Greaves, S	Forward	9/22/00	10/27/00	6	0	6	0	0	0	0	
Green, Blake	Stand-off	2/13/11	7/29/12	39	0	39	0	0	17	68	Australian
Green, James	Prop-forward	8/10/12	current	8	54	62	0	0	1	4	
Greenwood, James	Prop-forward	5/22/15	9/6/15	0	13	13	0	0	0	0	Loan from Wigan only
Grice, Ken	Prop-forward	11/17/51	5/6/63	194	0	194	0 *	0	18	54	
Griffett, Harry	Back-row forward	10/12/57	8/19/59	32	0	32	0	0	6	18	
Griffin, George	Back-row forward	7/29/12	9/14/13	12	8	20	0	0	0	0	
Gudzek, Josh	Full-back	9/8/13	current	1	0	1	0	0	1	4	
Guy, Billy	Stand-off	26/02/1898	3/25/05	110	0	110	2	0	12	40	
Hackling, C	Back-row forward	2/10/34	*	1	0	1	0	0	0	0	
Hackling, Gordon	Back-row forward	11/15/58	4/25/60	28	0	28	0	0	1	3	Welsh
Hadi, Steve	Wing	10/7/90	4/24/94	19	0	19	0	0	3	12	
Halafihi, Nick	Utility player	1/2/94	3/12/95	13	11	24	0	0	4	16	KR CEO 2001-04
Hall, Carl	Three-quarter	3/21/93	4/9/93	3	0	3	0	0	2	8	
Hall, Craig	Utility back	2/27/11	9/14/14	77	3	80	41	2	41	248	Son of David
Hall, David	Centre/utility	4/4/71	5/11/85	333	50	383	164	2	89	613	GB intl
Hall, J	Stand-off	9/1/27	3/3/28	32	0	32	0	0	6	18	
Hall, Jim	Prop-forward	10/11/68	1/18/69	11	2	13	0	0	0	0	Australian
Hall, John	2nd row	9/25/54	12/26/57	65	0	65	0	0	3	9	
Hall, Mike	Full-back	5/26/00	8/3/03	5	0	5	2	0	0	4	

Appendices

Player's name	Position	First	Last	Start	Sub	Total	Goals	D/g	Tries	Pts	Notes
			KR Appearances				**Scoring**				
Hallas, Graham	Centre	1/22/89	4/20/92	62	5	67	34	4	15	132	
Hallett, McAuley	Three-quarter	9/7/14	current	2	0	2	0	0	3	12	
Hambrecht, G J	Forward	12/25/05	4/9/10	76	0	76	0	0	5	15	
Hames, E	Wing	8/29/36	*	1	0	1	0	0	0	0	
Hamilton, George	2nd row	2/19/55	12/27/55	9	0	9	0	0	0	0	
Hancock, Norman	Three-quarter	12/26/55	8/31/57	54	0	54	0	0	7	21	
Harbour, Ken	Prop-forward	12/19/53	11/24/56	30	0	30	0	0	1	3	
Hardman, Ian	Full-back/wing	4/15/07	9/15/07	18	0	18	0	0	4	16	Loan from St Helens only
Hardy, Craig	Prop-forward	12/13/92	7/9/00	67	47	114	0	0	2	8	
Harkin, Paul	Scrum-half	2/18/79	3/25/87	167	18	185	0	38	27	134	GB intl
Harmon, Neil	Prop-forward	2/13/05	6/5/05	9	0	9	0	0	0	0	
Harper, Colin	Loose-forward	12/31/55	3/23/57	19	0	19	4	0	0	8	
Harris, Bob	Wing	8/13/60	12/11/65	128	0	128	0	0	77	231	
Harris, Louis	Wing	9/4/20	12/1/28	254	0	254	1	0	77	233	
Harrison, A	Wing	2/20/37	1/15/38	11	0	11	0	0	5	15	
Harrison, Chris	Prop-forward	4/16/86	7/21/96	136	23	159	0	0	19	76	Younger brother of Des
Harrison, David	Hooker	3/6/88	3/27/89	21	3	24	0	0	4	16	KR coach 1997-2000
Harrison, Des	Forward	4/14/85	8/29/99	191	104	295	0	0	29	116	
Harrison, Tom	Forward	11/5/55	1/14/56	6	0	6	0	0	0	0	
Harrison, Walter	Wing	1/30/04	2/6/04	2	0	2	0	0	0	0	
Hartley, A	Forward	9/9/11	*	1	0	1	0	0	0	0	
Hartley, Jez	2nd row	5/26/97	8/30/98	1	5	6	0	0	0	0	
Hartley, Len	Forward	4/20/46	9/25/48	47	0	47	0	0	4	12	
Hartley, Len	Half-back	10/23/54	9/12/55	4	0	4	0	0	0	0	
Hartley, Steve	Stand-off/centre	1/2/71	12/2/84	326	43	369	0	0	191	592	GB intl
Hasty, Phil	Half-back	2/1/04	9/11/05	32	10	42	3	1	27	115	
Hatch, Brian	Scrum-half	11/7/59	8/22/64	27	0	27	0	0	7	21	
Hatfield, A	Forward	1/25/00	*	1	0	1	0	0	0	0	
Hayes, Richard	Prop-forward	6/15/97	9/15/02	64	2	66	0	0	3	12	
Haynes, James	Full-back/wing	6/12/09	*	1	0	1	0	0	0	0	
Heil, Chris	Centre	7/29/12	9/8/13	4	0	4	0	0	2	8	
Helliwell, B	Forward	23/09/1899	30/09/1899	2	0	2	0	0	0	0	
Henry, Craig	Forward	9/7/03	*	0	1	1	0	0	0	0	
Henson, E W	Forward	04/11/1899	3/30/01	29	0	29	0	0	1	3	
Hepi, Tyla	Utility player	7/21/13	9/8/13	0	4	4	0	0	0	0	
Hepworth, J E	Wing	9/19/36	3/29/37	6	0	6	0	0	1	3	
Heslop, David	Hooker	2/26/72	10/21/79	134	5	139	0	0	1	3	
Hewitt, Mark	Scrum-half	12/27/99	7/9/00	29	1	30	108	0	4	232	
Hick, David	Utility player	9/6/72	4/15/74	35	4	39	0	0	8	24	
Hickman, Kevin	Scrum-half	12/14/80	1/11/81	2	0	2	0	0	0	0	
Hicks, Robert G	Three-quarter	9/7/12	10/3/14	60	0	60	0	0	19	57	
Hickson, John	2nd row	10/31/64	3/25/73	63	18	81	0	0	5	15	Cousin of John Taylor
Hill, Danny	2nd row	4/15/07	4/22/07	2	0	2	0	0	0	0	
Hill, Howard	Centre/2nd row	2/1/98	9/20/98	22	12	34	0	0	5	20	
Hill, Kenny	Prop-forward	8/28/94	10/9/94	4	4	8	0	0	1	4	
Hill, Roland	Three-quarter	12/21/29	12/21/35	148	0	148	2	0	40	124	
Hill, Viv	Prop-forward	12/22/45	4/3/48	47	0	47	1	0	1	5	
Hind, J	Full-back	3/9/35	3/21/36	12	0	12	2	0	0	4	
Hobson, Ron	Forward	11/9/57	4/8/58	8	0	8	0	0	0	0	KR's 1st Australian player
Hodgson, David	Wing	2/3/12	7/26/14	53	0	53	0	0	32	128	GB intl

The Robins

Player's name	Position	First	Last	Start	Sub	Total	Goals	D/g	Tries	Pts	Notes
				KR Appearances			Scoring				
Hodgson, Eddie	Wing	10/5/12	12/27/13	26	0	26	0	0	7	21	
Hodgson, F	Wing	3/7/08	*	1	0	1	0	0	0	0	
Hodgson, Josh	Hooker	3/12/10	9/14/14	104	30	134	0	0	35	140	England intl
Hodgson, R	Prop-forward	2/26/38	1/21/39	4	0	4	0	0	0	0	
Hoe, Sean	Hooker	8/19/90	9/7/97	99	36	135	0	0	19	76	
Hogan, Phil	Centre/back-row	12/10/78	12/7/88	229	25	254	53	1	65	316	Eng/GB intl
Holbrook, Eric	2nd row	12/30/73	8/19/79	2	1	3	0	0	0	0	
Holdstock, Alan	Hooker	8/29/61	9/15/65	30	0	30	0	0	7	21	
Holdstock, Dale	Utility player	2/1/04	9/11/05	36	1	37	0	0	10	40	Son of Roy
Holdstock, H	Forward	1/18/02	3/1/02	4	0	4	0	0	0	0	
Holdstock, H	Utility-back	10/24/31	4/16/32	3	0	3	0	0	0	0	
Holdstock, Robert	Hooker	12/27/58	9/2/59	5	0	5	0	0	0	0	
Holdstock, Roy	Forward	3/18/73	4/28/85	242	35	277	0	1	23	71	Eng/GB intl
Holdstock, Steve	Hooker	11/15/69	11/14/71	10	0	10	0	0	0	0	
Holland, Doug	Forward	12/25/57	4/16/60	58	0	58	0	0	9	27	
Holliday, Bill	Forward	1/16/65	9/2/68	143	2	145	139	0	18	332	GB intl
Holker, Steven	Back-row fwd	5/22/15	current	0	1	1	0	0	0	0	
Holmes, C	Scrum-half	2/23/07	*	1	0	1	0	0	1	3	
Holmes, F B	Utility	10/18/30	4/1/33	5	0	5	1	0	0	2	
Holt, Jack	Forward	11/14/53	12/18/54	35	0	35	0	0	4	12	
Hood, H	Forward	3/8/19	11/29/19	10	0	10	0	0	1	3	
Hornby, J	Full-back	9/29/34	*	1	0	1	0	0	0	0	
Horne, Graeme	Centre/2nd row	2/3/12	current	78	18	96	0	0	20	80	
Horner, W	Utility	12/18/09	12/26/13	5	0	5	0	0	0	0	
Hosking, David	Prop-forward	9/19/93	1/30/94	15	1	16	0	0	1	4	Australian
Hossell, David	Prop-forward	8/19/69	4/9/78	20	14	34	0	0	0	0	
Hotham, J	Forward	9/8/00	10/17/08	37	0	37	0	0	10	30	
Hough, D	Wing/scrum-half	3/16/46	4/13/46	5	0	5	0	0	1	3	
Houghton, C	Prop-forward	4/18/49	11/26/49	6	0	6	0	0	1	3	
Hoult, Jack	Centre/Stand-off	9/7/22	12/27/26	172	0	172	3	0	74	228	
Howard, Harvey	Prop-forward	3/23/03	7/27/03	10	7	17	0	0	5	20	GB intl; coach 2004/05
Howat, Bob	Full-back	10/5/68	10/25/68	5	0	5	13	0	0	26	
Hubbard, Steve	Wing	3/27/78	10/17/82	118	4	122	327	0	72	870	
Hudson, R	Centre	1/11/13	4/18/14	11	0	11	1	0	0	2	
Hudson, Terry	Scrum-half	10/22/71	10/20/74	100	6	106	13	0	20	86	
Hughes, Ian	2nd row	1/31/99	8/29/99	23	6	29	0	0	5	20	
Hughes, Mike	Back-row forward	3/2/75	12/30/78	74	28	102	0	0	10	30	
Hughes, R	Centre	1/16/09	4/8/13	145	0	145	5	0	32	106	
Huskins, William	Forward	9/2/09	9/27/19	222	0	222	0	0	17	51	
Hutchins, D	Three-quarter	9/8/45	4/3/48	25	0	25	0	0	7	21	
Hutchinson, Bernard	Three-quarter	3/12/38	12/29/45	29	0	29	0	0	8	24	
Hutchinson, Carl	Centre	4/11/86	4/22/86	2	1	3	0	0	0	0	
Hutchinson, Darren	Centre	7/28/96	9/7/97	28	12	40	2	0	6	28	
Hutchinson, Rob	Centre	11/15/92	4/24/94	40	3	43	0	0	11	44	
Hyam, W	Three-quarter	9/3/10	4/24/12	45	0	45	0	0	12	36	
I'Anson, Chas	Stand-off	9/15/07	5/2/10	19	14	33	0	0	4	16	
Idle, A	Forward	25/11/1899	1/1/00	4	0	4	0	0	0	0	
Ingram, Peter	Full-back	11/18/50	12/27/52	27	0	27	7	0	6	32	
Irvine, Jimmy	Utility back	1/2/89	10/21/90	24	23	47	0	0	14	56	
Jackson, A	Back-row forward	1/13/34	2/2/35	20	0	20	0	0	1	3	
Jackson, Bill	Centre	11/8/47	8/30/48	23	0	23	0	0	5	15	
Jackson, J	Back-row forward	1/8/21	2/5/21	2	0	2	0	0	0	0	
Jackson, R.W 'Ginger'	Wing	18/03/1899	4/10/02	21	0	21	0	0	8	24	

Appendices

Player's name	Position	First	Last	Start	Sub	Total	Goals	D/g	Tries	Pts	Notes
			KR Appearances					**Scoring**			
Jackson, Rod	Wing	12/1/70	12/5/70	2	0	2	0	0	0	0	Australian
Jackson, Wayne	Prop-forward	10/21/90	5/17/98	55	17	72	0	0	1	4	Also spell with Halifax
Jacques, Ray	Back-row forward	10/4/58	12/3/60	62	0	62	0	0	10	30	
Jenkin, Jim	2nd row	1/24/59	8/29/61	42	0	42	0	0	1	3	
Jennison, J	Forward	26/02/1898	02/12/1899	2	0	2	0	0	0	0	
Jessop, H	Wing	10/25/30	1/31/31	5	0	5	0	0	1	3	
Joe, Leroy	Half-back	12/27/99	7/9/00	29	1	30	0	1	9	37	Cook Is intl
Johnson, Dennis	Forward	5/2/55	1/5/57	22	0	22	0	0	0	0	
Johnson, G	Forward	9/9/09	*	1	0	1	0	0	0	0	
Johnson, G	Wing	10/17/25	12/12/25	3	0	3	0	0	1	3	
Johnson, G	Three-quarter	1/12/46	4/24/46	4	0	4	0	0	0	0	
Johnson, J	Forward	9/1/00	12/29/00	7	0	7	0	0	0	0	
Johnson, Lindsay	Prop-forward	9/22/85	4/22/86	7	4	11	0	0	0	0	Australian
Johnson, Nick	Wing	9/8/12	*	1	0	1	0	0	0	0	
Johnson, R	Stand-off	9/15/00	1/26/01	13	0	13	2	0	0	4	
Johnson, R	Forward	10/19/07	4/3/09	15	0	15	0	0	1	3	
Johnston, K	Forward	9/9/09	*	1	0	1	0	0	0	0	
Johnston, Peter	Prop-forward	10/13/85	5/3/86	23	0	23	0	0	1	4	Australian
Jones, Geoff	Front-row fed	4/30/75	4/2/76	5	7	12	0	0	0	0	
Jones, Mark	Half-back	10/9/88	2/12/89	3	5	8	0	1	2	9	Australian
Jones, Reginald	Half-back	2/5/10	2/18/11	27	0	27	0	0	6	18	
Jones, S	Utility-back	12/3/10	4/17/11	3	0	3	0	0	1	3	
Jones, T	Full-back	3/18/22	3/25/22	2	0	2	0	0	0	0	
Jones, William Gwyn	Hooker	3/29/30	9/13/30	9	0	9	0	0	0	0	
Jones, Windsor	Centre	1/25/08	4/13/08	11	0	11	0	0	1	3	Welsh
Jordan, A.J	Centre	3/19/27	10/11/30	112	0	112	0	0	13	39	
Jordan, Wilfred	Hooker	12/29/34	10/1/38	11	0	11	0	0	1	3	
Joseph, Phil	Utility player	2/12/06	8/20/06	4	15	19	0	0	7	28	Welsh intl
Jowett, W.F	Three-quarter	9/23/05	10/12/07	44	0	44	1	0	23	71	
Keable, J	Scrum-half	3/4/33	*	1	0	1	0	0	0	0	
Keating, Kris	Half-back	2/16/14	9/7/14	24	0	24	0	0	5	20	Australian
Keegan, Bob	Utility-back	12/13/19	4/3/20	16	0	16	0	0	1	3	
Keegan, John	Hooker	8/30/58	4/18/59	14	0	14	0	0	0	0	
Keen, George	Half-back	10/25/47	10/8/49	16	0	16	0	0	0	0	
Kellett, Cyril	Full-back	10/27/56	11/17/67	382	0	382	1194	0	35	2493	
Kelly, Albert	Half-back	2/8/15	current	24	0	24	2	0	17	72	Australian
Kelly, Andy	2nd row	8/22/82	10/4/87	125	46	171	0	1	48	183	England intl
Kelly, Pat	Back-row forward	4/27/80	*	0	1	1	0	0	0	0	USA gridiron player
Kemp, Albert	Forward	26/02/1898	4/29/05	162	0	162	25	0	9	77	KR's 1st capt in NU
Kemp, Dave	Hooker	11/24/69	*	1	0	1	0	0	0	0	
Kennedy, George M	Winger	10/3/64	2/20/65	4	0	4	0	0	0	0	
Kennedy, Jamie	Second-row	2/13/98	9/13/98	20	9	29	0	0	6	24	Australian
Kennedy, Phil	Second-row	5/1/00	5/21/00	3	1	4	0	0	1	4	
Key, Peter	Half-back	4/15/53	9/5/59	114	0	114	4	0	17	59	
Khan, Patrick 'Paddy'	Prop	10/4/94	12/11/94	6	2	8	0	0	1	4	
Kilby, Alan	Centre	4/22/64	*	1	0	1	0	0	0	0	
Kingsbury, Ken	Second-row	2/20/60	9/2/61	32	0	32	20	0	1	43	
Kirby, Harry	Half-back	10/14/50	9/11/54	45	0	45	1	0	10	32	
Kirby, J	Forward	11/6/20	*	1	0	1	0	0	0	0	
Kirchin, Terry	Second-row	2/4/73	3/6/73	5	1	6	0	0	0	0	
Kirk, G	Full-back	4/5/02	1/20/06	4	0	4	0	0	0	0	
Kirk, Malcolm	Prop-forward	11/5/60	12/3/60	4	0	4	0	0	0	0	On loan only

The Robins

Player's name	Position	First	Last	Start	Sub	Total	Goals	D/g	Tries	Pts	Notes
				KR Appearances			**Scoring**				
Kirke, Ian	Back-row forward	12/27/99	6/18/00	4	13	17	0	0	1	4	
Kirkham, J	Stand-off	1/19/24	*	1	0	1	0	0	0	0	
Kirkpatrick, George	Three-quarter	8/8/71	1/18/76	106	8	114	0	0	36	108	
Kitching, Chris	Utility back	5/26/97	7/15/01	50	21	71	13	1	20	107	
Kitson, H	Scrum-half	12/6/19	4/10/20	10	0	10	0	0	0	0	
Knapp, Ernie	Utility back	8/31/53	5/4/55	29	0	29	0	0	6	18	
Knight, Herbert	Centre	10/12/46	5/26/47	15	0	15	0	0	3	9	
Knowleden, Bryn	Centre/Stand-off	1/19/52	11/13/54	66	0	66	0	0	9	27	Eng/GB int; pl/coach
Kruger, H.A	Scrum-half	9/1/00	9/28/01	22	0	22	0	0	0	0	
Laithwaite, James	2nd row	7/8/12	7/29/12	1	2	3	0	0	1	4	Loan from Warr'tn only
Lamping, J	Prop-forward	4/28/51	*	1	0	1	0	0	0	0	
Langley, Jamie	Back-row forward	2/16/14	6/13/14	6	5	11	0	0	1	4	
Larroyer, Kevin	Back-row forward	2/16/14	current	43	10	53	0	0	10	40	French
Last, Cliff	Loose-forward	1/23/60	1/21/61	30	0	30	1	0	2	8	
Latus, Sam	Three-quarter	6/26/10	4/1/13	35	3	38	0	0	14	56	
Lavin, J	Forward	10/7/50	11/17/51	21	0	21	0	0	2	6	
Lawler, George	Back-row fwd	8/23/15	current	1	2	3	0	0	2	8	
Lawler, Kenny	2nd row	9/6/87	4/16/89	4	3	7	0	0	0	0	
Laws, David	Wing/Stand-off	2/1/81	3/24/89	177	17	194	0	0	75	289	GB intl
Lawton, J	Wing	18/03/1899	*	1	0	1	0	0	0	0	
Lazenby, Tracy	Loose-forward	2/20/83	4/18/93	19	7	26	0	0	6	20	Also spell with W'field
Leatham, James	2nd row	5/7/00	7/9/00	9	0	9	0	0	2	8	
Leftley, G	Prop-forward	12/3/49	9/30/50	10	0	10	0	0	0	0	
Leighton, Jamie	Back-row forward	4/20/92	6/29/97	23	28	51	0	0	6	24	Son of Steve
Leighton, Steve	Utility back	3/21/72	4/27/80	89	11	100	0	0	11	33	
Lennon, Mark	Full-back/wing	4/22/07	9/15/07	11	4	15	7	0	5	34	Australian
Levett, J	Half-back	02/09/1899	1/13/00	18	0	18	0	0	2	6	
Lewis, A	Utility	9/4/33	3/21/36	12	0	12	0	0	1	3	
Lewis, C	Centre	12/7/01	11/29/02	24	0	24	1	0	3	11	
Lewis, Dan	Forward	1/13/12	12/13/13	51	0	51	0	0	8	24	
Lewis, Harry	Centre	4/15/50	11/8/52	56	0	56	48	0	3	105	
Lewis, John H	Full-back	12/29/45	12/9/50	33	0	33	63	0	0	126	Welsh
Liddiard, David	Full-back	12/6/92	1/2/94	28	1	29	0	0	11	44	Australian
Lightfoot, David	Full-back	10/1/89	11/18/90	30	1	31	0	0	7	28	
Lindsay, J	Forward	05/03/1898	30/03/1898	4	0	4	0	0	0	0	
Lines, John	2nd row	9/26/70	10/6/70	4	0	4	0	0	0	0	
Lockwood, Alan	Hooker	4/7/62	5/27/63	31	0	31	1	0	1	5	
Lockwood, Brian	Prop-forward	2/5/78	5/3/80	75	1	76	0	0	11	33	Eng/GB intl; cousin of Millward
Lofthouse, A	Scrum-half	3/26/04	9/18/09	82	0	82	1	0	10	32	
Lofthouse, S	Stand-off	10/10/25	12/11/26	9	0	9	0	0	1	3	
Longstaff, Paul	Utility back	12/25/67	3/31/74	121	6	127	0	0	41	123	
Lord, Harold	Wing	9/6/13	4/19/19	64	0	64	0	0	39	117	
Lovegrove, Rhys	Centre/back-row	7/8/07	9/14/14	80	80	160	0	0	19	76	Australian
Lowe, Andrew	Prop-forward	12/13/92	*	1	0	1	0	0	0	0	Son of Phil
Lowe, James	Forward	9/12/14	4/10/15	36	0	36	0	0	2	6	
Lowe, Phil	Second-row	3/4/67	2/13/83	386	32	418	0	0	179	537	Eng/GB int; chair 92-94
Luckwell, David	Prop-forward	1/31/99	8/18/02	28	48	76	0	0	3	12	Australian
Luffman, Bob	Full-back/centre	9/2/61	11/2/63	6	0	6	0	0	2	6	
Lufford, Jim	Full-back	4/24/48	11/5/49	16	0	16	7	0	2	20	
Lumb, Tim	Scrum-half	3/12/95	8/27/95	11	1	12	1	2	3	16	

Appendices

Player's name	Position	First	Last	Start	Sub	Total	Goals	D/g	Tries	Pts	Notes
			KR Appearances				Scoring				
Lunt, Shaun	Hooker	3/15/15	current	17	3	20	0	0	7	28	England intl
Lydiat, John	Utility back	4/20/81	4/20/92	121	59	180	50	0	45	277	
Lyman, Paul	Loose-forward	1/8/89	9/19/93	82	17	99	0	0	39	156	
Lynch, W	Utility back	11/8/20	1/31/20	9	0	9	1	0	0	2	
Lynn, Terry	Scrum-half	3/7/76	10/17/76	4	0	4	0	0	1	3	
Lyons, N	Stand-off	11/22/24	12/5/25	20	0	20	0	0	3	9	
Lyons, Steve	Prop-forward	12/1/74	10/24/76	53	3	56	0	0	6	18	
McAvoy, Jock	Full-back/centre	12/1/51	4/30/53	50	0	50	4	0	9	35	
McBain, Fred	Wing	12/7/46	11/11/50	70	0	70	0	0	17	51	
McCarthy, Troy	Stand-off	10/6/91	1/26/92	12	1	13	0	0	4	16	Australian
McCarthy, Tyrone	Back-row fwd	2/8/15	9/27/15	30	1	31	0	0	6	24	
McClarron, Alasdair	Wing	3/4/01	6/19/05	101	4	105	0	0	67	268	
McCloud, Ernest	Wing	1/23/32	4/23/32	8	0	8	0	0	1	3	
McConnell, W	Three-quarter	3/22/02	4/10/02	3	0	3	0	0	0	0	
McCracken, John	Three-quarter	2/13/98	5/17/98	4	1	5	0	0	2	8	
McDermott, P	Forward	26/02/1898	*	1	0	1	0	0	0	0	
McDonald, C	Forward	9/10/10	4/10/20	105	0	105	0	0	20	60	
McDonnell, Shannon	Full-back	2/3/12	7/23/12	22	0	22	0	0	6	24	Australian
McGiever, Tommy	Half-back	10/11/13	12/27/22	157	0	157	0	0	26	78	
McGlone, Joe	Half-back	1/10/19	1/5/24	23	0	23	0	0	3	9	
McGowan, T	Half-back	1/5/35	3/12/38	67	0	67	0	0	13	39	
McHugh, Gary	Wing	2/25/79	10/18/81	39	1	40	0	0	7	21	
McIntyre, Jack	Half-back	9/23/22	2/6/32	298	0	298	1	0	41	125	
McKeough, Craig	Centre	10/28/92	1/10/93	11	0	11	0	0	3	12	Australian
McNamara, A	Forward	1/23/04	*	1	0	1	0	0	0	0	
McNamara, Ted	Full-back	12/7/63	12/18/65	15	1	16	0	0	1	3	KR first ever substitute
McNulty, James	2nd row	4/10/37	1/8/38	12	0	12	0	0	2	6	
McWatt, Ernie	Hooker	1/16/37	10/19/46	9	0	9	0	0	0	0	Brother of Wilf
McWatt, Wilf	Full-back	1/30/32	3/27/51	328	0	328	431	0	29	949	KR coach 1950-52
Madden, Len	Wing	9/16/50	10/7/50	4	0	4	0	0	0	0	
Madley, Ian	Forward	9/28/73	3/16/80	44	21	65	0	0	4	12	
Madley, W	Three-quarter	12/7/01	12/1/06	123	0	123	34	0	24	140	
Mageen, Joe	Centre	1/11/58	9/9/58	19	0	19	0	0	8	24	
Major, Terry	Centre/back-row	11/21/59	5/2/70	266	8	274	3	0	52	162	
Mann, Alfred	Forward	9/2/09	5/3/19	224	0	224	4	0	50	158	
Mansson, Paul	Half-back	7/27/03	9/25/05	71	0	71	0	5	35	145	N Zealander
Mantellato, Josh	Wing	2/8/15	current	32	0	32	115	0	27	338	Italian intl
Manu, Misili	Centre	7/24/05	7/31/05	2	0	2	0	0	0	0	N Zealander; Samoa intl
Marchant, Billy	2nd row	9/30/84	11/9/86	6	2	8	0	0	1	4	
Mariano, Frank	2nd row	5/10/09	8/15/10	0	4	4	0	0	0	0	
Markham, Ian	Full-back	9/2/68	8/18/72	133	4	137	0	0	15	45	
Marks, Tony	Wing	8/25/62	*	1	0	1	0	0	0	0	
Marrow, F	Centre	3/26/04	4/26/05	6	0	6	0	0	1	3	
Marrow, John	Wing	1/24/31	2/14/31	2	0	2	0	0	0	0	
Marsden, Lee	Forward	5/7/95	*	0	1	1	0	0	0	0	
Marsden, Tom	Half-back	3/26/55	4/2/56	10	0	10	0	0	0	0	
Marsh, Matthew	Half-back	6/30/15	current	4	1	5	0	0	1	4	
Marshall, David	Wing	11/8/13	9/19/14	12	0	12	0	0	2	6	
Marshall, W	Wing	12/5/08	12/19/08	3	0	3	0	0	0	0	
Mart, W	Forward	2/19/10	*	1	0	1	0	0	0	0	
Martindale, R	Hooker	9/15/45	1/4/47	10	0	10	0	0	0	0	
Martins, Sebastian	Prop-forward	5/7/06	6/4/06	1	3	4	0	0	1	4	French intl; loan only

The Robins

Player's name	Position	First	Last	Start	Sub	Total	Goals	D/g	Tries	Pts	Notes
				KR Appearances			Scoring				
Maskill, Raymond	Prop-forward	8/29/36	1/12/46	115	0	115	0	0	8	24	
Mason, Willie	2nd row	3/13/11	4/15/11	6	0	6	0	0	1	4	Australian intl
Matthews, Alan	2nd row	1/5/57	12/25/57	26	0	26	0	0	2	6	
Matthews, Brian	Stand-off	12/17/60	9/23/61	27	0	27	0	0	5	15	Brother - Alan
Matthews, E G	Stand-off	3/17/34	3/21/34	2	0	2	0	0	1	3	
Matthews, H	Centre	10/20/23	3/8/24	5	0	5	0	0	0	0	
Matthews, Lee	Back-row forward	9/20/87	10/4/87	0	2	2	0	0	0	0	
Maxwell, Bob	Forward	8/24/70	9/14/70	0	3	3	0	0	0	0	
Mayberry, Casey	Three-quarter	2/1/04	4/3/04	4	2	6	0	0	2	8	
Mead, Andrew	Centre	9/16/67	9/28/68	1	1	2	0	0	0	0	
Medcalf, Peter	Loose-forward	12/24/60	1/11/61	3	0	3	0	0	0	0	
Megson, H	Centre	4/22/46	3/22/47	9	0	9	0	0	5	15	
Mennell, Brian	Prop-forward	5/21/63	9/22/70	106	5	111	0	0	5	15	
Menzies, Luke	Prop-forward	3/15/08	4/20/08	0	2	2	0	0	0	0	
Merritt, E H	Wing	9/1/00	9/29/00	4	0	4	0	0	1	3	
Metcalf, E	Loose-forward	8/29/49	4/10/50	4	0	4	0	0	0	0	
Middleton, F	Forward	10/27/34	10/19/46	44	0	44	0	0	5	15	
Mika, Constantine	2nd row	2/3/12	9/14/13	46	6	52	0	0	10	40	N Zealander; Samoa intl
Miller, Bruce	Three-quarter	3/15/85	4/19/85	5	3	8	0	0	6	24	Australian
Miller, Gavin	Loose-forward	11/11/84	3/19/89	102	0	102	0	0	27	108	Australian intl
Millington, John	Prop-forward	11/28/70	4/14/85	371	47	418	0	0	32	97	England intl
Mills, David	Prop-forward	2/2/08	6/5/09	22	14	36	0	0	2	8	Welsh intl
Mills, Henry 'Ike'	Centre/Stand-off	12/7/46	3/21/53	155	0	155	0	0	35	105	
Mills, Ron	Centre/half-back	3/25/39	9/5/53	121	0	121	13	0	17	77	
Millward, Roger	Half-back	8/15/66	5/3/80	399	7	406	597	10	207	1825	Eng/GB int; coach 77-91
Milner, H	Forward	14/10/1899	3/16/01	3	0	3	0	0	0	0	
Milner, J C	Three-quarter	12/27/38	2/16/46	27	0	27	25	0	12	86	
Mitton, W	Stand-off	11/3/23	12/22/23	9	0	9	0	0	0	0	
Moat, Rowley	Wing/half-back	12/25/58	11/19/60	59	0	59	0	0	18	54	
Molloy, Gavin	Wing	7/25/99	4/22/01	21	8	29	0	0	10	40	
Moore, Arthur	Loose-forward	4/3/09	12/25/24	341	0	341	2	0	90	274	England intl
Moore, Frank	Prop-forward	10/28/50	5/7/55	133	0	133	0	0	22	66	
Moore, J	Centre	12/11/20	12/18/20	2	0	2	0	0	1	3	
Moore, J G	Centre	4/12/09	9/10/10	9	0	9	0	0	0	0	
Moore, John Ernest	Centre/Stand-off	4/26/52	9/29/56	42	0	42	2	0	7	25	
Moore, John Robert	Centre/utility	8/31/63	4/27/80	395	38	433	0	0	105	315	Asst coach 1980-86
Moore, Pete	Wing	9/16/73	*	0	1	1	0	0	0	0	
Moores, J.W	Loose-forward	1/14/33	9/7/35	33	0	33	0	0	8	24	
Moran, Asher	Half-back	8/23/69	*	1	0	1	0	0	0	0	
Moran, H	Forward	8/27/21	9/8/21	2	0	2	0	0	0	0	
Morfitt, Sammy	Centre	26/02/1898	3/21/03	83	0	83	9	0	29	105	England RU
Morgan, Stephen	Half-back	9/19/36	9/20/47	90	0	90	0	0	17	51	Welsh
Morrison, Iain	2nd row	2/12/06	9/9/07	32	7	39	0	0	5	20	Scottish intl
Mortimer, Albert	Centre	4/5/58	1/31/59	19	0	19	0	0	4	12	
Mortimer, Peter	Centre	10/4/87	3/23/88	22	0	22	0	0	5	20	Australian intl
Morton, Gareth	Centre/back-row	5/22/05	7/22/07	39	5	44	210	0	23	512	Scottish intl
Moss, A	Half-back	10/17/31	4/19/35	2	0	2	0	0	1	3	
Moss, T	Stand-off	1/26/24	3/8/24	7	0	7	0	0	1	3	
Moxon, R	Centre/2nd row	8/31/38	11/10/45	7	0	7	0	0	0	0	
Mullineux, D	Forward	12/17/04	9/22/06	56	0	56	0	0	2	6	
Mullins, Arthur	Utility player	8/29/59	9/28/68	109	2	111	8	0	16	64	
Mulvey, Harold	Wing	8/23/19	12/31/21	49	0	49	0	0	16	48	

Player's name	Position	First	Last	Start	Sub	Total	Goals	D/g	Tries	Pts	Notes
Murdock, Craig	Scrum-half	5/6/01	8/3/03	34	6	40	4	0	14	64	
Murphy, Peter	2nd row	4/3/61	2/19/66	34	2	36	0	0	2	6	
Murphy, S	Prop-forward	10/6/51	*	1	0	1	0	0	0	0	
Murray, D	Centre/scr-half	9/14/01	1/25/02	6	0	6	0	0	0	0	
Murray, Frank	Wing	2/8/19	3/18/33	17	0	17	0	0	2	6	
Murrell, Scott	Stand-off/l-fwd	2/12/06	8/10/12	152	25	177	36	4	41	240	
Muscroft, Peter	Wing	2/14/81	2/6/83	58	1	59	0	0	18	54	
Naylor, J	Half-back	9/3/38	3/6/46	35	0	35	0	0	10	30	
Neal, J	Wing	1/1/08	1/9/09	5	0	5	0	0	5	15	
Neal, W	Forward	10/5/07	*	1	0	1	0	0	0	0	
Neale, Jim	Prop-forward	1/21/72	4/29/73	35	3	38	0	0	1	3	
Needler, Tony	Hooker	4/12/87	*	0	1	1	0	0	0	0	
Neil, Thomas	Scrum-half	12/4/09	2/12/10	6	0	6	0	0	0	0	
Nelson, J	Forward	4/4/08		1	0	1	0	0	0	0	
Ness, Walter	Half-back	9/1/45	10/5/46	21	0	21	2	0	5	19	
Netherton, Jason	Forward	7/25/04	9/7/14	100	94	194	0	0	13	52	
Netherton, Kirk	Hooker	8/6/06	8/25/08	11	17	28	0	0	3	12	Cousin of Jason
Newton, Clint	2nd row	2/2/08	9/17/11	97	2	99	0	0	40	160	Australian
Nichol, G 'Syd'	Utility back	1/26/46	11/27/54	32	0	32	0	0	9	27	
Niebling, Brian	Prop-forward	9/24/89	3/31/91	53	3	56	0	0	3	12	Australian intl
Noble, J	Forward	16/09/1899	3/24/00	15	0	15	0	0	0	0	
Noble, Rob	Centre	4/18/86	4/22/86	2	0	2	0	0	0	0	
Nolan, E T	Wing	2/7/20	10/23/20	6	0	6	0	0	1	3	
Nolan, Robert	Centre	12/27/99	7/9/00	30	0	30	0	0	12	48	
Norrie, Ray	Centre	8/24/70	4/12/71	1	3	4	0	0	0	0	
Nuttall, Steve	S-half/hooker	12/26/73	3/22/81	15	1	16	0	0	1	3	
Oates, Len	Scrum-half	1/8/49	4/17/50	36	0	36	0	0	0	0	
O'Brien, Craig	2nd row	10/2/88	4/9/95	52	16	68	0	0	8	32	
O'Brien, Richard	2nd row	11/12/95	9/7/97	6	35	41	0	0	11	44	Brother - Craig
O'Connor, Hugh	Centre	9/30/50	10/13/51	21	0	21	0	0	1	3	
O'Connor, J	Wing	4/23/31	*	1	0	1	0	0	0	0	
O'Dell, Jeff	Utility player	8/19/79	3/7/82	3	2	5	0	0	0	0	
O'Hara, Ryan	Prop-forward	5/5/12	9/8/12	8	7	15	0	0	1	4	Australian
Okul, John	Centre	3/31/96	4/5/98	6	4	10	0	0	2	8	PNG intl
O'Leary, Pat	Full-back	10/30/54	2/15/56	28	0	28	8	0	0	16	
Oliver, F W	Utility back	12/6/13	3/20/15	46	0	46	1	0	4	14	
Oliver, Joe	Centre	3/19/38	2/25/39	34	0	34	36	0	4	84	
Oliver, Paul	Forward	6/1/97	9/7/97	0	2	2	0	0	0	0	
Oliver, Richard	Wing	11/28/93	5/5/96	14	0	14	0	0	12	48	
Ollett, Aaron	Forward	6/28/13	current	7	19	26	0	0	1	4	
Olsen, Steve	2nd row	4/16/86	4/22/86	3	0	3	0	0	0	0	
O'Neill, Mark	2nd row	2/25/07	9/9/07	17	0	17	0	0	5	20	Australian
Orr, David	Full-back	5/11/46	*	1	0	1	2	0	0	4	
Osborne, Laurie	Full-back	8/28/20	4/23/32	431	0	431	718	0	20	1496	England intl
Osborne, W T	Forward	9/3/04	4/16/06	66	0	66	0	0	2	6	Welsh RU intl
Owen, Paul	Full-back	7/25/04	9/26/04	10	0	10	0	0	1	4	
Paea, Micky	Prop-forward	2/3/12	9/14/13	37	17	54	0	0	6	24	Tongan intl
Palframan, Alf (jnr)	Prop-forward	3/6/48	1/23/54	161	0	161	0	0	7	21	Son of Alf (snr)
Palframan, Alf (snr)	Forward	12/27/13	10/23/20	14	0	14	0	0	1	3	
Palmer, Eric	2nd row	11/24/62	4/5/72	78	19	97	0	0	18	54	Also spell with Keighley
Park, A	Scrum-half	4/23/46	4/24/46	2	0	2	0	0	0	0	
Parker, Frank	Wing/2nd row	3/29/81	4/22/86	5	5	10	0	0	2	8	Brother - Wayne
Parker, J	Wing	2/4/22	*	1	0	1	0	0	0	0	
Parker, Johnny	Scrum-half	9/6/54	12/8/56	54	0	54	1	0	4	14	

The Robins

Player's name	Position	First	Last	Start	Sub	Total	Goals	D/g	Tries	Pts	Notes
Parker, Keith	Prop-forward	9/29/62	*	1	0	1	0	0	0	0	
Parker, Paul	Centre	1/19/03	3/26/06	73	5	78	0	0	37	148	
Parker, Wayne	Half-back	4/16/86	8/29/99	216	29	245	0	33	62	281	Spell at H'fax; asst coach
Parkes, R	Scrum-half	4/19/19	1/7/33	2	0	2	0	0	0	0	
Parkin, Jonty	Scrum-half	10/4/30	4/23/32	57	0	57	27	0	11	87	GB intl
Parr, V	Wing	2/23/07	*	1	0	1	0	0	1	3	
Paterson, Cory	2nd row	2/3/13	7/7/13	17	0	17	0	0	7	28	Australian
Pattison, H	Wing	10/23/09	*	1	0	1	0	0	0	0	
Paul, Graham	Wing	12/26/58	5/23/64	197	0	197	1	0	116	350	
Payne, Arthur	Centre	8/20/49	9/8/51	36	0	36	0	0	3	9	
Peak	Wing/Stand-off	3/29/19	4/21/19	5	0	5	0	0	0	0	
Perrott, W	Three-quarter	10/3/36	4/17/39	35	0	35	0	0	5	15	
Petersen, David	Loose-forward	4/9/12	9/8/12	2	2	4	0	0	1	4	
Pexton, H	Full-back	1/12/01	4/8/01	14	0	14	0	0	0	0	
Phillips, J	Scrum-half	8/29/36	9/12/36	4	0	4	0	0	0	0	
Phipps, Billy	Centre	12/22/00	1/4/08	172	0	172	2	0	32	100	
Pickering, James A	Forward	9/6/02	9/10/04	55	0	55	0	0	1	3	
Pickering, Paul	Hooker	1/19/03	9/11/05	52	13	65	0	0	19	76	
Pickersgill, Ken	Prop-forward	12/8/56	12/26/56	4	0	4	0	0	0	0	
Pinkney, Brian	Scrum-half	8/25/73	11/10/74	11	7	18	0	0	4	12	
Pinkney, Nick	Three-quarter	7/7/02	9/26/04	56	6	62	0	0	30	120	Eng intl
Plange, David	Wing	8/21/94	1/21/96	55	0	55	0	0	64	256	GB intl
Pollard, Keith	Prop-forward	12/28/64	3/25/66	20	2	22	0	0	1	3	
Poole, Harry	Back-row forward	2/18/61	9/24/65	123	0	123	0	0	27	81	GB intl; KR coach 1975-77
Poore, Justin	Prop-forward	2/16/14	4/21/14	7	0	7	0	0	0	0	Australian
Porter, J W	Forward	4/6/01	4/26/05	9	0	9	0	0	1	3	
Porter, Michael	Prop-forward	9/18/88	3/24/89	28	1	29	0	0	5	20	Australian
Poucher, Craig	Centre	1/19/03	6/5/05	53	4	57	58	0	22	204	
Pounder, J	Stand-off	9/29/38	8/25/45	3	0	3	0	0	0	0	
Pramil, Olivier	Forward	8/7/05	*	0	1	1	0	0	0	0	French; loan only
Pratt, C H	Forward	11/15/13	4/19/19	4	0	4	0	0	0	0	
Pratt, George	Wing/forward	10/15/04	12/17/10	84	0	84	4	0	25	83	
Pratt, Richard	Wing	11/6/88	10/1/89	28	0	28	0	0	5	20	
Prescott, John H	Half-back	9/12/14	10/13/19	39	0	39	0	0	10	30	
Price, Gareth	Prop-forward	3/12/06	7/16/06	5	13	18	0	0	1	4	Welsh intl
Price, Ray	Hooker	1/13/80	11/21/82	45	7	52	0	2	1	5	
Price, Sydney	Stand-off	3/15/24	4/18/24	6	0	6	0	0	1	3	
Prissick, H	Wing	4/24/09	*	1	0	1	0	0	0	0	
Proctor, Paul	Full-back/centre	12/14/80	4/22/84	31	16	47	0	0	6	18	
Prohm, Gary	Centre	9/22/82	5/3/86	145	2	147	0	0	104	399	NZ intl
Puletua, Tony	Prop	5/30/15	9/19/15	14	0	14	0	0	1	4	N Zealand / Samoa intl; loan
Rainey, Adrian	2nd row	3/10/02	5/12/02	4	2	6	0	0	3	12	Australian
Rainton, C 'Tacker'	Full-back	12/12/25	1/23/32	44	0	44	8	0	5	31	
Raleigh, Andy	2nd row	2/13/05	9/25/05	28	1	29	0	0	17	68	
Ramsden, Albert E	Winger	9/7/35	*	1	0	1	0	0	0	0	
Ramsden, Joe	Hooker	9/1/34	4/7/50	346	0	346	0	0	8	24	KR coach 1956/57
Ramshaw, Terry	Prop-forward	1/6/74	10/11/74	16	2	18	0	0	0	0	
Raper, Danny	Centre	4/17/64	9/24/66	3	0	3	1	0	2	8	
Raper, H	Wing	3/21/13	*	1	0	1	0	0	0	0	

Player's name	Position	First	Last	Start	Sub	Total	Goals	D/g	Tries	Pts	Notes
			KR Appearances					**Scoring**			
Ratu, Mike	Three-quarter	2/21/10	6/25/10	5	0	5	0	0	1	4	
Raynor, J	Wing/half-back	2/21/25	3/3/28	48	0	48	0	0	11	33	
Raywood, E	Wing	10/28/11	*	1	0	1	0	0	0	0	
Read, D	Forward	1/30/04	3/24/06	34	0	34	0	0	0	0	
Read, J W	Utility back	9/13/02	12/11/09	112	0	112	0	0	24	72	
Read, Stephen	Centre	1/23/04	10/5/07	33	0	33	0	0	6	18	
Reaston, J	Forward	3/8/05	4/26/05	2	0	2	0	0	0	0	
Redmond, Gerard	Wing	8/29/31	9/26/31	2	0	2	0	0	1	3	
Rees, Dan	Centre	10/21/05	10/19/07	54	0	54	5	0	10	40	Welsh RU intl
Rees, Rhys	Centre	1/2/22	1/5/24	82	0	82	1	0	17	53	Welsh
Rhoades, Ralph W	Centre	3/7/25	4/27/31	28	0	28	2	0	6	22	
Rhodes, A	Wing	1/25/00	*	1	0	1	0	0	0	0	
Rhodes, Jack	Forward	26/02/1898	3/22/02	70	0	70	0	0	6	18	
Riach, Fred	Prop-forward	12/29/34	11/2/35	21	0	21	0	0	0	0	
Ribbett, Walter	Wing	9/18/30	10/4/30	3	0	3	0	0	0	0	
Richards, Emlyn	Half-back/wing	12/22/45	3/18/50	112	0	112	0	0	46	138	Welsh
Richards, Gwyn	Stand-off	1/8/38	1/22/38	3	0	3	0	0	0	0	Welsh RU intl
Richardson, A	Forward	9/14/07	4/4/08	19	0	19	0	0	3	9	
Richardson, F	Full-back/3-qtr	9/12/08	1/9/09	7	0	7	4	0	0	8	
Richardson, Lee	Hooker	4/13/88	4/18/93	47	1	48	0	0	4	16	
Richardson, Steve	Centre/2nd row	9/27/92	9/11/94	7	9	16	0	0	1	4	
Richardson, T Edward	Half-back	4/24/09	12/10/10	20	0	20	0	0	3	9	
Richmond, F	Forward	1/25/00	1/27/00	2	0	2	0	0	0	0	
Riley, Bill	Centre	12/14/57	4/15/61	107	0	107	0	0	23	69	
Ripton, Thomas	Three-quarter	26/02/1898	10/18/02	21	0	21	0	0	1	3	
Rivett, Leroy	Three-quarter	4/24/05	10/8/06	39	5	44	0	0	16	64	
Roberts, C	Full-back	9/17/49	*	1	0	1	2	0	0	4	
Roberts, Fred	Utility	10/9/26	12/27/30	49	0	49	0	0	3	9	
Robinson, A W	Centre	09/12/1899	4/29/05	48	0	48	6	0	7	33	
Robinson, Conor	Half-back/hooker	7/26/14	current	0	2	2	0	0	0	0	
Robinson, Ian	Full-back/centre	10/12/75	1/19/86	184	35	219	40	0	50	245	
Robinson, N	Scrum-half	11/14/53	1/16/54	7	0	7	0	0	0	0	
Robinson, Steve	Half-back	1/15/89	3/10/91	17	3	20	0	0	5	20	
Robley, W	Wing	1/30/26	*	1	0	1	0	0	2	6	
Robson, Steve	Forward	12/13/92	*	0	1	1	0	0	0	0	
Rogers, Jack	Prop-forward	10/4/58	9/2/59	26	0	26	1	0	1	5	
Rooms, Max	Wing	4/7/70	10/12/75	57	5	62	0	0	17	51	
Rose, Paul	Forward	9/27/69	12/12/81	237	33	270	0	0	43	129	Eng/GB intl
Rouse, Paul	Wing	7/14/96	8/15/99	72	3	75	0	0	42	168	
Rowbottom, Ron	Prop-forward	9/12/59	1/23/60	17	0	17	0	0	0	0	
Rudd, Chris	Hooker	1/9/83	3/31/91	129	32	161	0	0	26	103	
Ruddeforth, S	Wing/forward	02/09/1899	2/24/00	10	0	10	0	0	1	3	
Rushton, Dennis	Full-back/centre	12/1/51	12/27/54	68	0	68	0	0	9	27	
Rushton, Nicky	Prop-forward	9/24/95	*	1	0	1	0	0	0	0	
Rushworth, T	Half-back	1/25/00	3/16/01	6	0	6	0	0	1	3	
Russell, J	Scrum-half	12/6/52	*	1	0	1	0	0	0	0	
Ryan, Glen	2nd row	12/18/87	4/10/88	19	0	19	0	0	2	8	Australian
Saddington, George	Back-rower	12/12/25	5/4/36	172	0	172	12	0	39	141	England intl
Sadler, J	Wing	11/24/23	*	1	0	1	0	0	0	0	
Sagar, Paul	Prop-forward	2/1/98	*	0	1	1	0	0	0	0	
Sage, Tim	Prop-forward	8/21/94	12/18/94	5	1	6	0	0	0	0	
Salter, J	Wing	1/31/31	*	1	0	1	0	0	0	0	
Salter, Liam	Centre	3/17/12	current	80	0	80	0	0	17	68	
Sanders, Len	Winger	11/9/46	11/30/46	4	0	4	0	0	0	0	
Sanderson, J 'Sammy'	Scrum-half	3/20/81	8/14/81	8	0	8	0	1	4	13	

The Robins

Player's name	Position	First	Last	Start	Sub	Total	Goals	D/g	Tries	Pts	Notes
			KR Appearances				**Scoring**				
Sanderson, R	Centre	4/14/34	1/5/35	8	0	8	0	0	2	6	
Sandham, William	Back rower	1/16/09	11/8/19	184	0	184	0	0	86	258	
Sapcote, E	Full-back	1/25/00	*	1	0	1	0	0	0	0	
Saul, G	Stand-off	1/8/26	11/17/28	30	0	30	0	0	5	15	
Scarborough, A	Wing	2/18/28	10/12/29	27	0	27	0	0	5	15	
Schofield, Ben	Wing	12/27/37	8/27/38	3	0	3	0	0	0	0	
Schofield, J	Centre	1/24/48	11/12/49	41	0	41	0	0	13	39	
Scholes, Dennis	Wing/back-row	5/12/47	12/26/58	129	0	129	0	0	24	72	
Schultz, Matthew	Back-row forward	4/1/01	9/15/02	41	4	45	0	0	3	12	
Schultz, Stuart	Half-back	12/7/88	2/6/91	2	1	3	0	0	0	0	
Scott, Jim	Centre	9/1/70	9/12/70	1	3	4	0	0	0	0	
Scott, Paul	Prop-forward	2/5/95	8/8/99	18	22	40	0	0	3	12	
Scruton, W	Centre	05/03/1898	*	1	0	1	0	0	0	0	
Sedgwick, F	Forward	14/10/1899	3/16/01	5	0	5	0	0	0	0	
Sedgwick, J	Wing	10/24/08	1/2/09	9	0	9	0	0	3	9	
Seibold, Anthony	2nd row	4/6/03	9/26/04	48	5	53	0	0	7	28	Australian
Senior, Arthur	Prop-forward	12/25/46	9/25/48	59	0	59	0	0	0	0	
Sharkett, W	Centre	10/19/46	5/26/47	4	0	4	0	0	1	3	
Sharpe, Leslie	Forward	11/17/28	3/21/34	182	0	182	0	0	13	39	
Shaw, Brian	Full-back/wing	8/22/53	4/22/61	84	0	84	6	0	34	114	
Shaw, John 'Joby'	Hooker	11/20/65	8/27/66	11	0	11	0	0	0	0	GB intl
Shaw, W	Scrum-half	25/11/1899	2/17/00	3	0	3	0	0	0	0	
Sheard, J	Forward	9/29/06	4/1/07	4	0	4	0	0	0	0	
Shepherd, A	Scrum-half	4/12/02	4/19/02	2	0	2	0	0	0	0	
Sheriffe, Louis	Full-back	4/25/11	9/8/12	9	0	9	0	0	4	16	
Sherwood, H	Forward	12/2/05	3/23/07	45	0	45	0	0	3	9	
Sherwood, Sam	Forward	11/20/06	9/19/07	19	0	19	1	0	1	5	
Shiel, W	Centre	9/6/13	1/2/15	22	0	22	0	0	3	9	
Shillito, F.W	Half-back	1/25/19	5/10/19	10	0	10	0	0	1	3	
Shillito, Fred	Prop-forward	10/29/32	10/15/38	116	0	116	0	0	10	30	
Shipp, T H	Full-back	12/15/34	1/26/35	9	0	9	0	0	0	0	
Shires, Jim	Back-rower	9/11/54	2/16/57	42	0	42	1	0	5	17	
Shoebottom, Gordon	Back-rower	4/12/57	11/2/57	7	0	7	0	0	2	6	
Sibary, Lee	Full-back	2/1/98	8/8/99	24	11	35	5	1	0	11	
Simpkin, D	2nd row	4/6/57	4/12/57	2	0	2	0	0	0	0	
Simpson, L	Stand-off	9/28/35	9/30/35	2	0	2	0	0	0	0	
Simpson, Mark	Half-back	12/4/83	*	0	1	1	0	0	0	0	Australian
Simpson, R E	Wing	3/5/32	3/19/32	3	0	3	0	0	4	12	
Sims, Brian	Forward	8/17/57	9/6/58	22	0	22	0	0	3	9	
Sims, Gary	Centre	4/14/85	12/6/92	18	6	24	0	0	2	8	
Sims, J	Scrum-half	4/13/59	8/29/59	4	0	4	0	0	0	0	
Sims, W	Forward	9/14/01	4/10/02	23	0	23	0	0	1	3	
Sinclair, Herbert	Full-back/centre	02/09/1899	10/16/09	148	0	148	6	0	3	21	
Sio, Ken	Full-back/wing	2/8/15	current	31	0	31	0	0	24	96	Australian
Sissons, Tony	Hooker	4/16/86	4/22/86	3	0	3	0	0	0	0	
Slater, Richard	Back-rower	12/27/99	7/15/01	44	2	46	0	0	2	8	
Sleep, E	Centre	9/5/03	11/21/03	11	0	11	0	0	1	3	
Small, J	Forward	1/1/02	4/19/02	4	0	4	0	0	0	0	
Small, Peter	Centre/back-row	1/25/69	5/2/70	35	8	43	0	0	3	9	GB intl
Smirk, Terry	Scrum-half	4/8/97	6/15/97	4	1	5	1	0	0	2	
Smith, A	Back-row forward	12/18/54	8/18/56	16	0	16	0	0	1	3	
Smith, Andrew	2nd row	2/1/98	9/26/04	147	26	173	1	0	18	74	
Smith, Cyril	Centre	8/23/47	2/17/51	63	0	63	0	0	17	51	Welsh
Smith, Gordon	Half-back/l-fwd	11/7/82	4/17/88	156	21	177	1	5	25	102	NZ intl
Smith, H W	Full-back/fwd	09/09/1899	9/12/08	79	0	79	1	0	5	17	

Player's name	Position	First	Last	Start	Sub	Total	Goals	D/g	Tries	Pts	Notes
		KR Appearances					**Scoring**				
Smith, J A	Full-back	2/15/13	4/18/14	4	0	4	6	0	0	12	
Smith, Jack	Centre	8/29/31	9/4/33	60	0	60	0	0	14	42	
Smith, Michael	2nd row	4/3/05	3/2/07	31	12	43	0	0	20	80	NZ intl
Smith, Mike	Centre/utility	3/28/75	3/31/91	481	8	489	2	3	140	493	Eng/GB intl
Smith, Richard	Full-back	3/29/98	8/29/99	49	0	49	0	0	21	84	
Smith, Sam	Hooker	3/18/50	1/23/54	117	0	117	0	0	0	0	Eng/GB intl
Smith, Steve	Wing	10/13/85	10/9/88	31	2	33	0	0	13	52	
Smith, T	Full-back/centre	9/19/01	10/18/02	23	0	23	28	0	0	56	
Smithies, Bob	Full-back	10/29/72	3/28/75	54	1	55	0	0	22	66	Australian
Snitch, A	Back-row forward	3/29/47	4/8/47	2	0	2	0	0	1	3	
Sodje, Bright	Wing	9/9/90	3/11/01	93	0	93	0	0	39	156	Two spells with KR
Spackman, Arthur	Forward	9/3/04	1/6/12	222	0	222	0	0	13	39	
Spamer, Bernard	Full-back	4/12/47	4/5/48	6	0	6	5	0	0	10	
Spamer, Jack	Centre/Stand-off	3/18/26	9/2/39	445	0	445	22	0	145	479	
Spaven, Scott	Scrum-half	4/25/10	7/24/10	0	2	2	0	0	0	0	
Spavieri, J	Full-back	26/02/1898	26/03/1898	3	0	3	9	0	0	18	
Speckman, Paul	Loose-forward	4/14/85	8/2/96	108	29	137	0	5	7	33	
Speckman, Ray	Back-row forward	2/16/57	12/25/59	3	0	3	0	0	0	0	
Spence, Brian	Stand-off	11/11/50	9/3/55	50	0	50	13	0	9	53	
Spiller, W	Wing	9/7/12	11/23/12	6	0	6	0	0	2	6	
Spivey, George	Wing	10/29/10	3/18/12	29	0	29	0	0	12	36	
Spivey, Mick	Prop-forward	12/17/72	12/30/73	0	2	2	0	0	0	0	
Standage, John	Wing	1/18/36	4/1/36	10	0	10	0	0	2	6	
Stark, Sid	Wing	12/26/56	4/24/59	34	0	34	0	0	16	48	
Starks, Anthony	Forward	26/02/1898	11/9/07	208	0	208	72	0	31	237	Eng intl
Starks, F	Forward	11/17/00	12/1/00	2	0	2	0	0	0	0	Brother of Anthony
Stead, Ray	Three-quarter	4/6/86	12/7/88	53	11	64	0	0	13	52	
Steel, Jon	Centre	2/13/05	9/7/08	65	2	67	15	0	40	190	Scottish intl
Steele, C A 'Gus'	Centre/Stand-off	9/15/45	9/5/50	73	0	73	0	0	28	84	
Stephenson, Chris	Stand-off	7/28/02	8/31/03	9	3	12	42	0	3	96	
Stephenson, Francis	Prop-forward	2/12/06	9/3/06	10	7	17	0	0	1	4	England intl
Stephenson, J	Forward	26/02/1898	4/26/05	117	0	117	1	0	4	14	
Stephenson, Mike	Half-back/wing	9/11/65	12/3/74	225	13	238	0	1	102	307	
Stewart, Sam	Back-row forward	8/20/95	9/1/96	46	0	46	0	0	9	36	NZ intl
Stocks, Terry	Wing	8/29/61	4/30/62	11	0	11	0	0	8	24	
Stokell, B	Scrum-half	4/2/04	*	1	0	1	0	0	0	0	
Stoker, J	Wing	8/31/35	9/5/36	5	0	5	0	0	2	6	
Storr, J	Back-row forward	10/27/51	4/6/53	16	0	16	0	0	0	0	
Stothard, R	Wing	1/2/22	1/14/22	3	0	3	0	0	0	0	
Stothard, Ronald B	Centre	8/21/50	*	1	0	1	0	0	0	0	
Stott, Lynton	Utility back	12/2/01	8/8/04	68	5	73	136	5	26	381	
Sullivan, Adam	Prop-forward	6/29/02	5/2/04	27	13	40	0	0	3	12	
Sullivan, Anthony	Wing	11/29/87	3/31/91	72	0	72	0	0	61	244	Son of Clive; W/GB intl
Sullivan, Clive	Wing	8/25/74	5/3/80	213	0	213	0	0	118	354	Welsh/GB intl
Surman, Tommy	Half-back	9/2/09	2/22/13	76	0	76	2	0	27	85	
Sutton, J	Forward	10/17/08	4/24/09	2	0	2	0	0	0	0	
Sutton, Tommy	Back-row forward	9/1/51	12/14/57	143	0	143	30	0	19	117	
Sykes, Cyril	Forward	4/9/71	4/12/71	2	0	2	0	0	0	0	
Sykes, Roger	Half-back	12/25/08	4/10/20	57	0	57	2	0	6	22	
Taewa, Whetu	Centre	1/31/99	9/15/02	131	0	131	0	0	59	236	NZ intl
Tandy, Ryan	Prop-forward	5/27/07	9/15/07	8	4	12	0	0	2	8	
Tangata-Toa, David	Prop-forward	2/13/05	9/9/07	53	24	77	0	0	14	56	Australian

The Robins

Player's name	Position	First	Last	Start	Sub	Total	Goals	D/g	Tries	Pts	Notes
Tate, E G 'Gerry'	Half-back	1/14/50	4/28/51	37	0	37	0	0	8	24	
Tattersfield, Ted	Back-row forward	2/14/31	1/23/37	147	0	147	44	0	27	169	
Tawhai, Latham	Scrum-half	1/26/03	9/28/03	25	1	26	3	4	7	38	N Zealander
Taylor, Andrew	Full-back	5/26/00	2/16/03	8	2	10	0	0	0	0	
Taylor, J	Hooker	8/27/32	9/7/32	3	0	3	0	0	0	0	
Taylor, J W	Forward	9/22/00	12/24/10	51	0	51	1	0	1	5	
Taylor, J W	Full-back	4/24/46	*	1	0	1	0	0	0	0	
Taylor, John	Forward	8/18/58	8/24/68	195	2	197	1	0	48	146	GB intl; 1st KR tourist
Taylor, Ross	Prop-forward	10/18/87	3/23/88	17	0	17	0	0	2	8	NZ intl
Taylor, Scott	Forward	8/18/09	9/8/12	21	31	52	0	0	9	36	
Taylor, Tom	Forward	11/16/07	1/2/09	34	0	34	0	0	4	12	
Tetlow	Back-rower	12/17/27	3/3/28	3	0	3	0	0	0	0	
Thomas, A E	Forward	4/5/24	11/29/24	6	0	6	1	0	0	2	
Thomas, D	Wing	9/22/45	10/13/45	3	0	3	0	0	1	3	
Thomas, Dai	Wing	10/23/09	11/20/09	5	0	5	0	0	1	3	Welsh
Thomas, Phil	Centre	1/16/09	11/29/13	104	0	104	0	0	28	84	
Thompson, Albert	2nd row	9/2/59	4/30/62	17	0	17	0	0	0	0	
Thompson, Alex	Prop-forward	6/29/97	8/29/99	69	4	73	0	0	5	20	
Thompson, Andy	2nd row	4/5/87	4/9/95	148	18	166	0	0	23	92	
Thompson, F	Prop-forward	3/23/35	1/22/38	76	0	76	0	0	1	3	
Thompson, H	Hooker	1/5/24	3/18/26	5	0	5	0	0	0	0	
Thompson, Peter	Centre/2nd row	5/2/55	1/12/57	11	0	11	0	0	1	3	
Thorburn, Scott	Scrum-half	2/15/04	7/25/04	14	5	19	37	0	7	102	Australian
Thornton, Maurice	Centre	11/14/53	4/22/57	62	0	62	0	0	10	30	
Tilse, Dane	Prop-forward	4/25/15	current	10	6	16	0	0	1	4	Australian
Tomlinson, W	Three-quarter	9/6/30	9/20/30	3	0	3	0	0	0	0	
Tong, Jim	Hooker	8/19/50	2/1/58	151	0	151	0	0	10	30	
Tonks, Les	Prop-forward	12/12/70	12/26/70	2	0	2	0	0	0	0	Loan from F'stone only
Tosney, Andy	Stand-off	4/11/86	4/16/86	2	0	2	0	0	0	0	
Townend, A	Full-back	9/14/01	9/28/01	3	0	3	0	0	0	0	
Townend, C S	Scrum-half	28/10/1899	2/24/00	7	0	7	0	0	0	0	
Townsley, R	Forward	9/6/02	1/1/06	82	0	82	0	0	1	3	
Trowell, Charlie	Prop-forward	4/29/60	8/29/61	21	0	21	0	0	0	0	
Trump, Leonard C	Forward	9/14/12	4/10/15	103	0	103	0	0	11	33	
Tuimavave, Evarn	Prop-forward	2/3/13	9/14/13	11	12	23	0	0	2	8	NZ intl
Tullock, Geoff	Wing	8/20/49	4/23/56	167	0	167	0	0	66	198	England intl
Tullock, Herbert	Wing	26/02/1898	12/13/02	49	0	49	14	0	16	76	
Turner, Derek 'Rocky'	Loose-f'd	9/5/51	8/24/55	140	0	140	0	0	27	81	GB intl
Turner, Glyn	Half-back	1/19/75	4/8/77	36	12	48	3	0	25	81	Welsh intl
Tyreman, Graham	Hooker	10/26/79	1/6/80	13	0	13	0	0	2	6	
Tyrer, Colin	Full-back	12/27/76	4/19/78	31	0	31	106	0	4	224	
Tyson, Brian	Prop-forward	2/18/61	4/29/67	231	0	231	0	0	16	48	GB intl
Ulugia, W	Three-quarter	5/4/14	6/13/14	3	0	3	0	0	1	4	New Zealander
Unsworth, G	Forward	1/12/07	4/17/09	32	0	32	0	0	0	0	
Upton, R	Centre	12/10/10	*	1	0	1	0	0	0	0	
Van Rooyen, George	Back-rower	9/7/22	10/27/23	35	0	35	0	0	8	24	S Africa RU intl
Vannet, Paul	Forward	10/8/89	1/29/95	32	13	45	0	0	4	16	
Vassilakopoulos, M	Loose-forward	4/25/99	5/23/99	4	0	4	0	0	0	0	
Vaughan, D	Centre	9/12/14	5/3/19	25	0	25	0	0	8	24	
Vella, Michael	Prop-forward	2/10/07	9/17/11	116	5	121	0	0	14	56	Australian intl
Wagstaffe, E W	Full-back	11/15/19	11/22/19	2	0	2	0	0	0	0	
Wainwright, David	Utility back	12/17/66	9/29/72	90	10	100	2	0	13	43	
Walker, A	Forward	9/6/02	11/1/02	2	0	2	0	0	0	0	

516

Player's name	Position	First	Last	Start	Sub	Total	Goals	D/g	Tries	Pts	Notes
			KR Appearances				Scoring				
Walker, Adam	Prop-forward	2/3/13	current	60	17	77	0	0	6	24	
Walker, C B	Wing	4/18/27	*	1	0	1	0	0	0	0	
Walker, Chev	Centre	2/2/08	9/18/09	26	8	34	0	0	5	20	Eng/GB intl
Walker, G	Hooker	4/24/46	*	1	0	1	0	0	0	0	
Walker, Gerald	Wing	10/24/53	4/26/54	5	0	5	0	0	1	3	
Walker, Jimmy	Half-back	1/23/01	9/11/05	52	43	95	0	1	32	129	
Walker, Jonny	Prop-forward	2/16/14	6/13/14	2	6	8	0	0	0	0	Brother - Adam
Walker, Peter	Hooker	4/17/65	12/2/67	16	1	17	0	0	3	9	
Wallace, Richard	Full-back	9/6/75	4/17/77	45	2	47	0	2	3	11	
Wallis, Cliff	Forward	4/17/64	1/1/77	138	12	150	2	0	14	46	Also spell with Cas'fd
Walsh, Jamie	Scrum-half	1/26/82	8/21/83	24	1	25	0	1	3	10	
Walsh, Mike	Scrum-half	4/23/85	*	0	1	1	0	0	0	0	Brother of Jamie
Walshaw, Harold	Centre	3/17/34	5/4/36	31	0	31	0	0	1	3	
Walters, Ralph	Hooker	9/25/54	9/20/58	37	0	37	0	0	0	0	
Ward, Danny	Prop-forward	2/10/07	8/17/07	12	9	21	0	0	0	0	GB intl
Ward, T	Full-back	02/09/1899	1/26/01	38	0	38	1	0	2	8	
Wardrobe, Neil	Half-back	10/4/92	4/8/96	24	12	36	1	0	9	38	
Warters, G	Centre	2/3/51	12/25/51	16	0	16	0	0	1	3	
Watene, Frank	Prop-forward	2/1/04	9/26/04	2	28	30	0	0	4	16	N Zealander
Waterworth, J	Stand-off	8/23/19	10/25/19	7	0	7	0	0	2	6	
Watkinson, David	Hooker	1/23/77	3/24/89	314	15	329	0	3	13	48	Eng/GB intl
Watson, A	Utility back	12/4/09	10/18/19	68	0	68	2	0	9	31	
Watson, Bernard	Centre	8/25/74	4/27/80	177	9	186	2	6	44	142	
Watson, David	Centre/half-back	9/2/90	3/31/91	29	0	29	0	0	13	52	NZ intl
Watson, Kevin 'Bobo'	Forward	12/23/79	12/4/83	20	15	35	0	0	3	10	
Watson, R H	Utility back	18/03/1899	3/17/00	15	0	15	0	0	3	9	
Watson, S E	Wing	2/15/19	3/15/19	5	0	5	0	0	3	9	
Watts, Liam	Forward	4/20/08	5/5/12	32	31	63	0	0	7	28	
Waxman, S	2nd row	9/27/47	*	1	0	1	0	0	0	0	
Webb, Charlie A	Half-back	1/20/23	11/28/25	42	0	42	0	0	3	9	
Webber, David	Loose-forward	3/14/97	4/20/97	1	5	6	0	0	0	0	Australian
Webster, Jake	Centre	2/2/08	9/2/12	104	1	105	7	0	41	178	NZ intl
Webster, James	Scrum-half	2/13/05	4/25/08	93	1	94	7	9	33	155	Australian
Weisner, Pat	Utility back	8/2/06	3/23/07	3	6	9	4	1	2	17	Australian; Irish intl
Welham, Kris	Centre	8/6/06	9/27/15	189	2	191	2	0	102	412	
Welham, Liam	Centre	8/6/06	8/20/06	2	0	2	0	0	0	0	Brother of Kris
Welsby, Harold	2nd row	4/24/48	8/3/50	46	0	46	0	0	4	12	
West, G H 'Tich'	Wing	4/6/01	10/10/08	218	0	218	45	0	98	384	
Westerdale, C W 'Bill'	2nd row	9/25/20	4/9/32	365	0	365	2	0	47	145	KR trainer 1935-40
Westerdale, Frank	Forward	3/29/24	11/7/31	42	0	42	1	0	4	14	Brother of Bill
Weyman, Mick	Prop-forward	2/16/14	9/14/15	23	1	24	0	0	7	28	Australian
Wheatley, A	Forward	11/28/31	*	1	0	1	0	0	0	0	
Wheeldon, L	Utility	9/17/21	10/5/35	3	0	3	0	0	0	0	
Wheeldon, Scott	Prop-forward	3/15/09	4/6/12	33	44	77	0	0	4	16	
Whitcombe, G	Forward	1/30/04	3/26/04	9	0	9	0	0	0	0	
White, Brendan	Prop-forward	4/10/83	4/30/83	3	1	4	0	0	0	0	Loan from York only
White, G	Full-back	10/30/35	9/4/48	73	0	73	0	0	1	3	
White, P	Wing	4/3/09	4/10/09	4	0	4	0	0	0	0	
Whiting, G	Wing	1/25/19	2/1/19	2	0	2	0	0	0	0	
Whittaker, Sam	Full-back	10/1/95	*	0	1	1	0	0	1	4	
Whittle, Jon	Three-quarter	7/22/06	8/20/06	4	1	5	0	0	1	4	

The Robins

Player's name	Position	First	Last	Start	Sub	Total	Goals	D/g	Tries	Pts	Notes
		KR Appearances					Scoring				
Whitton, G	Centre/half-back	11/16/35	3/29/37	32	0	32	5	0	1	13	
Whitworth, Wilfred	Utility back	2/18/39	4/23/46	43	0	43	12	0	6	42	
Wildbore, Loz	Full-back	8/29/04	9/11/05	11	3	14	40	0	3	92	
Wildridge, Mark	Wing	2/6/91	*	1	0	1	0	0	0	0	
Wiley, Steve	Prop-forward	11/24/69	9/6/74	88	7	95	0	0	8	24	
Wilkin, Jon	Back-row forward	5/26/00	9/15/02	21	18	39	0	0	8	32	Eng/GB intl
Wilkinson, Alfred E	Centre	11/29/19	10/16/20	18	0	18	3	0	3	15	
Wilkinson, J H 'Jack'	Prop-forward	1/10/20	11/3/28	263	0	263	2	0	17	55	
Wilkinson, J R 'Bob'	Prop-forward	3/13/20	11/3/28	273	0	273	0	0	8	24	
Willett, Ron	Centre	8/28/70	11/14/70	12	0	12	10	0	1	23	
Williams, C	Three-quarter	9/1/00	10/19/01	21	0	21	1	0	2	8	
Williams, Desi	Wing	3/5/06	4/9/06	3	0	3	0	0	1	4	
Williams, Harry	Back-row forward	10/5/29	3/16/35	133	0	133	0	0	29	87	
Wilmot, Arthur	Prop-forward	8/25/45	11/12/49	127	0	127	0	0	7	21	
Wilson, A H	Full-back	10/1/32	12/2/33	3	0	3	1	0	0	2	
Wilson, Colin	Forward	3/26/99	*	0	1	1	0	0	0	0	
Wilson, David	Forward	2/23/03	3/31/07	7	6	13	0	0	0	0	
Wilson, Ernie	Wing	8/19/57	1/23/60	50	0	50	0	0	12	36	
Wilson, George	Stand-off	9/13/30	10/25/30	7	0	7	0	0	0	0	WWII PoW
Wilson, H	Three-quarter	21/10/1899	4/20/01	20	0	20	0	0	0	0	
Wilson, R	Three-quarter	02/12/1899	4/26/05	7	0	7	0	0	0	0	
Wilson, Richard	Prop-forward	5/7/00	4/3/04	87	24	111	0	1	3	13	
Wilson, Robert	2nd row	4/8/96	7/7/02	68	12	80	0	0	22	88	
Wilson, W	Forward	1/14/28	1/13/34	2	0	2	0	0	0	0	
Wiltshire, H	Forward	1/30/04	3/5/04	7	0	7	0	0	0	0	
Wimpenny, A	Wing	9/3/04	4/26/05	14	0	14	0	0	2	6	
Windle, Andrew	Forward	02/09/1899	10/17/08	238	0	238	0	0	7	21	
Windley, Johan	Scrum-half	5/18/97	6/1/97	1	3	4	0	0	1	4	Loan from Hull FC only
Windley, Phil	Scrum-half	9/4/92	9/20/92	3	0	3	0	0	0	0	
Windmill, Derek 'Sam'	Prop	8/18/72	12/30/73	42	13	55	7	0	3	23	
Winfield	Prop-forward	12/7/46	12/14/46	2	0	2	0	0	0	0	
Winsor, F	Three-quarter	2/2/35	4/10/36	35	0	35	0	0	3	9	
Withers, Lincoln	Hooker	2/3/12	9/14/13	19	23	42	0	0	10	40	Australian
Wood, A	Wing	3/18/33	1/23/37	55	0	55	0	0	25	75	
Wood, Martin	Utility player	8/18/02	9/15/02	5	1	6	0	0	0	0	
Woodcock, John	Stand-off	8/26/33	3/31/34	31	0	31	0	0	9	27	
Woodhead, Bob	Back-row forward	4/23/73	4/15/74	1	4	5	4	0	1	11	
Woodhouse, Anthony	Prop	9/12/70	9/26/70	1	1	2	0	0	0	0	
Woods, Ryan	Prop	4/24/00	5/21/00	0	4	4	0	0	0	0	
Woolford, Billy	Hooker	2/28/70	9/26/70	6	0	6	0	0	0	0	
Wootton, W T	Forward	9/12/14	1/31/20	60	0	60	64	0	10	158	
Wray, A	Forward	12/15/00	1/5/01	4	0	4	0	0	0	0	
Wray, Jonathan	Wing	1/31/99	7/9/00	60	0	60	0	0	24	96	
Wrigglesworth, Brian	Centre	12/4/65	8/20/66	21	2	23	0	0	10	30	
Wright, J W	Wing	10/18/02	*	1	0	1	0	0	0	0	
Wrigglesworth, Geoff	Centre	11/9/68	5/2/70	51	0	51	0	0	17	51	GB intl
Yeaman, Scott	Scrum-half	8/22/99	4/29/01	11	7	18	5	0	3	22	
Young, A	Prop-forward	3/2/29	3/16/29	3	0	3	0	0	0	0	
Young, C	Wing/2nd row	3/27/51	8/29/51	2	0	2	0	0	0	0	
Young, Chris	Wing	5/18/64	8/26/69	163	1	164	0	0	85	255	GB intl
Young, George	Prop-forward	12/25/50	8/14/54	52	0	52	0	0	1	3	
Young, Gordon	2nd row	8/28/65	10/20/74	82	14	96	0	0	4	12	Son of George
Young, Vic	Stand-off/threeqtr	8/29/36	8/27/38	59	0	59	19	0	11	71	
Youngman, Wally	Wing	2/20/77	11/8/80	52	2	54	0	0	23	69	
Trailists				28	0	28	0	0	0	0	

The Author

Roger Pugh was born in Leeds, West Yorkshire, in 1952. He began following Hull Kingston Rovers in 1968 and moved to the city three years later. He worked for 37 years in the civil service, the last 18 in a communications and public relations, and was awarded the OBE for his work in the New Years' honours list in 2012.

Roger is known in East Yorkshire as a league cricket umpire and administrator. He retired from umpiring after 37 years in 2014 but, as a committee member of the Yorkshire County Premier League, is actively involved in the restructuring of Yorkshire cricket.

The paucity of literature about the Robins has always disappointed him. When, in 2012, he retired from the civil service, he resolved to address the gap by writing a club history. He is currently a member of the committee of the Hull Kingston Rovers Community Trust.

Roger is married to Kirsty and has a son Gavin, who is also a Rovers passholder.

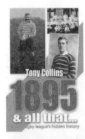  
 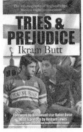 

Be inspired.

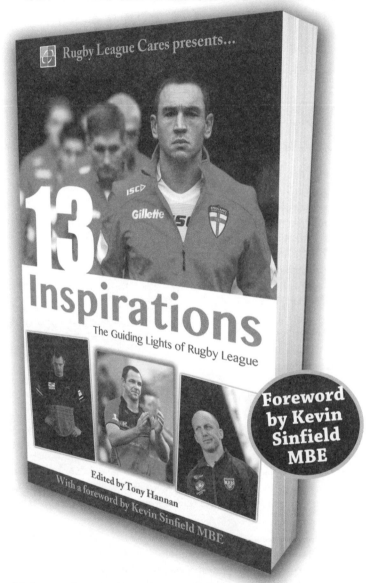

Rugby League Cares presents...

13 Inspirations
The Guiding Lights of Rugby League

Foreword by Kevin Sinfield MBE

Edited by Tony Hannan
With a foreword by Kevin Sinfield MBE

With contributions from many of the leading writers and personalities in the game, **13 Inspirations** is a lively literary collection in praise of the guiding lights of rugby league.

In aid of Rugby League Cares

Learning Curve

The Remarkable Story of Student League

Dave Hadfield

Learning Curve - Dave Hadfield's seventh book about rugby league - is devoted to one of the game's great untold stories.

The history of Student rugby league is marked by the defiance of prejudice and obstruction in building one of the code's most thriving sectors. Kicking off with the pioneers of the 1960s Hadfield traces the birth of the game in universities and colleges. From the founding fathers at Portsmouth and Leeds, he has gleaned the heroic truth behind those early years.

The spread of Student rugby league throughout England is highlighted by chapters on league development at Oxford and Cambridge - where sceptics said it would never penetrate.

From dozens of interviews with the most closely involved, alongside the author's inimitable observations of the state of play today, rugby league's best-loved writer captures the spirit of one of the sport's great successes - from the dedication at the elite level to humour in the lower echelons. Whether you played at university or college or not, *Learning Curve* is an unmissable read for those interested in the future of rugby.

www.scratchingshedpublishing.com